Negotiation Theory and Research

FRONTIERS OF SOCIAL PSYCHOLOGY

Series Editors:
Arie W. Kruglanski, *University of Maryland at College Park*
Joseph P. Forgas, *University of New South Wales*

Frontiers of Social Psychology is a new series of social psychology books, providing comprehensive, up-to-date reviews of the latest empirical, theoretical, and practical issues in major topics in the field. The editors and contributors are all internationally renowned scholars, whose work is at the cutting edge of research.

Scholarly, yet accessible, the volumes in the *Frontiers* series are an essential resource for senior undergraduates, postgraduates, researchers, and practitioners, and are suitable as texts in advanced courses in specific subareas of social psychology.

Forthcoming titles

Affective Influences on Social Cognition and Behavior, Forgas
Automatic Processes in Social Thinking and Behavior, Bargh
Close Relationships, Noller & Feeney
Culture, Chiu & Mallorie
Evolutionary Social Psychology, Schaller, Simpson, & Kenrick
Political Psychology, Krosnick
Science of Social Influence, Pratkanis
Social Cognition, Strack & Förster
Social Communication, Fiedler
The Self, Sedikides & Spencer

For continually updated information about published and forthcoming titles in the *Frontiers of Social Psychology* series, please visit: **www.psypress.com/frontiers**

Negotiation Theory and Research

Edited by Leigh L. Thompson

Psychology Press
New York • Hove

Published in 2006 by
Psychology Press
Taylor & Francis Group
270 Madison Avenue
New York, NY 10016

Published in Great Britain by
Psychology Press
Taylor & Francis Group
27 Church Road
Hove, East Sussex BN3 2FA

Printed in the United States of America on acid-free paper
10 9 8 7 6 5 4 3 2 1

International Standard Book Number-10: 1-84169-416-9 (Hardcover)
International Standard Book Number-13: 978-1-84169-416-0 (Hardcover)
Library of Congress Card Number 2005006912

Library of Congress Cataloging-in-Publication Data

Negotiation theory and research / edited by Leigh L. Thompson.
        p. cm. -- (Frontiers of social psychology)
  Includes bibliographical references and index.
  ISBN 1-84169-416-9 (hardback : alk. paper)
  1. Negotiation--Congresses. I. Title: Negotiation theory and research. II. Thompson, Leigh L. III. Series.

BF637.N4N445 2005
302.3--dc22   2005006912

Taylor & Francis Group
is the Academic Division of Informa plc.

Visit the Taylor & Francis Web site at
http://www.taylorandfrancis.com

and the Psychology Press Web site at
http://www.psypress.com

Contents

About the Editor

Leigh L. Thompson, PhD, is the J. Jay Gerber Distinguished Professor of Dispute Resolution & Organizations in the Kellogg School of Management at Northwestern University. Her research focuses on negotiation, team creativity, and learning. In 1991, Dr. Thompson received the multiyear Presidential Young Investigator award from the National Science Foundation for her research on negotiation and conflict resolution and has received several National Science Foundation grants for her research. In 1994–1995, Dr. Thompson was a Fellow at the Center for Advanced Study in the Behavioral Sciences in Stanford, California. She is the Director of the Kellogg Team and Group Research Center, the Leading High Impact Teams Executive Program at Kellogg, and the Behavioral Laboratory at Kellogg.

Leigh L. Thompson has published over 90 research articles, books, and chapters. She has authored five books: *The Mind and Heart of the Negotiator* (3rd ed.), *Shared Cognition in Organizations* (with John Levine and David Messick), *Making the Team* (2nd ed.), *The Social Psychology of Organizational Behavior: Key Readings,* and *Creativity in Organizations*. She is a member of the editorial boards of *Organizational Behavior and Human Decision Processes, Journal of Personality and Social Psychology, Journal of Experimental Social Psychology, Journal of Behavioral Decision Making*, and *International Journal of Conflict Management*.

Contributors

Linda Babcock
H. John Heinz III School of Public
   Policy and Management
Carnegie Mellon University
Pittsburgh, Pennsylvania

Bruce Barry
Owen Graduate School of
   Management
Vanderbilt University
Nashville, Tennessee

Max H. Bazerman
Harvard Business School
Harvard University
Cambridge, Massachusetts

Jeanne M. Brett
Kellogg School of Management
Northwestern University
Evanston, Illinois

Peter J. Carnevale
Department of Psychology
College of Arts and Sciences
New York University
New York, New York

Dolly Chugh
Harvard Business School
Harvard University
Cambridge, Massachusetts

Carsten K. W. De Dreu
Department of Psychology
Faculty of Social and
   Behavioral Sciences
University of Amsterdam
Amsterdam, The Netherlands

Alison R. Fragale
Department of Organizational
   Behavior and Strategy
Kenan-Flagler Business School
University of North Carolina
Chapel Hill, North Carolina

Ingrid Smithey Fulmer
Eli Broad Graduate School of
   Management
Michigan State University
East Lansing, Michigan

Michele J. Gelfand
Department of Psychology
College of Behavioral and Social Science
University of Maryland
College Park, Maryland

Nathan Goates
Owen Graduate School of Management
Vanderbilt University
Nashville, Tennessee

Laura Kray
Haas School of Business
University of California
Berkeley, California

Jeffrey Loewenstein
McCombs School of Business
University of Texas
Austin, Texas

Kathleen L. McGinn
Graduate School of Business
   Administration
Harvard University
Cambridge, Massachusetts

Janice Nadler
Northwestern University School of Law
   and American Bar Foundation
Chicago, Illinois

Margaret A. Neale
Department of Organizational Behavior
Graduate School of Business
Stanford University
Stanford, California

Donna Shestowsky
School of Law
University of California
Davis, California

Leigh L. Thompson
Kellogg School of Management
Northwestern University
Evanston, Illinois

Preface

The chapters of this book were presented at a conference held at the Kellogg School of Management in May 2004, titled, "Frontiers of Negotiation: Theory and Research." We were fortunate to secure the most prolific and influential negotiation scholars in the world to contribute to this book and to attend the conference. The conference was generously funded in full by Kellogg's Dispute Resolution Research Center.

Assistance with the coordination of the conference and preparation of this volume was provided initially by Rachel Claff, Sean McMillan, and Nancy McLaughlin, who ran the conference beautifully. Subsequent administrative and editorial assistance was spearheaded by Aarthi Kuppuswamy who worked with all of the authors and the reviewers on a breakneck production schedule.

This book is lovingly dedicated to the past, present, and future students of negotiation theory and research.

—Leigh L. Thompson

Negotiation: Overview of Theory and Research

LEIGH L. THOMPSON

U nlike so many subfields within a larger discipline, negotiation research seems to defy the typical pattern often witnessed: A new research area is identified; a small group of scholars conducts research in that area and excludes others who have not been steeped in their very particular methodologies. Eventually, the area of research withers and dies. So many areas of research are "hot" or "trendy" for a few years (perhaps even a decade) and then fade away. Negotiation research stands in sharp contrast to this pattern: By almost any count, negotiation research is even more popular today than it was in 1985.

Pfeffer (1993) argues that the success of a discipline can be measured by the degree of internal consistency and paradigm development. Negotiation as a sub-field of organizational behavior nearly meets all of Pfeffer's criteria. The suggested criteria by Pfeffer includes:

- The proportion of PhD graduates employed in university teaching
- The percentage of references in published works that were themselves published in the preceding five years
- The length of the longest chain of courses in a department, where a chain is defined as a course being a prerequisite to another course and that course being a prerequisite to another course and so on
- The preference for and use of graduate students and assistants in the research process

Unlike so many areas of research, negotiation has proliferated across a large body of social scientific inquiry. What is the key to the long-standing success of negotiation as a topic of scholarly inquiry? In this opening chapter, we identify five key reasons that sustain and grow negotiation as a field: adaptive supply and demand, clear and compelling dependent measures, underperformance by people who are highly motivated, pressing need for best practices, and the culture of the community of scholars.

ADAPTIVE SUPPLY AND DEMAND

For more than three decades, negotiation has been the most popular course in several top business schools. Consequently, business schools have hired scholars to teach negotiation courses. Many of the people hired to teach the courses have heretofore never conducted negotiation research. These scholars responded to the challenge by developing research programs on negotiation. Because the scholars are trained in different disciplines and have often conducted dissertation research on topics other than negotiation, each scholar brings a unique perspective to the timeless topic of negotiation. In short, many scholars have taken up the challenge to "reinvent" themselves postdissertation as a negotiation scholar. By agreeing to teach courses in negotiation, these scholars have thought deeply about how their own area of expertise might inform negotiation research. The research produced by these scholars then creates more excitement and demand for the course, which in turn leads to more hiring in the field, and so on.

CLEAR AND COMPELLING DEPENDENT MEASURES

Negotiation research has its roots in economic theory (see Nash, 1950; von Neumann & Morgenstern, 1947). Consequently, elegant measures for performance exist that are measurable and clear. Negotiation scholars, can, for example, measure the incidence and degree of "win-win" outcomes. (It should be noted that researchers do not use the term win-win, but rather, "integrative" agreement to refer to the fact that mutually beneficial outcomes are ones that satisfy both parties' interests.) Integrative outcomes are not compromises. Compromise agreements require both parties to abandon their most important interests and settle for something substantially less. The timeless example that scholars most often refer to is the case of the two sisters and the one orange (Follett, 1940). Both sisters demand a single orange for themselves. Finally, they agree to compromise and cut the orange in half. One sister uses the juice to make fresh-squeezed orange juice; the other uses the peel and discards the juice. In the heat of conflict, they overlooked the integrative solution of giving one sister all of the juice and the other all of the peel.

PEOPLE WHO CARE UNDERPERFORM

Another feature that is arguably even more important in terms of fueling research on negotiation is the fact that most people fail to reach integrative agreements (Thompson, 2005; Thompson & Hrebec, 1996). Hundreds of investigations have revealed that people leave hundreds of thousands of dollars "under the table" because they are unable to reach integrative agreements. The reason is not for lack of trying. The problem is fundamentally rooted in negotiators' mental models of the situation. In short, most negotiators have a competitive, fixed-pie perception of negotiation (Bazerman & Chugh, chapter 2; Bazerman & Neale, 1983).

NEED FOR BEST PRACTICES

We think that it is the cry for best practices and ways to improve performance that helps negotiation theory to be stronger. This logic would seem to defy the traditional notion of "basic research," which is considered to be more pure and noble than applied research. Negotiation research is applied, but also the essence of basic research.

COMMUNITY OF SCHOLARS

The negotiation community of scholars is an inclusive, rather than exclusive community. No negotiation researcher would ever suggest that unless one has dedicated several years of training in special laboratory methods, that they need not bother engaging in negotiation research. Quite the contrary. The negotiation community of scholars is welcoming to newcomers, who have interesting ideas that have not yet been applied to negotiation. For this reason, researchers with roots in social psychology, economics, sociology, and communication studies are part of the field. Moreover, the community comes together quite often in the form of classroom research projects (Loyd, Kern, & Thompson, 2005; Thompson, Kern, & Loyd, 2003). In short, communities of scholars across the globe collaborate on research projects that involve several laboratories. The community of scholars interacts regularly at national conference meetings and small, topical conferences (this book is a case in point).

The field of negotiation is noted for its bright superstars. These superstars graciously agreed to be a part of this book. And, in every case, they worked as a team. The cross-citation rate is very high, and the incidence of multiauthored papers is very high.

CONTENTS OF THE BOOK

In chapter 2, Max Bazerman (PhD, 1979, Carnegie-Mellon University) and Dolly Chugh (PhD in progress, Harvard University) elaborate on what some might refer to as the first descriptive theory of negotiation—bounded rationality and faulty decision making. In their chapter, Bazerman and Chugh focus on failures (see the point about underperformance above) as a point of departure. They provide a top-down view of the classic decision-perspective of negotiation in which negotiators are viewed as falling prey to a number of biases, such as framing effects, overconfidence, and anchoring. According to Bazerman and Chugh, the "bounded awareness" and "focusing failure" perspective not only accounts for the performance problems of negotiators, but provides a new way of thinking about ethical shortcomings of negotiators.

In chapter 3, Margaret Neale (PhD, 1982, University of Texas, Austin) and Alison Fragale (PhD, 2004, Stanford University) follow closely on the heels of

Bazerman and Chugh, but in their social cognitive view of negotiation, they take us out of the mind of the individual negotiator and into the social-interpersonal dynamics of two (or more negotiators). Their fundamental point of theorizing begins with the observation that negotiations are highly ambiguous and, consequently, negotiators must make assumptions and draw inferences about the other party, the situation, and themselves. Neale and Fragale deeply investigate the different types of uncertainty that negotiators experience and how each can then shape attitudes and behaviors at the negotiation table.

In chapter 4, Peter Carnevale (PhD, 1982, SUNY at Buffalo) and Carsten De Dreu (PhD, 1993, University of Groningen) heat up the study of negotiator judgment and decision making by considering the goals and motives that drive the negotiator. Carnevale and De Dreu distinguish key concepts of motivations, goals, aspirations, and tactics. They examine how goals and motives are expressed in strategies and tactics of negotiation. They present a taxonomy of motives and a framework for examining emotion, cognitive processes, and strategic choices in negotiation.

In chapter 5, Jeffrey Loewenstein (PhD, 2000, Northwestern University) and Leigh Thompson (PhD, 1988, Northwestern University) take up the question of just how and why negotiators might improve their performance. They provide stark evidence that negotiators—despite their position, intelligence, and motivation—routinely underperform, and they concomitantly make the point that most people should be experts at negotiation, at least judging by the frequency with which they negotiate. Loewenstein and Thompson review the major paradigms that have been used to study experience and expertise in negotiation and outline the key conditions that need to be in place for negotiators to learn. Loewenstein and Thompson specify what is meant by learning and distinguish superficial learning from deep learning.

In chapter 6, Bruce Barry (PhD, 1973, University of Wisconsin), Ingrid Fulmer (PhD, 2003, Vanderbilt University), and Nathan Goates (PhD in progress, Vanderbilt University) introduce the concept of emotion and mood to the study of negotiation. Barry, Fulmer, and Goates represent the new vanguard of scholars who realize that despite its somber economic roots, negotiation is anything but a coolheaded process. Barry et al. distinguish the constructs of mood, emotion, affect, and feeling and discuss the methods by which negotiation produces mood and the way in which affect influences the process and outcome of negotiation.

In chapter 7, Kathleen McGinn (PhD, 1992, Northwestern University) brings her social network training to the study of relationships in negotiations. McGinn heralds the new look of negotiation research that realizes that negotiation does not occur in a social vacuum. She methodically considers how past relationships affect negotiations and how choice of a negotiation partner influences the process and outcome of negotiations.

In chapter 8, Janice Nadler (PhD, 2000, University of Illinois, Urbana-Champaign) and Donna Shestowsky (PhD, 2003, Stanford University) focus on how information technology (e.g., phone, e-mail, Internet) affect the process and outcome of negotiation. Nadler and Shestowsky commandingly bring together the stockpile of negotiation research that has focused on non–face-to-face interaction. They distinguish economic measures of process and performance from social indicators of performance.

In chapter 9, Jeanne Brett (PhD, 1972, University of Illinois) and Michele Gelfand (PhD, 1996, University of Illinois, Urbana-Champaign) provide a state-of-the-art review of how negotiation process and outcomes are affected by cultural frameworks. They define culture and then identify five key cultural assumptions that pervade the common approach to negotiation. Many of their key assumptions cut to the very heart of the chapters in this book (e.g., the rationality assumption, assumptions about the appropriate display of emotions, etc.). Brett and Gelfand effectively take us behind the cultural curtain that so much negotiation research plays in front of to raise critical questions about the processes and outcomes of cross-cultural negotiations.

In chapter 10, Laura Kray (PhD, 1997, University of Washington, Seattle) and Linda Babcock (PhD, 1988, University of Wisconsin at Madison) take up the study of gender in negotiation. They do not rely on a narrow personality of sex differences approach. Rather, their point of departure is "motivated social cognition," which brings the social-cognitive view and the study of motivation and goals to the forefront of gender in negotiation. They provide compelling evidence of women's performance relative to that of men in negotiation and then analyze the underlying motivations.

SUMMARY AND CONCLUSION

The chapters in this book can be conceptualized as a 10-sided prism. It is possible for the simple act of negotiation (as it occurs every day in boardrooms, lunchrooms, and perhaps even bedrooms!) to be analyzed via behavioral decision theory, social-cognition, motivation, and so forth. However, rather than each approach being a competitor or threat to the other approaches (or lenses), each complements the other approaches. Thus, just as the different approaches complement one another, the scholars in this book complement each other. It is a testament to the scholars' versatility that nearly every scholar was fully capable or writing almost every chapter in this book.

REFERENCES

Bazerman, M. H., & Neale, M. A. (1983). Heuristics in negotiation: Limitations to dispute resolution effectiveness. In M. H. Bazerman & R. J. Lewicki (Eds.), *Negotiating in organizations*. Beverly Hills, CA: Sage.

Follett, M. P. (1940). Constructive conflict. In H. C. Metcalf & L. Urwick (Eds.), *Dynamic administration: The collected papers of Mary Parker Follett*. New York: Harper.

Loyd, D. L., Kern, M. C., & Thompson, L. (2005). Classroom research: Bridging the ivory divide. *Academy of Management Journal: Learning and Education, 4*(1), 8–21.

Nash, J. (1950). The bargaining problem. *Econometrica, 18,* 155–162.

Neumann, J. von, & Morgenstern, O. (1947). *Theory of games and economic behavior.* Princeton, NJ: Princeton University Press.

Pfeffer, J. (1993). Barriers to the advance of organizational science: Paradigm development as a dependent variable. *Academy of Management Review, 8*(4), 599–620.

Thompson, L. (2005) *The mind and heart of the negotiator* (3rd ed.). Upper Saddle River, NJ: Pearson Prentice Hall.

Thompson, L. & Hrebec, D. (1996). Lose-lose agreements in interdependent decision making. *Psychological Bulletin, 120*(3), 396–409.

Thompson, L., Kern, M., & Loyd, D. L. (2003). Research methods of micro-organizational behavior. In C. Sansone, C. Morf, & A. Panter (Eds.), *Handbook of methods in social psychology* (pp. 457–470). Thousand Oaks, CA: Sage.

2

Bounded Awareness: Focusing Failures in Negotiation

MAX H. BAZERMAN and DOLLY CHUGH

*R*ecent reviews have documented a shift over the last 25 years in the study of negotiation toward the decision-making process of the negotiator (Bazerman, Curhan, & Moore, 2000a; Bazerman, Curhan, Moore, & Valley, 2000b; Neale & Fragale, chapter 3; Neuberg & Fiske, 1987; Thompson & Fox, 2000). The decision perspective to negotiation has highlighted important ways in which negotiator judgment falls systematically short of rationality. This paper is broadly compatible with this perspective, but highlights an underexplored aspect of the judgmental failure—how decision makers and negotiators systematically ignore valuable information that is readily available.

Recent research in social and cognitive psychology has documented the ability of the human mind to focus on specific information while failing to incorporate other information that is readily available and relevant. We use this literature to integrate what we know about this failure, and organize this knowledge under our organizing construct of "bounded awareness." We define bounded awareness as an individual's failure to "see" and use accessible and perceivable information while "seeing" and using other equally accessible and perceivable information.

We believe that bounded awareness is relevant to both individual decision making and negotiation. Thus, after reviewing the decision perspective to negotiation, we develop the individual decision-making aspect of bounded awareness before identifying the specific application of the concept to negotiation. We conclude by suggesting future research directions on bounded awareness in negotiation.

A DECISION PERSPECTIVE TO NEGOTIATION

We date the decision perspective to negotiation with Howard Raiffa's classic 1982 work, *The Art and Science of Negotiation*. In contrast to game theory, which assumed the presence of fully rational negotiators, Raiffa argued for the importance of developing a prescriptive approach to improving negotiator effectiveness based on a realistic description of the behavior of the other side. Raiffa's notion that negotiation advice should be based on analysis implicitly acknowledged that negotiators themselves do not intuitively follow purely rational strategies. From an empirical perspective, Raiffa opened a dialogue between prescriptive and descriptive researchers. Along with other work in the decision perspective of negotiation (Bazerman, Neale, Valley, et al., 1992; Thompson & Fox, 2000), we aim to continue this dialogue by empirically identifying psychological patterns that inform the negotiator about his or her own behavior and the behavior of his or her opponents (Bazerman, 2005; Neale & Bazerman, 1991; Thompson & Fox, 2000).

The decision perspective to negotiation seeks to understand how negotiators actually make decisions, with a specific focus on the systematic ways in which decision makers deviate from optimality or rationality (Hastie & Dawes, 2001; Kahneman & Tversky, 1979; Tversky & Kahneman, 1974). Behavioral decision researchers assume that people attempt to act rationally, but are bounded in their ability to achieve rationality (Simon, 1957). Researchers predict, *a priori*, how people will make decisions that are inconsistent, inefficient, and based on normatively irrelevant information. A core argument is that humans rely on simplifying strategies or cognitive heuristics (Bazerman, 2005). While these heuristics are typically useful shortcuts, they also lead to predictable mistakes (Tversky & Kahneman, 1974).

To provide a flavor of this research, studies of two-party negotiations suggest that negotiators tend to be

- More concessionary in a negotiation that is positively framed than in a negotiation that is negatively framed (Bazerman Magliozzi, & Neale, 1985; Bottom & Studt, 1993; De Dreu & McCusker, 1997; Lim & Carnevale, 1995; Olekalns, 1997)
- Inappropriately affected by anchors in negotiation (Kahneman, 1992; Northcraft & Neale, 1987; Ritov, 1996; Thompson, 1995; Whyte & Sebenius, 1997)
- Overconfident and overly optimistic about the likelihood of attaining outcomes that favor themselves (Bazerman, Moore, & Gillespie, 1999; Bazerman & Neale, 1982).

They also tend to

- Falsely assume a "fixed pie" and miss opportunities for mutually beneficial tradeoffs between the parties (Bazerman et al., 1985; Fukuno & Ohbuchi, 1997; Thompson & DeHarpport, 1994; Thompson & Hastie, 1990)
- Falsely assume incompatibility in the preferences of negotiating parties (Thompson & Hrebec, 1996)
- Escalate conflict even when a rational analysis would dictate a change in strategy (Bazerman, 2005; Bazerman & Neale, 1983; Diekmann, Tenbrunsel, & Bazerman, 1999; Diekmann, Tenbrunsel, Shah, Schroth,

& Bazerman, 1996; Dijksterhuis, Macrae, & Haddock, 1999; Keltner & Robinson, 1993)

- Overweight interpretations of a dispute in ways that favor themselves (Babcock & Loewenstein, 1997; Bazerman & Neale, 1982; Diekmann, Samuels, Ross, & Bazerman, 1997)
- Reactively devalue any concession that their opponent makes (Curhan, Neale, & Ross, 1999; Ross & Stillinger, 1991)

In the 1990s, research emerged that added social psychological variables to research structures consistent with a behavioral decision research perspective. The judgment of individual negotiators is influenced by social context (Loewenstein, Thompson, & Bazerman, 1989), how social relationships within dyads can influence negotiation processes and outcomes (McGinn, Thompson, & Bazerman, 2003), and how relationships affect the broader network of actors (Shah & Jehn, 1993; Sondak & Bazerman, 1989; Tenbrunsel, Galvin, Neale, & Bazerman, 1996). Most people view themselves, the world, and the future in a considerably more positive light than reality can sustain (Taylor, 1989; Taylor & Brown, 1988) and this behavior generalizes to the negotiation context (Kramer, Newton, & Pommerenke, 1993; Messick, Bloom, Boldizar, & Samuelson, 1985). In addition, emotions can affect the wisdom of decisions. For example, positive moods tend to increase negotiators' tendencies to select a cooperative strategy (Forgas, 1998) and enhance their ability to find integrative gains (Carnevale & Isen, 1986). Angry negotiators are less accurate in judging the interests of opponent negotiators, achieve lower joint gains (Allred, Mallozzi, Matsui, & Raia, 1997), and are more self-centered in their preferences than control subjects (Loewenstein et al., 1989). Pillutla and Murnighan (1996) found that angry negotiators are more likely to reject profitable offers than control subjects in ultimatum games.

The decision perspective has also been enhanced by an understanding of how negotiators define the negotiation game. Specifically, Bazerman et al.'s (2000a, 2000b) overview describes how concerns about ethics, values, and norms of fairness affect the negotiator's definition of the game being played; the role of different forms of communication in the way the game is played; the impact of cross-cultural issues in perception and behavior on the negotiation game; and how negotiators cope with making decisions in negotiations involving more than two players.

A key feature of the decision perspective to negotiation is its reliance on a backdrop of rationality for assessing decisions. This feature is central to transforming descriptive research into useful prescriptions. Specifically, it gives the negotiator useful hints about the likely behavior of opponents and suggests ways in which the individual's own decisions may be biased. Consistent with these values, we aim to push the decision perspective in a new direction.

Specifically, we argue that (a) negotiators demonstrate bounded awareness when they systematically overlook critical, easily accessible information relevant to their negotiations; (b) we can identify the conditions under which bounded awareness is most likely to occur as well as the types of information most commonly ignored by negotiators in those conditions; and (c) we can train negotiators to more effectively broaden their awareness to include useful information. Before developing this argument within the domain of negotiation, we offer background on bounded awareness at the individual level. In the next section, we define what we mean by bounded awareness, summarize relevant evidence from a broad array of literatures, and, on the basis of this evidence, propose that "focusing failures" are most likely to occur under certain predictable conditions.

EVIDENCE FOR BOUNDED AWARENESS AND FOCUSING FAILURES

Herbert Simon offered the concept of bounded rationality as a "behavioral model [in which] human rationality is very limited, very much bounded by the situation and by human computational powers" (1983, p. 34). Boundedness has since come to represent the distinction between economists' normative and psychologists' descriptive views of human decision making. Thaler (1996, 2000) extended Simon's thinking when he described the three ways in which "Homo Economicus" and "Homo Psychologicus" vary; he argued that people are "dumber, nicer, and weaker" than classical economic theory predicts (Simon, 1983, pp. 227, 230). That is, Thaler proposed that human beings are characterized by bounded rationality, self-interest, and willpower into the equation. Chugh, Bazerman, and Banaji (2005) apply the concept of boundedness to ethical decision making, using the term "bounded ethicality" to describe the systematic constraints on decision making with ethical consequence.

Here, we argue that people have bounded awareness that prevents them from focusing on easily observable and relevant data. That is, bounded awareness is the phenomenon by which individuals do not "see" and use accessible and perceivable information during the decision-making process, while "seeing" and using other equally accessible and perceivable information. Thus, useful information remains out of focus for the decision maker. A "focusing failure" results from a misalignment between the information needed for a good decision and the information included in the decision-making process. Our less formal definition of a focusing failure is captured in the familiar "How could I miss that?" reaction to the realization that important information, despite being easily seen, has been ignored. We are deliberate and normative in our labeling of these instances as failures, as they represent costly errors. Researchers are just beginning to understand the systematic effects caused by our bounded awareness, particularly within the negotiation domain, but we can, and will, demonstrate suboptimality based on negotiators systematically ignoring important information. We argue that the focusing failures that arise from bounded awareness are indeed quite costly to negotiators.

We propose four conditions that correspond to the types of information or tasks that compete for the decision maker's attention and most likely to lead to a focusing failure. Specifically, we describe evidence of focusing failures that occur when the decision maker is faced with (a) another task competing for attention; (b) a seemingly clearly defined primary task with narrow default assumptions;

(c) affective information; or (d) information with self-relevance. The evidence we present is deliberately diverse in domain but shares the characteristic of being important, easily seen information that is ignored and that elicits the "How could I miss that?" reaction if and when the focusing failure is recognized.

The Condition of a Competing Task:
Inattentional Blindness

Ulric Neisser (1979) asked participants to observe a video of two visually super-imposed groups of players passing basketballs. In the video, one group of players wears white shirts and the other group wears dark shirts. Study participants were instructed to count the number of passes between members of one of the two groups. The task is moderately difficult, and study participants had to give it their full attention. Only 21% of Neisser's study participants reported seeing a woman who clearly and unexpectedly walked through the basketball court carrying an open umbrella. Our own experience using this video in the classroom is that even far fewer than 21% of students notice the woman. Yet when the video is shown again to demonstrate what most of the class missed, everyone sees the woman. Essentially, by focusing on one task, people miss very obvious information in their visual world. Simons and Chabris (1999) replicated this effect with a more contemporary video in which a person in a gorilla costume walks through a basketball game, thumping his chest, and is clearly and comically visible for more than 5 seconds. Simons provides a series of such demonstrations on a video available at www.viscog.com.

The common failure to see the obvious is surprising to many people, including the authors, and far exceeds most of our assumptions about visual awareness. Investigating the relationship between perception and attention, Mack and Rock (1998) demonstrate that people have a broad tendency to not see what they are looking at directly when they are focused on a different issue. This failure, known as "inattentional blindness," is nicely summarized in Mack and Rock and in the work of Daniel Simons and colleagues (Simons, 2000; Simons & Chabris, 1999; Simons & Levin, 2003). Mack (2003) suggests the implications of inattentional blindness for the airplane pilot who, attending to the controls, fails to see another airplane on his runway. Similarly, many car accidents undoubtedly result from drivers focusing on matters other than driving, such as talking on their cell phones. Often, the driver has the needed information visually available, but the attention to the person on the other end of the line keeps the driver from appropriately giving attention to the critical information that affects road safety.

Psychologists are conducting interesting research that connects inattentional blindness to neural regions in the brain (Moore & Egeth, 1997) and that identifies key independent variables that affect the probability of not seeing the obvious (Mack, 2003). Here, we ask whether inattentional blindness generalizes from the visual world to the broader array of information that is readily available in the environment, yet overlooked by most decision makers, including negotiators. As we later develop, we think that many negotiators often act close to rationally based on the information in their mental representation of the negotiation. However, due to inattentional blindness, they fail to act rationally as a result of not even assessing information that failed to be mentally represented.

The Condition of Narrow Assumptions

Dan Gilbert, Tim Wilson, and their colleagues (Gilbert & Wilson, 2000; Wilson, Wheatley, Meyers, Gilbert, & Axsom, 2000) use the term "focalism" to describe a related set of errors in human judgment. Focalism describes the tendency to focus too much on a particular event (the "focal event") and too little on other events that are likely to occur concurrently (Wilson et al., 2000). As a result, individuals overestimate the degree to which their thoughts will be occupied by the focal event and to overestimate the duration of their emotional response to the event. For example, people tend to overestimate the impact on their overall happiness of good and bad events (Wilson et al., 2000). Thus, we expect to be more affected emotionally than we really are when our preferred sports team or political candidate wins or loses, or when we are afflicted by a major medical condition.

Schkade and Kahneman (1998) use the term "focusing illusion" to describe the tendency of individuals making judgments to attend to only a subset of available information, to overweight that information, and to underweight unattended information. Using a causal mechanism very similar to that of Gilbert, Wilson, and colleagues, Schkade and Kahneman examined judgments of life satisfaction. They surveyed college students in the Midwest and southern California about their own life satisfaction and perceived life satisfaction of others. While Californians and Midwesterners reported similar levels of life satisfaction, when both groups were asked to rate the life satisfaction of a similar person living in the other location, both groups rated Californians as having greater life satisfaction than Midwesterners. That is, they found that differences between California and the Midwest, such as climate, strongly influenced nonresidents' judgments of residents' life satisfaction but did not predict the experienced life satisfaction of the citizens of the two locales. Schkade and Kahneman observe that when these citizens are asked specifically about the other location, weather is a salient factor in their responses, and all other life events affecting satisfaction swim out of focus.

The widespread human tendency to focus on certain events and ignore other events available in the environment also emerged in the basketball study of Fox and Tversky (1998). When the 1995 National Basketball Association championship series was down to eight teams, Fox and Tversky recruited basketball fans as subjects. The subjects were asked to assess the probability that each team (Chicago, Indiana, Orlando, New York, Los Angeles, Phoenix, San Antonio, and Houston) would win the championship, the probability that the winning team would come from each of the four divisions (Central [Chicago and Indiana], Atlantic [Orlando and New York], Pacific [Los Angeles and Phoenix], and Midwest [San Antonio and Houston]). They were also asked to assess the probability that the winning team would come from either the Eastern conference (comprising the Central and Atlantic divisions) or the Western conference (comprising the Pacific and Midwest divisions). Logically, the sum of the probabilities for the eight teams, the sum of the probabilities of the four divisions, and the sum of the probabilities for the two conferences should each add up to 100%. Indeed, the combined probabilities for the two conferences were close—102%. But the sum of the probabilities of the four divisions rose as high as 144%, and the sum of the probabilities of the eight teams was as much as 218%. Building off Tversky and Koehler's (1994) support theory, Fox and Tversky argue that as participants focus on each team, they can find support for that team winning while failing to focus on data that supports other teams winning. This conclusion parallels Tversky and Koehler's finding that medical doctors, when asked to assess the probabilities of four mutually exclusive prognoses for a patient, gave probabilities for the four diagnoses that totaled far in excess of 100%.

Research on creativity can also be understood from the perspective of focusing and narrow assumptions. Many well-studied creativity problems have the essential characteristic of being obvious once you see the solutions. These problems often are structured to put one set of features in focus and to put necessary features of the problem out of focus. People enact an overly narrow focus, often induced by the problem's presentation, and this narrow focus becomes the core barrier to solution (Thompson & Fox, 2000; Winklegren, 1974). Certain conditions, such as positive mood (Amabile, Barsade, Mueller, & Staw, 2002) and less time pressure (Amabile, Hadley, & Kramer, 2002) have been found to contribute to the flexible interpretation, divergent thinking, and greater ingenuity that is lacking in thinking characterized by bounded awareness. This research may offer possible prescription for negotiators seeking to reduce focusing failures.

The Condition of Affective Primacy

Loewenstein (1996) discusses the role of visceral influences on behavior. He highlights the essence of the conflict that people feel when choosing between alternative courses of action—for example, following what you want in the short term versus what would be best for you in the long term. Loewenstein argues that much human behavior is based on these sorts of visceral or transient responses that conflict with long-term self-interest.

More recently, Slovic, Finucane, Peters, and MacGregor (2002) coined the term "affect heuristic" to describe the rapid and automatic feelings that precede cognition and that often determine behavior. Loewenstein (1996) and Slovic et al. (2002) share the view that people often act on a limited set of data that prompts an affective response that cuts off cognitive deliberation. These reviews provide compelling evidence that "hot" affective responses are immediate, powerful, and often lead to the failure to consider a broader set of information that is often useful to a rational assessment. These authors argue against the common behavioral decision perspective in which people conduct an approximation of a rational assessment that is affected by a predictable set of biases. Rather, these authors argue that we are predictably influenced by affective considerations that are in focus while other cognitive considerations remain out of focus.

The Condition of Self-Relevant Information

Magicians rely heavily on the human mind's propensity for an overly narrow focus by relying on "misdirection" tactics to manipulate an audience's focus (Schneider, 2004). Misdirection can take many forms, but the type most relevant to our argument happens literally right before the audience's eyes. In this style, the audience looks directly at the "trick" part of the magic as it takes place, seeing everything needed to demystify the illusion, and yet fails to see the motions used to generate "magic."

The magician accomplishes such misdirection through techniques as simple as asking a question of the audience that requires self-relevant mental processing. That is, at precisely the moment of illusion the magician asks a casual question that relates to the trick being performed and requires the audience members to focus briefly on themselves (such as "Why did you select that card?" or, when performing a trick called The Matrix, asking "Does anyone know what a matrix is?"). The question shifts the awareness of each member of the audience from the magician's motions to an issue related to himself or herself; this shift leads them to fail to focus on information right before their eyes.

Chugh and associates (2005) propose a view of unethical behavior that relates well to the bounded awareness and focusing concepts. In other work, these authors (Banaji, Bazerman, & Chugh, 2003) explore how ethical people can nonetheless end up engaging in stereotyping, favoring their own group, being affected by conflicts of interest, and overclaiming credit. We argue that, in ethical contexts, a self-serving set of interpretations comes into focus, often leaving an objective assessment of the situation out of focus. Moore, Loewenstein, Tanlu, & Bazerman (2005) argue that in conflicts between acting in one's self-interest and acting ethically, self-serving options come into focus more naturally than do ethical concerns, which often involve other parties. Thus, we argue that ethical concerns are often out of focus rather than consciously ignored by the decision maker, whose focus is more likely drawn to concerns about the self.

What Focusing Is Not

On a surface level, bounded awareness overlaps with the better-known concept of availability (Tversky & Kahneman, 1974). Both concepts consider why certain information is more salient to the decision maker than other information. But, unlike the concept of bounded awareness, availability is a general cognitive heuristic; it explains the tendency for people to assume that more available information, such as vivid data, is more common than less available information. Research on bounded awareness, by contrast, examines specific conditions and identifies the specific groups of variables likely to be in or out of focus under each condition. Thus, the work on inattentional blindness demonstrates that leading people to focus their attention on a particular task blinds them to quite obvious and relevant information. Gilbert and Wilson (2000) and their colleagues (Wilson et al., 2000) and Schkade and Kahneman (1998) show that asking how specific events affect satisfaction leads to an overestimation of those events, which are in focus, while leaving other unmentioned events out of focus. Later, we identify the specific variables that tend to be in and out of focus in negotiations, variables that would not be obvious from even a sophisticated knowledge of the availability heuristic.

Cutcher-Gershenfeld, McKersie, Peace, and Segal (2004) use the term focusing in their prescriptive work on collective bargaining. In this model, focusing is a critical stage that is needed between the act of exploring options with the other side and reaching an agreement. Focusing is a deliberate and collective act of narrowing the pool of possible agreements, and represents a normative view of a negotiation. In our use of the term, focusing failure is a descriptive term. However, the stage that precedes "focus" in the Cutcher-Gershenfeld et al. model, exploration, is the very stage where we believe bounded awareness is likely to occur.

BOUNDED AWARENESS IN NEGOTIATION

Negotiators are overly affected by readily available information and are not aware of this influence on their decisions (Neale, 1984; Pinkley, Brittain, Neale, & Northcraft, 1995). In this section, we outline a framework for identifying which information can be predicted to be out of focus in negotiation. Much of this section is based on empirical work by Tor and Bazerman (2003) and Idson et al. (2004), and provides preliminary empirical support for our speculative claims about the conditions under which focusing failures are likely to occur.

Both Tor and Bazerman (2003) and Idson et al. (2004) identify the failure of competitive actors to focus on critical information known to be needed for negotiation effectiveness—the decisions of other parties and the rules of the game they are playing. This empirical work uses variations of three well-studied decision problems: the Monty Hall game (Friedman, 1998; Nalebuff, 1987), the Acquiring a Company problem (Ball, Bazerman, & Carroll, 1991; Carroll, Bazerman, & Maury, 1988; Samuelson & Bazerman, 1985), and Multi-Party Ultimatums (Messick, Moore, & Bazerman, 1997). In all three games, individuals typically make the wrong decision, although the games require no complex analytical reasoning. To overview the evidence from this research, we provide a summary of these experimental games.

The Monty Hall Game   In the once-popular television game show *Let's Make a Deal*, host Monty Hall would ask contestants to choose one of three doors. One of the doors led to a grand prize and the other two, known as "zonks," led to minor prizes or gag gifts. After the contestant chose a door and before it was opened, Monty would open one of the other two doors to reveal a zonk. The contestant then had the chance to trade their chosen door for the remaining unchosen, unopened door. Most contestants assumed that, with only two doors remaining, the odds of winning the grand prize are 50-50, and most of them preferred to stick with the door they originally chose.

Years after *Let's Make a Deal* went off the air, statisticians, economists, and journalists (Nalebuff, 1987; Selvin, 1975; vos Savant, 1990, 1991) analyzed contestants' decisions and noted that, in tending not to switch to the remaining unchosen door, they were making a systematic mistake. Assuming that Monty always opened an unchosen door (we will call this the "Monty always opens" condition) and then offered a switch, contestants should always have taken him up on it (Friedman, 1998; Nalebuff, 1987). The logic is simple. When they first choose their door, the contestants have a 1/3 chance of winning the prize. When Monty opens one unchosen door to reveal a zonk, there is still a 1/3 chance that the contestant chose the winner to start with and a 2/3 chance that the big prize is behind one of the other two doors. With one zonk revealed, the unopened, unchosen door now carries the 2/3 chance. To increase the odds of winning from 1/3 to 2/3, the contestant should therefore always switch doors. In a laboratory analog of this problem, Friedman's participants failed overall to make the correct decision and only exhibited limited learning through repeated trials.

A critical element in this analysis is the assumption that Monty always opened an unchosen door that did not contain the grand prize. Under that assumption, the correct contestant response would be to switch doors. One could make a very different assumption about Monty's behavior, however, if one assumed a "mean Monty"—one who knows where the grand prize is located and who wants to reduce the contestant's chance of winning. Imagine that after the contestant chooses a door, "Mean Monty" could either declare the game over or open one door and suggest a switch. Assuming that Monty wants to reduce the contestant's chance of winning the grand prize, the contestant should never accept Monty's offer to switch. Since Monty wants the contestant to lose, the fact that Monty makes the offer should tell the contestant that she has already picked the winning door.

In summary, a normative analysis suggests that contestants should always switch doors in the "Monty always opens" condition but never in the "Mean Monty" condition. Tor and Bazerman (2003) found, however, that the rules of the game and Monty's decision rules, even when carefully spelled out, are out of focus to contestants and are normatively evaluated. They also found that a consideration of these typically out-of-focus pieces of information is necessary to arrive at the correct answers to these problems. (Note: Despite the extensive reanalysis of this game show, no clear data exists on the actual decision rule that was used on the show.)

Acquiring a Company   Adapting Akerlof's (1970) "lemons" problem, Samuelson and Bazerman (1985) created a takeover game in which people systematically make offers with negative expected values—in other words, they make mistakes. In this problem, one firm (the Acquirer) is considering making an offer to buy out another firm (the Target). Participants, who play the role of the Acquirer, are uncertain about the ultimate value of the Target. They are told that its value under current management falls between $0 and $100, with all values equally likely. They also know that the Target is expected to be worth 50% more under the Acquirer's management than under its current ownership. Thus, it appears to make sense for the Acquirer to offer to buy the Target. The Target knows its exact current worth, but the Acquirer does not. The game begins with the Acquirer making one take-it-or-leave it offer. The Target responds, and the game ends.

How much should the Acquirer offer for the Target? Across a number of studies, the dominant range of responses falls between $50 and $75 (Ball et al., 1991; Bereby-Meyer & Grosskopf, 2002; Carroll et al., 1988). Carroll et al. used protocol analyses to identify cognitive patterns underlying these bids. They argue that the most common explanation for the $50 to $75 range is, "on average, the firm will be worth $50 to the Target and $75 to the Acquirer; consequently, a transaction in this range will, on average, be profitable to both parties."

In fact, it turns out that the correct answer to the problem is an offer of $0—no offer at all. Why? Because all offers have a negative expected value, with twice the chance of losing than of winning, and with the possibility of losing twice as much as the largest possible gain. The following analysis of an offer of $60 per share explains the negative expected value of any positive number.

> If I offer $60 per share, the offer will be accepted 60% of the time—whenever the firm is worth between $0 and $60 to the Target. Since all values between $0 and $60 are equally likely, the firm will, on average, be worth $30 per share to the Acquirer, resulting in a loss of $15 per share ($45 to $60). Consequently, a $60 per share offer is unwise. (Bazerman, 2005)

This reasoning can be applied to any positive offer. On average, the Target will be worth 25% less than the price the Acquirer pays when its offer is accepted. If the Acquirer offers $X and the Target accepts, the company is currently valued at anywhere from $0 to $X. Because any value in that range is equally likely, the expected value of the offer therefore equals $X/2. Since the company is worth 50% more to the Acquirer, its expected value is 1.5($X/2) = 0.75($X), or 75% of its offer price. Thus, for any value of $X, the Acquirer's best option is to not make an offer ($0 per share).

Clearly, the game is a trap. While in all circumstances the firm is worth more to the Acquirer than to the Target, any offer higher than $0 generates a negative expected return to the Acquirer. Nonetheless, the vast majority of participants bid positive values that can be explained systematically. Replications with accounting firm partners, CEOs, investment bankers, and many other groups of "experts" have achieved similar results (Bazerman, 2005). In addition, similar patterns were exhibited by participants who were paid on the basis of their performance and given multiple trials to foster learning (Ball et al., 1991; Bereby-Meyer & Grosskopf, 2002).

Multi-Party Ultimatums   The ultimatum game is one of the most common games studied by experimental economists (Guth, Schmittberger, & Schwarze, 1982; Roth, 1991). In the ultimatum game, Player 1 divides a known, fixed sum of money any way she chooses by filling out a form that states, "I demand X." Player 2 either accepts the offer and receives his portion of the money allocated by Player 1 or rejects the offer, leaving both sides with nothing. Models that assume that both actors will maximize profit predict that Player 1 will offer Player 2 only slightly more than zero and that Player 2 will accept any offer greater than zero. These models fail to account for the fairness considerations that players incorporate into their offers and choices. Across many studies, Player 1 typically demands less than 70% of the funds, while individuals in the role of Player 2 often reject profitable but unequal offers (Ochs & Roth, 1989).

Inspired by this problem and by a real-world situation in which a buyer made an offer to a selling group that consisted of multiple individuals, Messick et al. (1997) constructed a multiple-party ultimatum game. In this version of the game, six participants were assigned the roles of A, B, C, D, E, and F. Player A was given $60 and was told to allocate the money to herself and to the other five parties. She was told that her offers to B, C, D, E, and F had to be equal and had to be an integer. B, C, D, E, and F each recorded the minimum amount of money that they would accept from A. The game's decision rule was the key manipulation. In one variation, if the amount that A offered to B–F equaled or exceeded the smallest amount requested by B, C, D, E, or F, then A's allocation of A went into effect, and if it was not, all parties received zero (we will call this condition "dividing the pie—smallest"). In the other condition, if the amount that A offered to B–F equaled or exceeded the largest amount requested by B, C, D, E, or F, then A's allocation went into effect, and if it was not, all parties received zero (we will call this condition "dividing the pie—largest").

Just as in the two-party ultimatum game, a bi-modal response pattern emerges from the demands of players B–F. Many B–F players will accept an offer of $1 because $1 is better than turning down the offer and getting nothing. Another large group of players B–F demand $10—their "fair" share. Tversky and Kahneman (1974) have shown that individuals underestimate disjunctive events and overestimate conjunctive events. This phenomenon leads to the prediction that player A will underestimate how likely it is to get at least 1 out of 5 people to accept $1 and to overestimate the likelihood of all five individuals accepting anything less than $10. Messick et al. (1997) found empirically that player A's profit-maximizing strategy would be to divide the money 55-1-1-1-1-1 in the dividing the pie—smallest condition and to divide it 10-10-10-10-10-10 in the dividing the pie—largest condition. In fact, in the latter version, any allocation other than 10 always led to player A receiving $0.

The empirically best strategy for player A diverged dramatically between the two conditions (offers of $1 vs. $10), but the actual behavior of player A was much closer across the two conditions. On average, player A allocated $8.15 to the other players in the dividing the pie—smallest condition and allocated $8.47 to the other players in the dividing the pie—largest condition. Player A in dividing the pie—largest condition missed an easy opportunity to collect $10, while player A in dividing the pie—smallest condition passed up a significant opportunity to profit. Part of the failure of player A to maximize his or her expected value can be explained by fairness considerations, and perhaps by a very strong risk aversion in the dividing the pie—smallest condition. We will also test the possibility that much of the failure is due to the insensitivity of player A to the decision rule and to the heterogeneity of players B–F. To rule out fairness and risk aversion as alternative explanations, the current experiment will adapt the Messick et al. (1997) tasks.

Substantial research on the Acquiring a Company problem suggests that bounded awareness leads decision makers to ignore or simplify the cognitions of opposing parties as well as the rules of the game (Carroll et al., 1988; Messick et al., 1997). The decision makers are faced with several of the conditions likely to lead to such focusing failures: narrow assumptions and information relevant to the self. For example, in the Acquiring a Company problem, the participant is presented with information about his or her role as the Acquirer and with a problem that suggests an offer is expected. The emphasis on self-related (e.g., the Acquirer) information and the narrow assumption that an offer is greater than zero lead to robust errors, which are consistently found in the Acquiring a Company problem (Bazerman, 2005; Samuelson & Bazerman, 1985). When presented with this problem, the overwhelming majority of respondents provided solutions that yielded a negative expected return (Carroll et al., 1988).

Across all of the games described above, by focusing on their own thoughts and actions, study participants ignore other key factors that also influence their outcomes and fail to perform optimally in competitive settings (Messick et al., 1997; Tor & Bazerman, 2003). Tor and Bazerman used protocol analysis to show that people performed suboptimally because they ignored the rules of the game and the decisions of the opposing party. In addition, Tor and Bazerman found that the same errors existed and predicted failure across three seemingly different tasks—the Acquiring a Company problem, the Monty Hall problem, and the Multi-Party Ultimatum game. These problems are particularly good examples of instances in which the rules of the game and the decisions of others are out of focus, two absolutely central and often accessible pieces of information in a negotiation. In the negotiation domain, the conditions of a challenging task, narrow assumptions, self-relevant information, and affective considerations are to be expected; thus, the rules of the game and the decisions of others are outside of the bounds of awareness.

Idson et al. (2004) use the concept of bounded awareness (referred to as focusing failures in that work) to attack one of the chief limitations of the field of behavioral decision research—its past failure to improve decision making. Building off the analogical reasoning work of Thompson, Gentner, Loewenstein, and colleagues (Gentner & Markman, 1997; Loewenstein, Thompson, & Gentner, 1999; Thompson, Gentner, & Loewenstein, 2000), Idson et al. show that proper training can reduce bias in the Acquiring a Company problem, one of the most robust problems in the decision literature (Bereby-Meyer & Grosskopf, 2002). Idson et al. find that by allowing study participants to see and understand differences in seemingly unrelated decision problems (the two versions of the Monty Hall game and Multi-Party Ultimatums presented above) study participants can learn to focus more accurately on the decisions of other parties and the rules of the game—the keys to solving the Acquiring a Company problem.

Tor and Bazerman (2003) and Idson et al. (2004) focused on the three simplest decision problems (those described above) that we could identify as potential examples of the predicted focusing failures. But we believe that these documented focusing failures have far greater explanatory power. Ho, Camerer, and Weigelt (1998) examine a problem in which each player chooses a number from 0 to 100.

The winning number is the one closest to a half of the mean of all the entries. If the decisions of others and nuances of the rules of the game are entirely out of focus, 50 emerges as a naïve yet common submission. But Ho et al. note that even the simplest logic should lead people to think that if the average were 50, a better submission would be 25. Of course, this logic requires attention to the rules of the game. Yet when you consider the decisions of other players, it should become clear that others will follow this same logic; therefore, the mean might be 25, which means that you should submit 12.5. However, if others use this logic, you should submit 6.25, and so on, down to 0—the equilibrium solution. The winning answer is typically greater than 0. But simple numbers such as 50 and 25 are prevalent, and they derive from not fully focusing on the rules of the game and the thoughts of other players.

Camerer and Lovallo (1999) found that participants were insensitive to the quality of their competition, a phenomenon they label "reference group neglect." We would argue that these researchers are identifying a common pattern of the quality of competitors that typically falls outside the awareness of the decision maker. They found that participants largely ignore how the quality of competitors interacts with the rules of the competition to affect the wisdom of entering their experimental market. Their results show that focusing failures lead to decisions with negative expected values.

Moore (2000) finds bounded awareness in the context of negotiation deadlines. In a very simple negotiation between a buyer and seller, where if no agreement is reached both parties get zero payoff, Moore's procedure then imposes a publicly known deadline on one of the parties, which intuitively puts that party at a disadvantage. Of course, if one party has a deadline, so does the other. Objectively, the deadline affects the two parties symmetrically, but negotiators falsely believed that a deadline put them at an asymmetric disadvantage.

In another experiment, Moore imposes time-related costs on one of the two parties. This manipulation objectively does give the party without time-related costs an advantage. Moore then offers the party with time-related costs the option to impose a firm deadline on the negotiations, eliminating their own asymmetric time-related costs and creating symmetric costs for the failure to reach agreement. The majority of study participants passed on this option, despite the strategic benefit it would create. These participants failed to think through how the rules of the game would affect the other party, and they suboptimized as a result.

Massy and Wu (2001, unpublished) show that study participants exhibit "system neglect," undervaluing the importance of the more general context in which they are making their decision. We see one critical example of this type of focusing failure in the lack of concern exhibited by citizens of the United States to consider campaign-finance reform as a means of curbing the political influence of special-interest groups (Bazerman, Baron, & Shonk, 2001). When citizens are asked whether they support and care about this issue, they say "yes." But when asked to rank campaign-finance reform against other issues, they rank it very low. Bazerman et al. argue that voters undervalue campaign-finance reform because of a specific failure to focus on how the system influences important outcomes. Yet, people should care about such reform because it would affect virtually every other issue (and its effects could be enormous). But people do not tend to think through this process; instead, they value issues that are more clearly seen as end states or outcomes, rather than using broader awareness that would direct attention toward a set of important outcomes (Bazerman et al., 2001).

We see this chapter as being broadly compatible with the review of the negotiation literature by Bazerman et al. (2000b) that argues that a critical new research direction concerns how negotiators psychologically define the negotiation game. Bazerman et al. build off the game theoretic work of Brandenburger and Nalebuff (1996), who argued that how competitors define the game may be more important than the moves they make within the game. We offer bounded awareness as a more unique construct to explain how people may make systematic errors in how they define the negotiation game.

WHAT ELSE IS OUT OF FOCUS IN NEGOTIATION?

The initial negotiation studies reviewed above are meant to exemplify the potential to study and improve negotiations by considering what is outside the awareness of most negotiators who should be in focus. Other speculative writing has argued that negotiators often err by failing to add issues to the table, failing to look for contingent contracts, and overly defining the structure of the negotiation as fixed, all of which we can conceptualize as products of narrow assumptions. Often, wise agreements occur by changing the negotiators who are at the table, changing the agenda, adding parties to the table, and so forth. We would argue that these nontraditional solutions can be systemized by the development of a literature based on what is commonly outside of awareness in negotiation.

Like any new conceptual ideas, ours are loosely defined and will improve over time. Rather than offering a summary of a specific study or a tightly defined construct, we contribute the argument that the examination of what is and is not in focus in negotiation offers insight into the limitations in negotiation effectiveness and allows us to continue our search for strategies to help negotiators add value.

REFERENCES

Akerlof, G. (1970). The market for lemons: Qualitative uncertainty and the market mechanism. *Quarterly Journal of Economics*, 89, 488–500.
Allred, K. G., Mallozzi, J. S., Matsui, F., & Raia, C. P. (1997). The influence of anger and compassion on negotiation performance. *Organizational Behavior and Human Decision Processes*, 70(3), 175–187.
Amabile, T., Barsade, S. G., Mueller, J. S., & Staw, B. M. (2002). *Affect and creativity at work: A daily longitudinal test*. Unpublished manuscript.
Amabile, T., Hadley, C. N., & Kramer, S. (2002). Creativity under the gun. *Harvard Business Review*, 80(8), 52–61.
Babcock, L., & Loewenstein, G. (1997). Explaining bargaining impasse: The role of self-serving biases. *The Journal of Economic Perspectives*, 11(1), 109–126.

Ball, S. B., Bazerman, M. H., & Carroll, J. S. (1991). An evaluation of learning in the bilateral winner's curse. *Organizational Behavior and Human Decision Processes, 48*(1), 1–22.

Banaji, M. R., Bazerman, M. H., & Chugh, D. (2003). How (un)ethical are you? *Harvard Business Review,* December, 56–64.

Bazerman, M. H. (2005). *Judgment in managerial decision making.* New York: John Wiley & Sons.

Bazerman, M. H., Baron, J., & Shonk, K. (2001). *You can't enlarge the pie: Six barriers to effective government.* New York: Basic Books.

Bazerman, M. H., Curhan, J. R., & Moore, D. A. (2000a). The death and rebirth of the social psychology of negotiation. In M. Clark & G. Fletcher (Eds.), *Blackwell handbook of social psychology.* Cambridge, MA: Blackwell.

Bazerman, M. H., Curhan, J. R., Moore, D. A., & Valley, K. L. (2000b). Negotiation. *Annual Review of Psychology, 51,* 279–314.

Bazerman, M. H., Magliozzi, T., & Neale, M. A. (1985). Integrative bargaining in a competitive market. *Organizational Behavior and Human Decision Processes, 35*(3), 294–313.

Bazerman, M. H., Moore, D. A., & Gillespie, J. J. (1999). The human mind as a barrier to wiser environmental agreements. *American Behavioral Scientist, 42*(8), 1277–1300.

Bazerman, M. H., & Neale, M. A. (1982). Improving negotiation effectiveness under final offer arbitration: The role of selection and training. *Journal of Applied Psychology, 67*(5), 543–548.

Bazerman, M. H., & Neale, M. A. (1983). Heuristics in negotiation: Limitations to dispute resolution effectiveness. In M. H. Bazerman & R. J. Lewicki (Eds.), *Negotiating in organizations.* Beverly Hills, CA: Sage.

Bazerman, M. H., Neale, M. A., Valley, K. L., Zajac, E. J., & Kim, Y. M. (1992). The effect of agents and mediators on negotiation outcomes. *Organizational Behavior and Human Decision Processes, 53*(1), 55–73.

Bereby-Meyer, Y., & Grosskopf, B. (2002). *Overcoming the winner's curse: An adaptive learning perspective.* AoM Conflict Management Division Meetings No. 13496, August 8, 2002, Denver.

Bottom, W. P., & Studt, A. (1993). Framing effects and the distributive aspect of integrative bargaining. *Organizational Behavior and Human Decision Processes, 56*(3), 459–474.

Bradenburger, A. M., & Nalebuff, B. J. (1996). *Co-opetition.* New York: Doubleday.

Camerer, C., & Lovallo, D. (1999). Overconfidence and excess entry: An experimental approach. *The American Economic Review,* 306–318.

Carnevale, P. J., & Isen, A. M. (1986). The influence of positive affect and visual access on the discovery of integrative solutions in bilateral negotiations. *Organizational Behavior and Human Decision Processes, 37,* 1–13.

Carroll, J. S., Bazerman, M. H., & Maury, R. (1988). Negotiator cognitions: A descriptive approach to negotiators' understanding of their opponents. *Organizational Behavior and Human Decision Processes, 41*(3), 352–370.

Chugh, D., Bazerman, M. H., & Banaji, M. R. (2005). Bounded ethicality as a psychological barrier to recognizing conflicts of interest. In D. A. Moore, D. M. Cain, G. F. Loewenstein, & M. H. Bazerman (Eds.), *Conflicts of interest: Problems and solutions from law, medicine and organizational settings.* London: Cambridge University Press.

Curhan, J. R., Neale, M. A., & Ross, L. (1999). *Dynamic valuation: Preference change in the context of active face-to-face negotiations.* Paper presented at the Annual Meeting of the Academy of Management, Chicago.

Cutcher-Gershenfeld, J., McKersie, R., Peace, N., & Segal, Z. V. (2004). *Negotiating labor agreements.* Paper presented at the Program on Negotiation, Cambridge, MA.

De Dreu, C. K., & McCusker, C. (1997). Gain-loss frames and cooperation in two-person social dilemmas: A transformational analysis. *Journal of Personality and Social Psychology, 72*(5), 1093–1106.

Diekmann, K. A., Samuels, S. M., Ross, L., & Bazerman, M. H. (1997). Self-interest and fairness in problems of resource allocation: Allocators versus recipients. *Journal of Personality and Social Psychology, 72*(5), 1061–1074.

Diekmann, K. A., Tenbrunsel, A. E., & Bazerman, M. H. (1999). Escalation and negotiation: Two central themes in the work of Jeffrey Z. Rubin. In M. Aaron & D. Kolb (Eds.), *Essays in memory of Jeffrey Z. Rubin.* Cambridge, MA: Program on Negotiation & Jossey-Bass.

Diekmann, K. A., Tenbrunsel, A. E., Shah, P. P., Schroth, & Bazerman, M. H. (1996). The descriptive and prescriptive use of previous purchase price in negotiations. *Organizational Behavior and Human Decision Processes, 66*(2), 179–191.

Dijksterhuis, A., Macrae, C., & Haddock, G. (1999). When recollective experiences matter: Subjective ease of retrieval and stereotyping. *Personality and Social Psychology Bulletin, 25*(6), 760–768.

Forgas, J. P. (1998). On feeling good and getting your way: Mood effects on negotiator cognition and bargaining strategies. *Journal of Personality and Social Psychology, 74*(3), 565–577.

Fox, C. R., & Tversky, A. (1998). A belief-based account of decision under uncertainty. *Management Science, 44*(7), 879–895.

Friedman, D. (1998). Monty Hall's three doors: Construction and deconstruction of a choice anomaly. *The American Economic Review, 4*(88), 933–946.

Fukuno, M., & Ohbuchi, K.-i. (1997). Cognitive biases in negotiation: The determinants of fixed-pie assumption and fairness bias. *Japanese Journal of Social Psychology, 13*(1), 43–52.

Gentner, D., & Markman, A. B. (1997). Structure mapping in analogy and similarity. *American Psychologist, 52*(1), 45–56.

Gilbert, D. T., & Wilson, T. D. (2000). Miswanting: Some problems in the forecasting of future affective states. In Forgas, J. P. (Ed.), *Feeling and thinking: The role of affect in social cognition studies in emotion and social interaction* (2nd series). Cambridge: Cambridge University Press.

Guth, W., Schmittberger, R., & Schwarze, B. (1982). An experimental analysis of ultimatum bargaining. *Journal of Economic Behavior and Organizations, 3,* 367–388.

Hastie, R., & Dawes, R. M. (2001). *Rational choice in an uncertain world: The psychology of judgment and decision making.* Thousand Oaks, CA: Sage.

Ho, T. H., Camerer, C., & Weigelt, K. (1998). Interated dominance and interated best response in experimental 'p-beauty' contests. *American Economic Review, 88,* 44–69.

Idson, L. C., Chugh, D., Bereby-Meyer, Y., Moran, S., Grosskopf, B., & Bazerman, M. H. (2004). Overcoming focusing failures in competitive environments. *Journal of Behavioral Decision Making, 17,*159–172.

Kahneman, D. (1992). Reference points, anchors, norms, and mixed feelings. *Organizational Behavior and Human Decision Processes, 51*(2), 296–312.

Kahneman, D., & Tversky, A. (1979). Prospect theory: An analysis of decision under risk. *Econometrica, 47,* 263–291.

Keltner, D., & Robinson, R. J. (1993). Imagined ideological differences in conflict escalation and resolution. *International Journal of Conflict Management, 4*(3), 249–262.

Kramer, R. M., Newton, E., & Pommerenke, P. L. (1993). Self-enhancement biases and negotiator judgment: Effects of self-esteem and mood. *Organizational Behavior and Human Decision Processes, 56*(1), 110–133.

Lim, R. G., & Carnevale, P. J. (1995). Influencing mediator behavior through bargainer framing. *International Journal of Conflict Management, 6*(4), 349–368.

Loewenstein, G. F. (1996). Out of control: Visceral influences on behavior. *Organizational Behavior and Human Decision Processes, 65*(3), 272–292.

Loewenstein, G. F., Thompson, L. L., & Bazerman, M. H. (1989). Social utility and decision making in interpersonal contexts. *Journal of Personality and Social Psychology, 57*(3), 426–441.

Loewenstein, J., Thompson, L., & Gentner, D. (1999). Analogical encoding facilitates knowledge transfer in negotiation. *Psychonomic Bulletin and Review, 6*(4), 586–597.

Mack, A. (2003). Inattentional blindness: Looking without seeing. *Current Directions in Psychological Science, 12*(5), 180–184.

Mack, A., & Rock, I. (1998). *Inattentional blindness.* Cambridge, MA: MIT Press/Bradford Books.

Massey, C., & Wu, G. (2001). Detecting regime shifts: A study of over- and under-reaction. Unpublished manuscript.

McGinn, K. L., Thompson, L. L., & Bazerman, M. H. (2003). Dyadic processes of disclosure and reciprocity in bargaining with communication. *Journal of Behavioral Decision Making, 16*(1), 17–34.

Messick, D. M., Bloom, S., Boldizar, J. P., & Samuelson, C. D. (1985). Why we are fairer than others. *Journal of Experimental Social Psychology, 21*(5), 480–500.

Messick, D. M., Moore, D. A., & Bazerman, M. H. (1997). Ultimatum bargaining with a group: Underestimating the importance of the decision rule. *Organizational Behavior and Human Decision Processes, 69*(2), 87–101.

Moore, C. M., & Egeth, H. (1997). Perception without attention: Evidence of grouping under conditions of inattention. *Journal of Experimental Psychology: Human Perception and Performance, 23*(2), 339–352.

Moore, D. A. (2000). *The unexpected benefits of negotiating under time pressure.* Unpublished doctoral dissertation, Northwestern University, Evanston, IL.

Moore, D. A., Loewenstein, G. F., Tanlu, L., & Bazerman, M. H. (2005). Auditor independence, conflict of interest, and the unconscious intrusion of bias. Harvard Business School Working Paper 03-116.

Nalebuff, B. (1987). Puzzles: Choose a curtain, duel-ity, two point conversions, and more. *Economic Perspectives, 1*(1), 157–163.

Neale, M. A. (1984). The effects of negotiation and arbitration cost salience on bargainer behavior: The role of the arbitrator and constituency on negotiator judgment. *Organizational Behavior and Human Decision Processes, 34*(1), 97–111.

Neale, M. A., & Bazerman, M. H. (1991). *Cognition and rationality in negotiation.* New York: Free Press.

Neisser, U. (1979). The concept of intelligence. *Intelligence, 3*(3), 217–227.

Neuberg, S. L., & Fiske, S. T. (1987). Motivational influences on impression formation: Outcome dependency, accuracy-driven attention, and individuating processes. *Journal of Personality and Social Psychology, 53*(3), 431–444.

Northcraft, G. B., & Neale, M. A. (1987). Experts, amateurs, and real estate: An anchoring-and-adjustment perspective on property pricing decisions. *Organizational Behavior and Human Decision Processes, 39*(1), 84–97.

Ochs, J., & Roth, A. E. (1989). An experimental study of sequential bargaining. *American Economic Review, 79*, 335–385.

Olekalns, M. (1997). Situational cues as moderators of the frame-outcome relationship. *British Journal of Social Psychology, 36*(2), 191–209.

Pillutla, M. M., & Murnighan, J. (1996). Unfairness, anger, and spite: Emotional rejections of ultimatum offers. *Organizational Behavior and Human Decision Processes, 68*(3), 208–224.

Pinkley, R. L., Brittain, J., Neale, M. A., & Northcraft, G. B. (1995). Managerial third-party dispute intervention: An inductive analysis of intervenor strategy selection. *Journal of Applied Psychology, 80*(3), 386–402.

Raiffa, H. (1982). *The art and science of negotiation.* Cambridge, MA: Belknap.

Ritov, I. (1996). Anchoring in simulated competitive market negotiation. *Organizational Behavior and Human Decision Processes, 67*(1), 16–25.

Ross, L., & Stillinger, C. (1991). Barriers to conflict resolution. *Negotiation Journal, 7*(4), 389–404.

Roth, A. E. (1991). An economic approach to the study of bargaining. In M. Bazerman, R. J. Lewicki, & B. H. Sheppard (Eds.), *Handbook of negotiation research: Research in negotiation in organizations* (Vol. 3, pp. 35–67). Greenwich, CT: JAI Press.

Samuelson, W. F., & Bazerman, M. H. (1985). The winner's curse in bilateral negotiations. In V. Smith (Ed.), *Research in experimental economics* (Vol. 3). Greenwich, CT: JAI Press.

Schkade, D. A., & Kahneman, D. (1998). Does living in California make people happy? A focusing illusion in judgments of life satisfaction. *Psychological Science, 9*(5), 340–346.

Schneider, A. (2004). *The theory of magic.* Retrieved April 20, 2005 from http://www.worldmagiccenter.com/ (under construction).

Selvin, S. (1975). [Letter to the editor]. *American Statistician, 29*, 67.

Shah, P. P., & Jehn, K. A. (1993). Do friends perform better than acquaintances? The interaction of friendship, conflict, and task. *Group Decision and Negotiation, 2*(2), 149–165.

Simon, H. A. (1957). *Models of man; social and rational.* New York: Wiley.

Simon, H. A. (1983). Search and reasoning in problem solving. *Artificial Intelligence, 21*, 7–29.

Simons, D. J. (2000). Current approaches to change blindness. *Visual Cognition, 7*(1–3), 1–15.

Simons, D. J., & Chabris, C. F. (1999). Gorillas in our midst: Sustained inattentional blindness for dynamic events. *Perception, 28*(9), 1059–1074.

Simons, D. J., & Levin, D. (2003). What makes change blindness interesting? In D. E. Irwin & B. H. Ross (Eds.), *The psychology of learning and motivation* (Vol. 42). San Diego, CA: Academic Press.

Slovic, P., Finucane, M., Peters, E., & MacGregor, D. G. (2002). The affect heuristic. In T. Gilovich, D. Griffin, & D. Kahneman (Eds.), *Intuitive judgment: Heuristics and biases.* Cambridge: Cambridge University Press.

Sondak, H., & Bazerman, M. H. (1989). Matching and negotiation processes in quasi-markets. *Organizational Behavior and Human Decision Processes, 44*(2), 261–280.

Taylor, S. E. (1989). *Positive illusions: Creative self-deception and the healthy mind.* New York: Basic Books.

Taylor, S. E., & Brown, J. D. (1988). Illusion and well-being: A social psychological perspective on mental health. *Psychological Bulletin, 103*(2), 193–210.

Tenbrunsel, A. E., Galvin, T. L., Neale, M. A., & Bazerman, M. H. (1996). Cognitions in organizations. In S. R. Clegg, C. Hardy, & W. Nord (Eds.), *Handbook of organization studies* (pp. 313–337). Thousand Oaks, CA: Sage.

Thaler, R. H. (1996). Doing economics without *Homo Economicus*. In S. G. Medema & W. J. Samuels (Eds.), *Foundations of research in economics: How do economists do economics*. Northampton, MA: Edward Elgar Publishing.

Thaler, R. H. (2000). From homo economicus to homo sapiens. *Journal of Economic Perspectives, 14*(1), 133–141.

Thompson, L. (1995). The impact of minimum goals and aspirations on judgments of success in negotiations. *Group Decision and Negotiation, 4*(6), 513–524.

Thompson, L., & DeHarpport, T. (1994). Social judgment, feedback, and interpersonal learning in negotiation. *Organizational Behavior and Human Decision Processes, 58*(3), 327–345.

Thompson, L., & Fox, C. R. (2000). Negotiation within and between groups in organizations: Levels of analysis. In M. E, Turner (Ed.), *Groups at work: Advances in theory and research* (pp. 221–266). Hillsdale, NJ: Lawrence Erlbaum.

Thompson, L., & Hastie, R. (1990). Social perception in negotiation. *Organizational Behavior and Human Decision Processes, 47*(1), 98–123.

Thompson, L., & Hrebec, D. (1996). Lose-lose agreements in interdependent decision making. *Psychological Bulletin, 120*(3), 396–409.

Thompson, L., Gentner, D., & Loewenstein, J. (2000). Avoiding missed opportunities in managerial life: Analogical training more powerful than individual case training. *Organizational Behavior and Human Decision Processes, 82*(1), 60–75.

Tor, A., & Bazerman, M. H. (2003). Focusing failures in competitive environments: Explaining decision errors in the Monty Hall game, the acquiring a company problem, and multiparty ultimatums. *Journal of Behavioral Decision Making, 16*(5), 353–374.

Tversky, A., & Kahneman, D. (1974). Judgment under uncertainty: Heuristics and biases. *Science, 185,* 1124–1131.

Tversky, A., & Koehler, D. J. (1994). Support theory: A nonextensional representation of subjective probability. *Psychological Review, 101*(4), 547–567.

vos Savant, M. (1990, December 2). Ask Marilyn. *Parade.* New York.

vos Savant, M. (1991, February 17). Ask Marilyn. *Parade.* New York.

Whyte, G., & Sebenius, J. K. (1997). The effect of multiple anchors on anchoring in individual and group judgment. *Organizational Behavior and Human Decision Processes, 69*(1), 75–85.

Wilson, T. D., Wheatley, T., Meyers, J. M., Gilbert, D. T., & Axsom, D. (2000). Focalism: A source of durability bias in affective forecasting. *Journal of Personality and Social Psychology, 78*(5), 821–836.

Winklegren, W. A. (1974). *How to solve problems.* San Francisco: W. H. Freeman & Company.

3

Social Cognition, Attribution, and Perception in Negotiation: The Role of Uncertainty in Shaping Negotiation Processes and Outcomes

MARGARET A. NEALE and ALISON R. FRAGALE

*T*raditional economic theories, as well as conventional wisdom, suggest that negotiations should be rational transactions guided by the principle of utility maximization (Raiffa, 1982). That is, the economic perspective assumes that negotiators have stable, well-defined preferences, and that they attempt to fulfill these preferences during the course of their negotiations by striving to maximize their gains and minimize their losses. Unfortunately, in reality, negotiations are rarely this straightforward, and negotiations often fail to play out according to the predictions of rational choice models (Neale & Bazerman, 1991). As a result, negotiation researchers have demonstrated a growing interest in a social cognition approach to negotiation, which aims to understand the human psychological influences on negotiation processes and outcomes. Rooted in social psychology, social cognition concerns how individuals make sense of their environment and think about the world around them (Fiske & Taylor, 1991). In the context of negotiation, research on social cognition investigates how negotiators' perceptions and attributions affect their desires and behavior in negotiations and, subsequently, their negotiated agreements. Thus, unlike traditional economic models of negotiator behavior, the social cognition approach to negotiation recognizes that two negotiators, facing the same objective circumstances, may have different goals, express different behaviors, and obtain different benefits, simply because these two negotiators perceive their circumstances differently.

Understanding negotiators' perceptions is important because negotiations are generally characterized by a high degree of uncertainty on the part of the negotiating parties. Negotiators operate in a world of imperfect information. They often have limited knowledge of their opponents' skills, preferences, and strategies, and frequently even lack insight into their own desires and behaviors (e.g., Curhan, Neale, & Ross, 2004). As a result, negotiators are often unsure of who or what to believe, how to behave to get what they want, and how to anticipate the consequences of their actions. In an attempt to reduce these types of uncertainties, negotiators are likely to be sensitive to environmental cues and vulnerable to cognitive shortcuts that enable them to simplify a relatively complex problem and make sense of their situation. At the same time, this uncertainty implies that any given negotiation situation is likely to be open to multiple interpretations. In short, the uncertainty inherent in most negotiations opens the door for negotiators' attributions and perceptions to shape how negotiations unfold, and these negotiator cognitions are influenced by both the negotiators' dispositions and specific features of the bargaining context. Thus, negotiators may frequently fall prey to many decision-making biases and perceptual errors (see Bazerman & Chugh, chapter 2), depending on how particular dispositional and situational factors affect their interpretation of the bargaining situation (Neale & Bazerman, 1991).

In this chapter, we take a social cognition approach to negotiation and explore how negotiators' social perceptions shape their attitudes, behaviors, and negotiated outcomes. In particular, we focus on the role of uncertainty in shaping negotiator cognition. We outline the various types of uncertainties that negotiators are likely to face, and discuss the perceptual and behavioral consequences that result from negotiators' attempts to resolve these uncertainties. We organize this discussion around the types of uncertainties that negotiators face at various stages of a negotiation, talking first about uncertainties that negotiators encounter before and during a negotiation, and second about uncertainties that negotiators face subsequent to a negotiation. Finally, we conclude by discussing the costs and benefits of negotiator uncertainty and then discussing factors that influence whether negotiator uncertainty will lead to functional or dysfunctional negotiator behavior.

UNCERTAINTY BEFORE AND DURING A NEGOTIATION

Many of the ambiguities that negotiators face arise during the preparatory stages of a negotiation and persist, and often evolve, throughout their interactions. In this section, we focus on two main types of uncertainty that negotiators encounter during their interactions: *goal uncertainty*, or ambiguity regarding the objective of the negotiation, and *preference uncertainty*, or uncertainty regarding one's own preferences and the preferences of one's counterparts. In both cases, we focus on how negotiators' attempts to resolve these uncertainties affect their cognitions and perceptions in their negotiations.

Goal Uncertainty

One of the first uncertainties that negotiators need to resolve is deciding on a goal for the negotiation (see Carnevale & De Dreu, chapter 4, for a complete discussion of goals and motivations in negotiations). As mentioned previously, economic models often assume that negotiators are motivated by a single goal, the desire to maximize utility, but in actuality, there are multiple, and sometimes seemingly contradictory, goals that negotiators may try to achieve through the course of their negotiations. The decision about which goal, or set of goals, to adopt during a negotiation may stem partly from individuals' chronic preferences to pursue some goals over others (e.g., Higgins, 1997), but will also be affected by situational factors, such as which goals are made salient to the negotiators (e.g., Galinsky, Mussweiler, & Medvec, 2002a) or which goals negotiators assume that their opponents will pursue (e.g., Paese & Gilin, 2000). In this section, we discuss how negotiators choose among multiple goals in a negotiation, and how these choices shape their subsequent cognitions, behaviors, and outcomes.

Achieving Aspirations vs. Beating Reservations   One of the most basic goals that negotiators need to decide on is what constitutes an acceptable outcome from a negotiation. In most cases, negotiators are likely to agree to a deal within a certain range of outcomes, with an upper and lower bound, rather than just insisting on one specific outcome that must be achieved. However, within this range of acceptable solutions, negotiators can set different goals. On one hand, negotiators may focus on the upper bound of their outcome range (referred to as a negotiator's *aspiration price*) and think about the ideal outcome that they could obtain from the negotiation. On the other hand, negotiators may focus on their lower bound (referred to as a negotiator's *reservation price*) and think about the minimum outcome that they must obtain to reach a deal in the present negotiation. Of course, negotiators are not required to choose between these two goals, and could theoretically attempt to satisfy both goals simultaneously. However, we suggest that the complex and uncertain nature of negotiations motivates negotiators to simplify their situation, and as such, they are likely to focus on only one of these goals at any given time (Polzer & Neale, 1995).

Understanding when and why negotiators are likely to choose one of these goals—achieving one's aspirations or beating one's reservations—over the other is important, because research suggests that this decision often affects the outcomes that negotiators are able to achieve. In general, negotiators achieve better outcomes for themselves when they focus on their aspiration price than when they focus on their reservation price (Galinsky et al., 2002a). This difference in performance occurs because attempting to achieve one's highest expectations (i.e., focusing on one's aspiration price) is a more challenging goal than simply attempting to outperform one's minimally acceptable standard (i.e., focusing on one's reservation price). A large body of evidence indicates that negotiator's outcomes are influenced by the difficulty of their goals: The more difficult the goal a negotiator is trying to achieve, the better the outcome obtained from the negotiation

(Bazerman, Magliozzi, & Neale, 1985; Huber & Neale, 1986, 1987; Galinsky et al., 2002a; Neale & Bazerman, 1985; White & Neale, 1994).

Several factors may influence on which of these two goals, aspirations or reservations, negotiators focus. One possibility is that negotiators have chronic, dispositional preferences for focusing on one goal over the other. For example, research by Higgins (see Higgins, 1997, for a review) has demonstrated that individuals differ in their self-regulation strategies: Some individuals adopt a *promotion focus*, or a focus on aspirations and accomplishments, whereas other individuals adopt a *prevention focus*, or a focus on responsibilities and safety. Individuals with a promotion focus are generally motivated by a desire to achieve positive outcomes, while individuals with a prevention focus are generally motivated by a desire to avoid negative outcomes. Evidence suggests that these differences in regulatory focus affect individuals' goals and behaviors. For example, promotion-focused individuals, who are eager to obtain gains, have been found to perform better on tasks when successful performance is framed in terms of achieving a gain (e.g., gaining $1 for successful performance), than when performance is framed in terms of avoiding a loss (e.g., losing $1 for unsuccessful performance), whereas prevention-focused individuals exhibit the opposite pattern (Shah, Higgins, & Friedman, 1998). Relatedly, Crowe and Higgins (1997) found that promotion-focused individuals were more willing to take risks than prevention-focused individuals, who were more conservative. These differences in self-regulation strategies have also been shown to affect negotiators' choices of goals in a negotiation. Promotion-focused individuals are more likely to focus on the goal of achieving their aspiration price; prevention-focused individuals are more likely to focus on the goal of beating their reservation price (Galinsky, Leonardelli, Okhuysen, & Mussweiler, 2005). Consequently, chronic differences in negotiators' self-regulation tendencies affect their outcomes from a negotiation: Promotion-focused negotiators, who focus on their aspiration prices, systematically outperform prevention-focused negotiators, who focus on their reservation prices (Galinsky et al., 2005).

Beyond these chronic tendencies to focus on one's aspirations or one's reservations, a negotiator's decision about which goal to pursue may also be affected by situational forces that make one of these goals more salient than the other (Galinsky et al., 2002a). For example, a negotiator's decision to focus on aspirations or reservations may be affected by which party in a negotiation makes the first offer and what the value of this first offer is (Galinsky & Mussweiler, 2001). A negotiator who makes a first offer in a negotiation is likely to make an offer that is personally advantageous, that is, an offer that is close to the negotiator's aspiration price. To the extent that different parties to a negotiation are likely to have nonidentical preferences, the negotiator who receives a first offer may find that this offer is not particularly desirable (perhaps barely above, or even below, this negotiator's reservation price). Once this first offer is made, negotiators are likely to generate knowledge that is consistent with it (Galinsky & Mussweiler, 2001; Mussweiler & Strack, 1999a, 1999b, 2000). That is, all parties to a negotiation will selectively recall information that supports the validity of this offer. The negotiator who made the offer, in thinking about why this offer is a reasonable one, may focus on his aspiration price and conclude that his goal is to obtain a deal as close to his aspiration price as possible. In contrast, the negotiator who receives the offer (which may be closer to this negotiator's reservation price than aspiration price), may become quite pessimistic about her likely outcome in the negotiation, and subsequently focus on simply trying to obtain an outcome that is at least as good as her reservation price. As discussed above, these differences in negotiator goals should affect the quality of the outcomes that negotiators obtain from a negotiation. Indeed, research suggests that negotiators who make first offers in a negotiation, and as a result focus on their aspiration price, generally obtain better outcomes than negotiators who do not make the first offer (Galinsky & Mussweiler, 2001).

The tendency to focus on one's aspiration price versus reservation price may also be affected by structural factors, such as the power relationship between the negotiating parties. Most conceptions of power are based on Weber's (1947) classic definition of power as the probability that a person can carry out his or her own will despite resistance. That is, power is defined as the capacity to control one's own outcomes and the outcomes of others: The greater one's level of control, the more power one possesses. According to power-dependence theory (Blau, 1964; Emerson, 1962), a prominent theoretical framework for conceptualizing power, one's level of control, in turn, is based on the extent to which others *depend* on the focal individual for resources and rewards. Thus, given two individuals, A and B, A's power over B is directly related to the degree to which B is dependent on A. In the context of negotiation, negotiator power has been operationalized in several different ways. One frequently studied source of negotiator power is a negotiator's alternative to a given negotiation (Pinkley, Neale, & Bennett, 1994). A negotiator who possesses a valuable alternative to a negotiation (e.g., a job candidate who already has several appealing job offers) is less *dependent* on the focal negotiation than a negotiator with poor (or nonexistent) alternatives (since the negotiator with attractive alternatives can simply walk away and accept another job); and, therefore, the former negotiator is said to possess greater power in the negotiation than the latter. Alternatively, negotiator power has also been operationalized as the amount of value that a negotiator contributes to the present negotiation (Kim, 1997; Kim & Fragale, 2005). Negotiators who bring unique skills, attributes, and knowledge to a negotiation (e.g., a job candidate with specialized finance skills that no other candidate possesses) increase their counterparts' dependence on this relationship (e.g., to acquire the specialized finance skills, the recruiter is dependent on the job candidate accepting the job), and consequently possess greater power. Conversely, negotiators who lack such unique contributions will generate less dependence from their counterparts and will possess lower levels of power.

In some instances, all parties to a negotiation may be equally dependent on each other and thus possess equal power. However, in many cases, negotiators will be of unequal power; that is, the parties will differ in the extent to which they are dependent on the other negotiators to receive valued rewards, and thus one party in a negotiation may have a greater ability to exert control over his or her own outcomes and the outcomes of others. Evidence suggests that negotiators' power positions affect their reservation and aspiration prices: High-power negotiators set higher reservation and aspiration prices than their low-power counterparts (Pinkley et al., 1994). As a result, negotiators with high power generally obtain better outcomes from their negotiations than low-power negotiators (Komorita & Leung, 1985; Pinkley et al., 1994). However, in addition to affecting the values of their aspiration and reservation prices, evidence suggests that negotiators' power positions may also affect their likelihood of focusing on one of these values over the other. Related to the above discussion of the effects first offered in negotiations, research has demonstrated that negotiators who possess high power are more likely to make a first offer in a negotiation than negotiators who possess lower power (Magee, Galinsky, & Gruenfeld, 2004). As the above-mentioned research suggests, making the first offer may affect a negotiator's goal, such that negotiators who make the first offer may be more likely to focus on their aspiration prices, whereas negotiators who receive a first offer made by a counterpart may be more likely to focus on their reservation prices (Galinsky & Mussweiler, 2001). Thus, a negotiator's power may affect which goal, achieving aspirations or surpassing reservations, is most salient in a negotiation; high-power parties, who are more likely to initiate a first offer in a negotiation, may consequently focus on their aspiration prices, whereas low-power parties, who are more likely to be the recipient of a first offer, may focus on their reservation prices. This systematic difference in goals between high- and low-power parties may provide at least a partial explanation for the well-documented finding that high-power negotiators systematically outperform low-power negotiators.

Cooperating vs. Competing Another aspect of goal uncertainty derives from negotiators' decisions about whether to cooperate or compete. A negotiator may wonder if he or she should view an upcoming negotiation as a cooperative endeavor, in which all parties are concerned about the welfare and outcomes of other negotiators, or as a competitive encounter in which negotiators care only about their own outcomes. Although negotiators may perceive the decision to cooperate or compete as opposite poles of a single dimension, in actuality, cooperation and competition represent separate dimensions of behavior (Pruitt & Rubin, 1986; see Carnevale & De Dreu, chapter 4, for a discussion of dual-concern theory), and negotiators can, at least in theory, hold cooperative and competitive goals or display cooperative and competitive behaviors, simultaneously. In fact, most negotiations are "mixed-motive conflicts" in which negotiators need to cooperate to ensure that the supply of resources available for exchange is as large as possible and to compete to ensure that they are able to claim an acceptable share of these resources for themselves (Neale & Bazerman, 1991). As a result, evidence suggests that negotiators are able to reach the most integrative (i.e., mutually beneficial) agreements when they balance cooperation, which facilitates trust and information sharing, with competition, which fosters high aspirations and prevents negotiators from settling for suboptimal or compromise (i.e., 50/50 split) solutions (De Dreu, Weingart, & Kwon, 2000b). However, obtaining the optimal balance between cooperation and competition is not easy, and consequently, many negotiators fail to capitalize on full integrative potential available in their negotiations (Bazerman et al., 1985).

One reason that negotiators may have such difficulty in finding the most effective balance between cooperation and competition is that the desire to simplify a complex negotiation problem, combined with their personal preferences for one type of interaction over another, leads negotiators to categorize their interactions as either primarily competitive or cooperative and behave accordingly. One factor that influences negotiators' choices between these two goals is the dispositional tendencies that negotiators have for choosing one of these goals over the other. Researchers refer to such tendencies as *social value orientations* (Deutsch, 1960; McClintock, 1976; see also Carnevale & De Dreu, chapter 4, for a discussion of social value orientations) and distinguish among three types of negotiator orientations: a cooperative orientation (also known as a prosocial orientation), an individualistic orientation, and a competitive orientation. Cooperators are those individuals who focus on maximizing joint benefit (their own benefit plus the benefits of their negotiation counterparts), individualists focus on maximizing their own benefit with no regard for their counterparts, and competitors focus on maximizing their own benefit relative to their counterparts' (i.e., obtaining a better outcome than their counterparts). As the labels imply, individuals with cooperative social value orientations are more likely to pursue cooperative goals in their negotiations, and competitors are more likely to pursue competitive goals, with individualists falling somewhere in between. For example, social value orientations have been shown to affect the way that negotiators think about and plan for their upcoming negotiations. De Dreu and Boles (1998) demonstrated that cooperators perceived their upcoming negotiations to be more friendly and expected their opponents to be more cooperative than competitors. In addition, in planning for the negotiation, cooperators chose more cooperative heuristics, or rules of thumb, such as "an equal split is fair," whereas competitors chose more competitive heuristics, such as "winner takes all." Social value orientations also influence negotiators' behaviors once a negotiation has commenced. Several studies have demonstrated that cooperators exhibit lower levels of demand and make more conciliatory offers, are more trusting of their opponents, and perceive their opponents as more fair than competitors (De Dreu & Boles, 1998; De Dreu & Van Lange, 1995; Olekalns, Smith, & Kibby, 1996).

In addition to these chronic preferences that most negotiators bring with them to the bargaining table, the decision to adopt a cooperative or competitive goal in a negotiation can be affected by ephemeral states or situational aspects of the bargaining context. For one, the decision to cooperate or compete in a negotiation can be affected by something as simple, and transient, as one's mood (see Barry, Fulmer, & Goates, chapter 6, for a complete discussion of mood, emotion, and affect in negotiation). From a social-cognitive standpoint, the study of mood in negotiation explores how a negotiator's perceptions of his or her environment (self, others, and situation) are affected by the negotiator's affective state. Research by Forgas (1998) has demonstrated that negotiators' moods affect how negotiators think about their goals. Across a series of studies, Forgas found that negotiators who are in a good mood report greater intent to adopt cooperative bargaining strategies, achieve deals, and to honor deals in an upcoming negotiation; whereas negotiators who are in a bad mood report a greater intent to behave competitively.

Furthermore, the effects of negotiator mood extend beyond the planning stages of a negotiation: Negotiators in a positive mood report using more cooperative strategies during the negotiation and actually achieve better outcomes for themselves than negotiators in a bad mood, who report using more competitive strategies (Forgas, 1998).

The decision to cooperate or compete can also be affected by the medium through which the negotiation is conducted. Although a majority of the empirical research on negotiations has been conducted in face-to-face contexts, there has been a growing interest in understanding how society's increasing reliance on e-mail communication impacts negotiator behavior (see Nadler & Shestowsky, chapter 8). Evidence to date suggests that negotiators are more likely to behave cooperatively when negotiating face to face than when negotiating from a distance: Face-to-face negotiators are more likely to reveal truthful information (Valley, Moag, & Bazerman, 1998), more likely to disclose information about their interests (Bazerman, Gibbons, Thompson, & Valley, 1998), and more likely to use cooperative strategies and achieve higher joint gains (Drolet & Morris, 2000) than negotiators who interact over the phone or through some form of written communication (e.g., e-mail or notes). These researchers argue that lower levels of cooperative behavior in non–face-to-face contexts are driven by the difficulty of establishing trust and rapport (due to time delays in exchanging information and a lack of nonverbal cues), which are necessary for the formation of cooperative relationships. As a result, negotiations conducted face to face are generally more efficient (i.e., take less time) and are more satisfying for the parties involved than negotiations that occur at a distance (Purdy & Nye, 2000).

In addition to communication mediums, negotiators' preferences for pursuing cooperative or competitive goals may be affected by their evaluations of their skills and abilities. Negotiators may choose to view a negotiation as a competitive encounter because they view themselves as excelling in competitive situations, or may choose to approach a negotiation cooperatively because they seem themselves as good team players. Of course, negotiators may have a dispositional tendency to view themselves as either good cooperators or competitors, but information provided in the negotiation may also temporarily shift negotiators' self-perceptions. A study by Kim and his colleagues (Kim, Diekmann, & Tenbrunsel, 2003) demonstrated that negotiators who received positive-ability feedback (i.e., feedback that the negotiator seemed competent) from an opponent perceived themselves as better negotiators and reported greater intent to behave competitively in an upcoming negotiation than those who had received negative-ability feedback from an opponent. However, negotiators who received positive-ethicality feedback (i.e., feedback that the negotiator seemed honest) from an opponent perceived themselves as more ethical and reported a greater intent to behave cooperatively in an upcoming negotiation than negotiators that received negative-ethicality feedback.

In deciding whether to adopt a cooperative or competitive orientation, negotiators may also be influenced by the expected or observed behaviors of their counterparts. That is, deciding whether to behave cooperatively or competitively depends, in part, on how one expects one's negotiation counterparts to behave.

Research by Diekmann and her colleagues (Diekmann, Tenbrunsel, & Galinsky, 2003) suggests that negotiators are aware that the behaviors of their counterparts will influence their negotiation behaviors, but that they are not always accurate in forecasting how these counterpart behaviors will affect them. In a series of studies, these researchers found that negotiators expected that they would behave more competitively when negotiating against a competitive opponent than a cooperative opponent. However, in actual negotiations, this did not occur. Compared to participants who negotiated against a purportedly noncompetitive opponent, participants who negotiated against an opponent that they believed to be competitive actually became less competitive during the negotiation: They set less aggressive reservation prices (i.e., they were willing to settle for less), they made less aggressive counteroffers, and they were more likely to accept their opponent's final offer. Thus, it appears that negotiating against an opponent that one believes to be competitive actually reduces one's competitive behaviors in a negotiation. Negotiators are likely to respond differently, however, to expectations of cooperative behavior from one's opponent. Evidence suggests that when a negotiator's opponent signals that he or she has a cooperative orientation, negotiators are likely to become *more* cooperative (Liebert, Smith, Hill, & Keiffer, 1968; Paese & Gilin, 2000). For example, Liebert et al. found that when a negotiator knew that his or her opponent had made a conciliatory, as opposed to demanding, first offer, the negotiator responded in kind with a conciliatory counteroffer. Similarly, when a negotiator knows that an opponent has been honest about his or her alternatives, negotiators are more honest about their own alternatives, and make and accept less demanding offers (Paese & Gilin, 2000). Thus, it appears that signals of cooperation from one's opponent, such as revealing truthful information and making less self-interested offers, increase one's level of cooperative behavior in a negotiation.

This asymmetry in negotiator responses to competitive and cooperative opponents raises an interesting question: Why is it that a competitive opponent *decreases* a negotiator's competitiveness, whereas a cooperative opponent *increases* a negotiator's cooperativeness? A potential answer to this question may be found in related research examining interpersonal behavior in social interactions. As mentioned above, cooperative and competitive orientations represent two separate dimensions of negotiatior behavior (Pruitt & Rubin, 1986). Interpersonal circumplex theories (Carson, 1969; Kiesler, 1983; Leary, 1957; Wiggins, 1979, 1982) organize interpersonal behavior around two dimensions: an *affiliation* dimension (anchored by agreeableness and quarrelsomeness) and a *control* dimension (anchored by dominance and submission). Although affiliation and control are used to describe individual behavior across a wide variety of social settings, they generally correspond, respectively, to the dimensions of cooperation and competition discussed in negotiation contexts. Circumplex theories predict and empirical evidence suggests (e.g., Dryer & Horowitz, 1997; Tiedens & Fragale, 2003) that individuals are likely to assimilate to their interactional partners along the affiliation dimension but display contrasting behaviors along a control dimension. In other words, cooperative behaviors on the part of one's interaction partner are likely to increase one's level of cooperativeness (and uncooperative behaviors will reduce cooperativeness), whereas competitive behaviors from one's partner invite one to behave in a more submissive, less competitive fashion. These findings are consistent with the above findings on the effects of opponents' actions on negotiators' behaviors: Whereas cooperative behaviors from one's negotiation opponent can increase one's level of cooperativeness, competitive behaviors from one's opponent actually reduce one's level of competitiveness.

Preference Uncertainty

In addition to uncertainty surrounding the goals that negotiators should pursue, there is often considerable ambiguity regarding the preferences of the negotiating parties. To reach a deal, negotiators need to understand and respond to the preferences of their counterparts, yet negotiators often have little direct insight into what their counterparts actually value. More surprisingly, it is often the case that negotiators are not even aware of their own preferences (e.g., Curhan et al., 2004), in contrast to the fundamental assumption of rationalist economic accounts. As a result, negotiators are left having to deduce their own and others' preferences, often as the negotiation is progressing. The information and assumptions that negotiators use to assess these preferences shape their subsequent cognitions and behavior during negotiations.

Uncertainty About Counterparts' Preferences   It stands to reason that negotiators will often lack knowledge of their counterparts' desires and demands before a negotiation commences. In fact, one of the reasons individuals negotiate in the first place is to create a forum for exchanging information that will enable a mutually acceptable solution to emerge. However, negotiators often do not know how to seek out information from their counterparts, and may also worry that requesting information will oblige the requester to disclose proprietary information in kind, so they often just rely on assumptions or inferences about what their counterparts are likely to value. Unfortunately, negotiators often make systematically erroneous assumptions about their counterparts' preferences, which reduce their ability to achieve optimal negotiation agreements. One of the most common heuristics that negotiators rely on when assessing their counterparts' preferences is the *false consensus effect* (Ross, Greene, & House, 1977; see Marks & Miller, 1987, for a review), wherein individuals assume that their preferences and opinions are widely shared by others. Although this assumption is not always incorrect, and can even be functional and rational in some circumstances (see Dawes, 1989; Dawes & Mulford, 1996), it can also lead individuals to make erroneous assumptions about others' preferences and behaviors (e.g., Sherman, Presson, & Chassin, 1984). When negotiators are unsure of what their counterparts value, they are likely to assume that the issues their counterparts care about are the same as their own (e.g., "If I care a lot about how much salary I earn, my employer must also care a lot about this issue"). This leads to a further, and also frequently incorrect, assumption that any negotiation an individual enters is likely to be a win-lose negotiation in which negotiators fight over dividing a fixed pie of resources (known as the *fixed-pie bias*; Neale & Bazerman, 1991). That is, if a negotiator and his counterpart have identically weighted but oppositely valenced issue preferences in a negotiation (which the negotiator may assume due to the false consensus effect), there is no opportunity to find integrative, or win-win, agreements; one negotiator's gain is simply the other's loss. The fixed-pie bias, which results from negotiators' inferences about their counterparts' preferences, has been shown to affect the quality of outcomes that negotiators obtain. Even when opportunities to make mutually beneficial tradeoffs exist in a negotiation, negotiators frequently arrive at compromise, or "split down the middle," outcomes due to the erroneous assumption of a fixed-pie negotiation (Bazerman et al., 1985; De Dreu, Koole, & Steinel, 2000a).

The assumption that negotiators care about the same issues as their counterparts can also affect how negotiators react to offers proposed by their counterparts during the negotiation. Evidence suggests that negotiators are likely to succumb to *reactive devaluation* (Curhan et al., 2004; Ma'oz, Ward, Katz, & Ross, 2002; Ross, 1995; Ross & Ward, 1995), wherein one's preference for a proposal or idea decreases when the proposal is put forth by one's opponent. If negotiators assume that a negotiation is a zero-sum (my loss is your gain) activity, then any offer proposed by one's counterpart should be considered a bad deal by the negotiator receiving the offer. That is, negotiators reason that what is good for you is bad for me, and the offer you proposed must be good for you, so it must be bad for me. As a result, negotiators will often revise their preferences for outcomes in a negotiation and come to value a particular proposal less once it is offered by one's opponent (Curhan et al., 2004).

Thus, one reason that negotiators may arrive at erroneous conclusions about their counterparts' preferences is that, rather than seeking out information, negotiators make assumptions about what their counterparts value. However, even when negotiators inquire about their counterparts' preferences, they may still end up with inaccurate perceptions of their opponents' wishes due to a biased information search. Individuals often engage in a confirmatory information search, wherein they seek out information that would confirm their preexisting beliefs, while ignoring or not searching for information that would disconfirm their beliefs (Wason, 1960). Negotiators are likely to fall prey to this *confirmatory evidence bias* when assessing the preferences of their negotiation counterparts: A negotiator may make assumptions about her counterpart's preferences and then only ask questions of the counterpart designed to confirm that these original assumptions were correct. A study by van Kleef and De Dreu (2002) found support for the notion that negotiators engage in confirmatory information searches with regard to their opponents. The authors found that negotiators with a cooperative social value orientation, who generally assume that their counterparts will also be cooperative (De Dreu & Boles, 1998), were more likely to ask questions about their counterpart's intention to cooperate; whereas competitive negotiators, who assume that their counterparts will be similarly competitive, were more likely to ask questions about their counterpart's intention to compete. As a result, the negotiators believed that their counterpart shared the same social value orientation as themselves. Thus, even when negotiators seek out information about their counterparts' preferences, a biased information search may still lead negotiators to arrive at the erroneous conclusion that they share the same preferences as their counterparts.

Beyond the uncertainty that negotiators have about *what* their counterparts want, negotiators are also often uncertain as to *why* their counterparts have these preferences. As much of the research reviewed in this chapter suggests, negotiators' desires and behaviors are frequently situationally determined. That is, although negotiators' personalities undoubtedly play a role in shaping negotiations, the processes and outcomes of negotiations are substantially influenced by aspects of the bargaining context that affect negotiators' perceptions and behaviors. Just as negotiators' goals may be contextually determined, negotiators' preferences are also likely to be shaped by situational factors (Thompson, 1990). However, individuals are generally not very good at understanding the situational forces that shape the behaviors of others and consequently attribute the behavior of others to their personalities or dispositions. This tendency to overweight stable personality characteristics and underweight social situations when explaining others' behaviors has been termed the *fundamental attribution error* (Ross, 1977). Evidence suggests that negotiators, when assessing the preferences and behaviors of their counterparts, are likely to fall prey to this judgmental bias. In a series of studies, Morris and his colleagues (Morris, Larrick, & Su, 1999) demonstrated that negotiators' preferences and behaviors in a negotiation are likely to be shaped more by their situation than their personalities but that their counterparts' attribute their behavior more to the negotiators' personalities than their situation. The authors found that the value of a negotiator's alternative offer (a situational factor) was a better predictor of the negotiator's hard bargaining, or haggling, tactics, than was the negotiator's disposition, but that opponents were likely to attribute haggling behavior to the fact that the negotiator was an uncooperative or quarrelsome person. Similarly, the certainty of a negotiator's alternative affected the negotiator's tendency to waffle about his or her limits, such that negotiators with risky alternatives were more likely to be vague and inconsistent about their alternative options than negotiators with certain alternatives, but opponents attributed waffling behavior to traits of inconsistency or insincerity. Furthermore, these dispositional attributions affected the negotiators' predicted future behaviors. Negotiators who faced an opponent with a high alternative (who was therefore perceived as disagreeable) were more likely to prefer that a third party handle any future disputes with that opponent, rather than negotiating with the opponent again. In addition, negotiators' opinions about what jobs the opponent would and would not be suited for (the topic of the negotiation was a job candidate negotiating new employment) were affected by the opponent's alternative. Negotiators who negotiated with an opponent with a valuable alternative were more likely to recommend their opponent for external bargaining roles (which required assertiveness and competitiveness) and less likely to recommend their opponent for a relationship manager role (which required positive interpersonal skills), due to the inferences that negotiators made about their opponents' personalities.

Uncertainty About One's Own Preferences It is not entirely surprising that negotiators experience uncertainty regarding their counterparts' preferences. After all, individuals have only indirect access to the thoughts and feelings of another. What is more astounding, however, is that negotiators often experience uncertainty about their own preferences in a negotiation. Some degree of preference uncertainty may be unavoidable, since evidence suggests that individuals may lack access to their own higher order cognitive processes (Nisbett & Wilson, 1977). That is, individuals often lack self-knowledge in a variety of domains, including their preferences, because they cannot access the mental processes responsible for perception and attitudes (see Wilson & Dunn, 2004, for a review). Thus, negotiators may either not know what they want out of a negotiation, or if they do form preferences, they may be unable to introspect about why their preferred outcomes are actually preferred. Above and beyond this limitation, a negotiator's preference uncertainty may also stem from inadequate planning, if negotiators enter a negotiation without a thorough understanding of their relative preferences for various issues in a negotiation.

Uncertainty about one's own preferences can affect how negotiators interpret proposals made during a negotiation. In the above-mentioned study by Curhan and his colleagues (2004), they found that, in addition to devaluing offers made by one's opponent, negotiators also increased the value attributed to their own offers. That is, after making a specific outcome proposal to one's opponent, negotiators preferred that outcome more than immediately before the proposal was put on the table. Thus, the ambiguity that negotiators experienced regarding their own preferences gave them psychological freedom to alter these preferences as the negotiation progressed. Consistent with this explanation, the researchers found that negotiators were less likely to ascribe greater value to the proposals they made during the negotiation when they ranked their preferences for all possible outcome packages before the negotiation commenced.

These two preference effects, devaluing offers made by one's opponent and increasing value attributed to one's own offers, can create a barrier to the successful resolution of conflicts. As Curhan et al. (2004) point out

> If every offer made to resolve a conflict becomes more attractive to the party offering it, and less attractive to the party receiving it, then the "gap" to be bridged before a mutually acceptable agreement can be reached will be widened rather than narrowed by the very process of negotiation. (p. 143)

If this were always the case, the preference uncertainty experienced by negotiators would greatly impede their ability to reach negotiated agreements. Fortunately, some remedies exist that may enable negotiators to bridge this psychological gap between their offers and the offers of their opponents. As mentioned above, the increased attractiveness of a negotiator's own offers can be reduced when a negotiator prerates all possible outcomes from the negotiation, suggesting that prenegotiation planning may be sufficient to eliminate this effect. Furthermore, the devaluation of offers made by one's counterpart has been shown to be reduced by prenegotiation discussion, in which negotiators talk about their needs and priorities for a brief period before any offers are exchanged (Curhan et al., 2004).

UNCERTAINTY AFTER THE NEGOTIATION

With planning and preparation, negotiators can find strategies to deal with the goal and preference uncertainties that they experience during the negotiation and eventually arrive at mutually acceptable agreements. However, the uncertainty that negotiators experience generally does not end when the negotiation is completed. Regardless of the specific negotiation context, all negotiators, on conclusion of their negotiation, are usually left with the same question: Did I get a good deal? Determining if they got a good deal is another uncertainty that negotiators are motivated to resolve, and the ways that negotiators attempt to resolve this uncertainty are likely to have implications for their behavior in subsequent negotiations. Whether an individual chooses to negotiate with the same counterpart in the future, find a new counterpart, or avoid negotiating all together is likely to depend on the individual's perception of how he or she performed in the present negotiation (Barry & Oliver, 1996). In this section, we discuss the ways that negotiators attempt to determine if they obtained a good deal and the consequences of these strategies for negotiator satisfaction.

One obvious determinant of negotiator satisfaction should be the objective outcomes that negotiators obtain. Negotiators who achieve objectively better outcomes should feel better about their performance than negotiators who perform poorly (Gillespie, Brett, & Weingart, 2000), but this may not always be the case. For one, research suggests that individuals are not always able to forecast their emotional responses to events accurately, and consequently may overestimate the impact of future events, such as getting a good deal in a negotiation, on their happiness (e.g., Gilbert, Pinel, Wilson, Blumberg, & Wheatley, 1998; Gilbert & Wilson, 2000). Furthermore, negotiators may often lack sufficient information to evaluate their outcomes in objective terms, and as a result, negotiator satisfaction may be heavily influenced by negotiators' perceptions and assumptions about their negotiated outcomes. Consequently, negotiators' objective outcomes and their subjective evaluations of those outcomes often diverge; individuals who achieve objectively superior outcomes will frequently feel less satisfied with their performance than negotiators who achieve poorer outcomes (Galinsky et al., 2002a; Galinsky, Seiden, Kim, & Medvec, 2002b; Loewenstein, Thompson, & Bazerman, 1989; Oliver, Balakrishnan, & Barry, 1994).

The primary determinant of negotiators' satisfaction with their outcomes appears to be the particular social comparisons that negotiators make. That is, whether one is satisfied with a negotiation outcome will depend on the specific standard of comparison that a negotiator uses. As multiple social comparisons are likely to be available to a negotiator at any one time, two negotiators who achieve equivalent outcomes may experience differing levels of satisfaction based on the particular social comparisons that they invoke. Social comparisons generally take two forms: *intrapersonal* comparisons, in which individuals compare their outcomes to some personal standard, and *interpersonal* comparisons, in which individuals compare their outcomes to the outcomes of other negotiators. Below, we discuss the factors that influence the types of comparisons that negotiators make, and the effects of these different comparisons on negotiators' subjective evaluations of their outcomes.

Intrapersonal Comparisons During a negotiation, negotiators generate various points of reference, such as aspiration and reservation prices, which can serve as internal standards of comparison after the negotiation has concluded. As discussed earlier, the choice of which reference point to focus on can affect the outcomes that negotiators obtain: Galinsky et al. (2002a) found that negotiators who focused on their aspiration prices achieved significantly better outcomes than negotiators who focused on their reservation prices. However, these researchers also found that focusing on aspiration versus reservation prices resulted in opposite effects for negotiators' satisfaction with their outcomes: Even though they achieved objectively better outcomes, negotiators who focused on their aspiration prices during the negotiation were less satisfied with their performance after the negotiation than negotiators who focused on their reservation prices (see also Conlon & Ross, 1993). One explanation for these effects is that different reference points generate different counterfactual thoughts in negotiators' minds, or thoughts about what "might have been" (Kahneman & Miller, 1986). Negotiators who focus on their aspiration prices during a negotiation may be left with thoughts about how their outcome could have been better (if they had achieved their aspiration price), whereas negotiators who focus on their reservation prices may find themselves thinking about how their outcome could have been worse (if they had to settle for their reservation price).

The specific counterfactual thoughts that negotiators generate can be affected by their goal in a negotiation (i.e., whether they focus on their aspiration or reservation prices). These thoughts, and consequently the levels of satisfaction that negotiators experience, can also be affected by specific events that occur during the negotiation. For example, although negotiators often obtain better outcomes when they make the first offer in a negotiation (Galinsky & Mussweiler, 2001), they are generally unsatisfied when these offers are immediately accepted (Galinsky et al., 2002b). Negotiators often fear falling victim to the "winner's curse" (Akerloff, 1970; Bazerman & Carroll, 1987), or the possibility that an item is not worth as much as the winner paid for it. When a negotiator's first offer is immediately accepted, negotiators may worry that they have been plagued by the winner's curse and generate counterfactual thoughts about how they may have done better in the negotiation. Across a series of studies, Galinsky and colleagues (2002b) found that, holding the outcome of the negotiation constant, negotiators whose first offers were immediately accepted generated more upward counterfactuals (i.e., thoughts about how the negotiator could have obtained a better outcome) and were less satisfied with their negotiation outcomes than negotiators whose first offers were accepted after a delay (during which the negotiator's opponent made some calculations) or negotiators whose offers were accepted after several rounds of negotiation. Furthermore, the amount of counterfactual activation that negotiators experienced influenced their behavioral intentions for future negotiations. Negotiators whose first offers were immediately accepted reported that they were less likely to make a first offer in a subsequent negotiation. Given that research has shown that making a first offer can result in a bargaining advantage for the negotiator making the offer (Galinsky & Mussweiler, 2001), this reluctance to make first offers in the future is a dysfunctional consequence of negotiators' decreased satisfaction with their negotiation outcomes.

Interpersonal Comparisons   In addition to comparisons to a personal standard or referent, negotiators' levels of satisfaction are also influenced by the interpersonal comparisons they make—comparisons to another negotiator. These interpersonal comparisons can take two forms: *internal* comparisons, in which a negotiator compares his outcome to the outcome of his negotiation counterpart (e.g., a car buyer comparing his outcome to the car dealer's outcome); and *external* comparisons, in which a negotiator compares his outcome to other negotiators outside of the present negotiation (e.g., a car buyer comparing his outcome to his neighbor's recent car purchase; Novemsky & Schweitzer, 2004). In forming internal interpersonal comparisons, negotiators may focus on the relative outcomes of the parties. Loewenstein et al. (1989) found that when comparing one's own outcomes to those of one's opponent, perceptions of relative gain were a bigger determinant of one's satisfaction after a negotiation than the absolute value of the negotiated outcome. How well a negotiator performed did not determine satisfaction, but how well he or she performed in comparison to the negotiator on the other side of the table did. In assessing relative gain, negotiators can compare objective outcomes, if this information is available to both parties, but they can also use subtler cues to assess relative performance in cases where direct information is not accessible. For example, negotiators often use the emotions of their counterparts to judge their relative outcomes, and hence their satisfaction. Thompson and her colleagues (Thompson, Valley, & Kramer, 1995) found that negotiators felt more successful after their negotiation when they found out that their opponent was disappointed than when they found out that their opponent was happy, and that this effect was independent of negotiators' actual performance in the negotiation. Additionally, the researchers demonstrated that this effect could be moderated by the relationship between the negotiating parties. Individuals who negotiated against a disappointed opponent felt more successful and satisfied with their negotiation outcome when their opponent was an out-group member than when their opponent was a member of their own in-group.

Thus, negotiators' levels of satisfaction are influenced by comparisons to negotiators on the other side of the bargaining table, such that negotiators are more satisfied when these comparisons reveal that a negotiator gained a better outcome than his or her opponent. Interestingly, however, research has demonstrated that, regardless of how favorable the comparison is, internal comparisons generally reduce negotiator satisfaction compared to situations in which no internal social comparison information is available. Novemsky and Schweitzer (2004) found that negotiators who received favorable internal comparisons (i.e., they obtained a better outcome than their opponent) were more satisfied than negotiators who received unfavorable internal comparisons (i.e., they obtained a worse outcome than their opponent), but that both favorable and unfavorable comparisons reduced negotiator satisfaction compared to a situation in which negotiators were given no information about how well their opponent performed. They suggest that this pattern emerges because negotiators generally assume, unless told otherwise, that they have claimed the entire surplus available in a negotiation. As a result, regardless of whether one did better or worse than one's opponent, all internal social comparisons are essentially unfavorable, unless negotiators find that they did indeed claim all of the surplus. Consistent with this prediction, Novemsky and Schweitzer found that negotiators are most satisfied as a result of internal social comparisons when they find that the outcome was equal to the opponent's reservation price (and hence the opponent gained no surplus).

External comparisons are the second form of interpersonal social comparisons, in which negotiators compare their outcomes to similar negotiators in other negotiations. Although the negotiations literature to date has paid relatively little attention to the role of external social comparisons in determining negotiator satisfaction, Novemsky and Schweitzer (2004) have begun to explore these types of comparisons. They find that, similar to internal social comparisons, negotiators are more satisfied with their negotiated outcomes when they receive favorable external social comparisons (e.g., a buyer of a rare coin discovering that she paid less than another buyer of a similar coin) than when they receive unfavorable external comparisons (e.g., the coin buyer discovering that she paid more than the comparable buyer). However, unlike internal social comparisons, favorable external comparisons generally increase negotiator satisfaction relative to situations in which no external comparison information is available, whereas unfavorable external comparisons reduce satisfaction from this baseline condition. The authors suggest that, unlike internal social comparisons, external comparisons do not necessarily trigger thoughts of foregone negotiation opportunities, and consequently negotiators are satisfied when they found that they outperformed a comparable negotiator in another negotiation, even if this comparable negotiator still received some surplus. Furthermore, the authors compare the effects of internal and external social comparisons on negotiator satisfaction, as well as the effects of negotiators' objective outcomes, and find that external social comparisons are the biggest single predictor of negotiator satisfaction. Thus, although work on external social comparisons in negotiations is just beginning, evidence to date suggests that external comparisons are a critical determinant of negotiator satisfaction, and consequently future research should be directed toward further understanding the determinants and consequences of such comparisons.

THE COSTS AND BENEFITS
OF NEGOTIATOR UNCERTAINTY

Our discussion thus far concerning the effects of uncertainty on negotiators' cognitions and perceptions has painted a rather bleak picture of negotiator behavior. We have highlighted research that has demonstrated that, among other things, negotiators alter their negotiation strategies based on transient factors, such as their current emotional state (e.g., Forgas, 1998), make erroneous assumptions about their counterparts (e.g., De Dreu & Boles, 1998; Morris et al., 1999; van Kleef & De Dreu, 2002), and fail to have insight into their own preferences (e.g., Curhan et al., 2004). These findings may create the impression that the uncertainty inherent in negotiations is undesirable. Contrary to this conclusion, however, we suggest that the uncertainty inherent in the negotiation process is actually beneficial, and even necessary, for reaching optimal negotiation outcomes. Research on certainty and information processing has suggested that one's level of certainty affects the way one processes information. When individuals experience a feeling of certainty, they may process information in a heuristic fashion and rely on well-developed associations, mental shortcuts, or rules of thumb to evaluate information and make decisions. In contrast, the experience of uncertainty may cause individuals to process information more deeply, or systematically. That is, when individuals experience uncertainty they may consider multiple alternatives or points of view more carefully, scrutinize information longer, and ask more probing and insightful questions (Chaiken, Liberman, & Eagly, 1989; Tiedens & Linton, 2001; Weary & Jacobson, 1997). Research from negotiation contexts suggests that systematic processing of information is a critical factor for achieving integrative, or mutually beneficial, negotiation agreements (e.g., Anderson & Neale, 2004; De Dreu, 2003; Thompson, 1991). When negotiators process information carefully, they are more likely to ask the right questions, listen to the answers, and uncover opportunities for mutually beneficial tradeoffs. Thus, uncertainty may facilitate the formation of integrative negotiation agreements because uncertainty may enhance systematic thinking, and systematic thinking, in turn, enhances negotiation performance.

Research conducted by Anderson and Neale (2004) is consistent with the assertion that uncertainty in negotiations may enhance negotiation performance. In this study, participants first engaged in a computer-mediated ultimatum bargaining game in which their counterpart (in actuality, a computer program) behaved very selfishly. Subsequently, pairs of participants engaged in a face-to-face negotiation between a job candidate and a recruiter. One member of each dyad was given some information about his or her opponent, designed to manipulate the focal negotiator's level of certainty. In one condition (certainty condition), participants were led to believe that their opponent in the job negotiation was the same selfish individual they had negotiated with in the first negotiation. In another condition (uncertainty condition), participants were given no information about their opponent in the job negotiation, and consequently they were unsure if they were negotiating against the selfish opponent from the first negotiation or not. The researchers predicted that negotiators who felt certain of their opponent's likely behavior would exhibit less cognitive complexity in their negotiation strategies (i.e., use fewer integrative and more distributive strategies) than negotiators who felt uncertain about their opponent. The authors also predicted that these strategic differences would influence the outcomes that the negotiators obtained: Certain negotiators, as a result of their heuristic information processing, were predicted to achieve outcomes of lower value than uncertain negotiators. The results of the study supported these predictions. Negotiators in the uncertain condition demonstrated greater cognitive complexity in their prenegotiation strategies than negotiators in the certain condition, and dyads with an uncertain negotiator reached agreements of greater joint value than dyads with a certain negotiator. Furthermore, results of mediation analyses revealed that these differences in outcomes were partially mediated by the complexity of negotiators' prenegotiation strategies: Uncertain dyads achieved better outcomes than certain dyads due, in part, to the more complex information-processing strategies of the uncertain negotiators. Of course, this study raises additional questions that cannot be answered without further empirical research. For example, this study examines only one type of uncertainty, uncertainty about the malevolent motives of one's opponent. It remains an open question as to whether these findings would generalize to other types of uncertainties (e.g., goal uncertainties, preference uncertainties, etc.), and future research is needed to address these issues. However, the current research is consistent with the notion that uncertainty may be a necessary condition for the achievement of optimal negotiation outcomes.

We have argued that without some degree of uncertainty to motivate systematic information processing, negotiators are likely to settle on easy or obvious solutions, and avoid gathering information that would enable them to achieve a superior, mutually beneficial outcome. Yet, as the decision biases and heuristics documented in earlier sections of this chapter indicate, the presence of uncertainty alone is not *sufficient* to ensure that negotiators will engage in systematic information processing. In some cases, negotiators may address feelings of uncertainty by seeking out information that will enable them to resolve the uncertainty that they are experiencing. However, it is also possible that negotiators will react to uncertainty by refusing to seek out information, relying instead on assumptions and heuristics. Because the experience of uncertainty is likely to be aversive for most individuals, they are generally motivated to reduce this uncertainty as quickly as possible. One obvious strategy for reducing uncertainty is to employ heuristics, or mental shortcuts, than enable individuals to turn a complex problem into a simpler problem. Many of the biased perceptions that we have discussed in this chapter are simply effective ways of quickly reducing uncertainty. Heuristics such as the false consensus effect (Ross et al., 1977), the fixed-pie bias (Neale & Bazerman, 1991), and the fundamental attribution error (Ross, 1977) are all strategies that individuals employ to simplify their social world. It seems, then, that the effects of uncertainty on negotiated outcomes depends on whether negotiators respond to this uncertainty by becoming more vigilant and carefully processing all available information, or by shutting out information and relying mainly on mental shortcuts.

What, then, determines a negotiator's response to the experience of uncertainty in a negotiation? We suggest that the mechanism through which a negotiator manages uncertainty depends on the negotiator's available cognitive resources. Systematic information processing demands more cognitive energy than heuristic information processing, and consequently individuals will engage in systematic processing when cognitive resources are plentiful and heuristic processing when such resources are scarce (Dijker & Koomen, 1996; Gilbert & Hixon, 1991;

Gilbert, Pelham, & Krull, 1988). Thus, a negotiator's response to uncertainty should depend on his or her cognitive capacity; the greater the negotiator's mental resources, the greater the likelihood the negotiator will seek to reduce the experienced uncertainty by engaging in systematic information processing. A negotiator's cognitive resources, in turn, are influenced by a variety of dimensions. These resources are determined, in part, by the negotiator's disposition, and also by situational forces that increase or deplete the negotiator's cognitive energy. Below, we discuss three factors (need for closure, time pressure, and accuracy motivation) that should influence negotiators' cognitive resources, and hence their responses to uncertainty in negotiations.

Need for Closure Kruglanski (1989) posits that individuals differ in their desire for types and amounts of knowledge, a dimension that he terms "need for cognitive closure." Individuals high in need for closure are generally rigid in their thoughts and opinions, are quick to judge on the basis of incomplete evidence, and are generally cognitively impatient. Individuals low in need for closure are willing to entertain multiple interpretations or conflicting opinions, prefer to gather complete information before forming an opinion, and are more willing to suspend judgment. When encountering uncertainty, evidence suggests that high need for closure individuals will be more rushed to reduce the uncertainty and arrive at a decision, and will therefore use more heuristic processing strategies; whereas low need for closure individuals will be more content with postponing judgment until they have gathered a sufficient amount of information, and will therefore process information more systematically (Kruglanski & Webster, 1996; Mayseless & Kruglanski, 1987; Webster & Kruglanski, 1994). These chronic differences in individuals' preferences for closure should affect their responses to uncertainty in negotiation contexts. High need for closure individuals, who engage in heuristic information processing, may be more likely to rely on heuristics and fall prey to the decision biases outlined in this chapter than low need for closure individuals, who are likely to engage in more systematic information-gathering strategies. To the extent that mutually beneficial negotiation outcomes are facilitated by information exchange, as research suggests (Thompson, 1991), low need for closure negotiators should be expected to achieve agreements of higher joint value than high need for closure negotiators.

Time Pressure Negotiators' cognitive resources, and hence their information-processing strategies, may also be affected by the level of time pressure in the negotiation. Time is frequently a scarce resource in negotiations, and many negotiations take place under the shadow of a looming deadline. The time pressure that negotiators experience may be either real (e.g., a 2-hour time window in which to reach an agreement) or perceived (e.g., the feeling that one has very little time to accomplish the deal). Evidence suggests that time pressure, both real and perceived, can induce a situational need for closure that affects information processing. Kruglanski and Freund (1983) demonstrated that when real time pressure is high, individuals are more motivated to achieve cognitive closure and process information more heuristically than under low time pressure, where need for closure is lower (Kruglanski & Freund, 1983). Research by De Dreu (2003) has extended this logic to a negotiation context and has also explored the effects of perceived time pressure on negotiator behavior. In a series of studies, De Dreu demonstrated that perceived time pressure in a negotiation affects negotiators' information processing strategies. Negotiators who perceived a high level of time pressure took less time to propose counteroffers and to reach final agreements reported less motivation to process information, made less persuasive arguments, and used more heuristics than negotiators who perceived less time pressure, even though all negotiators had the same amount of actual time to complete their negotiations. Furthermore, De Dreu found that these differences in information processing affected the quality of the outcomes that negotiators achieved. Negotiators who perceived high time pressure, and hence used more heuristic processing strategies, achieved agreements of significantly lower joint value than negotiators who perceived low time pressure and processed information more systematically (see also Carnevale & Lawler, 1986; Yukl, Malone, Hayslip, & Pamin, 1976).

Accuracy Motivation Motivational differences may also play a role in determining negotiators' responses to uncertainty. Individuals differ in their accuracy motivation—or their desire to form accurate, rather than biased, judgments (Chaiken & Trope, 1999; De Dreu et al., 2000a). Differences in accuracy motivation may stem from dispositional preferences, or they may arise from situational constraints, such as one's level of accountability in a given situation (Lerner & Tetlock, 1999; Tetlock, 1992). These differences in accuracy motivation have been shown to affect individuals' information-processing strategies: In general, the higher one's level of accuracy motivation, the greater the likelihood that one will engage in systematic and thoughtful information processing (Petty & Cacioppo, 1986). Accuracy motivation has also been examined in negotiation contexts and has been found to reduce negotiators' reliance on simple heuristics and improve the accuracy of their perceptions (De Dreu et al., 2000a). Across a series of studies, De Dreu and colleagues found that negotiators who expected to have their negotiation behavior evaluated by an unknown third party (a manipulation intended to result in high accuracy motivation) were less likely to fall prey to the fixed-pie bias and also achieved outcomes of higher joint value than negotiators who did not expect such evaluation (and hence had a lower accuracy motivation).

CONCLUSION

The social cognition approach to negotiation aims to highlight the consequences of negotiators' perceptions and attributions for the processes and outcomes of negotiations. This perspective stands in contrast, but also complements, alternative approaches to the study of negotiation, such as traditional game theory approaches and the decision-making approach (see Bazerman & Chugh, chapter 2). Unlike the game theory approach, both the decision-making and social cognition approaches recognize that the negotiator is not always fully rational and often departs from rationality in predictable ways. However, unlike the decision-making approach, which focuses mainly on *intrapersonal* negotiator behavior (i.e., the decision-making processes occurring inside a negotiator's head), the social cognition approach is, as the name implies, inherently more social and focuses on understanding *interpersonal* negotiator behavior (i.e., how a negotiator is affected by his or her counterparts and the negotiation context). Although these approaches make different assumptions about the underlying capabilities of negotiators and attempt to answer different questions through their empirical investigations, we see these theoretical approaches as adjacent pieces in a larger negotiation puzzle; take away any one piece and our understanding of the negotiation picture would be incomplete.

In our review of the social cognition perspective, we have suggested that one reason that negotiations are so influenced by the psychologies of the negotiating parties is that the uncertainty inherent in most negotiations makes negotiators susceptible to a variety of cues that shape their thoughts and behaviors. Some of these cues may be internal to the negotiator, such as stable personality traits or ephemeral emotional states, whereas other cues may derive from the external circumstances of the negotiation, such as the power relationship between the negotiating parties or an opponent's behavior. The cues that negotiators rely on to shape their attributions and perceptions will likely change throughout the course of a negotiation, as negotiators encounter different forms of uncertainty at various stages of the negotiation process. Before and during a negotiation, negotiators may be unsure of what goal to pursue and how to assess their own preferences and the preferences of their counterparts. Subsequent to a negotiation, negotiators may be uncertain as to how to evaluate the quality of their negotiated agreement.

Although the uncertainty experienced by most negotiators leaves them vulnerable to a host of decision biases and perceptual errors, this does not imply that uncertainty is necessarily an impediment to the achievement of optimal negotiation agreements. On the contrary, we suggest that uncertainty is beneficial in negotiations, since it creates an opportunity for negotiators to provide and process information, which improves the quality of negotiated agreements (Thompson, 1991). The benefits or detriments of uncertainty will depend, then, on the degree to which negotiators capitalize on this opportunity to seek and share information. To the extent that negotiators can muster the necessary cognitive resources to resolve this uncertainty through systematic information processing, the experience of uncertainty should improve the quality of negotiators' outcomes. However, if negotiators do not possess such capacity (because of individual differences or situational forces that constrain ability or motivation), uncertainty is likely to be resolved in heuristic fashion, and consequently negotiators are likely to develop biased perceptions, make erroneous inferences, and fail to capitalize on the full integrative potential of their negotiations.

REFERENCES

Akerloff, G. (1970). The market for lemons. *Quarterly Journal of Economics, 89,* 488–500.

Anderson, N., & Neale, M. A. (2004). *The benefits of anger in negotiation: Where emotion meets uncertainty.* Unpublished manuscript, Stanford University, Stanford, CA.

Barry, B., & Oliver, R. L. (1996). Affect in dyadic negotiation: A model and propositions. *Organizational Behavior and Human Decision Processes, 67,* 127–143.

Bazerman, M. H., & Carroll, J. S. (1987). Negotiator cognition. In L. L. Cummings & B. M. Staw (Eds.), *Research in organizational behavior* (Vol. 9, pp. 247–288). Greenwich, CT: JAI Press.

Bazerman, M. H., Gibbons, R., Thompson, L., & Valley, K. L. (1998). Can negotiators outperform game theory? In J. J. Halpern & R. N. Stern (Eds.), *Debating rationally: Nonrational aspects in organizational decision making.* Ithaca, NY: ILP Press.

Bazerman, M. H., Magliozzi, T., & Neale, M. A. (1985). Integrative bargaining in a competitive market. *Organizational Behavior and Human Decision Processes, 35,* 294–313.

Blau, P. M. (1964). *Exchange and power in social life* (5th ed.). New Brunswick, NJ: Transaction Publishers.

Carnevale, P. J. D., & Lawler, E. J. (1986). Time pressure and the development of integrative agreements in bilateral negotiations. *Journal of Conflict Resolution, 30,* 636–659.

Carson, R. C. (1969). *Interaction concepts of personality.* Chicago: Aldine.

Chaiken, S., Liberman, A., & Eagly, A. H. (1989). Heuristic and systematic information processing within and beyond the persuasion context. In J. Uleman & J. Bargh (Eds.), *Unintended thought* (pp. 212–252.). New York: Guilford Press.

Chaiken, S., & Trope, Y. (Eds.). (1999). *Dual-process theories in social psychology.* New York: Guilford Press.

Conlon, D. E., & Ross, W. H. (1993). The effects of partisan third parties on negotiator behavior and outcome perceptions. *Journal of Applied Psychology, 78,* 280–290.

Crowe, E., & Higgins, E. T. (1997). Regulatory focus and strategic inclinations: Promotion and prevention in decision-making. *Organizational Behavior and Human Decision Processes, 69,* 117–132.

Curhan, J. R., Neale, M. A., & Ross, L. (2004). Dynamic valuation: Preference changes in the context of a face-to-face negotiation. *Journal of Experimental Social Psychology, 40,* 142–151.

Dawes, R. M. (1989). Statistical criteria for establishing a truly false consensus effect. *Journal of Experimental Social Psychology, 25,* 1–17.

Dawes, R. M., & Mulford, M. (1996). The false consensus effect and overconfidence: Flaws in judgment or flaws in how we study judgment? *Organizational Behavior and Human Decision Processes, 65,* 210–211.

De Dreu, C. K. W. (2003). Time pressure and closing of the mind in negotiation. *Organizational Behavior and Human Decision Processes, 91,* 280–295.

De Dreu, C. K. W., & Boles, T. L. (1998). Share and share alike or winner take all?: The influence of social value orientation upon choice and recall of negotiation heuristics. *Organizational Behavior and Human Decision Processes, 76,* 253 –276.

De Dreu, C. K. W., Koole, S., & Steinel, W. (2000a). Unfixing the fixed-pie: A motivated information processing of integrative negotiation. *Journal of Personality and Social Psychology, 79,* 975–987.

De Dreu, C. K. W., & Van Lange, P. A. M. (1995). Impact of social value orientation on negotiator cognition and behavior. *Personality and Social Psychology Bulletin, 21,* 1177–1188.

De Dreu, C. K. W., Weingart, L. R., & Kwon, S. (2000b). Influence of social motives on integrative negotiation: A meta-analytic review and a test of two theories. *Journal of Personality and Social Psychology, 78,* 889–905.

Deutsch, M. (1960). The effect of motivational orientation upon trust and suspicion. *Human Relations, 13,* 123–139.

Diekmann, K. A., Tenbrunsel, A. E., & Galinsky, A. D. (2003). From self-prediction to self-defeat: Behavioral forecasting, self-fulfilling prophecies, and the effect of competitive expectations. *Journal of Personality and Social Psychology, 85,* 672–683.

Dijker, A. J., & Koomen, W. (1996). Stereotyping and attitudinal effects under time pressure. *European Journal of Social Psychology, 26,* 61–74.

Drolet, A. L., & Morris, M. W. (2000). Rapport in conflict resolution: Accounting for how face-to-face contact fosters mutual cooperation in mixed-motive conflicts. *Journal of Experimental Social Psychology, 36,* 26–50.

Dryer, D. C., & Horowitz, L. M. (1997). When do opposites attract? Interpersonal complementarity versus similarity. *Journal of Personality and Social Psychology, 72,* 592–603.

Emerson, R. M. (1962). Power-dependence relations. *American Sociological Review, 27,* 31–40.

Fiske, S. T., & Taylor, S. E. (1991). *Social cognition* (2nd ed.). New York: McGraw-Hill.

Forgas, J. P. (1998). On feeling good and getting your way: Mood effects on negotiator cognition and bargaining strategies. *Journal of Personality and Social Psychology, 74,* 565–577.

Galinsky, A. D., Leonardelli, G. L., Okhuysen, G. A., & Mussweiler, T. (2005). Regulatory focus at the bargaining table: Promoting distributive and integrative success. *Personality and Social Psychology Bulletin, 31,* 1–12.

Galinsky, A. D., & Mussweiler, T. (2001). First offers as anchors: The role of perspective-taking and negotiator focus. *Journal of Personality and Social Psychology, 81,* 657–669.

Galinsky, A. D., Mussweiler, T., & Medvec, V. H. (2002a). Disconnecting outcomes and evaluations: The role of negotiator focus. *Journal of Personality and Social Psychology, 83,* 1131–1140.

Galinsky, A. D., Seiden, V. L., Kim, P. H., & Medvec, V. H. (2002b). The dissatisfaction of having your first offer accepted: The role of counterfactual thinking in negotiations. *Personality and Social Psychology Bulletin, 28,* 271–283.

Gilbert, D. T., & Hixon, J. G. (1991). The trouble of thinking: Activation and application of stereotypic beliefs. *Journal of Personality and Social Psychology, 60,* 509–517.

Gilbert, D. T., Pelham, B. W., & Krull, D. S. (1988). On cognitive busyness: When person perceivers meet persons perceived. *Journal of Personality and Social Psychology, 54,* 733–740.

Gilbert, D. T., Pinel, E. C., Wilson, T. D., Blumberg, S. J., & Wheatley, T. P. (1998). Immune neglect: A source of durability bias in affective forecasting. *Journal of Personality and Social Psychology, 75,* 617–638.

Gilbert, D. T., & Wilson, T. D. (2000). Miswanting. In J. Forgas (Ed.), *Thinking and feeling: The role of affect in social cognition* (pp. 178–197). Cambridge, UK: Cambridge University Press.

Gillespie, J. J., Brett, J. M., & Weingart, L. R. (2000). Interdependence, social motives, and outcome satisfaction in multiparty negotiation. *European Journal of Social Psychology, 30,* 779–797.

Higgins, E. T. (1997). Beyond pleasure and pain. *American Psychologist, 52,* 1280–1300.

Huber, V. L., & Neale, M. A. (1986). Effects of cognitive heuristics and goals on negotiator performance and subsequent goal setting. *Organizational Behavior and Human Decision Processes, 38,* 342–365.

Huber, V. L., & Neale, M. A. (1987). Effects of self and competitor's goals on performance in an interdependent bargaining task. *Journal of Applied Psychology, 72,* 197–203.

Kahneman, D., & Miller, D. T. (1986). Norm theory: Comparing reality to its alternatives. *Psychological Review, 93,* 136–153.

Kiesler, D. J. (1983). The 1982 Interpersonal Circle: A taxonomy for complementarity in human transactions. *Psychological Review, 90,* 185–214.

Kim, P. H. (1997). Strategic timing in group negotiations: The implications of forced entry and forced exit for negotiators with unequal power. *Organizational Behavior and Human Decision Processes, 71,* 263–286.

Kim, P. H., Diekmann, K. A., & Tenbrunsel, A. E. (2003). Flattery may get you somewhere: The strategic implications of providing positive vs. negative feedback about ability vs. ethicality in negotiation. *Organizational Behavior and Human Decision Processes, 90,* 225–243.

Kim, P. H., & Fragale, A. R. (2005). Choosing the path to bargaining power: An empirical comparison of the effects of BATNAs and contributions in negotiation. *Journal of Applied Psychology, 90,* 373–381.

Kleef, G. A. van, & De Dreu, C. K. W. (2002). Social value orientation and impression formation: A test of two competing hypotheses about information search in negotiation. *International Journal of Conflict Management, 13,* 59–77.

Komorita, S. S., & Leung, K., (1985). The effects of alternatives on the salience of reward allocation norms. *Journal of Experimental Social Psychology, 17,* 525–544.

Kruglanski, A. W. (1989). The psychology of being "right": The problem of accuracy in social perception and cognition. *Psychological Bulletin, 106,* 395–409.

Kruglanski, A. W., & Freund, T. (1983). The freezing and unfreezing of lay-inferences: Effects on impressional primacy, ethnic stereotyping, and numerical anchoring. *Journal of Experimental Social Psychology, 19,* 448–468.

Kruglanski, A. W., & Webster, D. M. (1996). Motivated closing of the mind: "Seizing and freezing." *Psychological Review, 103,* 263–283.

Leary, T. (1957). *Interpersonal diagnosis of personality.* New York: Ronald Press.

Lerner, J. S., & Tetlock, P. E. (1999). Accounting for the effects of accountability. *Psychological Bulletin, 125,* 255–275.

Liebert, R. M., Smith, W. P., Hill, J. H., & Keiffer, M. (1968). The effects of information and magnitude of initial offer on interpersonal negotiation. *Journal of Experimental Social Psychology, 4,* 431–441.

Loewenstein, G. F., Thompson, L., & Bazerman, M. H. (1989). Social utility and decision making in interpersonal contexts. *Journal of Personality and Social Psychology, 57,* 426–441.

Magee, J. C., Galinsky, A. D., & Gruenfeld, D. H. (2004). *Plunging headfirst with power: Power as a determinant of who moves first in competitive interaction.* Unpublished manuscript, New York University, New York.

Ma'oz, I., Ward, A., Katz, M., & Ross, L. (2002). Reactive devaluation of an "Israeli" vs. "Palestinian" peace proposal. *Journal of Conflict Resolution, 46,* 515–546.

Marks, G., & Miller, N. (1987). Ten years of research on the false-consensus effect: An empirical and theoretical review. *Psychological Bulletin, 102,* 72–90.

Mayseless, O., & Kruglanski, A. W. (1987). What makes you so sure? Effects of epistemic motivations on judgmental confidence. *Organizational Behavior and Human Decision Processes, 39,* 162–183.

McClintock, C. (1976). Social motivations in settings of outcome interdependence. In D. Druckman (Ed.), *Negotiations: Social psychological perspective* (pp. 49–77). Beverly Hills, CA: Sage.

Morris, M. W., Larrick, R. P., & Su, S. K. (1999). Misperceiving negotiation counterparts: When situationally determined bargaining behaviors are attributed to personality traits. *Journal of Personality and Social Psychology, 77,* 52–67.

Mussweiler, T., & Strack, F. (1999a). Comparing is believing: A selective accessibility model of judgmental anchoring. In W. Stroebe & M. Hewstone (Eds.), *European review of social psychology* (Vol. 10, pp. 135–168). Chichester, UK: Wiley.

Mussweiler, T., & Strack, F. (1999b). Hypothesis-consistent testing and semantic priming in the anchoring paradigm: A selective accessibility model. *Journal of Experimental Social Psychology, 35,* 136–164.

Mussweiler, T., & Strack, F. (2000). The use of category and exemplar knowledge in the solution of anchoring tasks. *Journal of Personality and Social Psychology, 78,* 1038–1052.

Neale, M. A., & Bazerman, M. H. (1985). The effect of externally set goals on reaching integrative agreements in competitive markets. *Journal of Occupational Behavior, 6,* 19–32.

Neale, M. A., & Bazerman, M. H. (1991). *Negotiator cognition and rationality.* New York: Free Press.

Nisbett, R. E., & Wilson, T. D. (1977). Telling more than we can know: Verbal reports on mental processes. *Psychological Review, 84,* 231–259.

Novemsky, N., & Schweitzer, M. E. (2004). What makes negotiators happy? The differential effects of internal and external social comparisons on negotiator satisfaction. *Organizational Behavior and Human Decision Processes, 95,* 186–197.

Olekalns, M., Smith, P. L., & Kibby, R. (1996). Social value orientations and negotiator outcomes. *European Journal of Social Psychology, 26,* 299–313.

Oliver, R. L., Balakrishnan, P. V., & Barry, B. (1994). Outcome satisfaction in negotiation: A test of expectancy disconfirmation. *Organizational Behavior and Human Decision Processes, 60,* 252–275.

Paese, P. W., & Gilin, D. A. (2000). When an adversary is caught telling the truth: Reciprocal cooperation versus self-interest in distributive bargaining. *Personality and Social Psychology Bulletin, 26,* 79–90.

Petty, R. E., & Cacioppo, J. T. (1986). The elaboration likelihood model of persuasion. In L. Berkowitz (Ed.), *Advances in experimental social psychology* (Vol. 19, pp. 123–205). New York: Academic Press.

Pinkley, R. L., Neale, M. A., & Bennett, R. J. (1994). The impact of alternatives to settlement in dyadic negotiation. *Organizational Behavior and Human Decision Processes, 57,* 97–116.

Polzer, J. T., & Neale, M. A. (1995). Constraints or catalysts? Reexamining goal setting within the context of negotiation. *Human Performance, 8,* 3–26.

Pruitt, D. G., & Rubin, J. Z. (1986). *Social conflict: Escalation, stalemate, and settlement.* New York: Random House.

Purdy, J. M., & Nye, P. (2000). The impact of communication media on negotiation outcomes. *International Journal of Conflict Management, 11,* 162–187.

Raiffa, H. (1982). *The art and science of negotiation*. Cambridge, MA: Belknap Press.

Ross, L. (1995). Reactive devaluation in negotiation and conflict resolution. In K. Arrow, R. H. Mnookin, L. Ross, A. Tversky, & R. Wilson (Eds.), *Barriers to conflict resolution* (pp. 26–42). New York: W. W. Norton.

Ross, L., Greene, D., & House, P. (1977). The "false consensus effect": An egocentric bias in social perception and attribution processes. *Journal of Experimental Social Psychology, 13*, 279–301.

Ross, L., & Ward, A. (1995). Psychological barriers to dispute resolution. In M. Zanna (Ed.), *Advances in experimental social psychology* (Vol. 27, pp. 255–304). San Diego, CA: Academic Press.

Ross, L. D. (1977). The intuitive psychologist and his shortcomings: Distortions in the attribution process. In L. Berkowitz (Ed.), *Advances in experimental social psychology* (Vol. 10, pp. 173–220). New York: Random House.

Shah, J., Higgins, E. T., & Friedman (1998). Performance incentives and means: How regulatory focus influences goal attainment. *Journal of Personality and Social Psychology, 74*, 285–293.

Sherman, S. J., Presson, C. C., & Chassin, L. (1984). Mechanisms underlying the false consensus effect: The special role of threats to the self. *Personality and Social Psychology Bulletin, 10*, 127–138.

Tetlock, P. E. (1992). The impact of accountability on judgment and choice: Toward a social contingency model. In L. Berkowitz (Ed.), *Advances in experimental social psychology* (Vol. 25, pp. 331–376). New York: Academic Press.

Thompson, L. L. (1990). Negotiation: Empirical evidence and theoretical issues. *Psychological Bulletin, 108*, 515–532.

Thompson, L. L. (1991). Information exchange in negotiation. *Journal of Experimental Social Psychology, 26*, 82–90.

Thompson, L., Valley, K. L., & Kramer, R. M. (1995). The bittersweet feeling of success: An examination of social perception in negotiation. *Journal of Experimental Social Psychology, 31*, 467–492.

Tiedens, L. Z., & Fragale, A. R. (2003). Power moves: Complementarity in dominant and submissive nonverbal behavior. *Journal of Personality and Social Psychology, 84*, 558–568.

Tiedens, L. Z., & Linton, S. (2001). Judgment under emotional certainty and uncertainty: The effects of specific emotions on information processing. *Journal of Personality and Social Psychology, 81*, 973–988.

Valley, K. L., Moag, J., & Bazerman, M. H. (1998). A matter of trust: Effects of communication on the efficiency and distribution of outcomes. *Journal of Economic Behavior and Organization, 34*, 211–238.

Wason, P. C. (1960). On the failure to eliminate hypotheses in a conceptual task. *Quarterly Journal of Experimental Psychology, 12*, 129–140.

Weary, G., & Jacobson, J. A. (1997). Causal uncertainty beliefs and diagnostic information seeking. *Journal of Personality and Social Psychology, 73*, 839–849.

Weber, M. (1947). *The theory of social and economic organization*. New York: Free Press.

Webster, D., & Kruglanski, A. W. (1994). Individual differences in need for cognitive closure. *Journal of Personality and Social Psychology, 67*, 1049–1062.

White, S. B., & Neale, M. A. (1994). The role of negotiator aspirations and settlement expectancies in bargaining outcomes. *Organizational Behavior and Human Decision Processes, 57*, 303–317.

Wiggins, J. S. (1979). A psychological taxonomy of trait-descriptive terms: The interpersonal domain. *Journal of Personality and Social Psychology, 37*, 395–412.

Wiggins, J. S. (1982). Circumplex models of interpersonal behavior in clinical psychology. In P. C. Kendall & J. N. Butcher (Eds.), *Handbook of research methods in clinical psychology*. New York: John Wiley & Sons.

Wilson, T. D., & Dunn, E. W. (2004). Self-knowledge: Its limits, value, and potential for improvement. *Annual Review of Psychology, 55,* 493–518.

Yukl, G. A., Malone, M. P., Hayslip, B., & Pamin, T. A. (1976). The effects of time pressure and issue settlement order on integrative bargaining. *Sociometry, 39,* 277–281.

4

Motive: The Negotiator's Raison d'Être

PETER J. CARNEVALE and CARSTEN K. W. DE DREU

Most would agree with the statement that *human behavior is goal directed*—that is, the human being is an *intentional system*, with needs, wants, purposes, desires, predispositions, and motives (Srull & Wyer, 1986, p. 503). The idea that goals and motives as well as prior expectations and values shape perception is, in psychology, broadly accepted and reflects a tradition that includes the early works of Freud (1900/1965) and experiments by Bruner and colleagues (e.g., Bruner & Postman, 1948) and Hastorf and Cantril (1954). Indeed, a keen interest of much modern social psychology is the manner in which the goals and motives that guide overt behavior also influence the cognitive and affective systems that mediate the generation of behavior (Srull & Wyer, 1986; see Eccles & Wigfield, 2002; Higgins, 1997; Kruglanski et al., 2002; Mook, 2000). How the situation is construed by the perceiver, and how goals and motives shape this construal process, is the central focus of much current social psychology and much of the modern social psychology of negotiation (Ross & Ward, 1995).

From the early days of the field to today, social psychologists consider goals and motives as central elements of negotiation, indeed, as the *raison d'être*, its *reason for being* (see Carnevale & Pruitt, 1992; Druckman, 1977). Thus, negotiation has been called "mixed-motive" interaction (Schelling, 1960) to reflect the fact that the parties involved simultaneously experience the motivation to cooperate and compete with each other. For example, a negotiator may prefer an agreement that satisfies her interests over one that favors her adversary's interests (an incentive to compete), while at the same time preferring any agreement over no agreement (an incentive to cooperate). In this chapter, we review social psychological work on negotiation and social conflict that considers goals and motives. We emphasize early, important studies conducted in the 1970s, and place them in context of current trends and developments. Much of our discussion reflects and supports a model of motivation and cognition in negotiation that we refer to as the *motivated information processing model of negotiation* (De Dreu & Carnevale, 2003).

TAXONOMY OF MOTIVES

The etymology of the term *motive* includes *motus*, Latin for *to move*, and the concept reflects an underlying process responsible for an overt behavior. Motivation thus refers to the arousal, persistence, and direction of behavior (Mook, 2000). In negotiation, the overt behaviors that are influenced by motivational include *demands*, the offers on the issues, as well as the form of agreement, if there is one, and these typically are classified on two dimensions: (1) cooperative versus noncooperative, the degree of movement on an issue in the direction of the other's interests (e.g., a "concession curve" as shown by Kelley, Beckman, & Fisher, 1967), and (2) integrativeness of the outcome, which often is measured in experiments on negotiation by the collective value of the agreement, as shown in Kelley (1966) and Pruitt and Lewis (1975). These studies were among the first to show that integrativeness of the outcome can reflect verbal processes of *problem solving*, statements that reflect the goal of generating an integrative agreement (e.g., a request for priority information as in "Which issue is most important to you?"). Problem solving is often contrasted with *contending*, statements designed to convince the other side to make a concession (including threats "Agree or we strike!"), commitments to a position ("This is my last offer, take it or leave it"), and derogatory statements about the other ("Only a . . . would make such an offer"). This distinction between problem solving and contending is at the heart of many frameworks of negotiation (e.g., Walton & McKersie's "subprocesses," 1965; Lax & Sebenius's "value creation" versus "value claiming," 1986), many of which leverage the insights of Mary Parker Follett (1942).

Motivation is a broad concept with many facets (Mook, 2000); here, we focus on *goal-achievement* and distinguish motivational strength and motivational orientation. Strength refers to the persistence of behavior; orientation refers to the direction of behavior. When we say that a negotiator is *motivated to reach agreement*, for example, we talk about motivational direction; compare this, for example, to the direction implied in the statement that a negotiator is *motivated to look tough in front of their constituent*. When we say that a negotiator is *very* motivated to reach agreement, the reference is to motivational strength. Although strength and orientation are conceptually distinct, and may have distinct antecedents and consequences, it is difficult to study them in isolation.[1] In this chapter we focus on goal-achievement and motivational orientation—and the central question is, *What is it that negotiators strive for?*

The set of motive orientations that drive negotiation behaviors is quite large; studies have examined aspirations for particular outcomes: the notion of resistance to making concession; face saving and the desire for a positive self-image; desire to be or appear consistent; fear of being taken advantage of; desire for respect, fairness, justice, and just treatment; desire to be responsive to the other's needs; egocentrism and self-enhancement, identity, cognitive closure; desire for a positive relationship; desire for a particular distribution of outcomes; a desire to satisfy the wishes of a constituent, and so on. Although a general taxonomy of negotiator motives is lacking, we suggest that, as a rough step in this direction, negotiator motives can generally be placed in four broad classes of motives. Before defining these, it is worth noting that motives can derive from characteristics of the person (e.g., personality, disposition, or trait, which might stem from socialization history), or from a person's perception of and reaction to situations and context. This reflects Srull and Wyer's (1986) notion of chronic and temporary goals. The four main classes of motives we consider in this chapter are:

1. *Aspirations* refer to preferences for a particular outcome or level of benefit (e.g., "I hope to get $10,000 for my used car"). It may also refer to a minimum level to be achieved lest one not participate in negotiation (reflected in the popular concept BATNA, see below). Tietz and Bartos (1983) identified more than a dozen forms of aspiration in negotiation.
2. *Social motives* refer to a preference for a particular distribution of outcomes, such as a desire to do better than the other, or a desire for fairness and equality. In the literature the terms "motivational orientation" or "social value orientation" are often used, with the former referring to reactions to situations and the latter referring to a generalized disposition or proclivity to engage in cooperation, or not.
3. *Identity motivation*, the desire to have a particular image of self in the negotiation, which can have an individual basis, for example "face saving," the desire to have a sense of personal strength (Brown, 1968, 1977), or it can have a group basis and stem from the relationship of the individual to a collective, as when the negotiator represents a group and thus the sense of shared identity with the group is a factor (Heider, 1958; van Knippenberg, 2000).
4. *Epistemic motivation*, the desire for understanding (Kruglanski, 1989). In negotiation, epistemic motivation is often reflected in truthful information exchange about the issues and the parties' true needs and interests (Olekalns, Smith, & Walsh, 1996; Pinkley, Griffith, & Northcraft, 1995; Pruitt & Lewis, 1975, Experiment 2; Thompson, 2004).

In addition, we identify a fifth category of motive, *initiation motivation*, which guides the start of negotiation. But we have only a little to say about initiation motivation later in this paper.

ASPIRATIONS IN NEGOTIATION

A main source of hypotheses and tests of effects in the social psychology of negotiation is combining one or another motive in an experimental design, and seeing how they interact to affect negotiation perceptions and behavior. This is seen in the classic work of Pruitt and Lewis (1975) and in more recent work such as the study by Bazerman, Magliozzi, and Neale (1985; see Neale & Bazerman,

1991) who examined gain/loss framing in combination with an experimental manipulation of negotiator aspirations.

Aspiration Level Theory and Goal Setting

The focus on aspirations in the empirical literature has an important foundation in the seminal work of Siegel and Fouraker (1960; see Smith, 2001). They developed a "Level of Aspiration Theory" that posited that negotiators make judgments of what they can get in negotiation, and the other's behavior can be a clue to this: If the other makes many concessions (the other is highly cooperative), this can cause aspirations to increase; that is, if the other appears to be a soft touch, negotiators give them fewer concessions. But if the other makes few or no concessions (the other is highly noncooperative), this can cause aspirations to decrease; that is, if the other appears to be tough, negotiators give them many concessions on the view that the gap needs filling for agreement to occur.

This notion of aspirations, concessions, and perception helped form what can be called the golden age of demands and concessions in the social psychology of negotiation, the late 1960s and 1970s, and studies by Yukl (1974), for example. It formed the basis of concepts such as "matching" and "mismatching" (Liebert, Smith, Hill, & Keiffer, 1968; Smith, Pruitt, & Carnevale, 1982), which extended the theory of *concession resistance*, "R," developed by Kelley et al. (1967).

Goal Setting and BATNA

Goal Setting Theory argues that goals promote performance when they are difficult but feasible (Locke & Latham, 1990). Higher aspirations in negotiation produce higher demands and smaller concessions but also closer scrutiny of the issues and negotiation problems, and thus sometimes promote both personal and joint gain (Huber & Neale, 1986; Zetik & Stuhlmacher, 2002). Similar effects have been found in work on limits, reservation prices, and so-called Best-Alternatives-to-Negotiated Agreement (BATNA; Fischer & Ury, 1981; Pinkley, Neale, & Bennett, 1994; White & Neale, 1994). Dozens of studies in which one or both parties to a negotiation were given a price below which they could not settle, showed that the higher this price, the higher their personal gain and, because oftentimes personal and joint gain are positively correlated, the higher the joint gain as well. The experiments by Yukl (1974) traced the location of *demands, goals, and limits* over time. His data suggest that at the early stages of negotiation, demands are placed well in advance of goals and limits (called *overbidding*, which may reflect negotiator efforts to create an image of firmness). But over time, overbidding diminishes, and demands come close to or identical with goals. Goals, in turn, tend to approach limits, as wishful thinking becomes eroded. The upshot of these trends is that limits are usually the most stable and demands the least stable of demands, goals, and limits.

A large body of work suggests that the impact of *goals* on negotiation is similar to those of *limits*. Higher goals produce higher demands, smaller concessions, and slower agreements; because higher goals produce higher demands, they lead to larger profits if agreement is reached (Pruitt, 1981; Siegel & Fouraker, 1960). Galinsky, Mussweiler, and Medvec (2002) found that negotiators were easily influenced to focus on either goals or limits, and that whichever was a central focus had a larger impact on outcomes. There is some evidence that an "anchoring-and-insufficient-adjustment" (Tversky & Kahneman, 1974) process may mediate the impact of goals on negotiation. People are affected by "anchor" information and adjust their thinking from that point. For example, Galinsky and Mussweiler (2001) report that negotiators sometimes anchor on their counterpart's opening offer and fail to adjust when making a counterproposal. Interestingly, these anchoring effects hold for individuals as well as groups of negotiators, and generalize across novices (e.g., students) and professionals (Whyte & Sebenius, 1997).

SOCIAL MOTIVES IN NEGOTIATION

Theory of Cooperation and Competition

Deutsch (1949, 1973) and Rubin and Brown (1975) were among the first to provide systematic treatment of motives in conflict and negotiation. Deutsch outlined the effects of cooperative or competitive social motivations on conflict resolution, with the latter associated with distrust, escalation, and destructive effects. The central element of this analysis was goal interdependence, with positive and negative interdependence referring to the correspondence of interests and the likelihood of each party achieving its goals: "In a cooperative situation the goals are so linked that everybody 'sinks or swims' together, while in the competitive situation if one swims, the other must sink" (1973, p. 20).

Deutsch defined three basic types of social motivations to social conflict: "cooperative—the party has a positive interest in the welfare of the other as well as its own; individualistic—the party has an interest in doing as well for itself and is unconcerned about the welfare of the other; and competitive—the party has an interest in doing better than the other as well as doing as well as it can for itself" (1994, p. 14). Over the years, research on social motivation has shown that an individualistically oriented dyad will move to either mutual cooperation or mutual competition depending on which is encouraged by situational variables and other external circumstances, or by the personality or predispositions of the subjects.

Dual Concern Theory

The Pruitt and Lewis (1975) study was a test of the "dual-concern model" (Pruitt, 1998; Pruitt & Rubin, 1986), a theoretical generalization of the combined impact of aspiration motivation and social motivation. In the model, shown in Figure 4.1, aspirations, that is, "resistance to making concessions" (Kelley et al., 1967), is called "concern for own outcomes"; the "concern for other's outcomes" represents social motivation. Pruitt and Lewis implemented social motivation via instructions to the negotiators to either disregard the other's welfare and maximize own profits, or to be concerned about the other's welfare and maximize collective profits. The result

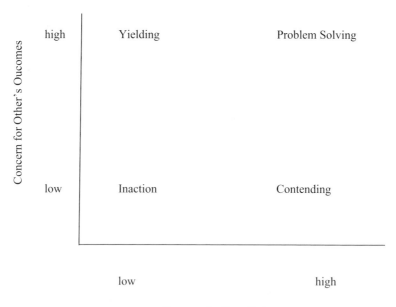

FIGURE 4.1   Dual-concern model.

was that both forms of outcome motivation were important for problem solving and attaining integrative agreements. Low other-concern, alone, encouraged contentiousness. High other-concern, alone, encouraged concession making (yielding).[2]

The dual-concern model is a theory about the impact of changing conditions on strategic choice in negotiation. Some of these conditions affect concern about own interests; others affect concern about the interests of the party with whom one is currently negotiating. Combinations of these conditions predict the strategies that will be chosen in a particular circumstance. For example, accountability to a constituent encourages own aspirations, which means that accountability will encourage problem solving if the parties have a positive relationship as, for example, when they expect a long-term relationship (Ben-Yoav & Pruitt, 1984). Of course, negotiation behaviors have many other antecedents in addition to these two concerns; but the dual-concern model is one basis for making predictions about strategic preference, and about organizing effects of seemingly disparate conditions. In an important empirical review (meta-analysis), Druckman (1994) reported that factors such as time pressure and accountability to constituents have effects that reflect resistance to yielding, and Carnevale and Lawler (1986) show that time pressure can sometimes have the opposite effect depending on motives.

The dual-concern model is also a theory of individual differences in conflict style, the way a person most commonly deals with conflict. This model has produced a psychometric tradition of research where peoples' judgments of the typical way they use various methods to handle conflicts are subject to scaling analyses (Ruble & Thomas, 1976; Van de Vliert, 1990).

But the bulk of the interest in negotiators' general preferences for particular outcome distributions between self and other, social value orientation, was stimulated by McClintock's (1977; see Messick & McClintock, 1968; McClintock & Van Avermaet, 1982) circumplex of social motives, shown in Figure 4.2. This model generates a plethora of motives—altruistic, competitive, cooperative, and so on—all derived from the combined positive or negative valuation of one's own outcomes and the other's outcomes. Thus a cooperator has a positive sense of their own outcome as well as the other's outcome; the competitor has just the former (for a comparison of this circumplex model to the dual-concern model, see Van de Vliert, 1997).

Many studies of social value orientations (e.g., De Dreu & Van Lange, 1995; Kuhlman & Marshello, 1975; Van Lange & Kuhlman, 1994) measure them using a decomposed game methodology developed by Messick and McClintock (1968; see Pruitt, 1967). It has reasonable test-retest reliability and construct validity (Van Lange, 1999); typically 50% of participants are classified as pro-social, 40% as individualistic, and about 10% as competitive. Researchers often use a "pro-self" category, a conglomeration of individualistic and competitive participants, who are people that try to maximize their own outcomes regardless of other's outcomes; and a "pro-social" category, who are people who tend to emphasize morality, fairness, and collective welfare.

In a meta-analysis, De Dreu, Weingart, and Kwon (2000b) tested the effects of (a) individual differences (mainly social value orientation), (b) incentives,

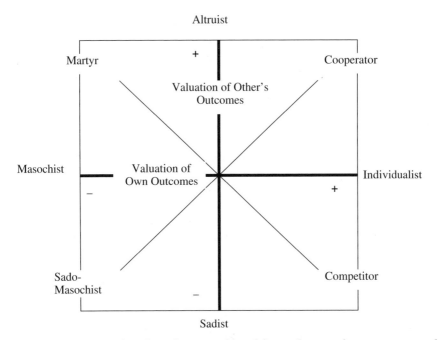

FIGURE 4.2 Circumplex of social motives derived from valuation of own outcomes and of other's outcomes (from McClintock & Van Avermaet, 1982).

(c) instructions, and (d) implicit cues (group membership, future interaction, friend vs. stranger) on joint outcomes. For all four, effect sizes indicated that pro-social negotiators achieved higher joint outcomes than selfish negotiators and, importantly, there were no differences between the different operationalizations of social motive. This latter finding indicates a *functional equivalence* of various ways of implementing social motivation in negotiation.

Social Motivation, Information Processing, and Emotions

The preceding discussion sets the stage for a review of current trends and tendencies in the study of goals and motives in negotiation. We focus our discussion on five sets of effects: motivation effects on negotiator cognition, epistemic motivation, fairness motivation, the effects of motivation on emotion in negotiation, and culture and motivation in negotiation.

Negotiator Cognition   There is evidence that social motivation alters the psychology of the person in the situation. For example, in an early study, Ajzen and Fishbein (1970) found that social motivation had different effects on attitudes and behavior: A cooperative social motivation enhanced the importance of social-normative beliefs, whereas a competitive social motivation enhanced the importance of the person's attitude about their own competitive behavior. Pruitt and Lewis (1975, Experiment 2) categorized participants on the basis of a personality variable, cognitive complexity, which reflects an individual's consideration of alternative conceptions of situations and use of more information for decisions. They found that asking and giving truthful information about the issues was positively related to integrativeness of the agreements but only for negotiators who were high in cognitive complexity. The overall level of information did not differ between high and low complexity negotiators, suggesting that the high complex negotiators had a lower threshold for information, understanding more with less.

A recent study by Olekalns and Smith (2003) found that different social motivations in negotiation dyads produce different paths to integrative agreement. In cooperatively oriented dyads, integrative outcomes were achieved when negotiators used much priority information and reciprocal sequences; in individualistically oriented dyads, integrative agreements were more likely when negotiators made multi-issue offers and avoided some reciprocal sequences. These patterns are consistent with earlier studies showing that pro-social individuals make greater concessions and see their opponent as more fair and trustworthy (De Dreu & Van Lange, 1995), and that pro-social individuals make more generous starting offers yet do better in the final agreement (Olekalns et al., 1996). These findings also comport with earlier results of Weingart, Bennett, and Brett (1993), who found that sequential treatment of issues was not a problem in four-person negotiation groups when the group had a cooperative social motivation. Here, the negotiators were more likely to note which party had the higher priority on the issues, something that did not occur when there was an individual, (see also Beersma & De Dreu, 1999, 2002). In addition, in the agreements, cooperatively motivated negotiators reported being m, than negotiators who were pro-self (Gillespie, Brett, & Weingart, 200\

Other evidence also supports the view that pro-social or pro-self n, .ion affects information processing. Camac (1992), for example, found that accuracy of recall was affected by social value orientation: pro-social individuals were more likely to correctly recall the joint-gain features of the task, whereas pro-self individuals were more likely to correctly recall the self-gain features. De Dreu and Boles (1998) reported similar effects of social value orientation on the recall of decision heuristics that reflected either cooperation or selfishness. Pro-social negotiators were more likely to recall heuristics such as "share and share alike"; selfish negotiators were more likely to recall heuristics such as "never trust your opponent." These results are consistent with van Kleef and De Dreu's (2002) finding that negotiators engage in confirmatory search consistent with their own social motives when goal information about the adversary is not known; when goal information was known (cooperative, competitive), this information guided their information search.

Social motivation produces a general, systemwide change in cognition that extends beyond cognition associated with the particular situation. Carnevale and Probst (1998) had people expect to enter a cooperative or conflictual negotiation; just before doing this, they were asked to evaluate material that assessed cognitive organization, for example, ratings of exemplars and a functional fixedness task. People expecting to enter conflict were less likely to see relationships among items and were less creative in these cognitive tasks (a person expecting conflict is less likely to see a "camel" as an example of the category "vehicle"). This is consistent with the notion that conflict can produce a "freezing" of cognition (see Lewin, 1951). The data also suggested that pro-social and pro-self individuals also differ in basic processes of cognitive organization, but that context can have important effects.

Fairness   Several studies suggest that social motivation and information interact to affect behavior in negotiation. O'Connor and Carnevale (1997), for example, found that cooperative social motivation inhibited the temptation to lie in negotiation (see also Steinel & De Dreu, 2004). Taken together, the bulk of the evidence suggests that motivational orientation has a profound impact on what is construed as fair and on how people react to violations of fairness.

In particular, social motivation interacts with the information features of the context. For example, one would think that information about payoffs would increase cooperation and increase the likelihood that people reach agreement. Such is not the case. In an early experiment, Messick and Thorngate (1967) found that information about other's payoffs led to no agreement; instead, knowledge of the other's payoffs affected own preferences. A similar effect is seen in work of Loewenstein, Thompson, and Bazerman (1989). Given a choice on division of a pie between self and other of (a) you: $300/other: $300 and (b) you: $500/other: $800, and how satisfactory is that division, many people preferred the equality distribution. A motive of fairness, in this case, for equality, was a problem. A similar effect was obtained by Pruitt (1970) in a demonstration of monetarily equivalent choices producing quite different motivations: When people thought that their best outcomes were controlled by another, they dropped their concern for a "fair" outcome and instead worked on getting the other to provide those outcomes. Results like this provided the foundation for the Pruitt and Kimmel (1977) goal-expectation theory of cooperation, which posits that two factors, a goal of mutual cooperation and trust (expectation that one's cooperation will be reciprocated), are fundamental elements of cooperation.

Another instance of the interaction of motivational orientation and information comes from a study by Carnevale and De Dreu (2005). They implemented three motivational orientations in face-to-face bilateral negotiation using the standard three-issue task: cooperative, individualistic, and competitive, defined by the payoffs to the negotiators, either joint gain, own gain, and in the competitive case a payoff based on the relative gain over the other in any final agreement. In addition, the level of information was varied, whether or not the negotiators had complete information about the payoff charts or the standard incomplete information. Figure 4.3 shows the values of the joint outcome as a function of information. As can be seen, having complete information helped negotiators achieve integrative agreements when they had an individualistic motivation. And it helped a little when they had a cooperative motivation, but those in the incomplete information condition talked about their payoff charts and developed an under-standing almost as good as those in the complete information condition. But when there was a competitive incentive, where payoffs were tied directly to doing better than the other, knowing how well the other would do in the agreement, having complete information lessened the likelihood of agreement. Here, negotiators

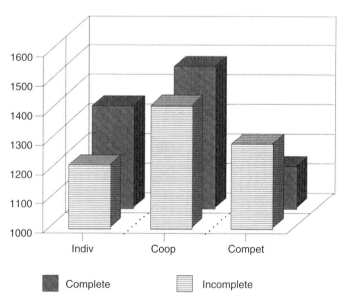

FIGURE 4.3   Effects of motivational orientation on joint outcome as a function of infor-mation (from Carnevale & De Dreu, 2005).

would rather not agree than let themselves be bested by the other, an effect akin to the rejection of an ultimatum offer. The latter effect is also consistent with an effect reported by Lamm and Rosch (1972).

Emotion   There is a growing body of evidence that moods and emotion play central roles in negotiation (see Barry, Fulmer, & Goates, chapter 6). There also is a link between emotion and cooperation, but not one that is always obvious. Several studies show a positive relationship between positive emotion and cooperation (Baron, 1990; Carnevale & Isen, 1986; Forgas, 1998; O'Quin & Aronoff, 1981). But sometimes cooperation goes along with anger. Hilty and Carnevale (1993) report that negotiators in some cases made the most concessions when forced to do so by an adversary who was completely uncooperative, and they felt quite angry about it; this is a case of a positive correlation of anger and cooperation (see also van Kleef, De Dreu, & Manstead, 2004a, b). But more often anger is associated with contentiousness and disagreement (Allred, Mallozzi, Matsui, & Raia, 1997; Forgas, 1998; Pillutla & Murnighan, 1996).

An interesting line of work reveals a relationship between social value orientation and emotion, or at least the facial display of emotion. Kuhlman and Carnevale (1984) reported that cooperative individuals had facial expressions that were more likely to be seen as happy, and competitors were more likely to be seen as angry, and these effects were obtained simply when the person was talking about personal life experiences in general. Shelley and Kuhlman (2003) reported that pro-social individuals were more likely to smile in a 30-second segment of interaction than were pro-self individuals. This work is intriguing for its suggestion that people of different motivational bents may signal their generalized proclivity to be cooperative, which may mediate relationship formation (Frank, 1988). As Shelley and Kuhlman asked it: Which comes first, the smiling or the social value orientation? Scharleman, Eckel, Kacelnik, and Wilson (2001) suggest that whatever the answer, trust will be a part of it.

EPISTEMIC MOTIVATION

Epistemic motivation, the need to understand one's world, provides a useful lens for understanding negotiation behavior (see Kruglanski, 1989). De Dreu, Koole, and Oldersma (1999) found that a negotiator's tendency to rely on cognitive heuristics is moderated by epistemic motivation. Heuristic, automatic information processing may be more efficient and faster, but controlled processing is typically more accurate (Chaiken & Trope, 1999). Thus, external forces such as time limits can lower epistemic motivation (De Dreu, 2003); the same for power (De Dreu & van Kleef, 2004).

Two studies further show the impact of motivation on information in negotiation: Galinsky and Mussweiler (2001) report that the first offer effect in negotiation—the greater impact of first offers on outcome—vanished when negotiators were given information that led them to think more deeply about the situation. The second is

Gallucci and Perugini (2003), who found that people with a high motivation to reciprocate were more likely to seek information about the other's past behavior; those with low motivation to reciprocate either favored no information about the other or information about the future.

Epistemic motivation increases systematic, effortful information search and processing. Combining this insight with work on social motives led to the formulation of a *motivated information-processing model* of negotiation (De Dreu & Carnevale, 2003; De Dreu, Koole, & Steinel, 2000a; De Dreu et al., 2000b; De Dreu et al., 1999; De Dreu & van Kleef, 2004; van Kleef et al., 2004b). The basic idea is that because negotiators often lack information about the task and about their counterpart, a motivated search for and provision of information provides new pieces of information on an almost continuous basis. Based on the research evidence discussed above, the model further assumes that social motivation drives the kind of information (i.e., either cooperative or competitive) that negotiators seek, provide, and consider. Epistemic motivation, in contrast, primarily determines the extent to which this "cooperative" or "competitive" information is being processed, and thus the extent to which this information impacts strategic choice, and the quality of agreement.

According to this motivated information-processing model, pro-social negotiators are more likely to develop trust, to engage in problem solving, and to reach high quality agreements than are selfish negotiators, but especially when epistemic motivation is high. Evidence for this central hypothesis was obtained in three experiments that showed that pro-social compared to selfish negotiators had better recall of cooperative information, developed more trust, engaged in more problem solving, and reached more integrative agreements when they had high but not when they had low levels of epistemic motivation (De Dreu, Beersma, Stroebe, & Euwema, 2004). The motivated information-processing model thus accounts for and integrates past research, and makes new and valid predictions about the interplay between basic classes of motives in conflict and negotiation.

IDENTITY MOTIVATION

Identity motivation is the desire to have a particular image of self in the negotiation. It has two general sources: an individual basis, for example, face saving (the desire to have a sense of personal strength) (Brown, 1968, 1977); or it can have a group basis and stem from the relationship of the individual to a collective, as when the negotiator represents a group and thus the sense of shared identity with the group is a factor (Heider, 1958; van Knippenberg, 2000). Some studies indicate that common identity across the negotiating table (measured by pronouns, "we" or "I," spoken in the negotiation), is an important mediator of effects (Carnevale, Pruitt, & Seilheimer, 1981). Baron (1985) found that an impression of strength is more likely to evoke cooperation if it is attributed to internal causes (one's own decision) rather than external causes (an organizational policy).

Often in negotiation there is a desire to create an impression of personal strength, of toughness (Sutton, 1991; Wall, 1991; see Hilty & Carnevale, 1993).

Indeed, there is evidence that conditions that help negotiators maintain this sense of strength, yet allow them to make concessions, such as the help of a third party, increase the likelihood of agreement (Pruitt & Johnson, 1970). Brown (1968, 1977) finds that people are willing to pay money to protect their sense of personal strength. Moreover, there is some reason to believe that certain conditions, for example surveillance by a constituent, will enhance the motivation to present an image of strength in negotiation (Carnevale, Pruitt, & Britton, 1979).

CULTURE AS A BASIS OF MOTIVES IN NEGOTIATION

Motivation and negotiation may have important ties to culture (see Brett & Gelfand, chapter 9). Much of culture is evolved social behavior in small groups, and small groups are involved in solving problems of coordination, cooperation, and bargaining. If humans are heavily reliant on imitation and social learning, then cultural transmission effects should be observed in small groups. That is, we should expect to observe differences in behaviors among people who have experienced social learning of cooperation in small groups. Such is the case. Robert and Carnevale (1997), using an ultimatum bargaining paradigm, had people make offers alone, and then as part of a small group. The group's mean level of offer was less cooperative than the individual's, and the best predictor of the groups ultimatum offer was the offer of the person who had been the least cooperative when alone (see Bornstein, 2003). But when the individuals later did an ultimatum offer, again, on their own, they were as uncooperative as when in the group. This suggests a cultural "meme" of uncooperative motivation, socially transmitted (Sperber, 1996).

There are other links of negotiator motivation to culture. Hulbert, Correa da Silva, and Adegboyega (2001) found that allocentrism was associated with cooperation, and idiocentrism was associated with noncooperation. These cultural values, measured via the IndCol (Singelis, Triandis, Bhawuk, & Gelfand, 1995), show consistent patterns of relationships with cooperation, and with the measures of social value orientation mentioned earlier (Probst, Carnevale, & Triandis, 1999). Figure 4.4 shows correlations between cultural values (VI, vertical individualism; HI, horizontal individualism; VC, vertical collectivism; and HC, horizontal collectivism) and social value orientation (cooperative, individualistic, and competitive), data collected recently by Carnevale and De Dreu at New York University (2005). As can be seen, pro-social individuals are especially likely to show characteristics of horizontal collectivism, and they are especially unlikely to show characteristics of vertical individualism. Pro-self individuals show the opposite pattern. This is perhaps not surprising given that the items that assess vertical individualism are all about competition ("Competition is the law of nature"), and the items that assess horizontal collectivism are about cooperation and sharing ("I like sharing little things with my neighbors"). A large question is, *What other motivational forces are present and important in understanding cultural variation in negotiation behavior?* (see Brett & Gelfand, chapter 9).

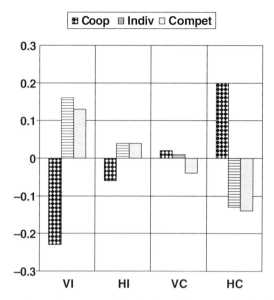

FIGURE 4.4   Correlations between cultural values (VI, vertical individualism; HI, horizontal individualism; VC, vertical collectivism; and HC, horizontal collectivism) and social value orientation (cooperative, individualistic, and competitive), $N = 404$. From Carnevale and De Dreu, 2005, unpublished data.

EXTENSIONS AND CONCLUSIONS

Two important agenda items for future work on motives in negotiation is what they are and how they relate to one another, in particular how they interact to affect negotiation. These are basic matters; and it may be a bit surprising that the field has not progressed further on these matters in the past 30 years or so. The first agenda item is about taxonomy. We presented a rough framework of four basic motives: aspiration, social motivation, identity motivation, and epistemic motivation—but these are hardly satisfactory. For example, research may start to take seriously another important class of motives, namely those having to do with *initiation*. *Initiation motivation* guides the start of negotiation and has three basic forms that reflect the notion that the situation is *ripe for negotiation* (Zartman, 1996): (1) a mutually hurting stalemate, where the parties are not winning and costs are mounting; (2) an impending or narrowly avoided catastrophe; and (3) a mutually enticing opportunity, where the divergent interests stand in the way of accomplishing important aims on both sides. All reflect the notion of negotiation as an adaptation to problems of interdependence (see Rusbult & Van Lange, 2003).

The links between our taxonomy and the framework offered by McClintock and colleagues (see Figure 4.2), is not at all clear. Looking at Figure 4.2, where should we locate the problem-solving negotiator? Are some motives more basic than others? However, there is reason to be optimistic in light of several encouraging signs, in particular the interest in cognitive models of motivation and the interest in relating important variables to their motivational under-pinnings. A great example is the link between gender effects and aspirations (Kray, Thompson, & Galinsky, 2001; see Kray & Babcock, chapter 10). We wonder about the links to other motivations, for example, possible gender effects in initiation motivation.

One would think that the four types of motives that we consider here would be interrelated. However, the evidence is mixed. For example, De Dreu et al. (1999) found no relationship between a measure of individual differences in need for cognitive closure and a measure of social value orientation. Also, in a study of negotiator accountability, De Dreu et al. (2000a) found it affected epistemic motivation but that it had no impact on a self-report measure of social motivation. One also wonders about mixtures of motives. Lax and Sebenius (1986) tell us that both cooperation and competition are necessary for optimal outcomes, and this too is the basic view of the dual concern theory.[3] Wall (1991) noted that negotiators should create an image of strength but at the same time be friendly and trust-worthy, which is reminiscent of the "firm but fair" notion presented by Pruitt (1981). We know from studies of mixed-strategies, such as the good-cop/bad-cop strategy, that mixtures can produce success. The critical question is what that mix should be, and when. Is epistemic motivation important in the mix with motiva-tional orientation?

There are important critiques of the negotiation literature that motivational models need to address. Zartman (1977), for example, noted that many complex negotiations are not about demands and concessions but rather are about stages of decision making. He identified two general stages, called formula and detail. In the formula stage, negotiators develop a general framework that assesses the global judgment that agreement is possible. Later, in the detail phase, negotiators work on specific issues. How can the models of motivation, or cognition, explain behavior in a stage model of negotiation?

It has long been recognized in the negotiation literature that people miss opportunities for gain because some "irrational force" leads people astray. Just one example is the irrational escalation of commitment (Brockner & Rubin, 1985), where people lose sight of actual value, and instead get caught in the trap of winning; another example is the notion of destructive efforts to punish the other (Deutsch, 1973, 2000), "cutting off one's nose to spite one's face" is the old adage. We suspect that a deeper understanding of motivational processes in negotiation and social conflict will provide greater understanding that has the potential of lessening the likelihood of destructive conflicts and unproductive negotiations.

NOTES

1. But there are interesting efforts along these lines, for example, Steigleder, Weiss, Bailing, Wenninger, and Lombardo (1980) show that conflict situations can produce a general aversive drive-like arousal state.

2. Previously, the dual-concern model was called the "flexible/rigidity model" on the notion that, to achieve integrative agreements, negotiators should be flexible with regard to means and rigid with regard to ends (Pruitt, 1981). The model is related to Blake and Mouton's (1964) *conflict grid*, which sees conflict management as a function of concern for the task (i.e., concern for self) and concern for people (i.e., concern for other). For a more elaborate discussion of this and related models, the reader is referred to Van de Vliert (1997).

3. Lax and Sebenius (1986) argued that negotiators must be both cooperative and competitive in negotiation, and achieve a balance; their concept of competitive ("claiming value") is akin to Siegal and Fouraker's (1960) notion of aspiration, and their notion of cooperation ("creating value") is akin to Pruitt's (1981) notion of problem solving, so their core idea is not dissimilar from the dual-concern model.

REFERENCES

Ajzen, I., & Fishbein, M. (1970). The prediction of behavior from attitudinal and normative variables. *Journal of Experimental Social Psychology, 6,* 466–487.

Allred, K. G., Mallozzi, J. S., Matsui, F., & Raia, C. P. (1997). The influence of anger and compassion on negotiation performance. *Organizational Behavior and Human Decision Processes, 70,* 175–187.

Baron, R. A. (1985). Reducing organizational conflict: An incompatible response approach. *Journal of Applied Psychology, 70,* 434–441.

Baron, R. A. (1990). Environmentally induced positive affect: It's impact on self-efficacy, task performance, negotiation, and conflict. *Journal of Applied Social Psychology, 20,* 368–384.

Bazerman, M. H., Magliozzi, T., & Neale, M. A. (1985). Integrative bargaining in a competitive market. *Organizational Behavior and Human Decision Processes, 35,* 294–313.

Beersma, B., & De Dreu, C. K. W. (1999). Negotiation processes and outcomes in prosocially and egoistically motivated groups. *International Journal of Conflict Management, 10,* 385–402.

Beersma, B., & De Dreu, C. K. W. (2002). Integrative and distributive negotiation in small groups: Effects of task structure, decision rule, and social motive. *Organizational Behavior and Human Decision Processes, 87,* 227–252.

Ben-Yoav, O., & Pruitt, D. G. (1984). Resistance to yielding and the expectation of cooperative future interaction in negotiation. *Journal of Experimental Social Psychology, 20,* 323–335.

Blake, R., & Mouton, J. S. (1964). *The managerial grid.* Houston, TX: Gulf.

Bornstein, G. (2003). Intergroup conflict: Individual, group, and collective interests. *Personality and Social Psychology Review, 7,* 129–145.

Brockner, J., & Rubin, J. Z. (1985). *Entrapment in escalating conflicts: A social psychological analysis.* New York: Springer-Verlag.

Brown, B. R. (1968). The effects of need to maintain face on interpersonal bargaining. *Journal of Experimental Social Psychology, 4,* 107–122.

Brown, B. R. (1977). Face-saving and face-restoration in negotiation. In D. Druckman (Ed.), *Negotiations: Social psychological perspectives* (pp. 275–300). Beverly Hills, CA: Sage.

Bruner, J. S., & Postman, L. (1948). Symbolic value as an organizing factor in perception. *Journal of Social Psychology, 27,* 203–208.

Camac, C. (1992). Information preferences in a two-person social dilemma. In W. B. G. Liebrand, D. M. Messick, & H. A. M. Wilke (Eds.), *Social dilemmas:Theoretical issues and research findings* (pp. 147–161). Elmsford, NY: Pergamon.

Carnevale, P. J., & De Dreu, C. (2005). *Information and motive in bilateral negotiation.* Unpublished manuscript, Department of Psychology, New York University, New York.

Carnevale, P. J., & Isen, A. M. (1986). The influence of positive affect and visual access on the discovery of integrative solutions in bilateral negotiation. *Organizational Behavior and Human Decision Processes, 37,* 1–13.

Carnevale, P. J., & Lawler, E. J. (1986). Time pressure and the development of integrative agreements in bilateral negotiation. *Journal of Conflict Resolution, 30,* 636–659.

Carnevale, P. J., & Probst, T. (1998). Social values and social conflict in creative problem solving and categorization. *Journal of Personality and Social Psychology, 74,* 1300–1309.

Carnevale, P. J., & Pruitt, D. G. (1992). Negotiation and mediation. *Annual Review of Psychology, 43,* 531–582.

Carnevale, P. J., Pruitt, D. G., & Britton, S. D. (1979). Looking tough: The negotiator under constituent surveillance. *Personality and Social Psychology Bulletin, 5,* 118–121.

Carnevale, P. J., Pruitt, D. G., & Seilheimer, S. (1981). Looking and competing: Account-ability and visual access in integrative bargaining. *Journal of Personality and Social Psychology, 40,* 111–120.

Chaiken, S., & Trope, Y. (Eds.). (1999). *Dual-process theories in social psychology.* New York: Guilford Press.

De Dreu, C. K. W. (2003). Time pressure and closing of the mind in negotiation. *Organizational Behavior and Human Decision Processes, 91,* 280–295.

De Dreu, C. K. W., Beersma, B., Stroebe, K., & Euwema, M. C. (2004). *Motivated information processing in negotiation.* Unpublished manuscript, University of Amsterdam.

De Dreu, C. K. W., & Boles, T. (1998). Share and share alike or winner take all? Impact of social value orientation on the choice and recall of decision heuristics in negotiation. *Organizational Behavior and Human Decision Processes, 76,* 253–267.

De Dreu, C. K. W., & Carnevale, P. J. (2003). Motivational bases of information processing and strategy in negotiation and social conflict. In M. P. Zanna (Ed.), *Advances in experimental social psychology* (Vol. 35, pp. 235–291). New York: Academic Press.

De Dreu, C. K. W., Koole, S., & Oldersma, F. L. (1999). On the seizing and freezing of negotiator inferences: Need for cognitive closure moderates the use of heuristics in negotiation. *Personality and Social Psychology Bulletin, 25,* 348–362.

De Dreu, C. K. W., Koole, S., & Steinel, W. (2000a). Unfixing the fixed-pie: A motivated information processing of integrative negotiation. *Journal of Personality and Social Psychology, 79,* 975–987.

De Dreu, C. K. W., Weingart, L. R., & Kwon, S. (2000b). Influence of social motives on integrative negotiation: A meta-analytical review and test of two theories. *Journal of Personality and Social Psychology, 78,* 889–905.

De Dreu, C. K. W., & Kleef, G. A. van (2004). The influence of power on the information search, impression formation, and demands in negotiation. *Journal of Experimental Social Psychology, 40,* 303–319.

De Dreu, C. K. W., & Lange, P. A. M. van (1995). The impact of social value orientations on negotiator cognition and behavior. *Personality and Social Psychology Bulletin, 21,* 1178–1188.

Deutsch, M. (1949). A theory of cooperation and competition. *Human Relations, 2,* 199–231.

Deutsch, M. (1973). *The resolution of conflict: Constructive and destructive processes.* New Haven, CT: Yale University Press.

Deutsch, M. (1994). Constructive conflict resolution: Principles, training, and research. *Journal of Social Issues, 50,* 13–32.

Deutsch, M. (2000). Cooperation and competition. In M. Deutsch & P. T. Coleman (Eds.), *The handbook of conflict resolution: Theory and practice.* San Francisco: Jossey-Bass.

Druckman, D. (Ed.). (1977). *Negotiations: Social-psychological perspectives.* Beverly Hills, CA: Sage.

Druckman, D. (1994). Determinants of compromising behavior in negotiation: A meta-analysis. *Journal of Conflict Resolution, 38,* 507–556.

Eccles, J. S., & Wigfield, A. (2002). Motivational beliefs, values, and goals. *Annual Review of Psychology, 53,* 109–32.

Fisher, R., & Ury. W. (1981). *Getting to yes.* Boston: Houghton Mifflin.

Follett, M. P. (1942). Constructive conflict. In H. C. Metcalf & L. Urwick (Eds.), *Dynamic administration: The collected papers of Mary Parker Follett.* New York: Harper.

Forgas, J. P. (1998). On feeling good and getting your way: Mood effects on negotiator cognition and behavior. *Journal of Personality and Social Psychology, 74,* 565–577.

Frank, R. H. (1988). *Passions within reason: The strategic role of the emotions.* New York: Norton

Freud, S. (1965). *The interpretation of dreams.* (James Strachey, Trans.) New York: Avon. (Original work published 1900).

Galinsky, A. D., & Mussweiler, T. (2001). First offers as anchors: The role of perspective-taking and negotiator focus. *Journal of Personality and Social Psychology, 81,* 657–669.

Galinsky, A. D., Mussweiler, T., & Medvec, V. H. (2002). Disconnecting outcomes and evaluations: The role of negotiator focus. *Journal of Personality and Social Psychology, 83,* 1131–1140.

Gallucci, M., & Perugini, M. (2003). Information seeking and reciprocity: A transformational analysis. *European Journal of Social Psychology, 33,* 473–495.

Gillespie, J. J., Brett, J. M., & Weingart, L. R. (2000). Interdependence, social motives, and outcome satisfaction in multiparty negotiation. *European Journal of Social Psychology 30,* 779–797.

Hastorf, A., & Cantril, H. (1954). They saw a game: A case study. *Journal of Abnormal and Social Psychology, 49,* 129–134.

Heider, F. (1958). *The psychology of interpersonal relations.* New York: Wiley.

Higgins, E. T. (1997). Beyond pleasure and pain. *American Psychologist, 52,* 1280–1300.

Hilty, J. A., & Carnevale, P. J. (1993). Black-hat/white-hat strategy in bilateral negotiation. *Organizational Behavior and Human Decision Processes, 55,* 444–469.

Huber, V., & Neale, M. (1986). Effects of cognitive heuristics and goals on negotiator performance and subsequent goal setting. *Organizational Behavior and Human Decision Processes, 38,* 342–365.

Hulbert, L. G., Correa da Silva, M. L., & Adegboyega, G. (2001). Cooperation in social dilemmas and allocentrism: A social values approach. *European Journal of Social Psychology, 31,* 641–657.

Kelley, H. H. (1966). A classroom study of the dilemmas in interpersonal negotiations. In K. Archibald, *Strategic interaction and conflict: Original papers and discussion.* Berkeley, CA: Institute of International Studies.

Kelley, H. H., Beckman, L. L., & Fischer, C. S. (1967). Negotiation the division of reward under incomplete information. *Journal of Experimental Social Psychology, 3,* 361–389.

Kleef, G. A. van, & De Dreu, C. K. W. (2002). Social value orientation and impression formation: A test of two competing hypotheses about information search in negotiation. *International Journal of Conflict Management, 13,* 59–77.

Kleef, G. A. van, De Dreu, C. K. W., & Manstead, A. S. R. (2004a). The interpersonal effects of anger and happiness in negotiations. *Journal of Personality and Social Psychology, 86,* 57–76.

Kleef, G. A. van, De Dreu, C. K. W., & Manstead, A. S. R. (2004b). The social effects of emotions in negotiation: A motivated information processing account. *Journal of Personality and Social Psychology, 87,* 510–528.

Knippenberg, D. van (2000). Work motivation and performance: A social identity perspective. *Applied Psychology: An International Review, 49,* 357–371.

Kray, L. J., Thompson, L., & Galinsky, A. (2001). Battle of the sexes: Gender stereotype confirmation and reactance in negotiations. *Journal of Personality and Social Psychology, 80,* 942–958.

Kruglanski, A. W. (1989). The psychology of being "right": The problem of accuracy in social perception and cognition. *Psychological Bulletin, 106,* 395–409.

Kruglanski, A. W., Shah, J. Y., Friedman, R., Fishbach, A., Chun, W. Y., & Sleeth-Keppler, D. (2002). *A theory of goal systems.* In M. P. Zanna (Ed.), *Advances in experimental social psychology* (pp. 331–378). San Diego, CA: Academic Press.

Kuhlman, D. M., & Carnevale, P. J. (1984). *Differences in nonverbal demeanor between cooperators, competitors, and individualists.* Paper presented at the Annual Meeting of the American Psychological Association, Toronto, Canada.

Kuhlman, D. M., & Marshello, A. (1975). Individual differences in game motivation as moderators of preprogrammed strategy effects in prisoner's dilemma. *Journal of Personality and Social Psychology, 32,* 922–931.

Lamm, H., & Rosch, E. (1972). Information and competitiveness of incentive structure as factors in two-person negotiation. *European Journal of Social Psychology, 2,* 459–462.

Lange, P. A. M. Van (1999). The pursuit of joint outcomes and equality in outcomes: An integrative model of social value orientations. *Journal of Personality and Social Psychology, 77,* 337–349.

Lange, P. A. M. Van, & Kuhlman, D. M. (1994). Social value orientations and impressions of partner's honesty and intelligence: A test of the might versus morality effect. *Journal of Personality and Social Psychology, 67,* 126–141.

Lax, D. A., & Sebenius, J. K. (1986). *The manager as negotiator: Bargaining for cooperation and competitive gain.* New York: Free Press.

Lewin, K. (1951). *Field theory in social science.* New York: Harper.

Liebert, R. M., Smith, W. P., Hill, J. H., & Keiffer, M. (1968). The effects of information and magnitude of initial offer on interpersonal negotiation. *Journal of Experimental Social Psychology, 4,* 431–441.

Locke, E. A., & Latham, G. P. (1990). *A theory of goal setting and task performance.* Upper Saddle River, NJ: Prentice Hall.

Loewenstein, G., Thompson, L., & Bazerman, M. (1989). Social utility and decision making in interpersonal contexts. *Journal of Personality & Social Psychology, 57,* 426–441.

McClintock, C. (1977). Social motives in settings of outcome interdependence. In D. Druckman (Ed.), *Negotiations: Social psychological perspective* (pp. 49–77). Beverly Hills, CA: Sage.

McClintock, C. G., & Van Avermaet, E. (1982). Social values and rules of fairness. In V. Darlega, J. Valerian, & J. Grzelak (Eds.), *Cooperation and helping behavior: Theories and research* (pp. 43–71). New York: Academic Press.

Messick, D. M., & McClintock, C. (1968). Motivational bases of choice in experimental games. *Journal of Experimental Social Psychology, 4*, 1–25.

Messick, D. M., & Thorngate, W. B. (1967). Relative gain maximization in experimental games. *Journal of Experimental and Social Psychology, 3*, 85–101.

Mook, J. (2000). *Motivation*. New York: Prentice Hall.

Neale, M. A., & Bazerman, M. H. (1991*). Rationality and cognition in negotiation*. New York: Free Press.

O'Connor, K. M., & Carnevale, P. J. (1997). A nasty but effective negotiation strategy: Misrepresentation of a common-value issue. *Personality and Social Psychology Bulletin, 23*, 504–515.

Olekalns, M., & Smith, P. L. (2003). Testing the relationships among negotiators' motivational orientations, strategy choices, and outcomes. *Journal of Experimental Social Psychology, 39*, 101–117.

Olekalns, M., Smith, P. L., & Walsh, T. (1996). The process of negotiating: Strategy and timing as predictors of outcomes. *Organizational Behavior and Human Decision Processes, 68*, 68–77.

O'Quin, K., & Aronoff, J. (1981). Humor as a technique of social influence. *Social Psychology Quarterly, 44*, 349–357.

Pillutla, M. M., & Murnighan, J. K. (1996). Unfairness, anger, and spite: Emotional rejections of ultimatum offers. *Organizational Behavior and Human Decision Processes, 68*, 208–224.

Pinkley, R. L., Griffith, T., & Northcraft, G. B. (1995). Fixed pie a la mode: Information availability, information processing, and the negotiation of sub-optimal agreements. *Organizational Behavior and Human Decision Processes, 62*, 101–112.

Pinkley, R. L., Neale, M. A., & Bennett, R. J. (1994). The impact of alternatives to settlement in dyadic negotiation. *Organizational Behavior and Human Decision Processes, 57*, 97–116.

Probst, T., Carnevale, P. J., & Triandis, H. C. (1999). Cultural values in intergroup and single-group social dilemmas. *Organizational Behavior and Human Decision Processes, 77*, 171–191.

Pruitt, D. G. (1967). Reward structure and cooperation: The decomposed prisoner's dilemma game. *Journal of Personality and Social Psychology, 7*, 21–27.

Pruitt, D. G. (1970). Motivational processes in the decomposed prisoner's dilemma game. *Journal of Personality and Social Psychology, 14*, 227–238.

Pruitt, D. G. (1981). *Negotiation behavior*. New York: Academic Press.

Pruitt, D. G. (1998). Social conflict. In D. Gilbert, S. T. Fiske, & G. Lindzey (Eds.), *Handbook of social psychology* (4th ed., Vol. 2, pp. 89–150). New York: McGraw-Hill.

Pruitt, D. G., & Johnson, D. F. (1970). Mediation as an aid to face saving in negotiation. *Journal of Personality and Social Psychology, 14*, 239–246.

Pruitt, D. G., & Kimmel, M. J. (1977). Twenty years of experimental gaming: Critique, synthesis, and suggestions for the future. *Annual Review of Psychology, 28*, 363–392.

Pruitt, D. G., & Lewis, S. A. (1975). Development of integrative solutions in bilateral negotiation. *Journal of Personality and Social Psychology, 31*, 621–633.

Pruitt, D. G., & Rubin, J. Z. (1986). *Social conflict: Escalation, stalemate, and settlement.* New York: Random House.

Robert, C., & Carnevale, P. J. (1997). Group choice in ultimatum bargaining. *Organizational Behavior and Human Decision Processes, 72*, 256–279.

Ross, L., & Ward, A. (1995). Psychological barriers to dispute resolution. In M. Zanna (Ed.), *Advances in experimental social psychology* (Vol. 27, pp. 255–304). San Diego, CA: Academic Press.

Rubin, J. Z., & Brown, B. (1975). *The social psychology of bargaining and negotiations.* New York: Academic Press.

Ruble, T. L., & Thomas, K. W. (1976). Support for a two-dimensional model of conflict behavior. *Organizational Behavior and Human Performance, 16*, 143–155.

Rusbult, C. E., & Lange, P. A. M. Van (2003). Interdependence, interaction, and relationships. *Annual Review of Psychology, 54*, 351–375.

Scharleman, J., Eckel, C., Kacelnik, A., & Wilson, R. (2001). The value of a smile: Game theory with a human face. *Journal of Economic Psychology, 22*, 617–640.

Schelling, T. C. (1960). *The strategy of conflict.* Boston, MA: Harvard University Press.

Shelley, G. P., & Kuhlman, D. M. (2003). Nonverbal encoding and decoding of social value orientation. Poster presented at the 10th international conference on social dilemmas, Marstrand, Sweden, August.

Siegel, A. E., & Fouraker, L. E. (1960). *Bargaining and group decision making.* New York: McGraw-Hill.

Singelis, T. M., Triandis, H. C., Bhawuk, D. P. S., & Gelfand, M. J. (1995). Horizontal and vertical dimensions of individualism and collectivism: A theoretical and measurement refinement. *Cross-Cultural Research, 29*, 240–275.

Smith, D. L., Pruitt, D. G., & Carnevale, P. J. (1982). Matching and mismatching: The effect of own limit, other's toughness, and time pressure on concession rate in negotiation. *Journal of Personality and Social Psychology, 42*, 876–883.

Smith, V. L. (2001). From old issues to new directions in experimental psychology and economics. *Behavioral and Brain Sciences, 24*, 428–429.

Sperber, D. (1996). *Explaining culture: A naturalistic approach*: Oxford, UK: Blackwell.

Srull, T. K., & Wyer, R. S., Jr. (1986). The role of chronic and temporary goals in social information processing. In R. M. Sorrentino & E. T. Higgins (Eds.), *Handbook of motivation and cognition.* New York: Guilford Press.

Steigleder, M. K., Weiss, R. E, Balling, S. S., Wenninger, V. L., & Lombardo, J. P. (1980). Drivelike motivational properties of competitive behavior. *Journal of Personality and Social Psychology, 38*, 93–104.

Steinel, W., & De Dreu, C. K. W. (2004). Social motives and strategic misrepresentation in social decision making. *Journal of Personality and Social Psychology, 86*, 419–434.

Sutton, R. (1991). Maintaining norms about expressed emotions: The case of bill collectors. *Administrative Science Quarterly, 36*, 245–268.

Thompson, L. (2004). *The mind and heart of the negotiator.* New York: Prentice Hall

Tietz, R., & Bartos, O. J. (1983). Balancing of aspiration levels as fairness principle in negotiations. In R. Tietz (Ed.), *Aspiration levels in bargaining and economic decision making.* Berlin: Springer-Verlag.

Tversky, A., & Kahneman, D. (1974). Judgment under uncertainty: Heuristics and biases. *Science, 185*, 1124–1131.

Vliert, E. Van de (1990). Positive effects of conflict: A field assessment. *International Journal of Conflict Management, 1,* 69–80.

Vliert, E. Van de (1997). *Complex interpersonal conflict behavior.* London: Psychology Press.

Wall, J. A. (1991). Impression management in negotiations. In R. A. Giacalone & P. Rosenfeld (Eds.), *Applied impression management: How image-making affects managerial decisions.* London: Sage.

Walton, R. E., & McKersie, R. (1965). *A behavioral theory of labor negotiations: An analysis of a social interaction system.* New York: McGraw-Hill.

Weingart, L. R., Bennett, R. J., & Brett, J. M. (1993). The impact of consideration of issues and motivational orientation on group negotiation process and outcome. *Journal of Applied Psychology, 78,* 504–517.

White, S. B., & Neale, M. A. (1994). The role of negotiator aspirations and settlement expectancies in bargaining outcomes. *Organizational Behavior and Human Decision Processes, 57,* 303–317.

Whyte, G., & Sebenius, J. K. (1997). The effect of multiple anchors on anchoring in individual and group judgment. *Organizational Behavior and Human Decision Processes, 69,* 75–85.

Yukl, G. A. (1974). The effects of situational variables and opponent concessions on a bargainer's perception, aspirations, and concessions. *Journal of Personality and Social Psychology, 29,* 227–236.

Zartman, I. W. (1977). Negotiation as a joint decision-making process. *Journal of Conflict Resolution, 21,* 619–638.

Zartman, I. W. (1996). Bargaining and conflict resolution. In E. A. Kolodziej & R. E. Kanet (Eds.), *Coping with conflict after the Cold War* (pp. 271–290). Baltimore, MD: Johns Hopkins Press.

Zetik, D. C., & Stuhlmacher, A. F. (2002). Goal setting and negotiation performance: A meta-analysis. *Group Processes and Intergroup Relations, 5,* 35–52.

5

Learning to Negotiate: Novice and Experienced Negotiators

JEFFREY LOEWENSTEIN and
LEIGH L. THOMPSON

INTRODUCTION

*E*veryone negotiates, and everyone could stand to learn to negotiate better. Effective negotiation requires understandings and skills that tend not to be intuitive (Loewenstein & Thompson, 2000). People exhibit a large number of cognitive and social foibles that limit and misguide them (see Bazerman & Chugh chapter 2; and Neale & Fragale, chapter 3). And yet, our hopes for what effective negotiation can bring about are high—more value creation, less strife, more peace. Negotiation training might also increase academic achievement (Stevahn, Johnson, & Johnson, 2002). Accordingly, we should have the goal of understanding how people learn to negotiate, what they learn from negotiation experience, and how to instill more effective negotiation practices.

Two linked studies in many ways began the field's experimental examination of learning and experience in negotiation. First, Bazerman, Magliozzi, and Neale (1985) found that undergraduates in a market simulation learned to logroll issues (concede on a low-value issue to gain on a priority issue; Froman & Cohen, 1970) and thereby increase their gains as they repeatedly bargained over the same three issues with new partners. Second, Neale and Northcraft (1986) found that corporate real estate negotiators with about 10 years of experience also learned to logroll issues in the same market simulation, although their initial rates of logrolling exceeded that of the undergraduates. The real estate negotiators also completed more transactions in the same amount of time than did the undergraduates. Finally, both groups were influenced by a framing manipulation (values reported as losses or gains) and a goal-setting manipulation (on the number of transactions to complete).

These studies are foundational both because they provided compelling data and because they stimulate a host of questions. First, is it a general truth that with repeated experiences people learn to logroll to secure joint gains? If so, how? And what about learning other means for creating value? Second, does experience also have an effect on bargaining to claim value, and if so, how and in what ways? Third, might experience confer any protection from decision biases (such as framing)? Fourth, does it matter whether people negotiate in the context within which they acquired their experience (e.g., do corporate real estate negotiators perform differently in corporate real estate negotiations than other kinds of negotiations)? Fifth, does experience influence the process negotiators use at the table—does it matter, for example, that corporate real estate negotiators bargained only with each other? In what follows we review the literature's current answers to these questions. We then analyze learning processes and what we know about novice negotiators' understandings of negotiation.

WHAT NEGOTIATION EXPERIENCE BRINGS

Learning to Create Value

It seems clear that repeated experience within similar negotiations allows people to logroll effectively. The initial studies asked people to repeatedly engage in the same negotiation within a market of other negotiators. This means that increased logrolling could be due to learning the structure of the negotiators preferences, or trial and error followed by imitation (among other alternatives). Accordingly, in a subsequent stream of research, Thompson (1990a, 1992; Thompson & Hastie, 1990; see also Roloff & Jordan, 1991) showed logrolling still increased across negotiating rounds in a series of studies using negotiations written in different situational contexts (e.g., buying a computer, renting a house, forming a job contract) but with a consistent issue structure (two equally preferred distributive issues, two unequally preferred issues that could be traded off, and a similarly preferred compatible issue). Logrolling levels increased even if only one negotiator engaged in prior rounds of negotiating (Thompson, 1990b). Increased logrolling was associated with setting higher goals, implying that negotiators learned as an indirect result of increased motivation to find agreements that allowed them to create enough value to meet their own targets. Increased logrolling was also associated and with drawing more accurate inferences about one's counterpart's preferences. This was confirmed in a later experiment: Negotiators who were provided outcome information were less effective in learning to logroll than negotiators who were also provided with information about the other party's preferences (Thompson & DeHarpport, 1994).

In contrast to logrolling, there is little evidence that people learn many other forms of value creation from repeated negotiation. We have found no data on whether repeated experience yields learning to add issues, to unbundle issues to find tradeoffs, to generate contingent contracts, to bridge issues by reframing them to allow agreement, or other forms of creating value, with the following two exceptions. First, in the same series of studies just discussed, Thompson found that negotiators did not improve in maximizing value on compatible issues.

They also did not improve their insight into this aspect of their counterpart's preferences, implying that inferring preferences related to logrolling is easier than inferring compatible issues. This difference is useful because it sheds light on how people learn from experience. It is hard to imagine a learning mechanism that would show that issue valuations would be easier to understand than positions on issues, given that positions are more concrete and more likely to be discussed explicitly. Rather, as novice negotiators share information and offers, they might assume that a proposal on a compatible issue is a concession or an unthinking mistake, or even simply fail to notice it because they do not need to discuss it further if it is set at their preferred outcome. That is, studies of compatible issues provide indirect evidence that learning takes place against a backdrop of assumptions about negotiations and the structure of parties' preferences.

The second and final kind of value creation about which there is evidence of learning through experience is cooperation in bargaining games. With a finite round repeated game, players show a moderate tendency to coordinate on cooperation (a mean rate of about 50% cooperation; Rapoport, 1988) until the final rounds, when they largely defect (Ledyard & Palfrey, 1995). Across games, players learn to cooperate more during the early rounds, and thereby create more value (Loewenstein, Zhong, & Murnighan, 2003).

Thus far, we have discussed prior experience as if it were only a positive. Yet one's negotiation experience may also lead to less value creation. There are at least three kinds of reasons. First, prior experience with a skewed sample of negotiation situations (e.g., pure distributive haggling) may lead people to assume that value creation is not possible—and assuming it is not possible should make it less likely to occur (cf. Kelley & Stahelski, 1970). Second, prior experience with one kind of counterpart may make it difficult to create value with other kinds of counterparts because of misunderstandings—an issue we pursue in discussing the cultural specificity of negotiation experience. Third, O'Connor and Arnold (2001) found that after an impasse, relative to those not experiencing an impasse, negotiators were less interested in working with their counterparts again, planned to share less information in the future, planned to behave less cooperatively, and felt that negotiation was a less effective means for resolving conflicts. And people appear to follow through with these behavioral intentions (O'Connor, Arnold, & Burris, in press), creating a self-reinforcing cycle of poor negotiated outcomes. In short, prior experience can yield lessons that are counterproductive.

Learning to Claim Value

Surprisingly few studies have addressed learning to claim value in negotiation simulations, perhaps because of the substantial number of studies of bargaining games, whose central purpose is to examine value claiming (Camerer, 2003). The negotiation simulation data reveal the principal finding that one would expect. People can learn to use tactics (Gist & Stevens, 1998), and people who have engaged in several negotiation simulations claim more value than their counterparts without such experience (Murnighan, Babcock, Thompson, & Pillutla, 1999). However, if the less experienced counterparts are warned that they will be negotiating with someone with a reputation for value claiming—even though this reputation is randomly assigned and not told to the negotiator supposedly possessing the reputation—no discrepancy in actual value claimed across parties results (Tinsley, O'Connor, & Sullivan, 2002). It is unclear how strong this effect of knowing about another's reputation is—the difference between experienced and inexperienced negotiators was a matter of a few days' work, not months or years, and neither party was particularly experienced with the particular bargaining context. It is still possible that the average person on the street will be fleeced by a wily salesperson, even knowing to watch out for wily salespeople.

As for the literature on bargaining games, the base finding concerning learning is that inexperienced players often do not know how to maximize their value, but often improve across trials. Depending on the game, they might initially start with fair divisions (e.g., in ultimatum bargaining games and coalition games, as discussed shortly). They might instead rely on a personal tendency or situational cue to make a cooperative or competitive choice (e.g., in prisoners' dilemma games; Bettenhausen & Murnighan, 1985; Liberman, Samuels, & Ross, 2004). They might also choose based on risk preferences, be they stable or situationally induced (Roth & Malouf, 1979). Critically for learning, across trials they might learn to coordinate (following Schelling, 1960, e.g., Van Huyck & Battalio, 2002), or they might learn they can claim more value. For example, Bottom, Holloway, McClurg, and Miller (2000) found that players in a coalition game tended to pursue less risky strategies initially, but then examined riskier strategies in search of claiming more value in a subsequent round. Slonim and Roth (1998) found a similar pattern with an ultimatum bargaining game with reasonably high stakes (12 to 62 times hourly wages). They found players generally started by making roughly even split offers, then learned to offer less across trials. We will return to these studies when we discuss learning processes.

The Limits of Learning From Experience

The Neale and Northcraft (1986) study with corporate real estate negotiators showed they were influenced by a framing effect (although they were not in their usual setting of real estate negotiation). In a subsequent study, Northcraft and Neale (1987) showed that real estate agents were influenced by an anchoring effect based on (a manipulated) sale price. This raises the question of whether experts are affected by decision biases, just as novices are (see Bazerman & Chugh, chapter 2). The Northcraft and Neale (1987, Experiment 2) study showed that real estate agents were influenced by sale prices set above and below the actual appraised value. The listed sale prices (manipulated between subjects) were roughly $120,000, $130,000, $140,000, and $150,000, and the appraised value was in the middle, about $135,000. Novices (students) reported estimates ranging from about $110,00 to about $140,000. Real estate agents averaging 9 years of experience responded with estimates ranging from about $112,000 to about $128,000, with higher sale prices producing higher estimates. Both groups were clearly influenced by the listed sale prices, but it is also clear that real estate agents were influenced differently than the novice group. Perhaps adjustment strategies take domain knowledge into consideration (e.g., some houses just have optimistic sellers so are priced artificially high, while other houses are priced low either because they are nonobvious problems or because they want to sell quickly).

More broadly, there are two important conclusions and two large open questions concerning expertise and decision biases. First, practitioners with years of experience nonetheless show decision biases (see Camerer, 2001, for a review). Second, decision biases are surely more consequential for practitioners than novices because the former make more consequential decisions. This leads to the open questions. Can people be taught to minimize decision biases (Fischoff, 1982)? There are some signs of hope (for a review, see Larrick, 2004). For example, being held accountable for one's decision can ameliorate some decision biases (Lerner & Tetlock, 1999), as can considering the opposite of one's initial judgment (Arkes, 1991). Formal instruction is effective (for what it sets out to teach; Nisbett, 1993). Yet debiasing remains a fragmented set of partial cures. Indeed, Diekman, Tenbrunsel, Shah, Schroth, and Bazerman (1996) argued that expert negotiators should take others' biases into consideration because other parties think and behave according to those biases, and accordingly they are consequential for forming negotiated agreements. Second, and most broadly, there is little attempt to define what constitutes expertise in decision making. For example, in the Northcraft and Neale (1987) study, the expert population was real estate agents with about 9 years of experience, engaging in about 16 transactions per year. This is only 144 total transactions—by contrast, Chase and Simon (1973) estimated that chess experts knew at least 50,000 chess patterns. Further, a given transaction does not provide all that much clear feedback, and there is little in the way of formal training to serve as a substitute. This is typical for negotiation as well—feedback is typically poor and subject to misinterpretation (e.g., Morris, Larrick, & Su, 1999), and formal training rarely exceeds a course or two. Impoverished training and poor feedback are troublesome because people's intuitions are not particularly well honed for effective negotiation (Loewenstein & Thompson, 2000), and expertise appears to require planning, monitoring, analyzing, and reflecting on one's practice, not merely repeated performance (Ericsson & Lehman, 1996).

The Situational Specificity of Experience

Most negotiators are neither novices nor experts. They have negotiated repeatedly in a particular setting defined by national, regional, and professional cultures, and the particular contexts of bargaining (e.g., real estate agents over property sales, company purchasing agents with suppliers, or union leaders over employment contracts). For this reason, negotiators likely use situated, not general, concepts of negotiation (see Medin & Ross, 1989). Thus, it may be unrealistic to assume that context-specific negotiating experience leads to domain general effective understanding and performance. For example, although it is obvious to management consultants that they could charge a client based on how valuable their advice turns out to be ("value billing"), it is not at all obvious that they could set a sales price for a television show contingent on its Nielsen ratings, despite these being analogous contingent contracts (Gentner, Loewenstein, & Thompson, 2004).

Thus, experience negotiating can lead to effective performance and even provide the fodder for general insights, but typically the result is learning that is bound to the situations in which it was acquired.

The situated nature of most knowledge has daunting implications for learning to negotiate. Because negotiations occur in a wide variety of settings, people's knowledge about negotiating is fragmented across situations, as the value billing example suggests. Not only are sophisticated negotiation strategies artificially limited in scope, people are also limited because they do not think of their actions in a variety of settings as all being negotiations. Therefore they approach situations in different fashions based on what they think the situation calls for, even if they all appear to be negotiations to an expert and warrant a more consistent approach. One result is that people's assumptions about what a negotiation is are shaped by the limited situations they actually think about as being negotiations. For example, people may fail to claim value because they do not realize a situation is a negotiation and simply agree to another's proposal (Babcock, Gelfand, Small, & Stayn, 2002). But people may also fail to be contentious if they were spontaneously thinking of a situation as a problem-solving opportunity, rather than as a negotiation, and perhaps create more value (O'Connor & Adams, 1999). We will examine further results of situated knowledge when we later consider learning processes.

The Cultural Specificity of Experience

Prior experience negotiating shapes one's expectations about whether an event is a negotiation, and what is likely to occur, how one should act, what will likely result, and so forth. That is, experience breeds expectations (Schank & Abelson, 1977). Negotiation research has documented a wealth of such expectations. For example, novice negotiators are looking for another party, a monetary issue or two, an argument, and concessions leading to an agreement (O'Connor & Adams, 1999). McGinn and Keros (2002) examined negotiation transcripts and found that parties tended to enact one of three social scripts: haggling, opening up (full honest information exchange), and working together (respectful problem solving). Expectations also differ according to structural aspects of context (e.g., one-time encounters or repeated negotiations), probably the most interesting of which are differences across national cultures (Brett, 2001; Brett & Gelfand, chapter 9). For example, one might expect others to communicate directly (e.g., in the United States), or indirectly (e.g., in Japan); one might expect others to be individualistic (France) or collectivist (Chile); one might expect others to talk as equals (Turkey) or as part of a status hierarchy (Singapore). This is a simplistic fragment of cultural differences and glosses over underlying mechanisms (see Hong, Benet-Martinez, Chiu, & Morris, 2003). The point is that negotiators have a wealth of expectations about what negotiations are and how they are supposed to be carried out; these expectations are rich, have many implications, and are largely implicit.

There are multiple implications of negotiator expectations for learning. One classic claim is that one's expectations may limit learning by shaping one's experiences: Kelley and Stahelski (1970) argued that people playing prisoners' dilemma games who defected would lead their counterparts to defect and, hence, would confirm their beliefs that defection was the only plausible choice. Players who tended to cooperate realized that both joint cooperation and joint defection were stable outcomes. De Dreu and Boles (1998) extended this finding. Cooperative negotiators not only choose more cooperative than competitive negotiating strategies when presented with both during preparation, but they recall the cooperative strategies better later and feel they are morally appropriate. Competitive negotiators choose competitive strategies, recall them better later, and prefer them because they are seen as effective. That is, expectations guide choices and what one later remembers, and these are shaped by broader motivations. And because expectations may be specific to social groups, the same situations may engender different interpretation, performance, and learning.

As a result of generating varied expectations about negotiations, experience can disrupt otherwise effective negotiators if they are negotiating with someone whose expectations clash. McGinn and Keros (2002) showed that negotiators who could not get in sync with one another did not develop rapport, shared less information than those who did, and created less value as a result. This seems of fundamental concern for learning to negotiate across cultures effectively (see Earley & Peterson, 2004).

CHARACTERIZING LEARNING PROCESSES

Experienced negotiators were once novices. We turn to examining classes of learning processes that cause novices to become more expert. One approach is to examine how people use feedback to update probabilities that actions will be successful. These models assume learners have a small amount of knowledge and that their goal is to maximize value within the limits of a boundedly rational information processing system. A second approach is to examine how people learn from examples. This approach assumes people have considerably more knowledge and focuses on how people construe situations. A third approach is to examine people's motivations. This approach assumes broad classes of motivations that provide different goals, and lead to different kinds of learning strategies.

Feedback-Driven Learning

People update their beliefs based on their perception of what has happened. That is, people learn from feedback about the results of their (and others') behavior. Several different theoretical models attempt to explain the process whereby a person's future behavior can be affected by knowledge of the outcome of their past behavior (Balzer, Doherty, & O'Connor, 1989; Brunswik, 1955; Einhorn & Hogarth, 1978; Hammond, McClelland, & Mumpower, 1980; Hogarth, 1981). From the research we have already reviewed, it is clear that people sometimes derive inappropriate lessons from feedback.

People in bargaining games make unambiguous choices, receive unambiguous feedback, and then make somewhat different patterns of choices. This setting is useful for modeling, and behavioral economics researchers have been active in proposing learning models that use outcome feedback to update their likelihoods of making choices. We revisit the Slonim and Roth (1998) study to show the benefits and limitations of such models for research on negotiation. Slonim and Roth showed that with sufficiently high stakes, a population of ultimatum bargaining players generally starts by making mostly even split offers, then learns to offer less across trials. The authors' explanation is that people making offers learn that responders will accept less, then fit their data to a reinforcement learning model (Roth & Erev, 1995) to explain how people come to offer less. The model assumes a probability distribution for making a given offer based on the actual population distribution of offers made in the initial two rounds of their behavioral study. Learning is a matter of drawing by chance from the initial distribution of choices, then updating based on the choice's success. Alternative learning models in this literature, nicely reviewed by Camerer (2003), instead might adjust differently off of a prior choice (learning direction theory), consider other information, such as opponents' choices (belief learning models, anticipatory models, and imitation models) or use a blend of information about one's own and one's opponent's choices (Camerer's own EWA models). All of these learning models are used for predicting changes in play across repeated, identical game situations, with unambiguous known choices and clear outcome feedback after each choice. Thus, even before we examine the models more closely, we should note that their value for understanding learning in negotiation situations suffers from several substantial caveats. Negotiators do not make single pure choices under dictated and severely constrained social conditions, but rather multiple simultaneous and hence confounded choices. Thus, whatever feedback they receive will be problematic to interpret. Second, negotiators do not receive unambiguous feedback, and thus people, in contrast to these learning models, have considerable leeway in generating attributions. Third, negotiators are not making identical choices in repeated games but rather making a series of different choices. The choices are path dependent. This presents a considerable categorization challenge to assessing what feedback should adjust what prior choice. These are nontrivial challenges to generalization.

One modeling improvement would be to consider learning at higher levels of analysis than choices. To return to the Slonim and Roth (1998) paper, they take a distribution of choices made by a population as a model of a given individual's likelihood of making various offers. However, it is just as plausible that individuals each consider a few strategies for generating offers that collectively produce a distribution of offers broader than any individual member actually considers. To consider the simplest example, perhaps some people try even split offers because they are fair, they value being fair, and feel these offers are likely to be accepted, and other people try low offers because they feel the stakes are high enough that responders will overlook the disparity in gains because something is better than nothing. The point is to examine plausible strategies bearing some causal logic and then to examine how people come to learn, select, and adapt various strategies (e.g., Siegler, 1995). Examining strategies as well as choices provides a natural route to transfer across situations, namely that the strategies remain the same although available choices change with the game one is playing. Rule learning models within behavioral economics come closest to using this approach (Stahl, 2000). However, they still have the problems of needing unambiguous choices and feedback, they take in considerable information about other players that negotiators likely ignore, and they require knowing all possible strategies in advance (Bazerman & Carroll, 1987). Yet it is possible to generate new strategies, and it is possible to choose strategies based on less information, but based on changing goals. To return to Slonim and Roth's (1998) data on ultimatum games, it is plausible that learning over trials is driven by people for whom lower offers are only considered after discovering that even offers are accepted. This is essentially the logic of a postsettlement settlement in negotiations (Raiffa, 1985): Once people have an agreement, their reservation point shifts, and they generate new goals and use new strategies to explore new alternatives. This logic is also consistent with a motivational shift (Higgins, 1997): Novices may initially be prevention focused, concerned with getting their offers accepted, and only after they have resolved that uncertainty will they shift to being promotion focused and accordingly consider strategies for maximizing their gains.

To summarize, learning models in behavioral economics are useful for specifying testable claims, yet at least at the moment, the strong ties to the specifics of the bargaining games limit providing novel general insights. Doing better seems to mean adding complexity, such as considering not just choices, but strategies that would lead to those choices and goals that would lead to those strategies. An advantage of generating these learning models is that they have required little learning about what people actually know. However, the utility of such models may ultimately be limited. People do have knowledge and expectations, and generate not just probabilistic leanings, but assumptions about causes (which are not just probabilities; e.g., Dennis & Ahn, 2001).

There have already been several demonstrations that could be interpreted as showing the limitations of simple outcome feedback in the absence of thought about what people actually know. For example, in a repeated decision situation, Ball, Bazerman, and Carroll (1991) found that outcome feedback was ineffective to curb poor bidding choices in a decision scenario (as did Foreman & Murnighan, 1996, in a follow-up study). This is because making better choices required most people to develop more complex interpretations of the situation, and outcome feedback was unable to prompt such thoughts. People had an alternative attribution, namely their lack of success could be due to anticipated variability in what outcomes would occur (i.e., bad luck). And in a very different kind of study, Morris and associates (1999) examined negotiator attributions about competitive behavior in a negotiation simulation. Negotiators given more valuable alternatives were viewed as less agreeable than those given less valuable alternatives. Negotiators made both situational and personality attributions and generated behavioral intentions purely about the person. Thus, people both under-learn and over-learn from experience. We suspect this is due to prior knowledge.

It is possible to integrate learning from feedback with an understanding of people's prior knowledge. Several studies show that people can learn from counterfactual reasoning. Outcomes that are close to category boundaries can prompt counterfactual reasoning (if we had not gotten stuck in traffic we would have made our flight; if we had not offered a pay increase up front, we would have been able to keep under our spending cap; and so forth; see Medvec & Savitsky, 1997). For example, with respect to negotiation, negotiators who have their first offers accepted feel worse despite gaining more than negotiators who start with the same offer but haggle and make further concessions (Galinsky, Seiden, Kim, & Medvec, 2002). The claim is that having one's first offer accepted inspires regret because one realizes one could have asked for more, and this kind of feedback would prompt learning in the sense that negotiators would, for example, plan to make higher first offers in the future. Of the various kinds of counterfactuals one might generate, there is some evidence that counterfactuals concerning how one could do better next time (as opposed to, say, how if the situation had been different one would have done worse) are most likely to lead to learning that transfers (Morris & Moore, 2000). Finally, as regret is not an emotion people wish to feel, there is evidence that people make riskier choices in a bargaining game after experiencing regret in an earlier game (Zeelenberg & Beattie, 1997).

A second approach to self-guided learning that regards feedback to be critical is case-based reasoning (Kolodner, 1993). The claim is that when people's expectations turn out to be incorrect, they will attempt to explain why their expectations failed (Chi, 1996; Schank, 1982). Thus, expectation failures prompt reflection and self-explanation, which provides a trigger and a mechanism for changing one's mental models. Although there are computational models of negotiation that use this approach (e.g., Sycara, 1990), there is little behavioral negotiation research that does so.

Example-Driven Learning

Although we discussed studies showing that negotiators learn to logroll across rounds (e.g., Thompson, 1990a), we did not present a theory to explain how people did so. Surely people had experienced some form of negotiation in the past. What experience did they have across a few rounds of negotiating that they had not already had? We suspect people drew comparisons across the negotiations that occurred in such close proximity. People negotiated case after case, and any learning about the structure of the negotiation issues would have transferred to subsequent rounds. The common format of the payoff charts, people's presumed focus during the negotiations, might have pushed the contextual information more to the background than it normally would be, allowing people to focus on issue structure and value creation. A parallel argument was made by Van Huyck and Battalio (2002), who showed that people derived an abstract structure of a bargaining game by playing variants in close succession. Both of these lines of research suggest that people can learn by accumulating examples and comparing across them, yielding abstract principles.

People compare two examples either because they are presented together ("notice how negotiating for a used car is not quite the same as negotiating a job offer"), or because we are reminded of one when thinking about another ("this job candidate thinks he is negotiating with a used car dealer!"; Gentner & Loewenstein, 2002). No matter how two examples become juxtaposed, once people initiate a comparison, they are likely to focus on the richest commonalities they can find, even if that is not what they began the comparison to discover (Gentner & Markman, 1997). Thus, learning by drawing comparisons can yield new insights people did not intend to discover.

Remindings People are reminded of prior experiences and draw on them as analogies to understand their current situations (Ross, 1984). The key question is what kinds of similar prior cases people are reminded of, and do these yield useful analogies. Gentner and associates (2004) gave undergraduates, university alumni, MBA students, and managers an example of negotiators forming a contingent contract. Unsurprisingly, people with more professional negotiation experience were more likely to recall an example of negotiating a contingent contract. A goal of learning then would be to develop a case library categorized by underlying principles to serve as useful analogies. Yet relying on remindings to generate such principles in the first place should be slow at best.

Analogical Encoding As we discussed in opening this section, another use of comparing examples to yield learning is for people to actively consider multiple examples at once. People are better at finding nonobvious similarities between examples they are actively considering than at generating remindings based on such a similarity (e.g., Gentner, Rattermann, & Forbus, 1993). Put another way, knowing two examples does not yield the same gains as comparing them. For example, Thompson, Gentner, and Loewenstein (2000) presented MBA students learning to negotiate with brief cases describing negotiators forming contingent contracts. Because the cases were set in different contexts (the timing of a shipment from an Asian merchant to a U.S. buyer, and two brothers considering a crop sale), only 10% of MBA students asked to analyze each one separately noticed any similarities between them. They were also unlikely to remark on the general usefulness of the contingent contract structure exemplified by the cases. In contrast, MBA students asked to compare the two examples focused on the contract structure. As a result of these case-processing differences, the two groups performed quite differently on a subsequent negotiation—those who compared cases were about three times more likely to form (appropriate and effective) contingent contracts in a negotiation simulation than MBA students who analyzed cases separately. Further research showed that people who analyze cases separately are no more likely to use the principles from the cases when later negotiating than are people never shown the cases (Loewenstein, Thompson, & Gentner, 2003). Additional studies also showed that more novice negotiators (undergraduates) benefited from being guided through comparing examples (Gentner, Loewenstein, & Thompson, 2003). Drawing comparisons across cases as a means of learning them, or *analogical encoding*, is a route to acquiring domain principles that facilitates their later use. Examples may otherwise be inert knowledge.

Motivation

Stepping back from the particular routes by which people obtain new information, we should also note that informal learning is facilitated by a motivation to learn. This may seem obvious, but then people are not always motivated to learn, and being in stressful negotiation situations may lower the likelihood that people take on this motivation. As Dweck (1986; Dweck & Leggett, 1988) has argued, people tend to take on either mastery goals, engaging metacognitive strategies to further learning, or performance goals, engaging strategies to demonstrate their effectiveness. These goals alter how one approaches a task.

Consider the basic finding that, due to outcome feedback across repeated trials, people who engage in the same negotiation situation repeatedly will discover available value-added tradeoffs and reach agreements worth more than their initial attempts (Bazerman et al., 1985). The opportunity for feedback and the demonstration of improved performance does not imply people have a general abstract understanding of the tradeoff contract structure nor that they have mastered the art of finding tradeoffs. As shown by a replication and extension of the Bazerman et al. (1985) study by Bereby-Meyer, Moran, and Unger-Aviram (2004), participants encouraged to have performance goals did form effective tradeoffs through repeated experience on a first negotiation task, but failed to form tradeoffs on a subsequent negotiation task at a rate greater than a baseline group just receiving the second negotiation task. In contrast, participants encouraged to have mastery goals learned to form tradeoffs on the first negotiation task and transferred that learning—they formed tradeoffs on the second negotiation task more than the baseline and performance goals groups did. Gist and Stevens (1998) reported a similar finding, showing greater transfer of new negotiation skills by negotiators with mastery goals than those with performance goals when put in particularly stressful negotiations. They also found that transfer was partially mediated by measures of cognitive learning. Thus, motivations provide enabling conditions for cognitive learning, which in turn leads to performance advantages.

CHARACTERIZING NOVICE NEGOTIATORS

If learning is set against a backdrop of motivations and expectations based on prior experiences, then it would be helpful to know people's typical starting point. Several studies shed light on this (O'Connor & Adams, 1999; Rackham & Carlisle, 1978a, b; Van Boven & Thompson, 2003), but nonetheless the picture is far from complete. The best examined aspect of untrained negotiators is the assumption that negotiators are haggling over a fixed sum because people's preferences are perfectly opposed (Bazerman & Neale, 1983; Thompson & Hastie, 1990). This "fixed-pie" assumption has a host of implications that combine to drastically simplify novice's interpretations of negotiation situations. Equal and opposite preferences over a fixed set of issues implies the value of the contract is a fixed sum (hence the name of the assumption). This in turn implies that tradeoffs are useless, compatible issues (i.e., those on which both parties want the same outcome) are unthinkable (Thompson & Hrebec, 1996), and value creation impossible. Thus, for example, novices can be convinced by a supposed negotiation expert to accept a poor agreement that fails to create value (Arnold & O'Connor, 1999). It also implies that discussing multiple issues at a time just needlessly complicates the conversation (see Balakrishnan, Patton, & Lewis, 1993), and thus it should be unsurprising that novices assume people should negotiate one issue at a time (O'Connor & Adams, 1999). The assumption implies that the only possible outcomes are standing firm on one's positions and prevailing, compromising, and meeting part way, or yielding completely to the other party's demands. Thus, negotiators are tough, fair, or soft. This and the previous implication, combined, may be responsible for the tendency of novice negotiators to focus on a single, salient issue such as price. The fixed-pie assumption also implies that there is no information to share other than one's positions and the arguments in favor of them; other information might just provide a basis for the other side to demand concessions or persuade one out of one's own positions. Further, given the fixed-pie assumption, one's major concerns must be power (ability to gain concessions, including through tactics and deceit), fairness (equal size concessions and value gained—which in this framework are perfectly complementary), and relationships (or lack thereof; i.e., what value one places on being fair and on the other party attaining value). What is striking is how much it follows from a core assumption about negotiation issue and preference structure, and how much it simplifies negotiations (though obviously not beneficially so).

Given the fixed-pie logic, we can generate predictions about how negotiators will interpret negotiation situations. For example, if one reaches agreement and one's counterpart is happy, then one will infer that they must have claimed more value (i.e., attribute their happiness to their satisfaction with their outcome), and hence one will be less satisfied with the outcome than if the counterpart is not happy (Thompson, Valley, & Kramer, 1995). This effect is driven by perceptions of emotion, which then drives interpretations about outcomes. In this situation one might additionally infer that they will appreciate the relationship, which, for prosocial cooperators, may inspire relief and confirm one's justification for conceding. Furthermore, one might actively seek out friends to negotiate with to avoid hard bargaining and foster fair concession making, despite the concomitant loss in value creation that comes with a rush to making concessions (Fry, Firestone, & Williams, 1983; Tenbrunsel, Wade-Benzoni, Moag, & Bazerman, 1999). With respect to learning, what is important is that negotiators may more readily remember their interpretations about their negotiation than the perceptions on which the interpretations were based. This impedes learning, as the more one abstracts away from what happened, the more one is assimilating the experience to old categories (Argyris & Schon, 1996).

A natural next concern would be to characterize expert negotiators. However, available research provides mostly tests of specific manipulations that result in better performance, as well as prescriptions from wise observers (see Roloff, Putnam, & Anastasiou, 2003, for a review). This may be because it is challenging to identify and observe expert negotiators. There are also inherent issues of content, context, and cultural specificity; we should not expect to find negotiators who are general experts but rather experts in, say, U.S. industrial labor contract negotiations, or diplomacy with the French, or possibly still more limited settings. Although it seems hard to argue that less value creation would be better than more, we should not expect to find consensus elsewhere, such as how to share value, how to value social relationships, or how to value reputations. Thus, there may be no single expert model to articulate.

IMPLICATIONS FOR INSTRUCTION

Instructors have choices as to how to present material (see, e.g., Galbraith, 2004, for evaluations of forms of pedagogical practice). Negotiation classes commonly blend the use of simulations, games and role plays, demonstrations (live or on film), case study analysis, and discussion (Lewicki, 1986, 1997). The logic behind these various techniques is to foster planning such that students are motivated, committed, and encouraged to translate concepts into behavioral intentions; to foster attempts at new behaviors both for personal and classroom exploration of potential approaches, the reactions they engender, and confidence through sheer exposure; and to foster reflection and analysis to alter people's understanding of negotiation.

To summarize our suggestions for pedagogy, we examine the most common particular forms of learning interventions in negotiation training (Table 5.1). Clearly, an important part of an instructor's role is to attempt to teach by discussing principles and articulating the domain principles that play important roles in an expert mental model. However, instructors should recognize that brief abstract descriptions are best thought of as morals to a story. They should be substantiated and explicated through multiple concrete examples and not expected to stand on their own. People often fail to learn from abstractions alone (Gentner et al., 2004).

Perhaps the opposite of principle training is encouraging trial and error, so learning can occur through feedback. There are benefits of self-guided exploration for fostering motivation and exploration. However, trial and error is likely to be inefficient, can lead to misunderstandings, and is in itself a poor means of fostering reflection and reframing, given the paucity of information feedback alone provides. Negotiation simulations alone do not yield substantial learning (Druckman, 1995). As a result, feedback should be viewed as an instructional tool to prompt reflection and explanation.

Observational learning can allow unbiased viewers to notice possible actions and outcomes that the actors themselves fail to see. However, although watching a negotiation might allow others to notice differences in preferences that could be logrolled, if people are partisans and prefer one party over another, they will be unlikely to notice (Thompson, 1995). Learners can also imitate what they see, and learn what good (or bad) performance and outcomes are possible (Tournadre & Villeval, 2004). The key challenge is that typically the only information available is behavioral, and cognitive or motivational aspects are hidden. It is also common for people to choose poor models to imitate, or to imitate without understanding. Ideally, expert models would share their interpretations, expectations, and attributions as well as their behaviors.

TABLE 5.1   Key Types of Learning and Teaching Methods in
Negotiation

	Advantages	Disadvantages	Prescriptions
Principle Learning	Articulate expert model	Likely to be misunderstood, perhaps distrusted, or discounted Inert knowledge problem	Link principles to concrete examples, provide clear labels
Trial-and-Error Learning	Can yield creative strategies	Inefficient, mostly leads to repeating prior others' errors	Foster exploration of many offers (brainstorming, removing assumptions)
Observational Learning	Can learn good actions and strategies	Cognitions and motivations may not be observable Companies may use poor models (=sampling on dependent variable)	Make expert interpretations and consideration of options explicit
Learning via Feedback	Can catch people ready to learn	Does not in itself provide new interpretation	Should be coupled with explanation, reflection, and some tool for generalization
Analogy	Facilitates understanding and generalization	People may use wrong analogy (based on surface rather than structural likeness) Risk of deriving an overly simplified model	Provide multiple good analogies; foster critical evaluation

Finally, instructors often use stories or examples to illustrate what they teach, and these are often quite useful to facilitate understanding. However, it often requires more than one example of the same underlying point for learners to understand the idea sufficiently that they can integrate it with what they already know and transfer it to solve new problems. Examples can be misunderstood just as principles can, and experts should not have illusions about how obviously an example illustrates an idea. Explicit guidance to draw comparisons across multiple examples and critical evaluation of those analogies are useful additions to the instructional use of analogy.

CONCLUSION

Learning to negotiate requires more than just experience, and studying learning requires more than just suggesting mechanisms for changing beliefs. Most negotiators possess an understanding of negotiation that protects and maintains their current system of beliefs. If they believe themselves to be capable adults who have negotiated in a professional context for years, they may have a sufficiently strong performance motivation that they fail to notice learning opportunities. Few novices become experts.

If people are open to the possibility of learning, they may learn from their own experiences as well as in formal instructional settings. Learning from feedback and examples, although studied in formal settings, may occur in everyday life. People receive some degree of feedback (they did or did not reach a deal; they can evaluate their agreements; they can compare themselves to others), generate counterfactuals, experience failed expectations, are reminded of prior negotiations when engaged in one, and compare previous negotiations. There is no guarantee that they will draw appropriate lessons from these experiences, but then again, there is often no such guarantee or even assessment in formal training settings either.

Learning to negotiate effectively requires developing a complex, nuanced, and broadly applicable understanding of negotiation. This in turn requires challenging and modifying a novice mental model that is simplistic, coarse, and narrowly applied. There are both cognitive and motivational factors that facilitate acquiring negotiation expertise, and fortunately in pedagogical practice, it seems feasible to combine them.

REFERENCES

Argyris, C., & Schon, D. A. (1996). *Organizational learning II: Theory, method, and practice*. Reading, MA: Addison-Wesley.

Arkes, H. R. (1991). Costs and benefits of judgment errors: Implications for debiasing. *Psychological Bulletin, 110*, 486–498.

Arnold, J. A., & O'Connor, K. M. (1999). Ombudspersons or peers? The effect of third-party expertise and recommendations on negotiation. *Journal of Applied Psychology, 84*(5), 776–785.

Babcock, L., Gelfand, M. J., Small, D., & Stayn, H. (2002). *Propensity to initiate negotiations: A new look at gender variation in negotiation behavior*. Paper presented at the 15th Annual Conference of the International Association of Conflict Management, Park City, Utah.

Balakrishnan, P. V., Patton, C., & Lewis, P. A. (1993). Toward a theory of agenda setting in negotiations. *Journal of Consumer Research, 19*(4), 637–654.

Ball, S. B., Bazerman, M. H., & Carroll, J. S. (1991). An evaluation of learning in the bilateral winner's curse. *Organizational Behavior and Human Decision Processes, 48*, 1–22.

Balzer, W. K., Doherty, M. E., & O'Connor, R. (1989). Effects of cognitive feedback on performance. *Psychological Bulletin, 106*, 410–433.

Bazerman, M. H., & Carroll, J. S. (1987). Negotiator cognition. *Research in Organizational Behavior, 9*, 247–288.

Bazerman, M. H., Magliozzi, T., & Neale, M. A. (1985). Integrative bargaining in a competitive market. *Organizational Behavior and Human Decision Processes, 35*, 294–313.

Bazerman, M. H., & Neale, M. A. (1983). Heuristics in negotiation: Limitations to effective dispute resolution. In M. H. Bazerman & R. J. Lewicki (Eds.), *Negotiating in organizations* (pp. 51–67). Beverly Hills, CA: Sage.

Bereby-Meyer, Y., Moran, S., & Unger-Aviram, E. (2004). When performance goals deter performance: Transfer of skills in integrative negotiations. *Organizational Behavior and Human Decision Processes, 93,* 142–154.

Bettenhausen, K., & Murnighan, J. K. (1985). The emergence of norms in competitive decision-making groups. *Administrative Science Quarterly, 30,* 350–372.

Bottom, W. P., Holloway, J., McClurg, S., & Miller, G. J. (2000). Negotiating a coalition: Risk, quota shaving, and learning to bargain. *Journal of Conflict Resolution, 44*(2), 147–169.

Boven, L. van, & Thompson, L. (2003). A look into the mind of the negotiator: Mental models in negotiation. *Group Processes and Intergroup Relations, 6*(4), 387–404.

Brett, J. M. (2001) *Negotiating globally: How to negotiate deals, resolve disputes, and make decisions across cultural boundaries.* San Francisco: Jossey-Bass.

Brunswik, E. (1955), Representative design and probabilistic theory in functional psychology. *Psychological Review, 62,* 193–217.

Camerer, C. F. (2001). Prospect theory in the wild: Evidence from the field. In D. Kahneman & A. Tversky (Eds.), *Choices, values, and frames* (pp. 288–300). Cambridge, UK: Cambridge University Press.

Camerer, C. F. (2003). *Behavioral game theory: Experiments on strategic interaction.* Princeton, NJ: Princeton University Press.

Chase, W. G., & Simon, H. A. (1973). Perception in chess. *Cognitive Psychology, 4,* 55–81.

Chi, M. T. H. (1996). Constructing self-explanations and scaffolded explanations in tutoring. *Applied Cognitive Psychology, 10,* 33–49.

De Dreu, C. K. W., & Boles, T. (1998). Share and share alike or winner take all? Impact of social value orientation on the choice and recall of decision heuristics in negotiation. *Organizational Behavior and Human Decision Processes, 76,* 253–267.

Dennis, M. J., & Ahn, W.-K. (2001). Primacy in causal strength judgments: The effect of initial evidence for generative versus inhibitory relationships. *Memory and Cognition, 29*(1), 152–164.

Diekman, K. A., Tenbrunsel, A. E., Shah, P. P., Schroth, H. A., & Bazerman, M. H. (1996). *Organizational Behavior and Human Decision Processes, 66*(2), 179–191.

Druckman, D. (1995). The educational effectiveness of interactive games. In D. Crookall & K. Arai (Eds.), *Simulation and gaming across disciplines and cultures.* Thousand Oaks, CA: Sage.

Dweck, C. S. (1986). Motivational processes aecting learning. *American Psychologist, 41,* 1040–1048.

Dweck, C. S., & Leggett, E. L. (1988). A social cognitive approach to motivation and personality. *Psychological Review, 95,* 256–273.

Earley, P. C., & Peterson, R. S. (2004). The elusive cultural chameleon: Cultural intelligence as a new approach to intercultural training for the global manager. *Academy of Management Learning and Education, 3*(1), 99–116.

Einhorn, H. J., & Hogarth, R. M. (1978). Confidence in judgment: Persistence of the illusion of validity. *Psychological Review, 85,* 395–416.

Ericsson, K. A., & Lehman, A. C. (1996). Expert and exceptional performance: Evidence of maximal adaption to task constraints. *Annual Review of Psychology, 47,* 273–305.

Fischoff, B. (1982). Debiasing. In D. Kahneman, P. Slovic, & A. Tversky (Eds.), *Judgment under uncertainty: Heuristics and biases* (pp. 422–444). Cambridge, UK: Cambridge University Press.

Foreman, P., & Murnighan, J. K. (1996). Learning to avoid the winner's curse. *Organizational Behavior and Human Decision Processes, 67,* 170–180.

Froman, L. A., & Cohen, M. D. (1970). Compromise and logroll: Comparing the efficiency of two bargaining processes. *Behavioral Science, 15,* 180–186.

Fry, W. R., Firestone, I. J., & Williams, D. L. (1983). Negotiation process and outcome of stranger dyads and dating couples: Do lovers lose? *Basic and Applied Social Psychology, 4,* 1–16.

Galbraith, M. W. (Ed.). (2004). *Adult learning methods: A guide for effective instruction* (3rd ed.). Malabar, FL: Kreiger Publishing.

Galinsky, A. D., Seiden, V., Kim, P. H., & Medvec, V. H. (2002). The dissatisfaction of having your first offer accepted: The role of counterfactual thinking in negotiations. *Personality and Social Psychology Bulletin, 28,* 271–283.

Gentner, D., & Loewenstein, J. (2002). Relational language and relational thought. In J. Byrnes & E. Amsel (Eds.), *Language, literacy, and cognitive development* (pp. 87–120). Mahwah, NJ: Lawrence Erlbaum.

Gentner, D., Loewenstein, J., & Thompson, L. (2003). Learning and transfer: A general role for analogical encoding. *Journal of Educational Psychology, 95*(2) 393–408.

Gentner, D., Loewenstein, J., & Thompson, L. (2004). *Analogical encoding: Facilitating knowledge transfer and integration.* Proceedings of the 26th Annual Meeting of the Cognitive Science Society, Chicago, IL.

Gentner, D., & Markman, A. B. (1997). Structure-mapping in analogy and similarity. *American Psychologist, 52*(1), 45–56.

Gentner, D., Rattermann, M. J., & Forbus, K. D. (1993). The roles of similarity in transfer: Separating retrievability from inferential soundness. *Cognitive Psychology, 25,* 524–575.

Gist, M. E., & Stevens, C. K. (1998). Effects of practice conditions and supplemental training method on cognitive learning and interpersonal skill generalization. *Organizational Behavior and Human Decision Processes, 75,* 142–169.

Hammond, K. R., McClelland, G. H., & Mumpower, J. (1980). *Human judgment and decision-making: Theories, methods, and procedures.* New York: Praeger Press.

Higgins, E. T. (1997). Beyond pleasure and pain. *American Psychologist, 52,* 1280–1300.

Hogarth, R. M. (1981). Beyond discrete biases: Functional and dysfunctional aspects of judgmental heuristics. *Psychological Bulletin, 90,* 197–214.

Hong, Y., Benet-Martinez, V., Chiu, C., & Morris, M. W., (2003). Boundaries of cultural influence: Construct activation as a mechanism for cultural differences in social perception. *Journal of Cross-Cultural Psychology, 34,* 453–464.

Huyck, J. van, & Battalio, R. (2002). Prudence, justice, benevolence and sex: Evidence from similar bargaining games. *Journal of Economic Theory, 104,* 227–246.

Kelley, H. H., & Stahelski, A. J. (1970). Social interaction basis of cooperators' and competitors' beliefs about others. *Journal of Personality and Social Psychology, 16*(1), 66–91.

Kolodner, J. L. (1993). *Case-based reasoning.* San Mateo, CA: Kaufmann.

Larrick, R. P. (2004). Debiasing. In D. J. Koehler & N. Harvey (Eds.), *Blackwell handbook of judgment and decision making.* Oxford, UK: Blackwell.

Ledyard, J. O., & Palfrey, T. R. (1995). Experimental game theory introduction. *Games and Economic Behavior, 10,* 1–5.

Lerner, J. S., & Tetlock, P. E. (1999). Accounting for the effects of accountability. *Psychological Review, 125,* 225–275.

Lewicki, R. J. (1986). Challenges of teaching negotiation. *Negotiation Journal, 2,* 15–27.

Lewicki, R. J. (1997). Teaching negotiation and dispute resolution in colleges of business: The state of the practice. *Negotiation Journal, 13,* 253–269.

Liberman, V., Samuels, S. M., & Ross, L. (2004). The name of the game: Predictive power of reputations versus situational labels in determining prisoner's dilemma game moves. *Personality and Social Psychology Bulletin, 30*, 1175–1185.

Loewenstein, J., & Thompson, L. (2000). The challenge of learning. *Negotiation Journal, 16*(4), 399–408.

Loewenstein, J., Thompson L., & Gentner, D. (2003). An examination of analogical learning in negotiation teams. *Academy of Management Learning and Education, 2*(2), 119–127.

Loewenstein, J., Zhong, C., & Murnighan, J. K. (2003, August). *Speaking the same language: The cooperative effects of labeling in the prisoners' dilemma.* Paper presented at the 2003 meeting of the Academy of Management, Seattle, WA.

McGinn, K. L., & Keros, A. T. (2002). Improvisation and the logic of exchange in socially embedded transactions. *Administrative Science Quarterly, 47*, 442–473.

Medin, D. L., & Ross, B. H. (1989). The specific character of abstract thought: Categorization, problem-solving, and induction. In R. J. Sternberg (Ed.), *Advances in the psychology of human intelligence* (Vol. 5, pp. 189–223). Hillsdale, NJ: Erlbaum.

Medvec, V. H., & Savitsky, K. (1997). When doing better means feeling worse: The effects of categorical cutoff points on counterfactual thinking and satisfaction. *Journal of Personality and Social Psychology, 72*(6), 1284–1296.

Morris, M. W., Larrick, R. P., & Su, S. K. (1999). Misperceiving negotiation counterparts: When situationally determined bargaining behaviors are attributed to personality traits. *Journal of Personality and Social Psychology, 77*(1), 52–67.

Morris, M. W., & Moore, P. C. (2000). The lessons we (don't) learn: Counterfactual thinking and organizational accountability after a close call. *Administrative Science Quarterly, 45*(5), 737–765.

Murnighan, J. K., Babcock, L., Thompson, L., & Pillutla, M. (1999). The information dilemma in negotiations: Effects of experience, incentives, and integrative potential. *International Journal of Conflict Management, 10*(4), 313–339.

Neale, M. A., & Northcraft, G. (1986). Experts, amateurs, and refrigerators: A comparison of expert and amateur negotiators in a novel task. *Organizational Behavior and Human Decision Processes, 38*, 305–317.

Nisbett, R. E. (Ed.). (1993). *Rules for reasoning.* Hillsdale, NJ: Erlbaum.

Northcraft, G., & Neale, M. A. (1987). Experts, amateurs, and real estate: An anchoring-and-adjustment perspective on property pricing decisions. *Organizational Behavior and Human Decision Processes, 39*, 84–97.

O'Connor, K. M., & Adams, A. A. (1999). What novices think about negotiation: A content analysis of scripts. *Negotiation Journal, 15*(2), 135–147.

O'Connor, K. M., & Arnold, J. A. (2001). Distributive spirals: Negotiation impasses and the moderating role of disputant self-efficacy. *Organizational Behavior and Human Decision Processes, 84*, 148–176.

O'Connor, K. M., Arnold, J. A., & Burris, E. R. (2005). Negotiators' bargaining experiences and their effects on future negotiations. *Journal of Applied Psychology, 90*(2), 350–362.

Rackham, N., & Carlisle, J. (1978a). The effective negotiator—Part I: The behaviour of successful negotiators. *Journal of European Industrial Training, 2*(6), 6–10.

Rackham, N., & Carlisle J. (1978b). The effective negotiator—Part II: Planning for negotiations. *Journal of European Industrial Training, 2*(7), 3–5.

Raiffa, H. (1985). Post-settlement settlements. *Negotiation Journal, 2*(1), 9–12.

Rapoport, A. (1988). Experiments with n-person social traps I: prisoner's dilemma, weak prisoner's dilemma, volunteer's dilemma, and largest number. *Journal of Conflict Resolution, 32*, 457–472.

Roloff, M. E., & Jordan, J. M. (1991). The influence of effort, experience and persistence on the elements of bargaining plans. *Communication Research, 18*(3), 306–332.

Roloff, M. E., Putnam, L. L., & Anastasiou, L. (2003). Negotiation skills. In J. O. Greene, & B. R. Burleson (Eds.), *Handbook of communication and social interaction skills* (pp. 801–833). Mahwah, NJ: Lawrence Erlbaum.

Ross, B. H. (1984). Remindings and their effects in learning a cognitive skill. *Cognitive Psychology, 16*, 371–416.

Roth A. E., & Erev, I. (1995). Learning in extensive-form games: Experimental data and simple dynamic models in intermediate term. *Games and Economic Behavior, 8*, 164–212.

Roth, A. E., & Malouf, M. W. K. (1979). Game-theoretic models and the role of bargaining. *Psychological Review, 86*, 574–594.

Schank, R. C. (1982). *Dynamic memory: A theory of reminding and learning in computers and people.* New York: Cambridge University Press.

Schank, R. C., & Abelson, R. P. (1977). *Scripts, plans, goals, and understanding: An inquiry into human knowledge structures.* Hillsdale, NJ: Lawrence Erlbaum.

Schelling, T. C. (1960). *The strategy of conflict.* Cambridge, MA: Harvard University Press.

Siegler, R. S. (1995). How does change occur: A microgenetic study of number conservation. *Cognitive Psychology, 28*(3), 225–273.

Slonim, R., & Roth, A. E. (1998). Learning in high stakes ultimatum games: An experient in the Slovak Republic. *Econometrica, 66*(3), 569–596.

Stahl, D. (2000). Rule learning in symmetric normal-form games: Theory and evidence. *Games and Economic Behavior, 32*, 105–138.

Stevahn, L., Johnson, D. W., & Johnson, R. T. (2002). Effects of conflict resolution training integrated into a high school social studies curriculum. *Journal of Social Psychology, 142*(3), 305–331.

Sycara, K. (1990). Persuasive argumentation in negotiation. *Theory and Decision, 28*(3), 203–242.

Tenbrunsel, A. E., Wade-Benzoni, K. A., Moag, J., & Bazerman, M. H. (1999). The negotiation matching process: Relationships and partner selection. *Organizational Behavior and Human Decision Processes, 80*, 252–284.

Thompson, L. (1990a). The influence of experience on negotiation performance. *Journal of Experimental Social Psychology, 26*, 528–544.

Thompson, L. (1990b). An examination of naive and experienced negotiators. *Journal of Personality and Social Psychology, 59*, 82–90.

Thompson, L. (1992). A method for examining learning in negotiation. *Group Decision and Negotiation, 1*, 71–74.

Thompson, L. (1995). The impact of minimum goals and aspirations on judgments of success in negotiations. *Group Decision Making and Negotiation, 4*, 513–524.

Thompson, L., & DeHarpport, T. (1994). Social judgment, feedback, and interpersonal learning in negotiation. *Organizational Behavior and Human Decision Processes, 58*, 327–345.

Thompson, L., Gentner, D., & Loewenstein, J. (2000). Avoiding missed opportunities in managerial life: Analogical training more powerful than individual case training. *Organizational Behavior and Human Decision Process, 82*, 60–75.

Thompson, L., & Hastie, R. (1990). Social perception in negotiation. *Organizational Behavior and Human Decision Processes, 47*, 98–112.

Thompson, L., & Hrebec, D. (1996). Lose-lose agreement in interdependent decision making. *Psychological Bulletin, 120,* 396–409.

Thompson, L., Valley, K. L., & Kramer, R. M. (1995). The bittersweet feeling of success: An examination of social perception in negotiation. *Journal of Experimental Social Psychology, 31,* 467–492.

Tinsley, C. H., O'Connor, K. M., & Sullivan, B. A. (2002). Tough guys finish last: The perils of a distributive reputation. *Organizational Behavior and Human Decision Proceses, 88,* 621–642.

Tournadre, F., & Villeval, M.-C. (2004). Learning from strikes. *Labour Economics, 11,* 243–264.

Zeelenberg, M. & Beattie, J. (1997). Consequences of regret aversion 2: Additional evidence for effects of feedback on decision making. *Organizational Behavior and Human Decision Processes, 72,* 63–78.

6

Bargaining with Feeling: Emotionality in and Around Negotiation

BRUCE BARRY, INGRID SMITHEY FULMER, and NATHAN GOATES

*T*he primary aim of this chapter is to provide a comprehensive review of research on emotion in the specific social context of negotiation—a manageable task given that most research on the subject has appeared in the last decade or so. In contrast to the relatively modest body of work examining emotion in negotiation, the broader literature on emotion is vast and diverse, grounded in various subdisciplines of psychology, biology, and sociology. This imposing conceptual breadth inevitably translates into an expansive array of theoretical perspectives—more than 150 theories pertaining to the psychology of emotion, by the measure of one review (Strongman, 1996). Accordingly, this chapter rests on something of a paradox: We can thoroughly review research on negotiation that considers the role of emotion, but we cannot account comprehensively for theories and findings on the psychology of emotion that may have something to say about negotiation.

To tackle the subject and manage this paradox, we divide this chapter into five segments. We begin with definitions of key terms. The terms "emotion," "affect," and "mood" are commonly used interchangeably, but, as we will explain, these terms have distinctive meanings for researchers studying emotions. We then offer a narrative review of published studies, both conceptual and empirical, that address emotional processes in the psychology of bilateral negotiation. A third section examines emotion in two important applied negotiation contexts: crisis negotiation and third-party conflict resolution. The fourth major segment of the chapter looks forward, highlighting emotion research in areas that offer promise for an analysis of negotiation. These include intraindividual processes grounded in psychobiology involving the experience of emotion, and research on emotional expression and regulation. In a final section, we argue for a broader, subjectivist view of emotion in negotiation and offer some concluding thoughts about ways in which this might be accomplished.

DEFINING EMOTION, OR RATHER, AFFECT

A singular definition is elusive because to define emotion is to put forth or adopt a particular theory of emotion (Plutchik, 2003; Strongman, 1996). Indeed, diverse theoretical perspectives on the subject offer substantially different definitions. For example, in psychophysiological theories, emotions are biological responses that people experience as a consequence of arousal (e.g., Darwin, 1965/1872; James, 1983/1890; and later work on facial expression: Ekman, 1993; Tomkins, 1975). Theories exploring emotion terms (sometimes called "language analytic" approaches; Metts and Bowers, 1994) identify and define emotions in terms of underlying taxonomic dimensions; prominent examples include Russell's (1980) two-dimensional circumplex and the inventory of prototypical emotions identified by Shaver, Schwartz, Kirson, and O'Connor (1987). Psychosocial, or interactionist, theories define emotional experience in terms of an individual's cognitive appraisal of the context in which it arises (e.g., Lazarus, 1982). Theories grounded in social constructivism (e.g., Averill, 1980) define emotion as culturally determined social roles that we enact and employ to make sense of social environments.

It is possible to define the expansive notion of emotions in very broad terms that bridge these theoretical perspectives. This is arguably what Parrott (2001) has in mind when he describes emotions as "ongoing states of mind that are marked by mental, bodily, or behavioral symptoms" (p. 3). Yet the very use of the term *emotion* poses conceptual problems from the outset because it is properly seen as one of a constellation of terms referring to related notions of noncognitive behavioral responding. In particular, the terms emotion, mood, and affect are interdependent and interrelated, if not at times, interchangeable. Among psychologists, however, these terms carry discrete meanings, and so should be differentiated.

Following some emotion theorists (Gross, 1998b; Scherer, 1984) and prior work on its relevance for negotiation (Barry & Oliver, 1996), we regard *affect* as the overarching construct that encompasses various types of "valenced states," including both emotions and moods (Gross, 1998b, p. 273). The distinction between emotions and moods is commonly based on differences in stimulus and pervasiveness. Stimulus refers to the object of an affective state, which may arise in response to situational stimuli of greater or lesser specificity. Emotions typically arise as a consequence of identifiable triggering stimuli, whereas moods are less differentiated and "lack this quality of object directedness" (Parrott, 2001, p. 3). With respect to pervasiveness, emotions are typically of shorter duration, whereas moods are more enduring and sustained, if typically not as high in intensity (Forgas, 1992; Gross, 1998b). Despite these distinctions, emotions and moods can and should be thought of as interdependent and (at times) mutually reinforcing

(Davidson, 1994; Diener, Smith, & Fujita, 1995). Beyond encompassing ephemeral valenced *states*, affect is also meant to include stable tendencies to encounter moods and emotions that have their basis in dispositions, or trait affect (e.g., Watson, Clark, & Tellegen, 1988).

RESEARCH ON AFFECT IN NEGOTIATION

Numerous scholars have observed that affect is a neglected area of study in the field of negotiation (see, for example, Brief & Weiss, 2002), and none of the following conceptual and empirical pieces fails to make that point. Encouragingly, the volume of conceptual and empirical research that specifically addresses the role of affect in negotiations has increased steadily over the last two decades. For instance, among the papers reviewed here, 19 were published since 2000, one more than the number published in all of the 1990s. In this section we first review theoretical and/or conceptual work on emotion in negotiation, then we review major empirical findings where emotion is studied in the context of negotiation or conflict resolution. (There have been two other recent reviews of this literature: Barry, Fulmer, & van Kleef [2004]; and Thompson, Medvec, Seiden, & Kopelman [2001].)

Conceptual/Theoretical Approaches

Seven published conceptual pieces (Allred, 1999; Barry & Oliver, 1996; Davidson & Greenhalgh, 1999; George, Jones, & Gonzalez, 1998; Lawler & Yoon, 1995; Morris & Keltner, 2000; Thompson, Nadler, & Kim, 1999) have specifically and extensively focused on theoretical development of affective processes in negotiation. We review them here and then provide an analysis of how they relate together and how they relate to the empirical research reviewed below.

Lawler and Yoon's (1995) model of affective commitment relies on multiple encounters between parties whose interdependence generates the need to negotiate repeatedly. The experience of agreement yields mild positive emotions, and consequently the development of a dyadic emotional link. Negotiators come to "credit their relationship, at least in part, for the sense of control and related positive feeling" (Lawler & Yoon, 1995, p. 155). The affective commitment that results sets the stage for subsequent interaction.

Barry and Oliver (1996) analyzed the role of affect within various phases of a dyadic bargaining encounter. They propose that the interaction of emotions, moods, dispositional affect, and negotiation context sets the stage for the emotional states and behaviors at the beginning of the negotiating encounter. Emotions and behaviors at the outset will affect how events transpire within the process of negotiating, such as tactics employed, concessions made, and changed expectations. Experienced affect, in turn, affects economic outcomes as well as satisfaction, desire for future interaction, and compliance with settlement terms.

Building on Forgas's (1995) affect infusion model (AIM), George et al. (1998) discuss how emotions brought to the table and developed during interaction influence negotiators' information processing, which in turn drives negotiation processes and outcomes. For example, in the AIM, an individual overwhelmed with new information that is ambiguous and complex, yet seems important, engages in selective learning and sensemaking. Affect primes information processing by biasing individual processing toward information that is consistent with one's affective state. George et al. argue that cross-cultural negotiating contexts, often complex and uncertain, are ripe with potential for this kind of biased processing and, as a result, susceptible to negative (or positive) affective spirals.

Focusing on negative emotion, Allred's (1999) model of retaliatory conflict outlines the attributional and cognitive appraisal mechanisms that must be triggered and aligned (between parties) in order for a party to retaliate against a harm doer. First, a party must perceive that she was the target of harmful behavior. Second, the harmed party places the blame for the behavior on a specific other party (rather than herself), and the harm must be of significant magnitude to incite anger. Finally, the harmed party chooses to retaliate. Allred's model expands on game theoretic notions such as the tit-for-tat strategy (Axelrod, 1984) by providing an explanation of the emotional (and therefore human and realistic) elements that would motivate such behavior.

Thompson et al. (1999) proposed a conceptual approach with prescriptive implications. Emotions are an inevitable part of human interaction and therefore negotiation; accordingly, negotiators who understand emotional experience and expression will be better equipped to act strategically in a context that is inherently emotional. Thompson et al. explain that emotion is experienced through emotional contagion, and that by mimicry (imitation of another's physical emotional expressions) and through "catching" others' emotions (genuine experience of the other party's affective state), emotional information is transmitted. Negotiators can influence others' experienced emotions by "tuning" their emotional expression, manipulating their opponent's emotional experience to strategic advantage.

Davidson and Greenhalgh (1999) argued that an appropriate understanding of emotion in real-world disputes leads to a paradigmatically distinct view of negotiation. Traditionally, negotiation is treated as a vehicle for utility gain (an outcome), with emotion one of a host of variables that influence outcome. Davidson and Greenhalgh propose that the experience of disputes depends on the meaning one constructs around the issues at stake—meaning that varies given the nature of the relationship between disputing parties. Emotional experience emanates from how a dispute is understood.

Moving away from the decision-making perspective that prevails in research on affect and negotiation, Morris and Keltner (2000) adopt a social-functionalist view of emotions (Keltner & Haidt, 1999; Keltner & Kring, 1998), a basic premise of which is that emotion-behaviors "help people respond to the basic problems presented by social living" (Morris & Keltner, 2000, p. 8). Particular classes of social problems call for particular classes of emotion-behaviors. For example, a need to maintain a cooperative climate might prompt emotions like gratitude, which rewards cooperation; anger, which punishes defection; or guilt, which motivates reflexivity and change. Morris and Keltner elucidate a four-stage model of negotiation (opening moves, positioning, problem solving, and endgame) and discuss the functional element of various emotion-behaviors in solving problems specific to each stage.

While we have chronologically summarized the conceptual work on emotion in negotiation here, the reader will also notice that with each new attempt to conceptualize emotion's role in negotiation, the theoretical models become more sophisticated and nuanced. However, it is often the earlier models (perhaps because they were published earlier) that prove the most useful in explaining the empirical results reviewed in the next section. The models proposed by Lawler and Yoon (1995) and Barry and Oliver (1996) are perhaps most consistent with the empirical literature. They offer complementary models that take emotional meaning as a given; their emphasis is on the prediction of consequent affective states and behavior. George et al. (1998) build on this by explaining how emotional experience can disrupt information processing and rational decision making. Allred (1999) and Thompson et al. (1999) focus on the process through which emotion-driven behavior occurs. However, the models developed by Davidson and Greenhalgh (1999) and Morris and Keltner (2000) differ paradigmatically from the others. They add richness to the literature by delving into the construction of emotional meaning (Davidson & Greenhalgh) and how emotions transmit meaning (Morris & Keltner), and it may be that they change the landscape of empirical work to come. The articulation of the social-functional role of emotions (Morris & Keltner, 2000) in particular seems to be picking up steam among negotiation researchers. In the empirical studies published in 2002, 2003, and 2004 reviewed below (of which there are six), the Morris and Keltner piece published in 2000 was cited by one half. Allred (1999), Barry and Oliver (1996), and Davidson and Greenbaugh (1999) were each cited once within the same sample, while Lawler and Yoon (1995), Thompson et al. (1999), and George et al. (1998) were not cited.

Empirical Work

In this section, we review recent empirical work on affect, emotion, and mood in negotiation. We segment this literature into four parts. The first and lengthiest part focuses on affective experience as a predictor of other process and/or outcome variables. The second section reviews work that treats affective state as an outcome, including work on negotiator satisfaction. In the third part we consider affect as a mediating variable. In the fourth part we discuss research treating emotional expression as a negotiation tactic.

Affect Predicts   Social psychologists have argued that positive moods affect information processing in ways that may enhance individuals' ability to navigate negotiation problems (Isen, 1987). Several studies substantiate this argument, relating positive affective experience with more cooperative, integrative negotiating behaviors and outcomes. Good mood or trait-positive affect have been linked to higher joint gains (Anderson & Thompson, 2004; Carnevale & Isen, 1986; Forgas, 1998; Kramer, Newton, & Pommerenke, 1993), higher prenegotiation confidence (Carnevale & Isen, 1986), more elaborative (less evasive) communication tactics (Forgas & Cromer, 2004), more concession giving (Baron, 1990), and an inclination toward more cooperative, problem-solving strategies (Forgas, 1998; Rhoades, Arnold, & Clifford, 2001).

If positive affect facilitates cooperative behavior, we might expect the opposite effect when negotiators experience negative affect. In a study focused exclusively on negative emotion, Allred, Mallozzi, Matsui, and Raia (1997) found that angry subjects had less regard for opponent's interests, which in turn distorted judgments of the other party's interests and, ultimately, reduced joint gains. Negative emotional regard also reduced desire for future interaction with the other party, which is consistent with theoretical expectations (Barry & Oliver, 1996; Lawler & Yoon, 1995). Furthermore, while angry subjects behaved more competitively, the experimental results failed to support a prediction that anger would help negotiators claim more value for themselves.

van Kleef, De Dreu, and Manstead (2004) tested a pair of competing theoretical perspectives—*social contagion* and *strategic choice*—on affect's influence on negotiation behavior. The social contagion perspective (Levy & Nail, 1993) predicts that an angry negotiator will provoke anger in an opponent and that the opponent will retaliate with higher demands; displays of happiness will trigger happiness in an opponent and the opponent will lower demands. The strategic-choice hypothesis predicts that negotiators will opportunistically make higher demands when their opponent appears conciliatory but are more likely to make concessions when opponents appear tough or competitive. Unlike the studies of good mood reviewed above, van Kleef and his colleagues' manipulation of happiness is unique in that it is, like anger, distinctly other-directed and discrete. In other words, participants' feelings are produced in reaction to comments by their opponents in the process of interacting with them, not by a prior nontask-related manipulation such as a film, cartoon, or odor.

Results supported the emotional contagion hypothesis, in that anger did indeed provoke anger; happiness was responded to with happiness. But they also found that behavior was more consistent with the strategic-choice hypothesis. Negotiators made higher demands of more conciliatory opponents and conceded more to aggressive opponents. It may be that the decision to act strategically is influenced by personality; Forgas (1998) found that good mood was linked with cooperative behavior, but that those scoring high on Machiavellianism and need for approval deviated from this pattern.

A study of online auction buyers and sellers in mediation over transactions gone sour provides further support for the social contagion hypothesis (Friedman et al., 2004). Expressions of anger by complainants stimulated expressions of anger by the other party, which in turn reduced the chances of settlement. However, reputation was an important moderator. Anger by a complainant impeded settlement only when the party responding to the complaint had a good reputation, suggesting that in certain contexts anger may promote cooperation.

The idea that negative feelings can trigger cooperative behavior and that positive feelings may be detrimental to reaching optimal outcomes received support in two other recent studies. Ketelaar and Au (2003) show that those who experience guilt for competitive decisions in previous rounds of prisoner and ultimatum games behave more cooperatively in later rounds. They argue that those who experience guilt "may be using this feeling state as 'information' about the future costs of pursuing an uncooperative strategy" (p. 429). Hertel, Neuhof, Theuer, and Kerr (2000), in a two-experiment study using a chicken dilemma game (similar to prisoner dilemma, but the worst outcome for both parties occurs when both compete) found that positive affectivity moderates the relationship between decision making and behavior. When participants felt secure, they were more likely to follow a simple consensus or reciprocity norm. However, when participants felt less secure, they demonstrated more rational analysis and critical decision making. Therefore, while positive affectivity may foster the cooperative behavior associated with the give and take necessary for integrative outcomes, it may also hinder individuals from engaging in the kind of high-effort cognitive work that facilitates finding integrative outcomes.

Conlon and Hunt (2002) argue that affective state is less important than the affective intensity of that state. Manipulating mood by associating payoffs with happy or sad faces (☺ or ☹), they found that increased emotional involvement, be it positive or negative, resulted in less cooperative outcomes. Affective involvement, particularly when generated by happy faces, was related to longer negotiation times and lower levels of trust and cooperation. Negative feelings experienced during the negotiation were also associated with longer negotiation times and less advantageous individual outcomes.

Other work suggests the relationship between affect, competition, and cooperation is even more nuanced. Sanna, Parks, and Chang (2003), using both state- and trait-based measures of affect, found interactions between affect and cognitive goals. In their studies of resource dilemma and prisoner dilemma games, participants in bad moods (manipulated by film, music, or measured dispositionally) were less satisfied with goal attainment, regardless of whether goal orientation was competitive or cooperative. Participants with positive moods were more satisfied that behavior was goal-consistent.

McGinn and Keros (2002) observed that when a party becomes cornered or disadvantaged during the course of a negotiation, an intense emotional outburst, called an "emotional punctuation," can help the distressed party regain control of a negotiation's course and prompt cooperation from the other party. This observation came in a study investigating how the logic of exchange differs in negotiations between friends and negotiations between strangers. Emotional punctuation, described as an abrupt transition analogous to Gersick's (1988) punctuated equilibrium, occurs when one party begins to feel cornered or at a disadvantage.

In summary, we can say that positive affect contributes to cooperative behavior and negative affect disrupts it (Isen, 1987), notwithstanding evidence that certain manifestations of affect, in certain contexts, yield an opposite conclusion. What seems to be a contradiction may be explained by the observation that those who have reached the first conclusion (positive affect elicits cooperative behavior and higher joint outcomes, while negative affect leads to competitive behavior) measured broad, umbrella-like constructs, while those whose work seems to contradict the proposition measured specific, discrete emotions (e.g., guilt, security, anger). As scholars continue to describe and examine the social effects of more specific emotions (such as anger, fear, excitement, and surprise) on negotiation processes and outcomes, we expect that results will not map neatly onto the conclusions of earlier work.

Predicting Affect
A number of negotiation studies (we review 10 here) have explicitly treated affective states as dependent variables. Eight of these 10 studies model satisfaction as an outcome variable. Satisfaction is appropriately included within a discussion of affective outcomes given its presence within several prominent typologies of emotion (e.g., Plutchik, 1980; Russell, 1980; Watson & Tellegen, 1985; see Oliver, 1997, chapter 11, for an extensive review and analysis of links between satisfaction and emotion). Research on negotiator satisfaction has generally pursued an explanation of the mechanism through which actors leave a negotiation more or less satisfied in one of two ways: expectancy disconfirmation (negotiated outcomes differ from prenegotiation expectations) or social comparison (negotiated outcomes compare [un]favorably to those of other parties inside or outside the negotiation).

Oliver, Balakrishnan, and Barry (1994) modeled outcome satisfaction as a function of objective and subjective evaluations of outcome criteria contrasted with prenegotiation aspirations. More formally, expectations disconfirmed objectively lead to a subjective disconfirmation of expectations, which in turn spawns dissatisfaction. An empirical study supported the model: to the extent that high aspirations led to a sense of having achieved an outcome that was less than expected, negotiators were less satisfied with outcomes. This supports previous research demonstrating that negotiators are more satisfied when their expectations are exceeded (Conlon & Ross, 1993).

Other researchers have argued that in the absence of objective performance indicators, negotiator satisfaction is related to perceived opponent performance. Galinsky, Seiden, Kim, and Medvec (2002) demonstrated that negotiators whose first offers are immediately accepted (rather than accepted after some temporal delay or further negotiation) are less satisfied with their outcomes. Naquin (2003) reported that negotiators faced with more issues are also less satisfied with outcomes. In both of these studies, less satisfied negotiators may have engaged in a sort of posthoc reflection on *what might have been*, or counterfactual thinking—a lingering concern than an opportunity to increase surplus was missed. Evaluating one's opponent as happy or unhappy with an outcome may also trigger counterfactual thinking. Thompson, Valley, and Kramer (1995) found that negotiators who believed their opponent (un)happy with his or her outcome expressed less (more) satisfaction with outcomes (this effect only held for out-group opponents).

Gillespie, Brett, and Weingart (2000) linked both individual and group outcomes to satisfaction in a multiparty, multi-issue simulation experiment. However, when controlling for individual outcomes, better group performance was associated with diminished individual satisfaction. Gillespie and colleagues surmise that negotiators (consciously or unconsciously) invoke a fixed-pie bias (e.g., Thompson & DeHarpport, 1994), which is to say that when a negotiator believes other parties to have done well she will evaluate her own performance negatively. Pillutla and Murnighan (1996) showed that participants in an ultimatum game who received less-than-equal shares of the pie expressed more anger (and rejected more offers), providing support to the argument that perceptions of outcome fairness effect postnegotiation affective state.

The prior studies on social comparison deal only with internal social comparisons (internal to the negotiation, i.e., a buyer comparing her outcome to that of the seller's). Novemsky and Schweitzer (2004) tested models that included measures for external social comparison (i.e., a buyer comparing her outcomes to similar buyers) and found that external social comparison explained negotiator satisfaction even when controlling for internal social comparison and expectancy disconfirmation.

O'Connor and Arnold (2001) investigated the affective consequences of impasse. Negotiators who failed to settle experienced more negative emotions (frustration, anger, and spite) and lower levels of satisfaction. They explain that negotiators who reached an impasse were caught in "distributive spirals," felt unsuccessful, and attributed their lack of success to external factors, whereas negotiators who reached a settlement felt more successful and took credit for their success. This is consistent with findings of Hegtvedt and Killian (1999), who found that perceptions of the fairness of an outcome were related to lower levels of negative affect and higher levels of positive affect. However, O'Connor and Arnold (2001) also report that self-efficacy moderated the relationship between impasse and negative feelings/dissatisfaction such that high self-efficacy participants were less prone to negative feelings due to impasse.

Taken together, the articles reviewed here demonstrate that negotiators evaluate their own performance based both on their prenegotiation expectations and their perceptions of how opponents and similar (by role) others performed. These findings are consistent with predictions made by early equity theorists (Adams, 1963; Homans, 1961) and likely informed by a fixed-pie bias, yet contradict propositions by others (e.g., Brett, Northcraft, & Pinkley, 1999) who argued that outcome satisfaction is a function of individual economic utility rather than a consequence of concessions one obtains from an opponent. Rationally, it should not matter how one's opponent fares in a negotiation if one's own interests are met, however, the empirical evidence reviewed above indicates that negotiators, quite irrationally, weigh their own success in negotiation against the perceived success of others.

We raise one caveat. The social comparison literature reviewed here paints a picture of a rather insecure negotiator, one unable to make reliable self-evaluations of performance based on relevant objective criteria. Because these experiments are studying almost exclusively young, inexperienced negotiators, these effects may be somewhat exaggerated. It seems likely that among more mature, experienced negotiators, the economic utility hypothesis (Brett et al., 1999) might better explain negotiator satisfaction: More confidently tuned to their interests, negotiators would report more satisfaction when their interests are met and less satisfied when they are not, irrespective of the performance of others.

Affect as Mediator Two studies have examined interpersonal rapport as a marker for emotional activity in the negotiating dyad that mediates between contextual antecedents and bargaining outcomes. Drolet and Morris (2000) defined rapport as a form of dyadic or group-level emotional cognition. They found that rapport between negotiators mediates the facilitative effect that face-to-face negotiation contact (versus side-by-side or telephone) has on the achievement of joint gain. Moore, Kurtzberg, Thompson, and Morris (1999), investigating negotiation via e-mail, manipulated group affiliation (in-group vs. out-group dyads) and self-disclosure (availability or not of personal information about opponent). Results indicate that a basis for a relationship (in-group status or self-disclosure) elicits positive affect within the negotiation, enhancing rapport and diminishing the likelihood of impasse. Looking further at what Moore et al. label "the prophylactic power of social lubrication" (p. 93), they found that e-mail negotiators who prefaced their negotiation with a brief "schmoozing" telephone conversation felt more rapport, were more trusting, and experienced better economic and social outcomes (Morris, Nadler, Kurtzberg, & Thompson, 2002). The implication is that even trivial relationships facilitate rapport among negotiators, which may result in more cooperative behavior and better outcomes.

Tactical Use of Emotion   The use of emotion-behaviors as tactical maneuvers in negotiation is often commented on and more frequently implied in discussion of emotion in negotiation. We are aware of just one published empirical paper (an edited volume chapter) that explicitly addressed the topic. Barry (1999) found that negotiators perceive the falsification of emotion (e.g., feigning pleasure, shock) more ethically appropriate than other deceptive negotiation tactics. Findings also suggest that negotiators differentiate between the strategic use of positive versus negative emotions, where feigning a negative emotion was considered less ethically appropriate than feigning a positive emotion. In an unpublished study, Kopelman, Rosette, and Thompson (2004) compared alternative styles of strategic emotion. They found that negotiators adopting a positive emotional style were more likely to reach interest-based agreements and create the basis for future interaction. In addition, recipients of ultimatums were more likely to accept terms when the demander engaged in strategically positive emotional behavior.

Summary   Empirical literature on emotion in bargaining supports the hypothesis that positive affect elevates expectations, a cooperative negotiating climate, and higher joint gains, while negative affect has the opposite effect. These findings have been attributed to demonstrated links between positive affect and creativity in problem solving, flexible thinking, cooperative motives, information processing, confidence, and risk-taking behavior (Barry & Oliver, 1996; Forgas, 1998; Kramer et al., 1993; Kumar, 1997; Sanna et al., 2003; Thompson et al., 1999). However, evidence supporting a strategic-choice hypothesis (Friedman et al., 2004; van Kleef et al., 2004) suggests an alternative view of negative emotion: Negative emotions can serve productive social functions (Morris & Keltner, 2000). Negotiator satisfaction appears to be a function of how outcomes match up with pre-negotiation expectations (Conlon & Ross, 1993; Oliver et al., 1994) and compare with outcomes of socially proximal others (e.g., Galinsky et al., 2002; Naquin, 2003; Novemsky & Schweitzer, 2004).

BEYOND THE LABORATORY: CONTEXTS FOR AFFECT IN NEGOTIATION

The findings discussed to this point have emerged mainly from a research paradigm that relies on laboratory simulation of negotiation behavior. In this section we describe research in two applied contexts where emotion has played a significant role in understanding conflict resolution: crisis negotiation and third-party dispute resolution.

Crisis Negotiation

Crisis negotiations occur in conflict situations where tensions are high, coercive strategies dominate, and violent outcomes are possible (Rogan & Hammer, 1995). They involve elevated levels of anxiety and uncertainty; prime examples are hostage, barricade, terrorist, or suicide situations (Hammer and Rogan, 1997, p. 9). Emotion is a central component of crisis negotiation; in hostage situations, for instance, emotional instability often precipitates the event that results in hostage negotiation (Taylor, 2002). Rogan (1997) went as far as to speculate that "crisis negotiation is an entirely emotion-laden event…. In fact, the word 'crisis' denotes emotionality" (p. 25). We recognize that a crisis is merely a context for bargaining that commonly features emotionality, not itself a form of emotional interaction. We include this topic in our review, however, because researchers studying crisis negotiation have analyzed the role of emotion in ways that laboratory researchers (working within the prevailing paradigm in negotiation research) have not and arguably cannot. Crisis negotiation differs fundamentally from the kind of deal-making with which most negotiation research is concerned in that the fundamental objective is not necessarily an agreement honestly brokered that creates value for both parties, but rather an end to the crisis.

The resolution of conflict in crisis situations is a process of creating momentum away from coercion and toward honest exchanges of information and good faith problem solving—away from emotionality and toward rationality (Taylor, 2002). Unstable crisis situations are defused as involved parties are moved out of harm's way, volatile emotions are brought under control, and a transition from crisis bargaining to "normative bargaining" ensues (Donohue & Roberto, 1993). These shifts depend in significant measure on the ability of parties to comprehend and adjust to each other's emotionality (Rogan & Hammer, 1995). Rogan (1997) observed that the practice of crisis negotiation historically has placed substantial emphasis on psychological profiling as a basis for "determining perpetrator affective propensity and volatility" (p. 36). This approach is built on an assumption of dispositional stability—that past behavior will predict reactions in the present context. Such a view has its limits, however, and Rogan reviews law enforcement literature on the role of active listening as a means to diagnose perpetrator actions and emotions in the crisis bargaining context at hand.

Affective processes may have figured more prominently in crisis negotiation research, compared to laboratory-based work on negotiator psychology, because of the importance of relational context to the successful resolution of these kinds of conflict situations. Donohue and Roberto (1993) drew on negotiated order theory (e.g., Strauss, 1978), which addresses how in the course of interaction negotiators generate and maintain social structure, in a study of FBI hostage negotiation transcripts. Effective law enforcement negotiators in these situations defused negative arousal on the part of hostage takers and worked to "establish a more affectively positive definition of the relationship" (Donohue & Roberto, 1993, p. 196). According to Donohue and Roberto, there is a predictable one-sidedness to this dynamic: The police negotiator tends to be the party that instigates relational transitions leading to a more positive affective climate, with hostage takers abdicating that role.

Emotional processes have figured prominently in research models and studies that focus on *communication stages* in crisis negotiation. For example, in hostage negotiations, some phase models see anger and frustration as an inherent and predictable step that precedes impasse or resolution (Holmes & Sykes, 1993, review these models). However, the implication that emotion is confined to particular, limited phases of crisis negotiation may represent an oversimplification. Rogan and Hammer (1995) measured message affect in the utterances of perpetrators and law enforcement negotiators in three authentic crisis negotiations (two barricade situations and one hostage situation). Exploring both language intensity and message valence, their data suggested patterns of emotional arousal at different stages of negotiation. Rogan and Hammer speculated that real-time analysis of message affect can yield insights that "enable a negotiator to more effectively control a perpetrator's level of emotional arousal, such that a negotiator could take actions to reduce a perpetrator's highly negative and intense emotionality in an effort to negate potentially violent behavior" (p. 57).

Other research has focused on the communication *goals* in crisis negotiation. An analysis by Taylor (2002) of transcripts from resolved hostage negotiations reveals emotional communication serving identity goals and relational goals at different stages of the encounter—avoidance stages, distributive (contentious) stages, and integrative (cooperative) stages. Rogan and Hammer (1994) investigated communication that addresses the desire of individuals involved in crisis negotiation to maintain a desired social image and avoid embarrassment or humiliation (so-called issues of "face"). Their findings suggested that face-related messages are clues to an individual's propensity to let a crisis negotiation spiral or end badly. They surmised that crisis negotiators who are sensitive to face-related messages may be in a better position to respond with appropriate emotional support that can defuse a difficult situation.

Third Parties

Practitioners of third-party dispute resolution have had a lot to say about managing the emotions of disputing parties, but the academic literature has been sparse, prompting calls for research to fill this gap (Jones & Bodtker, 2001). In this section we review academic research and relevant practitioner literature that has discussed emotion in the context of mediation and arbitration.

By the time conflicts reach the mediation or arbitration stage, emotions may be highly charged. Conflict interveners are expected to recognize different kinds of concerns that arise—especially the distinction between substantive issues, which engage mainly cognitive processes, and emotional issues, which engage affective processes (Walton, 1969, p. 75). Understandably, practitioners and academic researchers have focused predominantly on disputant emotions that are negatively valenced, which commonly include anger, frustration, betrayal (e.g., Moore, 2003), and grief (e.g., Evans & Tyler-Evans, 2002). Conventional wisdom in the practitioner literature recommends that mediators defuse disputants' anger so that more positive feelings arise and attention can be focused on problem solving (Moore, 2003).

There is some empirical evidence supporting the view that strong emotions impede mediation outcomes, attenuating agreement as well as satisfaction with agreement and with process (Zubek, Pruitt, Peirce, McGillicuddy, & Syna, 1992). In a study of divorce mediation, Donohue (1991) found that couples who came to an agreement were more likely to have focused conversation on factual issues versus "relational" issues (which include emotional discourse). Where the dispute is about interpersonal hostility between the participants, mediator tactics aimed at facilitating the process appear to result in better outcomes (Posthuma, Dworkin, & Swift, 2002). Lastly, Thompson and Kim (2000) explored how participant relationships influence perceptions of third parties. Observers in a laboratory watched videotaped interactions between disputants exhibiting either a positive or a negative relationship. Observers perceived negotiators' interests with greater accuracy and proposed more mutually beneficial settlements when the parties exhibited a positive relationship compared to a negative relationship.

Caucusing is a mediation tactic that seems particularly useful in helping disputants focus on issues instead of emotions. One study found fewer direct emotional displays (swearing, yelling, hitting the table) and fewer hostile questions (denoted by vocal tone) in caucus sessions compared with joint sessions (Welton, Pruitt, & McGillicuddy, 1988).

A separate question concerns the emotions of the mediator. The practitioner literature gives a nod to the importance of the emotions of the third party (Jones & Bodtker, 2001), but empirical research on mediator/arbitrator emotions is rare. Posthuma et al. (2002) found that negotiator friendliness as a disposition/tactic may be related to settlement perceptions of the mediators, although results were only marginally significant; correlational analyses also suggest a relationship between mediator avoidance of negative emotions and negotiation success, but this relationship disappears when other variables are included in a regression analysis.

Practitioners recommend emotion-focused training as an aspect of broader mediator training (e.g., Schreier, 2002), and there is some empirical evidence to corroborate its value. In a study of mediation in a community dispute resolution center, mediator empathy was associated with reaching an agreement and with participant satisfaction, even after controlling for difficulty of the case (Zubek et al., 1992). Mediators also stand to benefit from awareness of the link between gender and emotion: A study of divorcing couples in mediation found gender differences in conflict communication style, with women tending to be more emotional and men more reserved (Pines, Gat, & Tal, 2002).

Academics and practitioners have begun to consider the relatively new phenomenon of electronic mediation, pondering the role of emotion in this context. Nadler (2001) notes that online mediation, generally like online communication, creates a context where it is difficult to exchange nonverbal informational cues and where people may be less inhibited about "flaming" or otherwise expressing negative emotion. The sometimes frustratingly asynchronous nature of electronic mediation can exacerbate the situation further. In a study of disputant anger in online mediation (Friedman et al., 2004), complainants' anger was positively related to responder anger and negatively related to settlement, consistent with the view that anger sometimes inhibits dispute settlement. Although still relatively rare, the use of electronic mediation is likely to expand, and its inherent archival capabilities make it a promising venue for researchers exploring conflict and emotion.

NEGOTIATION AND THE SCIENCE OF INTRAINDIVIDUAL EMOTION

The foregoing review makes it clear that research on affective components and processes of negotiation is generating significant theoretical and empirical progress. However, as we noted at the outset, the science of affect is a vast enterprise. Numerous perspectives on emotion have yet to be considered as directly relevant to or informative within the specific social context of negotiation. In this final major section of the chapter, we focus on intraindividual affect as an area that is ripe for deeper exploration by psychologists who study negotiation. There are two parts to this discussion. First, we address the science of emotional *experience* from two angles: (a) a psychological perspective and (b) a physiological/psychophysiological perspective. Second, we review research on individual emotional *expression* and *regulation* that is potentially useful for understanding affect in negotiation.

Emotional Experience—Psychological Approaches

The classic social cognitive view of emotional experience takes the perspective that emotion is not only manifested physically as visceral sensation but is also accompanied by cognitive processes. Appraisal theories presume that emotion cannot be fully experienced without cognitions (e.g., Arnold, 1960; Lazarus, Averill, & Opton, 1970; Schachter, 1964; Schachter & Singer, 1962). Others question this view, suggesting that emotion may be experienced directly without cognitive mediation (Zajonc, 1980, 1984). The debate continues (see Lazarus, 1984; Zajonc, 1984), but the important point is that as a practical matter, the two are quite interrelated (Roseman & Smith, 2001; Zajonc, 1984).

An extensive literature has explored the effects of experienced mood or emotion on cognitive processes such as memory, information processing, and judgment. Several general patterns emerge from this research and may be summarized as follows (Fiske & Taylor, 1991; for reviews, see Forgas, 2001): Affective experiences impact memory encoding and later recall; emotional impressions are often remembered more vividly than other details of social encounters. In addition, mood state during recall biases memory retrieval. Generally, happy (sad) memories are recalled when people are in positive (negative) moods. Information processing also seems to be guided by mood state; individuals in a given mood often seek out and pay greater attention to information that is congruent with that mood. Other research finds an increase in creativity and flexible problem solving when people are happy. Recent research suggests that there may be differential effects of specific emotions on judgment and decision making, even if the specific emotions are similarly valenced (e.g., sadness, disgust, anger) (DeSteno, Petty, Wegener, & Rucker, 2000; Lerner, Small, & Loewenstein, 2004). Individual differences in personality and in attentiveness to emotions have been found to moderate some of these relationships between mood and cognitive processes (e.g., Forgas, 1998; Gasper & Clore, 2000; Rusting, 1999, 2001).

A number of theoretical accounts has been offered that attempt to explain the role of affect in cognitive processes. The affect-as-information perspective suggests that affect is a source of unconscious evaluative information in decision making (Schwarz, 1990; Schwarz & Clore, 1983). A slightly different perspective proposes that individuals engage in heuristic processing as a function of mood; those in a happy mood are more likely to rely on heuristic processing, while those in sad moods are more likely to engage in motivated, effortful processing (for reviews of related research, see Bless, 2000, 2001; Ruder & Bless, 2003). Yet another view, the affect infusion model (Forgas, 1995) proposes that mood effects on cognition will be moderated by the information processing strategy required by the task at hand, with stronger effects observed when the task calls for extensive information search and integration.

Historically, decision-making research has focused on cognitions and cognitive biases in decision making, but contemporary work is beginning to view cognition and emotion as co-processes in decision making. Studies of patients with prefrontal cortex brain lesions by Damasio and colleagues (Damasio, 1994; Bechara, Damasio, Tranel, & Damasio, 1997) suggest that the resulting inability to receive affective feedback inhibits the ability to make decisions. In normal people, not only does emotion enable decision making, but some suggest that it has a greater influence on decisions than has been previously thought. This view has been articulated in the "risk-as-feelings" hypothesis (Loewenstein, Weber, Hsee, & Welch, 2001). Drawing on the affect as information perspective (Schwarz & Clore, 1983), this theory argues that "anticipatory emotions" at the time of the decision impact judgments of risk; such affective evaluations may be unconscious and, at times, dominate cognitive evaluations of probabilities associated with outcomes. Since much of the negotiation research over the last 20 or so years has been framed from a decision-making perspective (e.g., Neale & Bazerman, 1991, 1992; Raiffa, 1982), this line of research is particularly germane for negotiation researchers.

Also relevant for the study of negotiation is research that considers the temporal dimensions of intraindividual emotion, including stability and rate of change (e.g., Eaton & Funder, 2001; Eid & Diener, 1999). Hemenover (2003) presents evidence of individual differences in the deterioration rate of state affect. Extraversion, emotional stability, and perceived efficacy in regulating negative mood are associated with faster decay of negative affect and slower decay of positive affect. The converse is true for introverts, those low in emotional stability and those with low negative mood regulation efficacy. Researchers have begun to consider methods for studying affective variability in interactive dyadic relationships (Ferrer & Nesselroade, 2003). While it is plausible to believe that the intraindividual affective variability of negotiators would impact the emotional ebb and flow of at least some bargaining encounters, this question has not been explicitly studied. In addition to the actual variability and stability of emotion over time, one's predictions about affect in response to future events—"affective forecasting"—is likely to be important for decision making in negotiation. Gilbert, Wilson, and colleagues find consistent support for the theory that people overestimate the intensity and duration of their future emotional reactions to a particular event (e.g., Dunn, Wilson, & Gilbert, 2003; Gilbert, Pinel, Wilson, Blumberg, & Wheatley, 1998; Wilson, Wheatley, Meyers, Gilbert, & Axsom, 2000). Bazerman and Chugh (chapter 2) link these heightened expectations to a broader tendency on the part of negotiators and others to overfocus on a narrow subset of information.

Psychological approaches to negotiation research thus far have focused mainly on the effects of mood on information processing and creativity/flexibility. We would challenge researchers to expand their approach and consider some relatively underdeveloped areas. Largely missing from negotiation research has been consideration of the relationship between affect and long-term memory in negotiation processes. We suspect that accurate encoding and recall of information in lengthy real-world negotiations are likely to be influenced by emotion, especially given that such situations are also often highly emotionally charged (e.g., divorce settlement, child custody negotiation, significant business transactions). Also scarce is negotiation research that directly considers whether "gut feelings" influence individuals' perceptions of the riskiness of negotiation tactics or of various possible outcomes, including impasse. Finally, as researchers expand their study of dynamic and extended negotiation encounters, we would encourage them to consider temporal dimensions of emotionality as well. Thus far, we know a bit about how *levels* of various emotions relate to various negotiation behaviors, cognitions, and outcomes, but virtually nothing about how intraindividual emotional *variability*, rate of change, pattern of change, and so on affect the bargaining process.

Emotional Experience—Physiological and Psychophysiological Approaches

William James noted, "If we fancy some strong emotion, and then try to abstract from our consciousness of it all the feelings of its characteristic bodily symptoms, we find that we have nothing left behind" (James, 1884, p. 193, cited in Cornelius, 1996). In the years since, psychologists have sought to tease apart the relationships between physiological responses and the subjective experience of emotion, debating such diverse issues as whether specific emotions are related to specific visceral sensations, and whether emotional experience can be manipulated by manipulating facial expression (e.g., Cannon, 1927, 1931; Ekman, 1993; Izard, 1971;

James, 1983/1890; Lange, 1922/1885; Levenson, 1992; Tomkins, 1962; also see Cornelius, 1996, for a review).

It is commonplace in emotion research to monitor physiological and somatic responses as an indicator of emotional reactivity; typical measures include heart rate, respiration, skin conductance, facial electromyography (EMG), and blood pressure. Early researchers assumed a one-to-one correspondence between physiological measures and psychological processes, an assumption that has proven to be overly simplistic. Contemporary researchers who utilize these measures are more careful to theoretically delineate the reasons why specific physiological responses are expected and to empirically substantiate their assumptions (Winkielman, Berntson, & Cacioppo, 2001; for an overview of current research and measures, see Bradley & Lang, 2000).

Going beyond visceral experience and autonomic responses, emotion researchers are increasingly exploring affective experience as it is manifested in the central nervous system itself (Borod, 2000; Hagemann, Waldstein, & Thayer, 2003; Lane & Nadel, 2000). Much of this research has been conducted by studying individuals with brain lesions and through animal studies, but increasingly, neuroimaging techniques (functional magnetic resonance imaging [fMRI] and positron emission tomography [PET]) are used to study human brain function related to emotional experience.

Advances both in methods for assessing physiological responses and in the theoretical understanding of how those responses are linked to psychological processes have reinvigorated the field of psychophysiology (Winkielman et al., 2001). Psychophysiology takes a multilevel perspective by viewing social psychological constructs and theories in conjunction with biological/neurological phenomena (Berntson & Cacioppo, 2000). Neuroimaging techniques have provided unique opportunities for researchers to compare psychological models of emotion with central nervous system manifestations of emotion (e.g., Murphy, Nimmo-Smith, & Lawrence, 2003). This line of research has led to the development of the branch of psychophysiology referred to as social neuroscience or social cognitive neuroscience (Cacioppo & Berntson, 1992; Cacioppo et al., 2002).

While seemingly remote from current approaches used to study emotion in negotiation, physiologically and psychophysiologically oriented emotion research actually has a number of implications for future studies of negotiation. First, we note that most laboratory studies of negotiation have relied on self-report measures to assess experienced emotion. The monitoring of physiological responses like blood pressure, skin conductance, and so on, provides an alternative means of assessing emotion that, depending on the measurement approach chosen, may provide either periodic or continuous information on emotional reactivity over time. Such monitoring is currently feasible, has been employed regularly in mainstream emotion research, and has been recommended as a corroborative technique for assessing emotional experience in negotiation (Barry & Fulmer, in press).

In addition, we expect that psychophysiological research will have increasing relevance for the study of negotiation insofar as it contributes to the understanding of and theory development related to sociocognitive processes, including those related to emotion (Willingham & Dunn, 2003; see Winkielman et al., 2001, for a brief review of this research related to emotion). For example, LeDoux (2002) suggests that the knowledge of the anatomical underpinnings of fear responses may inform the cognitive appraisal debate (i.e., whether cognition is required prior to the experience of an emotion), as well as broaden our understanding of why strong emotions influence cognitive processes, a psychological phenomenon that has begun to receive attention in research on the effects of anger on negotiation (Allred et al., 1997).

Emotion Expression and Regulation

In addition to experiencing emotion, individuals also engage in emotion expression, often moderated by self-regulatory processes. Emotions may unconsciously "leak" out in facial expressions and vocal and physical cues that are difficult to control. People are also often motivated to actively communicate emotion for goal-directed purposes, such as expressing affection (Planalp, 1998) or engaging in deception (Buller & Burgoon, 1998). On the other hand, individuals may be motivated to regulate their emotional behavior as a result of a desire to comport with appropriate social norms (i.e., self-monitoring; Snyder, 1974), or for other strategic reasons (e.g., Barry, 1999).

Empirical evidence confirms what our everyday experience tells us: some people are more emotionally expressive than others. For example, women perceive themselves to be more skilled at expressing emotion, where men view themselves as more skilled at controlling emotion (Guererro & Reiter, 1998). And indeed, women do tend to be more facially expressive of emotions than men (e.g., Hall, Carter, & Horgan, 2000; Kring & Gordon, 1998). Men, on the other hand, report hiding their emotions more than women (Gross & John, 1998). Dispositional emotional expressivity may also moderate the relationship between experienced and expressed emotion (Gross, John, & Richards, 2000), and various conceptualizations of emotional intelligence incorporate dimensions related to emotion perception, expression, and regulation (Mayer & Salovey, 1997; Salovey & Mayer, 1990).

Emotion regulation has been defined as "the process by which individuals influence which emotions they have, when they have them, and how they experience or express these emotions" (Gross, 1998b, p. 275). Gross (1998a, b) describes two types of deliberate emotion regulation: antecedent-focused and response-focused. The former involves controlling stimuli that generate emotional responses while the latter focuses on dealing with the experienced emotion. Two specific emotion regulation strategies that have been studied include reappraisal (reconstrual of a situation to lessen its emotional impact) and suppression (emotion masking) (Gross, 1998a; Gross & John, 2003).

Emotional suppression is physically challenging for the suppressor, resulting in increases in cardiovascular activation and blood pressure (Butler et al., 2003; Gross & Levenson, 1997; Richards & Gross, 1999). Suppression is also cognitively demanding, negatively impacting memory (Richards & Gross, 1999, 2000; Richards, Butler, & Gross, 2003), an effect that is not found when reappraisal is used as a mode of regulation (Richards & Gross, 2000). Particularly relevant for negotiation is research suggesting that emotional suppression inhibits relationship formation. Butler and colleagues found that when one individual in a previously unacquainted dyad engages in emotion suppression, *both* the suppressor and the partner experience increases in blood pressure. Furthermore, partners of suppressors felt less rapport with the suppressors and were less interested in having a future relationship with them.

Both emotional expression and regulation are relevant for the study of negotiation. For example, Barry (1999) empirically studied attitudes toward the strategic use of emotional deception in negotiation; in this context, emotional deception could include either portraying an emotion not felt or suppressing some emotion that is felt. He found that people are generally more approving of and more confident about their ability to use emotional tactics compared to cognitive tactics of deception. Suppression of experienced emotion may be a poor tactical choice for a negotiator, however, if it disrupts memory or results in decreased rapport with the other negotiator, as has been found in studies by Gross and colleagues; this remains an empirical question to be explored. In addition, reviews by Thompson, Nadler, and Kim (1999) and Barry, Fulmer, and van Kleef (2004) consider the interpersonal effects of emotion in negotiation. An underlying assumption of such phenomena as mimicry and emotional contagion is that emotion can be effectively communicated by a given individual in such a way as to actually be influential on another person. Individual differences in ability to express and regulate emotion related to gender, dispositional expressivity, and emotional intelligence are likely to moderate the extent to which emotion is transmitted back and forth in negotiation, both intentionally and unintentionally.

TO CONCLUDE: BROADENING HORIZONS

We have reviewed the nascent literature on emotion in negotiation and proposed avenues for adapting research on affect in other domains to the study of bargaining. Reflecting on the research to date, we make the general observation that investigations of affect in negotiation are expanding in volume, but not necessarily in scope. Accordingly, we conclude this chapter with a few "big picture" thoughts on potential novel directions for negotiation researchers studying emotion.

In much of the negotiation research reviewed here, emotional expression is aggregated into broad categories of positive and negative affect, focusing primarily on valence. A principal aim of this research has been to identify factors that complement or transcend rational/cognitive processes in negotiation, and in this pursuit a basic model of positive and negative emotion has been adequate. However, as we evolve from the basic cognition-versus-emotion discussion to a more nuanced view that acknowledges the ongoing interplay between cognition and emotion, finer-grained conceptualizations of emotion become necessary. We urge negotiation researchers to look to the work of emotion scholars who go beyond global dimensions (e.g., negative affect) to differentiate effects of discrete emotions (e.g., anger versus sadness [DeSteno, Petty, Rucker, Wegener, & Braverman, 2004; DeSteno et al., 2000], or disgust versus sadness [Lerner et al., 2004]).

Second, we see merit in exploring situations where negotiators anticipate *mixed* feelings. In the social psychological literature on emotion, there is long-standing and ongoing debate about whether affect is a univariate/bipolar or bivariate construct (e.g., Cacioppo & Berntson, 1994; Russell, 1980; Russell & Carroll, 1999; Watson & Tellegen, 1985). Put simply, is it possible for people to feel both happiness and sadness at the same time? It is intuitively reasonable to assume that people typically express affect at one end of the spectrum or the other, consistent with a univariate model. In some circumstances, however, people report more complex combinations of simultaneous emotions related to various life events (Larsen, McGraw, & Cacioppo, 2001) and to winning and losing in the presence of counterfactual information (Larsen, McGraw, Mellers, & Cacioppo, 2004). Many bargaining situations entail some combination of winning and losing (e.g., the sale of the old family home) or are related to events that elicit mixed emotions (e.g., divorce), making this line of research quite relevant for practical application in the field of negotiation.

Last, we urge attention to broader perspectives on affect in negotiations that reflect *social constructivist* approaches to emotion. Constructivist theories begin with the observation that humans are social beings living in dynamic social environments and that the propriety of or entitlement to certain patterns of emotion and emotion-behavior vary by social context (see Harre, 1983, 1986; Sabini & Silver, 1982; Tavris, 1982). For example, Averill (1980) defined an emotion as "a transitory social role (a socially constituted syndrome) that includes an individual's appraisal of the situation and that is interpreted as a passion rather than as an action" (p. 312). Emotional experience and expression are elements of the social roles people play. Averill does not reject the possibility that social norms might at some level be informed by biological fact, but maintains that the model that best explains emotionally linked behavior is informed by cognitive appraisal in relation to accepted norms, rather than innate, biological impulse. Alternatively, rather than pitting biology against constructivism, other perspectives synthesize the two; Keltner and Haidt (2001) describe both "primordial" (biological) and "elaborated" (socially constructed) emotions as elements of an integrative social functional emotion system. We suggest that constructivist approaches may provide deeper theory—fundamental explanations for the emotion-behavioral patterns that we observe in the lab. Negotiation offers an ideal context for the study of emotion-behavior as role-playing, and we encourage the development of a social-constructionist thread in the epistemological tapestry of conflict management.

In closing, we see expanding research attention to the psychology of emotion in many domains, and note that the field of conflict and negotiation provides an especially rich context for the study of affect. Evidence for this assertion is found in emotion's presence as a meaningful element in virtually every chapter in this collection: the influence of emotions on the wisdom of decisions (Bazerman & Clugh, chapter 2); variations in emotionality across cultures (Brett & Gelfand, chapter 9); the motivational implications of emotional responses to conflict (Carnevale & De Dreu, chapter 4); connections between emotion and gender differences in negotiation (Kray & Babcock, chapter 10); emotion's influence on situational judgments that impel learning (Loewenstein & Thompson, chapter 5);

emotional aspects of negotiator relationships (McGinn, chapter 7); how emotions in negotiation are evoked by communication channels in use (Nadler & Shestowsky, chapter 8); and emotional effects on attributions, judgments, and strategies (Neale & Fragale, chapter 3). Social psychologists and others who study negotiation should seize this momentum to improve on existing research paradigms, broaden their conceptualizations of emotion, and take advantage of the vast and ever-growing array of theoretical and methodological approaches we have sampled here.

REFERENCES

Adams, J. S. (1963). Toward an understanding of inequity. *Journal of Abnormal and Social Psychology, 67,* 422–436.

Allred, K. G. (1999). Anger and retaliation: Toward an understanding of impassioned conflict in organizations. In R. J. Bies, R. J. Lewicki, & B. H. Sheppard (Eds.), *Research on negotiation in organizations* (Vol. 7, pp. 27–58). Stamford, CT: JAI Press.

Allred, K. G., Mallozzi, J. S., Matsui, F., & Raia, C. P. (1997). The influence of anger and compassion on negotiation performance. *Organizational Behavior and Human Decision Processes, 70,* 175–187.

Anderson, C., & Thompson, L. L. (2004). Affect from the top down: How powerful individuals' positive affect shapes negotiations. *Organizational Behavior and Human Decision Processes, 40,* 125–139.

Arnold, M. B. (1960). *Emotion and personality* (Vol. 1, *Psychological aspects*). New York: Columbia University Press.

Averill, J. R. (1980). A constructivist view of emotion. In R. Plutchik & H. Kellerman (Eds.), *Emotion: Theory research, and experience* (Vol. 1., pp. 305–339). New York: Academic Press.

Axelrod, R. (1984). *The evolution of cooperation.* New York: Basic Books.

Baron, R. A. (1990). Environmentally induced positive affect: Its impact on self-efficacy, task performance, negotiation, and conflict. *Journal of Applied Social Psychology, 20,* 368–384.

Barry, B. (1999). The tactical use of emotion in negotiation. In R. J. Bies, R. J. Lewicki, & B. H. Sheppard (Eds.), *Research on negotiation in organizations* (Vol. 7, pp. 93–121). Stamford, CT: JAI Press.

Barry, B., & Fulmer, I. S. (in press). Methodological challenges in the study of negotiator affect. *International Negotiation.*

Barry, B., Fulmer, I. S., & Kleef, G. van (2004). I laughed, I cried, I settled: The role of emotion in negotiation. In M. J. Gelfand & J. M. Brett (Eds.), *The Handbook of negotiation and culture: Theoretical advances and cross-cultural perspectives* (pp. 71–94). Palo Alto, CA: Stanford University Press.

Barry, B., & Oliver, R. L. (1996). Affect in dyadic negotiation: A model and propositions. *Organizational Behavior and Human Decision Processes, 67,* 127–143.

Bechara, A., Damasio, H., Tranel, D., & Damasio, A. R. (1997). Deciding advantageously before knowing the advantageous strategy. *Science, 275,* 1293–1295.

Berntson, G. G., & Cacioppo, J. T. (2000). Psychobiology and social psychology: Past, present, and future. *Personality and Social Psychology Review, 4,* 3–15.

Bless, H. (2000). Mood and the use of general knowledge structures. In L. L. Martin & G. L. Clore (Eds.), *Theories of mood and cognition: A user's handbook* (pp. 9–26). Mahwah, NJ: Lawrence Erlbaum Associates.

Bless, H. (2001). The consequences of mood on the processing of social information. In A. Tesser & N. Schwartz (Eds.), *Blackwell handbook of social psychology: Intraindividual processes* (pp. 391–412). Malden, MA: Blackwell Publishers, Inc.

Borod, J. C. (Ed.). (2000). *The neuropsychology of emotion*. New York: Oxford University Press.

Bradley, M. M., & Lang, P. J. (2000). Measuring emotion: Behavior, feeling, and physiology. In R. D. Lane & L. Nadel (Eds.), *Cognitive neuroscience of emotion* (pp. 242–276). Oxford, UK: Oxford University Press.

Brett, J. F., Northcraft, G, B., & Pinkley, R. L. (1999). Stairways to heaven: An interlocking self-regulation model of negotiation. *Academy of Management Review, 24,* 435–451.

Brief, A. P., & Weiss, H. M. (2002). Organizational behavior: Affect in the workplace. *Annual Review of Psychology, 53,* 279–307.

Buller, D. B., & Burgoon, J. K. (1998). Emotional expression in the deception process. In P. A. Andersen & L. K. Guerrero (Eds.), *Handbook of communication and emotion* (pp. 381–402). San Diego, CA: Academic Press.

Butler, E. A., Egloff, B., Wilhelm, F. H., Smith, N. C., Erickson, E. A., & Gross, J. J. (2003). The social consequences of expressive suppression. *Emotion, 3,* 48–67.

Cacioppo, J. T., & Berntson, G. G. (1992). Social psychological contributions to the decade of the brain: Doctrine of multilevel analysis. *American Psychologist, 47,* 1019–1028.

Cacioppo, J. T., & Berntson, G. G. (1994). Relationship between attitudes and evaluative space: A critical review with emphasis on the separability of positive and negative substrates. *Psychological Bulletin, 115,* 401–423.

Cacioppo, J. T., Berntson, G. G., Adolphs, R., Carter, C. S., Davidson, R. J., McClintock, M. K., et al. (2002). *Foundations in social neuroscience*. Cambridge, MA: MIT Press.

Cannon, W. B. (1927). The James-Lange theory of emotions: A critical examination and an alternative theory. *American Journal of Psychology, 39,* 106–124.

Cannon, W. B. (1931). Again the James-Lange and the thalamic theories of emotion. *Psychological Review, 38,* 281–295.

Carnevale, P. J. D., & Isen, A. M. (1986). The influence of positive affect and visual access on the discovery of integrative solutions in bilateral negotiation. *Organizational Behavior and Human Decision Processes, 37,* 1–13.

Conlon, D. E., & Hunt, C. S. (2002). Dealing with feeling: The influence of outcome representations on negotiation. *International Journal of Conflict Management, 13,* 38–58.

Conlon, D., & Ross, W. (1993). The effects of partisanship on negotiator behavior and outcome perceptions. *Journal of Applied Psychology, 78,* 280–290.

Cornelius, R. R. (1996). *The science of emotion: Research and tradition in the psychology of emotions*. Upper Saddle River, NJ: Prentice Hall.

Damasio, A. R. (1994). *Descartes' error: Emotion, reason, and the human brain*. New York: HarperCollins.

Darwin, C. (1965). *The expression of the emotions in man and animals*. Chicago: University of Chicago Press. (Original work published 1872)

Davidson, M. N., & Greenhalgh, L. (1999). The role of emotion in negotiation: The impact of anger and race. In R. J. Bies, R. J. Lewicki, & B. H. Sheppard (Eds.), *Research on negotiation in organizations* (Vol. 7, pp. 3–26). Stamford, CT: JAI Press.

Davidson, R. J. (1994). On emotion, mood, and related affective constructs. In P. Ekman & R. J. Davidson (Eds.), *The nature of emotion: Fundamental questions* (pp. 51–55). New York: Oxford University Press.

DeSteno, D., Petty, R. E., Rucker, D. D., Wegener, D. T., & Braverman, J. (2004). Discrete emotions and persuasion: The role of emotion-induced expectancies. *Journal of Personality and Social Psychology, 86,* 43–56.

DeSteno, D., Petty, R. E., Wegener, D. T., & Rucker, D. D. (2000). Beyond valence in the perception of likelihood: The role of emotion specificity. *Journal of Personality and Social Psychology, 78,* 397–416.

Diener, E., Smith, H., & Fujita, F. (1995). The personality structure of affect. *Journal of Personality and Social Psychology, 69,* 130–141.

Donohue, W. A. (1991). *Communication, marital dispute, and divorce mediation.* Hillsdale, NJ: Lawrence Erlbaum.

Donohue, W. A., & Roberto, A. J. (1993). Relational development as negotiated order in hostage negotiation. *Human Communication Research, 20,* 175–198.

Drolet, A. L., & Morris, M. W. (2000). Rapport in conflict resolution: Accounting for how face-to-face contact fosters mutual cooperation in mixed-motive conflicts. *Journal of Experimental Social Psychology, 36,* 26–50.

Dunn, E. W., Wilson, T. D., & Gilbert, D. T. (2003). Location, location, location: The misprediction of satisfaction in housing lotteries. *Personality and Social Psychology Bulletin, 29,* 1421–1432.

Eaton, L. G., & Funder, D. C. (2001). Emotional experience in daily life: Valence, variability, and rate of change. *Emotion, 1,* 413–421.

Eid, M., & Diener, E. (1999). Intraindividual variability in affect: Reliability, validity, and personality correlates. *Journal of Personality and Social Psychology, 76,* 662–676.

Ekman, P. (1993). Facial expression and emotion. *American Psychologist, 48,* 384–392.

Evans, M. J., & Tyler-Evans, M. (2002). Aspects of grief in conflict: Re-visioning response to dispute. *Conflict Resolution Quarterly, 20,* 83–97.

Ferrer, E., & Nesselroade, J. R. (2003). Modeling affective processes in dyadic relations via dynamic factor analysis. *Emotion, 3,* 344–360.

Fiske, S., & Taylor, S. E. (1991). *Social cognition.* New York: McGraw-Hill.

Forgas, J. P. (1992). Affect in social judgments and decisions: A multiprocess model. *Advances in Experimental Social Psychology, 25,* 227–275.

Forgas, J. P. (1995). Mood and judgment: The Affect Infusion Model (AIM). *Psychological Bulletin, 117,* 39–66.

Forgas, J. P. (1998). On feeling good and getting your way: Mood effects on negotiator cognition and behavior. *Journal of Personality and Social Psychology, 74,* 565–577.

Forgas, J. P. (Ed.). (2001). *Handbook of affect and social cognition.* Mahwah, NJ: Lawrence Erlbaum Associates.

Forgas, J. P., & Cromer, M. (2004). On being sad and evasive: Affective influences on verbal communication strategies in conflict situations. *Journal of Experimental Social Psychology, 40,* 511–518.

Friedman, R., Anderson, C., Brett, J., Olekalns, M., Goates, N., & Lisco, C. C. (2004). The positive and negative effects of anger on dispute resolution: Evidence from electronically mediated disputes. *Journal of Applied Psychology, 89,* 369–376.

Galinsky, A. D., Seiden, V. L., Kim, P. H., & Medvec, V. H. (2002). The dissatisfaction of having your first offer accepted: The role of counterfactual thinking in negotiations. *Personality and Social Psychology Bulletin, 28,* 271–283.

Gasper, K., & Clore, G. L. (2000). Do you have to pay attention to your feelings to be influenced by them? *Journal of Personality and Social Psychology, 6,* 698–711.

Gersick, C. J. (1988). Time and transition in work teams: Toward a new model of group development. *Academy of Management Journal, 31,* 9–41.

George, J. M., Jones, G. R., & Gonzalez, J. A. (1998). The role of affect in cross-cultural negotiations. *Journal of International Business Studies, 29,* 749–772.

Gilbert, D. T., Pinel, E. C., Wilson, T. D., Blumberg, S. J., & Wheatley, T. P. (1998). Immune neglect: A source of durability bias in affective forecasting. *Journal of Personality and Social Psychology, 75,* 617–638.

Gillespie, J. J., Brett, J. M., & Weingart, L. R. (2000). Interdependence, social motives, and outcome satisfaction in multiparty negotiation. *European Journal of Social Psychology, 30,* 779–797.

Gross, J. J. (1998a). Antecedent- and response-focused emotion regulation: divergent consequences for experience, expression and physiology. *Journal of Personality and Social Psychology, 74,* 224–237.

Gross, J. J. (1998b). The emerging field of emotion regulation: An integrative review. *Review of General Psychology, 2,* 271–299.

Gross, J. J., & John, O. P. (1998). Mapping the domain of expressivity: Multimethod evidence for a hierarchical model. *Journal of Personality and Social Psychology, 74,* 170–191.

Gross, J. J., & John, O. P. (2003). Individual differences in two emotion regulation processes: Implications for affect, relationships and well-being. *Journal of Personality and Social Psychology, 85,* 348–362.

Gross, J. J., John, O. P., & Richards, J. M. (2000). The dissociation of emotion expression from emotion experience: A personality perspective. *Personality and Social Psychology Bulletin, 26,* 712–726.

Gross, J. J., & Levensen, R. W. (1997). Hiding feelings: The acute effects of inhibiting negative and positive emotion. *Journal of Abnormal Psychology, 106,* 95–103.

Guererro, L. K., & Reiter, R. L. (1998). Expressing emotion: Sex differences in social skills and communicative responses to anger, sadness, and jealousy. In D. J. Canary & K. Dindia (Eds.), *Sex differences and similarities in communication: Critical essays and empirical investigations of sex and gender in interaction* (pp. 321–350). Mahwah, NJ: Lawrence Erlbaum Associates.

Hagemann, D., Waldstein, S. R., & Thayer, J. F. (2003). Central and autonomic nervous system integration in emotion. *Brain and Cognition, 52,* 79–87.

Hall, J. A., Carter, J. D., & Horgan, T. G. (2000). Gender differences in nonverbal communication of emotion. In A. H. Fischer (Ed.), *Gender and emotion: Social psychological perspectives* (pp. 97–117). Cambridge, UK: Cambridge University Press.

Hammer, M. R., & Rogan, R. G. (1997). Negotiation models in crisis situations: The value of a communication-based approach. In R. G. Rogan, M. R. Hammer, & C. R. Van Zandt (Eds.), *Dynamic processes of crisis negotiation: Theory, research, and practice* (pp. 9–23). Westport, CT: Praeger.

Harre, R. (1983). *Personal being.* Oxford, UK: Basil Blackwell.

Harre, R. (1986). An outline of the social constructionist viewpoint. In R. Harre, (Ed.), *The social construction of emotions.* (pp. 2–14). Oxford, UK: Basil Blackwell.

Hegtvedt, K. A., & Killian, C. (1999). Fairness and emotions: Reactions to the process and outcomes of negotiations. *Social Forces, 78,* 269–303.

Hemenover, S. H. (2003). Individual differences in rate of affect change: Studies in affective chronometry. *Journal of Personality and Social Psychology, 85,* 121–131.

Hertel, G., Neuhof, J., Theuer, T., & Kerr, N. L. (2000). Mood effects on cooperation in small groups: Does positive mood simply lead to more cooperation? *Cognition and Emotion, 14,* 441–472.

Holmes, M. E., & Sykes, R. E. (1993). A test of the fit of Gulliver's phase model to hostage negotiations. *Communication Studies, 44,* 38–55.

Homans, G. C. (1961). *Social behavior: Its elementary forms.* New York: Harcourt.

Isen, A. M. (1987). Positive affect, cognitive processes, and social behavior. In L. Berkowitz (Ed.), *Advances in experimental social psychology* (Vol. 20, pp. 203–253). New York: Academic Press.

Izard, C. E. (1971). *The face of emotion.* New York: Appleton-Century-Crofts.

James, W. (1884). What is an emotion? *Mind, 19,* 188–205.

James, W. (1983). *The principles of psychology.* Cambridge, MA: Harvard University Press. (Original work published 1890)

Jones, T. S., & Bodtker, A. (2001). Mediating with heart in mind: Addressing emotion in mediation practice. *Negotiation Journal, July,* 217–244.

Keltner, D., & Haidt, J. (1999). Social functions of emotions at four levels of analysis. *Cognition and Emotion, 13,* 505–521.

Keltner, D., & Haidt, J. (2001). Social functions of emotions. In T. Mayne & G. Bonanno (Eds.), *Emotions: Current issues and future directions* (pp. 192–213). New York: Guilford Press.

Keltner, D., & Kring, A. M. (1998). Emotion, social function, and psychopathology. *Review of General Psychology, 2,* 320–342.

Ketelaar, T., & Au., W. T. (2003). The effects of feelings of guilt on the behavior of uncooperative individuals in repeated social bargaining games: An affect-as-information interpretation of the role of emotion in social interaction. *Cognition and Emotion, 17,* 429–453.

Kleef, G. A. van, De Dreu, C. K., & Manstead, A. S. R. (2004). The interpersonal effects of anger and happiness in negotiations. *Journal of Personality and Social Psychology, 86*(1), 57–76.

Kopelman, S., Rosette, A. S., & Thompson, L. (2004). *The three faces of Eve: An examination of strategic positive, negative, and neutral emotion in negotiations.* (Unpublished working paper).

Kramer, R. M., Newton, E., & Pommerenke, P. L. (1993). Self-enhancement biases and negotiator judgment: Effects of self-esteem and mood. *Organizational Behavior and Human Decision Processes, 56,* 110–133.

Kring, A. M., & Gordon, A. H. (1998). Sex differences in emotion: Expression, experience, and physiology. *Journal of Personality and Social Psychology, 74,* 686–703.

Kumar, R. (1997). The role of affect in negotiations. *Journal of Applied Behavioral Science, 33,* 84–100.

Lane, R. D., & Nadel, L. (Eds.). (2000). *Cognitive neuroscience of emotion.* New York: Oxford University Press.

Lange, C. G. (1922). *The emotions.* Baltimore: Williams & Wilkins. (Original work published 1885)

Larsen, J. T., McGraw, A. P., & Caccioppo, J. T. (2001). Can people feel happy and sad at the same time? *Journal of Personality and Social Psychology, 81,* 684–696.

Larsen, J. T., McGraw, A. P., Meller, B. A., & Cacioppo, J. T. (2004). The agony of victory and the thrill of defeat. *Psychological Science, 15,* 325–330.

Lawler, E. J., & Yoon, J. (1995). Structural power and emotional processes in negotiation. In R. M. Kramer & D. M. Messick (Eds.), *Negotiation as a social process* (pp. 143–165). Thousand Oaks, CA: Sage.

Lazarus, R. S. (1982). Thoughts on the relations between emotion and cognition. *American Psychologist, 37,* 1019–1024.

Lazarus. R. S. (1984). On the primacy of cognition. *American Psychologist, 39,* 124–129.

Lazarus, R. S., Averill, J. R., & Opton, E. M., Jr. (1970). Toward a cognitive theory of emotions. In M. Arnold (Ed.), *Feelings and emotions* (pp. 207–232). New York: Academic Press.

LeDoux, J. E. (2002). Emotion: Clues from the brain. In J. T. Cacioppo, G. G. Berntson, R. Adolphs, C. S. Carter, R. J. Davidson, M. K. McClintock et al. (Eds.), *Foundations in social neuroscience* (pp. 389–410). Cambridge, MA: MIT Press.

Lerner, J. S., Small, D. A., & Loewenstein, G. (2004). Heart strings and purse strings: Carry-over effects of emotions on economic decisions. *Psychological Science, 15,* 337–341.

Levenson, R. W. (1992). Autonomic nervous system differences among emotions. *Psychological Science, 3,* 23–27.

Levy, D. A., & Nail, P. R. (1993). Contagion: A theoretical and empirical review and reconceptualization. *Genetic, Social, and General Psychology Monographs, 119,* 235–285.

Loewenstein, G. F., Weber, E. U., Hsee, C. K., & Welch, N. (2001). Risk as feelings. *Psychological Bulletin, 127(2),* 267–286.

Mayer, J. D., & Salovey, P. (1997). What is emotional intelligence? In P. Salovey & D. J. Sluyter (Eds.), *Emotional development and emotional intelligence: Educational implications* (pp. 3–31). New York: Basic Books.

McGinn, K. L., & Keros, A. T. (2002). Improvisation and the logic of exchange in socially embedded transactions. *Administrative Science Quarterly, 47,* 442–474.

Metts, S., & Bowers, J. W. (1994). Emotion in interpersonal communication. In M. L. Knapp & G. R. Miller (Eds.), *Handbook of interpersonal communication* (pp. 508–541). Thousand Oaks, CA: Sage.

Moore, C. W. (2003). *The mediation process.* San Francisco: Jossey-Bass.

Moore, D. A., Kurtzberg, T. R., Thompson, L. L., & Morris, M. W. (1999). Long and short routes to success in electronically mediated negotiations: Group affiliations and good vibrations. *Organizational Behavior and Human Decision Processes, 77,* 22–43.

Morris, M. W., & Keltner, D. (2000). How emotions work: The social functions of emotional expression in negotiations. *Research in Organizational Behavior, 22,* 1–50.

Morris, M., Nadler, J., Kurtzberg, T., & Thompson, L. (2002). Schmooze or lose: Social friction and lubrication in e-mail negotiations. *Group Dynamics: Theory, Research, and Practice, 6,* 89–100.

Murphy, F. C., Nimmo-Smith, I., & Lawrence, A. D. (2003). Functional neuroanatomy of emotions: A meta-analysis. *Cognitive, Affective, and Behavioral Neuroscience, 3,* 207–233.

Nadler, J. (2001). Electronically-mediated dispute resolution and e-commerce. *Negotiation Journal, 17,* 333–347.

Naquin, C. E. (2003). The agony of opportunity in negotiation: Number of negotiable issues, counterfactual thinking, and feelings of satisfaction. *Organizational Behavior and Human Decision Processes, 91,* 97–107.

Neale, M. A., & Bazerman, J. H. (1991). *Cognition and rationality in negotiation.* New York: Free Press.

Neale, M. A., & Bazerman, J. H. (1992). Negotiator cognition and rationality: A behavioral decision theory perspective. *Organizational Behavior and Human Decision Processes, 51,* 157–176.

Novemsky, N., & Schweitzer, M. E. (2004). What makes negotiators happy? The differential effects of internal and external social comparisons on negotiators satisfaction. *Organizational Behavior and Human Decision Processes, 95,* 186–197.

O'Connor, K. M., & Arnold, J. A. (2001). Distributive spirals: Negotiation impasses and the moderating role of disputant self-efficacy. *Organizational Behavior and Human Decision Processes, 84*, 148–176.

Oliver, R. L. (1997). *Satisfaction: A behavioral perspective on the consumer.* New York: McGraw-Hill.

Oliver, R. L., Balakrishnan, P. V., & Barry, B. (1994). Outcome satisfaction in negotiation: A test of expectancy disconfirmation. *Organizational Behavior and Human Decision Processes, 60*, 252–274.

Parrott, W. G. (2001). Emotions in social psychology: Volume overview. In W. G. Parrott (Ed.), *Emotions in social psychology* (pp. 1–19). Philadelphia: Psychology Press.

Pillutla, M. M., & Murnighan, J. K. (1996). Unfairness, anger, and spite: Emotional rejections of ultimatum offers. *Organizational Behavior and Human Decision Processes, 68*, 208–224.

Pines, A. M., Gat, H., & Tal, Y. (2002). Gender differences in content and style of argument between couples during divorce mediation. *Conflict Resolution Quarterly, 20*, 23–50.

Planalp, S. (1998). Communicating emotion in everyday life: Cues, channels, and processes. In P. A. Andersen & L. K. Guerrero (Eds.), *Handbook of communication and emotion* (pp. 29–48). San Diego, CA: Academic Press.

Plutchik, R. (1980). *Emotion: A psychoevolutionary synthesis.* New York: Harper & Row.

Plutchik, R. (2003). *Emotions and life: Perspectives from psychology, biology, and evolution.* Washington, DC: American Psychological Association.

Posthuma, R. A., Dworkin, J. B., & Swift, M. S. (2002). Mediator tactics and sources of conflict: Facilitating and inhibiting effects. *Industrial Relations, 41*, 94–109.

Raiffa, H. (1982). *The art and science of negotiation.* Cambridge, MA: Harvard University Press.

Rhoades, J. A., Arnold, J., & Clifford, J. (2001). The role of affective traits and affective states in disputants' motivation and behavior during episodes of organizational conflict. *Journal of Organizational Behavior, 22*, 329–345.

Richards, J. M., & Gross, J. J. (1999). Composure at any cost? The cognitive consequences of emotion suppression. *Personality and Social Psychology Bulletin, 25*(8), 1033–1044.

Richards, J. M., Gross, J. J. (2000). Emotion regulation and memory: The cognitive costs of keeping one's cool. *Journal of Personality and Social Psychology, 79*, 410–424.

Richards J. M., Butler, E. A., & Gross, J. J. (2003). Emotion regulation in romantic relationships: The cognitive consequence of concealing feelings. *Journal of Social and Personal Relationships, 20*, 599–620.

Rogan, R. G. (1997). Emotion and emotional expression in crisis negotiation. In R. G. Rogan, M. R. Hammer, & C. R. Van Zandt (Eds.), *Dynamic processes of crisis negotiation: Theory, research, and practice* (pp. 25–43). Westport, CT: Praeger.

Rogan, R. G., & Hammer, M. R. (1994). Crisis negotiations: A preliminary investigation of facework in naturalistic conflict discourse. *Journal of Applied Communication Research, 22*, 216–231.

Rogan, R. G., & Hammer, M. R. (1995). Assessing message affect in crisis negotiations: An exploratory study. *Human Communication Research, 21*, 553–574.

Roseman, I. J., & Smith, C. A. (2001). Appraisal theory: Overview, assumptions, varieties, controversies. In K. Scherer, A. Schorr, & T. Johnstone (Eds.), *Appraisal process in emotion: Theory, methods, research* (pp. 3–19). Oxford, UK: Oxford University Press.

Ruder, M. I., & Bless, H. (2003). Mood and the reliance and the ease of retrieval heuristic. *Journal of Personality and Social Psychology, 85*, 20–32.

Russell, J. A. (1980). A circumplex model of affect. *Journal of Personality and Social Psychology, 39*, 1161–1178.

Russell, J. A., & Carroll, J. M. (1999). On the bipolarity of positive and negative affect. *Psychological Bulletin, 125*, 3–30.

Rusting, C. L. (1999). Interactive effects of personality and mood on emotion-congruent memory and judgment. *Journal of Personality and Social Psychology, 77*, 1073–1086.

Rusting, C. L. (2001). Personality as a moderator of affective influences on cognition. In J. P. Forgas (Ed.), *Handbook of affect and social cognition* (pp. 371–391). Mahwah, NJ: Lawrence Erlbaum Associates.

Sabini, J., & Silver, M. (1982). *Moralities of Everyday Life.* Oxford, UK: Oxford University Press.

Salovey, P., & Mayer, J. D. (1990). Emotional intelligence. *Imagination, Cognition and Personality, 9*, 185–211.

Sanna, L. J., Parks, C. D., & Chang, E. C. (2003). Mixed-motive conflict in social dilemmas: Mood as input to competitive and cooperative goals. *Group Dynamics: Theory, Research, and Practice, 7*(1), 26–40.

Schachter, S. (1964). The interaction of cognitive and physiological determinants of emotional state. In L. Berkowitz (Ed.), *Advances in experimental social psychology* (Vol. 1, pp. 49–82). New York: Academic Press.

Schachter, S., & Singer, J. E. (1962). Cognitive, social and physiological determinants of emotional state. *Psychological Review, 69*, 379–399.

Scherer, K. R. (1984). On the nature and function of emotion: A component process approach. In K. R. Scherer & P. Ekman (Eds.), *Approaches to emotion* (pp. 293–317). Hillsdale, NJ: Erlbaum.

Schreier, L. S. (2002). Emotional intelligence and mediation training. *Conflict Resolution Quarterly, 20*, 99–119.

Schwarz, N. (1990). Feelings as information: Informational and motivational functions of affective states. In E. T. Higgins & R. M. Sorrentino (Eds.), *Handbook of motivation and cognition: Foundations of social behavior* (Vol. 2, pp. 527–561). New York: Guilford Press.

Schwarz, N., & Clore, G. L. (1983). Mood, misattribution, and judgments of well-being: Informative and directive functions of affective sates. *Journal of Personality and Social Psychology, 45*, 513–523.

Shaver, P. R., Schwartz, J. C., Kirson, D., & O'Connor, C. (1987). Emotion knowledge: Further explorations of a prototype approach. *Journal of Personality and Social Psychology, 52*, 1061–1086.

Snyder, M. (1974). Self-monitoring of expressive behavior. *Journal of Personality and Social Psychology, 30*, 526–437.

Strongman, K. T. (1996). *The psychology of emotion* (4th ed.). Chicester, UK: Wiley.

Strauss, A. L. (1978). *Negotiations: Varieties, contexts, processes, and social order.* San Francisco: Jossey Bass.

Tavris, C. (1982). *Anger: The misunderstood emotion.* New York: Simon & Schuster.

Taylor, P. J. (2002). A cylindrical model of communication behavior in crisis negotiations. *Human Communication Research, 28*, 7–48.

Tomkins, S. S. (1962). *Affect, imagery, and consciousness* (Vol. 1, *The positive affects*). New York: Springer.

Tomkins, S. S. (1975). The phantasy behind the face. *Journal of Personality Assessment, 39*, 550–562.

Thompson, L., & DeHarpport, T. (1994). Social judgment, feedback, and interpersonal learning in negotiation. *Organizational Behavior and Human Decision Processes, 58,* 327–345.

Thompson, L., & Kim, P. H. (2000). How the quality of third parties' settlement solutions is affected by the relationships between negotiators. *Journal of Experimental Psychology: Applied, 6,* 3–14.

Thompson, L., Medvec, V. H., Seiden, V., & Kopelman, S. (2001). Poker face, smiley face, and rant 'n' rave: Myths and realities about emotion in negotiation. In M. A. Hogg & R. S. Tindale (Eds.), *Blackwell handbook of social psychology: Group processes* (pp. 139–163). Malden, MA: Blackwell.

Thompson, L., Nadler, J., & Kim, P. H. (1999). Some like it hot: The case for the emotional negotiator. In L. Thompson, J. Levine, & D. Messick (Eds.), *Shared cognition in organizations* (pp. 139–161). Mahwah, NJ: Lawrence Erlbaum Associates.

Thompson, L., Valley, K. L., Kramer, R. M. (1995). The bittersweet feeling of success: An examination of social perception in negotiation. *Journal of Experimental Social Psychology, 31,* 467–492.

Walton, R. E. (1969). *Interpersonal peacemaking: Confrontations and third-party consultation.* Reading, MA: Addison-Wesley.

Watson, D., Clark, L. A., & Tellegen, A. (1988). Development and validation of brief measures of positive and negative affect: The PANAS scales. *Journal of Personality and Social Psychology, 54,* 1063–1070.

Watson, D., & Tellegen, A. (1985). Toward a consensual structure of mood. *Psychological Bulletin, 98,* 219–235.

Welton, G. L., Pruitt, D. G., & McGillicuddy, N. B. (1988). The role of caucusing in community mediation. *Journal of Conflict Resolution, 32,* 181–202.

Willingham, D. T., & Dunn, E. W. (2003). What neuroimaging and brain localization can do, cannot do, and should not do for social psychology. *Journal of Personality and Social Psychology, 85,* 662–671.

Wilson, T. D., Wheatley, T., Meyers, J. M., Gilbert, D. T., & Axsom, D. (2000). Focalism: A source of durability bias in affective forecasting. *Journal of Personality and Social Psychology, 78,* 821–836.

Winkielman, P., Berntson, G. G., & Cacioppo, J. T. (2001). The phychophysiological perspective on the social mind. In A. Tesser, & N. Schwarz (Eds.), *Blackwell handbook of social psychology: Intraindividual processes* (pp. 89–108). Malden, MA: Blackwell Publishers.

Zajonc, R. B. (1980). Feeling and thinking: Preferences need no inferences. *American Psychologist, 35,* 151–175.

Zajonc, R. B. (1984). On the primacy of affect. *American Psychologist, 39,* 117–123.

Zubek, J. M., Pruitt, D. G., Peirce, R. S., McGillicuddy, N. B., & Syna, H. (1992). Disputant and mediator behaviors affecting short-term success in mediation. *Journal of Conflict Resolution, 36,* 546–572.

7

Relationships and Negotiations in Context

KATHLEEN L. MCGINN

R elationships, any form of social tie between parties, have become a common theme in negotiation research. A query in PsychINFO for articles between 1995 and 2005 that included both "negotiation" and "relationships" as keywords resulted in 422 citations.[1] In social psychological studies, friends are compared to strangers (e.g., Halpern, 1994; McGinn & Keros, 2003; Thompson & DeHarpport, 1998), those from the same school are compared to those from different schools (e.g., Thompson, Valley, & Kramer, 1995), and those negotiating face to face are compared to those dealing with nameless, faceless others (e.g., McGinn, Thompson, & Bazerman, 2003; Moore, Kurtzberg, Thompson, & Morris, 1999). In sociology, arm's-length transactions—those between actors who share little familiarity or affect and no prolonged past or expected future social ties—are differentiated from socially embedded transactions—those facilitated by either direct or indirect social relationships between the actors (Coleman, 1988; Granovetter, 1974; Uzzi, 1999). Even economists are starting to view social ties between parties in economic transactions as within their purview (Manski, 2000).

The hundreds of studies on relationships and negotiation encompass a broad range of definitions of relationships. The most common approach in social psychological research is to conceptualize and operationalize relationships as dichotomous, for example, friends are compared to strangers. Greenhalgh and Chapman (1998) criticize dichotomous operationalizations of relationships as inadequate tools for exploring fully the effects of relationships on negotiations. To capture the complexities of interpersonal relationships, they created a composite relationship index, comprised of 15 constructs, including scope, common interests, trust and openness/disclosure, aggregating to one overall relationship score. While Greenhalgh and Chapman's multiattribute measure of relationships goes far beyond dichotomous, relationship/no-relationship distinctions, it collapses across types of relationships, and thereby misses the rules that come with the content of the tie, for example, friendship, peer, parent–child.

Research on specific types of relationships suggests that important differences may be found across types. Interactions between people who have previously existing relationships reflect the rules and norms in place for those ongoing relationships (Rusbult & Arriaga, 1997). Negotiations between parents and children, for example, are guided by the social roles of mother, father, and child: Mothers tend to defer when negotiating with their teenage sons, while fathers in similar negotiations are deferred to (Steinberg, 1981). Similarly, the presence of a friendship between the parties imposes guidelines for negotiations: Friends set lower prices when selling to, and are willing to pay higher prices when buying from, friends relative to strangers (Halpern, 1997). Relationships between people who work together within organizations or interact in professional settings reflect tensions between coworker and friend roles, and conflicting expectations for appropriate behavior across these roles (Sias, Krone, & Jablin, 2002). Explicitly restricting the sample to strangers does not eliminate the question of relationships from the research; it simply limits the relationships studied to one type.

No one definition of relationship can capture all of the important research on relationships and negotiation carried out over the past decade. This chapter restricts its purview to positive, ongoing relationships, giving special attention to the social rules occurring within specific types of relationships. This restriction is consistent with the underlying assumptions in most recent studies, but it does exclude a growing body of research focusing on negative relationships (e.g., Labianca, Brass, & Gray, 1998).

A CONCEPTUAL FRAMEWORK FOR STUDYING RELATIONSHIPS IN NEGOTIATIONS

Rather than asking the circumscribed question of how relationships affect negotiated outcomes, this chapter takes a broader perspective, asking how relationships between the parties fit into the larger picture of negotiations in context. One conclusion that is quickly reached from even the most cursory review of the last ten years of negotiation research is that negotiations affect and are affected by (for better and for worse, as this review will go on to discuss) the form and content of the relationship between the parties. To acknowledge this fundamental result, a negotiated order perspective (Strauss, 1978) is offered as an organizing structure for this chapter.

The negotiated order perspective depicts organizations and other social units (such as families or societies) as continuously changing via negotiations, and negotiations as continuously evolving in response to the organization or social unit in which they take place. Viewed through this lens, relationships are shaped by the social and economic context. In turn, relationships influence the occurrence as well as the process and outcome of negotiations, negotiation outcomes alter or reinforce the social and economic context, and the cycle continues (Figure 7.1). In short, relationships shape negotiations, and negotiations shape relationships through the socially driven and situated definition, enactment, and interpretation of conflict and exchange (Blumer, 1969; Uzzi, 1997).

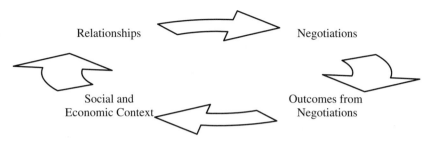

FIGURE 7.1   Cycle of influence between relationships and negotiations from a negotiated order perspective.

Relationships Influence the Process of Negotiating

The process of negotiating includes all of the verbal and nonverbal actions of and interactions between the involved parties while they search for a mutually agreeable solution. Like other social issues in organizational life, the process of negotiation is not objectively determined and experienced. It rests on the coconstruction that takes place during the interaction (McGinn & Keros, 2003). Relationships affect this coconstruction in a number of ways: through the choice of interaction partner; through attributions and emotions; through shared knowledge structures; through procedural rules and norms; and through coordinated action and information sharing.

Relationships Influence Process Through the Choice of Interaction Partner
The first step in any negotiation is choosing the party or parties with whom to try to shape a deal. Deciding whom to bring to or allow at the bargaining table can be thought of as a matter of search. A bounded rationality argument would assert that parties attempt to reduce search costs, just as they attempt to reduce other information-processing costs (March & Simon, 1958). Turning to someone with whom ties are already established reduces the cost of search. In situations in which trust is critical to successful negotiations, selecting known others as partners can not only reduce costs but also bring additional benefits (DiMaggio & Louch, 1998; Miller & Rempel, 2004).

Sociologists have long asserted that social ties drive partner choice (Baker, 1984; Granovetter, 1974). Recent empirical work on embeddedness in organizational and market contexts provides evidence of the benefits and costs of limiting partner selection. Embeddedness creates a logic of exchange with close others that saves time, increases joint gains, and enhances adaptation (Uzzi, 1999). But only to a point—beyond that, embeddedness can derail negotiations by insulating parties from critical information available only outside close ties. In the financial sector, Mizruchi and Stearns (2001) found that bankers attempting to close risky deals with corporate customers tended to rely on close, trusted colleagues for advice and support during negotiations (Mizruchi & Stearns, 2001). While this reduced search ensures trust, it comes at a cost, reducing the likelihood that multiple points of view will be conveyed and incorporated into the deal. In a study of auditor–client interactions, Seabright and colleagues found that positive personal relationships between boundary spanners reduced the likelihood of negotiating a contract with a new auditor, even when there were economic forces suggesting a change could benefit the client (Seabright, Levinthal, & Fichman, 1992).

Restricting search to close ties also occurs in negotiations within consumer markets. DiMaggio and Louch, studying large item negotiations, such as those over houses and cars, found higher satisfaction for deals achieved through within-network ties. They conclude that "consumers use social networks in much the same way as firms use hierarchy" to protect against opportunistic agents (1998, p. 619). But restricting negotiations in markets to trusted others may generate costs, as well as benefits, for the involved parties. Tenbrunsel and her colleagues, in an experimental simulation of markets, found that power and friendship ties interact such that high-power players realize less profit, while low-power players realize more profit, when negotiating with friends than when negotiating with others (Tenbrunsel, Wade-Benzoni, Moag, & Bazerman, 1999).

In some cases, selection of close others as negotiation partners becomes an end in itself, and economic gains from a deal are traded for maintaining or enhancing the relationship. Commitment to one's partner can lead to a conscious derogation of alternatives (Johnson & Rusbult, 1989). But relationship effects on partner selection may also work in the opposite direction. There may be occasions in which negotiators will take steps to avoid bargaining with close friends or colleagues, because doing so could restrict profit-maximization or could be socially uncomfortable. Alternatively, parties may choose to maintain an arm's length relationship, and not develop the relationship further, when interacting with some-one with whom they may have to engage in potentially contentious negotiations in the future.[2] These possibilities, as yet unexplored, deserve investigation in future research.

Relationships Influence Process Through Attributions and Emotions in Negotiations
Relationships create emotions that in turn shape negotiations. Barry, Fulmer, and Goates (chapter 6) provide a comprehensive review of the roles emotions play in negotiations. In an earlier paper, Barry and Oliver (1996) argued that positive relationships lead parties to expect more from one another, setting the parties up for negative emotional responses if these expectations are not met. In negotiations involving positive relationships, aspirations reflect heightened importance attached to fair treatment and distribution, though the potential negative consequences of these heightened aspirations may be mitigated by perspective taking (Drolet, Larrick, & Morris, 1998).

People hold positive general images (or illusions, depending on your perspective) of those they are close to (Murray & Holmes, 1996). A generalized positive image of the other provides the canvas on which a negotiator can paint negative conflict behaviors as positive attributes (Miller & Rempel, 2004). What might be viewed as stubborn, obstructionist behavior in a stranger or an enemy, for example, may be seen as a strong commitment to values when there are close ties between the parties. These positive attributions provide a cushion of trust when things go poorly in negotiations, reducing the likelihood of reciprocity of negative behaviors (Rubin, Pruitt, & Kim, 1994) and increasing the stability of the relationship (Murray & Holmes, 1996). Over four experiments, Dunn and Schweitzer (2005) found that negative emotions do not color trust judgments of close others, while they have measurable deleterious effects on judgments of strangers.

Relationships Influence Process Through Knowledge Structures
Parties in close, positive relationships develop and share their own, unique way of interacting with one another and interpreting the social world around them (Berger, 2002). These shared systems of meanings or understandings facilitate agreement on how to make sense of the issues in and surrounding a negotiation between close parties (Fletcher & Fitness, 1996; Wegner, Erber, & Raymond, 1991). In a study revealing the extent of presumed knowledge sharing between friends, Keysar, Carter, and Swanson (2004) presented participants with an assortment of items, including a roll of scotch tape and an audiotape. With a physical barrier separating the parties so they could not see one another, the focal participant was instructed to place the scotch tape into a small paper bag and to put the bag back on the table with the other items. The barrier was then removed and either a friend or stranger instructed the focal participant to pick up one item at a time, as written on an index card, eventually getting to "the tape." If the party giving instructions was a friend rather than a stranger, the participant was significantly more likely to initially reach for the scotch tape in the bag when told to pick up "the tape." The participants naturally and without conscious thought assumed their friends shared the same knowledge that they held. If this same assumption occurs in negotiations between parties with close positive relationships, the parties will negotiate with a shared understanding of what to expect from one another, enhancing coordination and easing interaction (McGinn & Keros, 2003). On the other hand, close parties may fail to communicate differences in preferences, valuations, expectations or interests, and therefore fail to identify opportunities for mutual gain. Taken-for-granted assumptions of what the other knows and wants may limit the amount of exploration of novel approaches and alternatives, restricting outcomes to those fitting the preconceived notions of the parties.

Relationships Influence Process Through Procedural Rules and Norms
When the relationship is left unspecified, there is wide variation in how people expect others to behave in a negotiation. O'Connor and Adams (1999) asked a group of undergraduates to "list the typical things that occur when two people negotiate" (p. 137). Thirty-five actions were listed by their respondents, only two of which were named by more than a very small minority—"attempt to compromise" and "reach agreement." The majority of the actions were listed by only one respondent, indicating a broad and varied range of "typical" negotiation behavior. But within socially embedded negotiations, acceptable behavior is often narrowly prescribed. Social norms or rules develop naturally through repetition, and specify that certain behaviors should occur, while others are off limits (Argyle & Henderson, 1985).

People within relationships act in ways that are consistent with situated role structures (Rusbult & Arriaga, 1997, p. 221). Situated role structures reflect broadly held norms for the relationship type, as well as situated norms for the specific relationship. Relationship categories, such as friend or spouse, are already psychologically represented as prototypes when parties begin a new relationship. Entering into a given type of relationship, for example, becoming friends, implies agreement with the norms accompanying such a relationship. As the tie matures, the parties begin to mold behavior to their unique relationship, adjusting and changing from the original prototype (Reis & Knee, 1996). Through this ongoing process of naming, assimilating, and habituating, mutually understood behavioral norms evolve. These norms result in regularity of one's own behavior and expectations for the other's. Mutually held norms for interaction, in turn, promote trust and further enhance the relationship (Olson & Olson, 2000).

Within negotiations, norms and rules for certain relationships result in predictable processes and outcomes. Halpern (1997) asserts that friends have a script for transactions, including being generous and not asking for large portions of the available surplus. Others have also shown consistently generous behavior, such as accommodation (Rusbult, Verette, Whitney, & Slovik, 1991) and willingness to sacrifice (Van Lange & Rusbult, 1995), in mixed-motive interactions between friends.

Relationships Influence Process Through Coordinated Action and Information Sharing

A positive relationship between the parties in a negotiation affects not just the specific norms that are in play, but the very presence of coordinated action. McGinn and Keros (2003), comparing negotiation processes between strangers and friends, found that strangers often failed to coordinate on a shared logic of exchange, but such asymmetry was rare between friends. The relational, procedural, and informational acts within a negotiation between friends are coordinated in ways that enhance information sharing and accurate interpretation of information (McGinn & Keros, 2003; Walther, 1995). Through field interviews of bankers, Uzzi (1999) revealed that transactions among socially embedded actors entailed detailed information exchange and joint problem solving, features not present in transactions among actors without network ties.

The benefits of information sharing among related parties in negotiation settings are multifold. Greenhalgh and Chapman (1998) showed experimentally that information sharing rose with the closeness of the relationship between the parties, while coercive behavior fell correspondingly, leading to higher joint gain in close dyads. In an examination of a company's archival human resources data, Seidel, Polzer, and Stewart (2000) found that increases from initial offers in starting salary negotiations were positively associated with having a friend already working in the organization. African Americans, who were less likely to have within-firm ties, negotiated smaller increases than whites, but the salary differences across racial groups were no longer significant when controlling for social ties. The authors speculate that those without ties to others in the organization had less information about the acceptability of asking for additional compensation and therefore failed to ask for significant increases.

Research has shown that coordination and information sharing is enhanced not only by positive relations between the parties, but also by friendly actions within the negotiation, regardless of prior ties. People are cooperative in response to cooperative acts (Fehr & Gächter, 2000). Even a modicum of social information about the other party increases self-disclosure and enhances rapport (Moore et al., 1999), which sets into motion the cycle of positive reciprocity. The additional benefits of a prior positive relationship occur through increases in the likelihood of the initial cooperative act and the ensuing prosocial reciprocity.

RELATIONSHIPS INFLUENCE OUTCOMES

As relationships influence the process of negotiations, they inevitably affect outcomes. In addition to the process-mediated effects discussed above, the relationship between the parties also influences agreements through objectives for, utilities for, and interpretations of the outcomes themselves. The value placed on long-term relatedness goals often guides behavior more directly than the desire for maximizing one's own economic payoffs (Tyler, 1989). Both Rabin (1993) and Bolton and Ockenfels (2000) provide theoretical arguments suggesting how a prior relationship results in each party placing a positive value on the outcomes of the other. Friendship may also create a positive utility for genial interaction over instrumental outcomes. Friends are willing to sacrifice economic payoffs to reduce the conflict and negative externalities of negotiations (Barry & Oliver, 1996; Halpern, 1994; Polzer, Neale, & Glenn, 1993).

Regardless of the objective payoffs, positive relationships influence parties' interpretations of those payoffs (Rusbult & Arriaga, 1997). The utility assigned to an outcome is mediated by the attributions the parties make about the process and the agreement, and what these say about the relationship (Tyler, 1999). Long-term, stable relationships elicit "stable, pattern-contingent transformational tendencies" (Rusbult & Arriaga, 1997, p. 241), in the Kelley (1979) sense of transformed payoff matrices. In other words, related parties transform the outcome of a negotiation to reflect not only economic payoffs, but also relational returns, as discussed below. Social scientists, particularly organizational scholars, may want to argue that the objective payoff should be considered primary, but this is akin to arguing that money matters more than happiness, more than relatedness. How many who make this assumption in experimental investigations would take on this preference ordering in their own negotiations?

NEGOTIATIONS INFLUENCE RELATIONSHIPS

The economic payoff to the parties is generally treated as the pertinent outcome variable in negotiation research. But three other dimensions of outcomes increase in importance as one moves away from experimental research and toward actual negotiations involving parties with past and future ties. The process itself becomes an important product of negotiations, because ethical, efficient processes have long-term relational and reputational benefits and unethical, inefficient processes have parallel costs, independent of the parties' immediate economic payoffs. Similarly, the ease and success in implementing the agreement is a critical outcome variable in negotiations between parties who plan to continue their relationship and negotiate again in the future. Finally, the continuity of, satisfaction with, and intimacy within the relationship itself is fundamental to what most would consider success in negotiations. Salacuse (1998) goes so far as citing the establishment and/or maintenance of relationships as the key purpose of business negotiations: "The essence of the deal between the parties is their relationship, not the contract" (p. 5).

The idea that relationships are a key outcome variable is explicit in the Group Values model of conflict resolution (Tyler, 1989). Negotiations can be seen as externalizing the substance and strength of the relationship itself (Burleson, Metts, & Kirch, 2000). The way in which conflict is handled is a defining element of interpersonal relationships, affecting the development, maintenance, and erosion of the ties between the parties (Canary & Messman, 2000; Gottman, 1994). Fair treatment in conflict situations matters most when the respondent values the relationship with the authority. In these situations, treatment matters because the relationship with the other is defined by the interaction (Tyler, 1999). The negotiation sends a status message—the way we interact is a message to me about how much you value me and our relationship (Tyler, 1999).

Under some conditions, negotiations may harm relationships. Greenhalgh and Chapman (1998) found that coercive tactics were negatively associated with relationship continuity. Other research has revealed how disruption of trust in a negotiation may trigger closer scrutiny of the underlying relationship. Bottom and his colleagues, in a series of dilemma exercises, show that relationships are fragile and easily disrupted by competitive moves (Bottom, Gibson, Daniels, & Murnighan, 1996). Luckily, they also find that small amends can reinstate trust when there is a prior relationship between the parties.

NEGOTIATION OUTCOMES (INCLUDING RELATIONSHIPS) SHAPE SOCIAL AND ECONOMIC CONTEXT

Mutual agreement on a set of payoffs is the end of the story in experimental research, but only one stage in an ongoing cycle of negotiations in organizations, markets, and other social systems. While social psychological research is essentially silent on the dynamic, cyclical nature of negotiations and the social contexts in which they take place, the ongoing evolution of social structure is foundational for anthropologists. More than 20 years ago, in a comparative study across tribes in Africa, Scott (1976) revealed how parties negotiate conflict in ways that reify the existing social structure. When disputes take place between closely tied parties (related, or in the same tribe), the chosen settlements reinforce social integration; when disputes take place between distant parties, settlements emphasize social distance and heighten animosities.

While negotiation outcomes often further solidify the social and economic structure in place prior to the interaction—"them that has, gets"—negotiations have the potential to alter the social and economic order. Buchalter (2003) offers a compelling illustration of this in a study of an elite neighborhood in Philadelphia. The borders of the neighborhood were being "challenged" and had to be negotiated. This negotiation, guided by relational and spatial ties, played out in the day-to-day interactions in the neighborhoods. As a new social agreement was formed, the modified border took on objectivity beyond the social construction. This, in turn, affected the social and economic context, from interpersonal relationships to real estate values.

CHALLENGES AND NEW FRONTIERS FOR STUDYING RELATIONSHIPS IN NEGOTIATIONS

In the years between 1995 and 2005, social psychological research has moved toward studying natural relationships in negotiations, if not toward studying naturally occurring negotiations. And sociologists have increasingly turned to negotiations in organizations and markets as arenas for investigation. The new learning that these forays have garnered, reviewed above, is substantial. But the challenges introduced by considering a negotiated order perspective in negotiation research are also substantial.

To study the multiple and dynamic aspects of relationships and negotiations in a negotiated order requires treating relationships or interactions, rather than the individual negotiators or the negotiation outcomes, as the unit of analysis. This raises the issue of nonindependent data—because of the mutual influence and knowledge processes in negotiation, party A's preferences, behavior, outcomes, and so forth cannot be considered independently of party B's. In economics, interdependence of behavior is responded to by game theory, but even here, underlying interests and preferences are assumed to be unaltered by the interaction. In sociology, network analytic methods have been developed to handle the statistical anomalies arising from interdependence. Social psychologists studying negotiations must also tackle this critical theoretical and empirical issue.

Taking a negotiated order lens to questions at the intersection of negotiations and relationships introduces issues of temporality that are difficult to reconcile with traditional experimental approaches. Long-term relationships are steeped in history that drives processes, understandings, and norms for distribution (Fichman & Levinthal, 1991). The emotions involved in both negotiations and relationships, and the ways in which these emotions affect attributions, vary in form and intensity over the course of a prolonged negotiation. The presence of a relationship, which exists over time across multiple negotiations, allows parties to adjust negotiated outcomes over time if one or both of the parties wish to do so (Sacks, Reichart, & Proffitt, 1999). Actual relationships make possible temporal tradeoffs not observable in one-shot interactions or cross-sectional studies. If changing emotions alter interpretations, parties add or eliminate issues during the negotiation, and payoffs are adjusted as negotiated agreements are implemented over time, measuring outcomes at the end of a negotiation session, based on stated preferences at the beginning of a negotiation, may lead to erroneous conclusions regarding the positive or negative effects of relationships on negotiated outcomes. Sacks and associates suggest longitudinal studies that explore actual negotiator relationships before and after negotiations.

Even the fundamental constructs of integration and distribution present a conundrum when the negotiation is viewed from the perspective of the larger social order in which parties may have positive, long-term relationships. Because parties with positive, enduring relationships tend to engage in truthful exchange and positive reciprocity, "efficiency questions and questions of distribution are inseparable" (Fehr & Gächter, 2000, p. 171). Field studies by Uzzi (1997, 1999), DiMaggio and Louch (1998), and Mizruchi and Stearns (2001) have shown that embedded ties facilitate the honest information exchange and problem solving that leads to high joint gains, equitably distributed (allowing for temporal tradeoffs). Even after the deal is made, relationships continue to create value and affect its distribution simultaneously. Shapiro, Sheppard, and Cheraskin (1992) assert that trust in business relationships enhances the efficiency of the deal and dealmaking, results in greater flexibility in the implementation of deals, and reduces the need for ongoing monitoring. The accompanying costs and benefits, and how these are distributed, depend on the basis of trust between the parties (Shapiro et al., 1992). Separating the efficiency of deals between embedded parties from the payoff each party achieves simply breaks one factor into two variables.

Another important concern that is brought to the fore when examining negotiation research through a negotiated order lens is the long-standing distinction between disputes and transactions (Gulliver, 1979). Once relationships are in the picture, the likelihood that any negotiation is a pure transaction falls precipitously. Brett and her colleagues (e.g., Brett, Goldberg, & Ury, 1990; Karambayya & Brett, 1989) attend to this distinction, but the bulk of social psychological research on negotiations focuses almost exclusively on transactions, ignoring disputes in general as well as the potential for disputes to erupt during transactions. In pure transactions, the critical outcomes are the parties' economic payoffs. In disputes, the critical outcomes include relationship continuity, intimacy, self-identity, self-worth, and reputation. Experimental and field methods relying on quantitative measures can easily accommodate payoffs in pure transactions, but the variables of interest in disputes pose challenges to these methods. Kurtzberg and Medvec (1999) cite a number of indirect ways of quantitatively measuring noneconomic effects of negotiations between related parties (e.g., how far apart the parties stand afterwards). Combinations of qualitative and quantitative measures, like those used by Jehn (1997) in her studies of group conflict, may open up opportunities for studying negotiated disputes as well as transactions. In an older study, Morrill (1991) used a combination of ethnographic, social network, and perceptual data to study conflict management among corporate executives, providing a promising methodological example for studying negotiated disputes among related parties.

In the field of close relationship research, theoretical and methodological challenges such as those discussed above are being tackled head-on (see Kashy & Levesque, 2000, for review of quantitative issues in close relationship research; Allen & Walker, 2000, for review of qualitative issues in close relationship research). For example, Kashy and Levesque apply a social relations model (SRM) to an analysis of friendship networks. The SRM allows dyadic variables to be separated into four distinct components: actor effects, partner effects, relationship effects, and group effects. These components have direct applications in negotiation research: The actor effect would measure one party's consistency in behavior and/or payoffs across multiple negotiation partners; the partner effect would measure the extent to which an actor elicits the same responses from others across negotiations; the relationship effect would measure the degree to which a behavior or outcome is unique to the dyadic negotiation; and the group effect would measure the mean of a variable across all negotiations within a particular group or organization. Turning to qualitative approaches in close relationship research, Allen and Walker describe ways of quantifying qualitative data, for example, taking the transcripts of narratives or interactions and coding them numerically for quality, valence, or frequency, and using these variables in statistical analyses. Recent research on relationships in negotiation has begun to move in this direction, but more work in this vein may allow deeper understanding of relationship issues.

There are many avenues that promise exciting adventures in future explorations of relationships and negotiations. The roads taken are likely to expose more of the underlying processes that precede, make up, and follow bargaining between related parties. Investigations into the critical normative, economic, and historical features of the social and organizational contexts in which negotiations take place are also likely to take a front seat, for these contextual features drive relationships, and negotiations are inexorably altered along the way. What we should be aiming for is not just a deeper understanding of each branch of the highway—relationships, negotiation processes, payoffs, perceptions, and so forth—but a comprehensive map of the negotiated order in the social systems around us.

NOTES

1. Boolean query, performed on PsychINFO, a database of articles from 1,944 academic and professional journals. Retrieved October 2004 from http://www.apa.org/psycinfo/
2. I am grateful to an anonymous reviewer for suggesting that relationships might in some circumstances cause negotiators to search outside of their personal relationships for negotiation partners.

REFERENCES

Allen, K. R., & Walker, A. J. (2000). Qualitative research. In C. Hendrick & S. S. Hendrick (Eds.), *Close relationships: A sourcebook* (pp. 19–30). Thousand Oaks, CA: Sage.

Argyle, M., & Henderson, M. (1985). The rules of relationships. In S. Duck & D. Perlman (Eds.), *Understanding personal relationships: An interdisciplinary approach* (pp. 63–84). Beverly Hills, CA: Sage.

Baker, W. E. (1984). The social structure of a national securities market. *American Journal of Sociology, 89*(4), 775–811.

Barry, B., & Oliver, R. L. (1996). Affect in dyadic negotiation: A model and propositions. *Organizational Behavior and Human Decision Processes, 67*(2), 127–143.

Berger, C. R. (2002). Goals and knowledge structures in social interaction. In M. Knapp & J. Daly (Eds.), *Handbook of interpersonal communication* (3rd ed., pp. 181–212). Thousand Oaks, CA: Sage.

Blumer, H. (1969). *Symbolic interaction.* Englewood Cliffs, NJ: Prentice Hall.

Bolton, G., & Ockenfels, A. (2000). A theory of equity, reciprocity, and competition. *American Economic Review, 90*, 166–193.

Bottom, W. P., Gibson, K., Daniels, S., & Murnighan, J. K. (1996). *Rebuilding relationships: Defection, repentance, forgiveness, and reconciliation.* Olin School of Business Working Paper, OLIN-96-06, St. Louis, MO.

Brett, J. M., Goldberg, S. B., & Ury, W. L. (1990). Designing systems for resolving disputes in organizations. *American Psychologist, 45*, 162–170.

Buchalter, R. (2003). Negotiating (im)permeable neighborhood borders. In L. R. Frey (Ed.), *Group communication in context: Studies of bona fide groups* (2nd ed., pp. 57–82). Mahwah, NJ: Lawrence Erlbaum Associates.

Burleson, B. R., Metts, S., & Kirch, M. W. (2000). Communication in close relationships. In C. Hendrick & S. S. Hendrick (Eds.), *Close relationships: A sourcebook* (pp. 245–258). Thousand Oaks, CA: Sage.

Canary, D. J., & Messman, S. J. (2000). Relationship conflict. In C. Hendrick & S. S. Hendrick (Eds.), *Close relationships: A sourcebook* (pp. 261–270). Thousand Oaks, CA: Sage.

Coleman, J. S. (1988). Social capital in the creation of human capital. *American Journal of Sociology, 94*, S95–S120.

DiMaggio, P., & Louch, H. (1998). Socially embedded consumer transactions: For what kinds of purchases do people most often use networks? *American Sociological Review, 63*(5), 619–638.

Drolet, A., Larrick, R., & Morris, M. W. (1998). Thinking of others: How perspective taking changes negotiators' aspirations and fairness perceptions as a function of negotiator relationships. *Basic and Applied Social Psychology, 20*(1), 23–31.

Dunn, J., & Schweitzer, M. (2005). Feeling and believing: The influence of emotion on trust. *Journal of Personality and Social Psychology, 88*(6), 736–748.

Fehr, E., & Gächter, S. (2000). Cooperation and punishment in public goods experiments. *American Economic Review, 90*(4), 980–995.

Fichman, M., & Levinthal, D. A. (1991). History dependence in professional relationships: Ties that bind. *Research in the Sociology of Organizations, 8*, 119–153.

Fletcher, G. J. O., & Fitness, J. (Eds.). (1996). *Knowledge structures in close relationships: A social psychological approach.* Mahwah, NJ: Lawrence Erlbaum.

Gottman, J. M. (1994). *What predicts divorce? The relationship between marital processes and marital outcomes.* Hillsdale, NJ: Lawrence Erlbaum.

Granovetter, M. (1974). *Getting a job.* Cambridge, MA: Harvard University Press.

Greenhalgh, L., & Chapman, D. I. (1998). Negotiator relationships: Construct measurement, and demonstration of their impact on the process and outcomes of negotiation. *Group Decision and Negotiation, 7*, 465–489.

Gulliver, P. H. (1979). *Disputes and negotiations: A cross-cultural perspective.* New York: Academic Press.

Halpern, J. J. (1994). The effect of friendship on personal business transactions. *Journal of Conflict Resolution, 38*(4), 647–664.

Halpern, J. J. (1997). Elements of a script for friendship in transactions. *Journal of Conflict Resolution, 41*(6), 835–868.

Jehn, K. (1997). A qualitative analysis of conflict types and dimensions in organizational groups. *Administrative Science Quarterly, 42*, 530–557.

Johnson, D. J., & Rusbult, C. E. (1989). Resisting temptation: Devaluation of alternative partners as a means of maintaining commitment in close relationships. *Journal of Personality and Social Psychology, 57*(6), 967–980.

Karambayya, R., & Brett, J. (1989). Managers handling disputes. *Academy of Management Journal, 32*, 687–704.

Kashy, D. A., & Levesque, M. J. (2000). Quantitative methods in close relationships research. In C. Hendrick & S. S. Hendrick (Eds.), *Close relationships: A sourcebook* (pp. 3–17). Thousand Oaks, CA: Sage.

Kelley, H., H. (1979). *Personal relationships: Their structures and processes*. Hillsdale, NJ: Laurence Erlbaum.

Keysar, B., Carter, T. J., & Swanson, A. T. (2004). *Perspective taking among friends and strangers in communication: Who is more egocentric?* Paper presented at the 44th annual meeting of the Psychonomic Society, Minneapolis, MN.

Kurtzberg, T., & Medvec, V. H. (1999). Can we negotiate and still be friends? *Negotiation Journal, 15*(4), 355–361.

Labianca, G., Brass, D. J., & Gray, B. (1998). Social networks and perceptions of intergroup conflict: The role of negative relationships and third parties. *Academy of Management Journal, 41*(1), 55–67.

Lange, P. A. M. Van, & Rusbult, C. E. (1995). My relationship is better than—and not as bad as—yours is: The perception of superiority in close relationships. *Personality and Social Psychology Bulletin, 21*(1), 32–44.

Manski, C. F. (2000). Economic analysis of social interactions. *Journal of Economic Perspectives, 14*(3), 115–136.

March, J., & Simon, H. A. (1958). *Organizations*. New York: Wiley.

McGinn, K. L., & Keros, A. T. (2003). Improvisation and the logic of exchange in embedded negotiations. *Administrative Science Quarterly, 47*, 442–473.

McGinn, K. L., Thompson, L. L., & Bazerman, M. H. (2003). Dyadic processes of disclosure and reciprocity in bargaining with communication. *Journal of Behavioral Decision Making, 16*, 17–34.

Miller, P. J. E., & Rempel, J. K. (2004). Trust and partner-enhancing attributions in close relationships. *Personality and Social Psychology Bulletin, 30*(6), 695–705.

Mizruchi, M. S., & Stearns, L. B. (2001). Getting deals done: The use of social networks in bank decision making. *American Sociological Review, 66*(5), 647–671.

Moore, D. A., Kurtzberg, T. R., Thompson, L. L., & Morris, M. W. (1999). Long and short routes to success in electronically mediated negotiations: Group affiliations and good vibrations. *Organizational Behavior and Human Decision Processes, 77*(1), 22–43.

Morrill, C. (1991). The customs of conflict management among corporate executives. *American Anthropologist, 93*(4), 871–893.

Murray, S., & Holmes, J. (1996). The construction of relationship realities. In G. J. O. Fletcher & J. Fitness (Eds.), *Knowledge structures in close relationships: A social psychological approach*. Mahwah, NJ: Lawrence Erlbaum Associates.

O'Connor, K., & Adams, A. A. (1999). What novices think about negotiation: A content analysis of scripts. *Negotiation Journal, 15*, 135–147.

Olson, G. M., & Olson, J. S. (2000). Distance matters. *Human–Computer Interaction, 15*(2 & 3), 139–178.

Polzer, J. T., Neale, M. A., & Glenn, P. O. (1993). The effects of relationships and justification in an interdependent allocation task. *Group Decision and Negotiation* 2: 135–148.

Rabin, M. (1993). Incorporating fairness into game theory and economics. *American Economic Review, 83*, 1281–1302.

Reis, H. T., & Knee, C. R. (1996). What we know, what we don't know, and what we need to know about relationship knowledge structures. In G. J. Fletcher & J. Fitness (Eds.), *Knowledge structures in close relationships: A social psychological approach.* (pp. 169–191). Hillsdale, NJ: Lawrence Erlbaum Associates.

Rubin, J. Z., Pruitt, D. G., & Kim, S. H. (1994). *Social conflict: Escalation, stalemate, and settlement* (2nd ed.). New York: McGraw-Hill.

Rusbult, C. E., & Arriaga, X. B. (1997). Interdependence theory. In S. Duch (Ed.), *Handbook of relationships: Theory, research and interventions* (pp. 221–250). Chichester, UK: John Wiley & Sons.

Rusbult, C. E., Verette, J., Whitney, G. A., & Slovik, L. F. (1991). Accommodation processes in close relationships: Theory and preliminary empirical evidence. *Journal of Personality and Social Psychology, 60*(1), 53.

Sacks, M. A., Reichart, K. S., & Proffitt, W. T. (1999). Broadening the evaluation of dispute resolution: Context and relationships over time. *Negotiation Journal, 15*(4), 339–345.

Salacuse, J. W. (1998). So, what is the deal anyway? Contracts and relationships as negotiating goals. *Negotiation Journal, 14*(1), 5–12.

Scott, R. A. (1976). Deviance, sanctions, and social integration in small-scale societies. *Social Forces, 54*(3), 604–620.

Seabright, M. A., Levinthal, D. A., & Fichman, M. (1992). The role of individual attachments in the dissolution of interorganizational relationships. *Academy of Management Journal, 35*(1), 122–160.

Seidel, M.-D. L., Polzer, J. T., & Stewart, K. J. (2000). Friends in high places: The effects of social networks on discrimination in salary negotiations. *Administrative Science Quarterly, 45*(1), 1–24.

Shapiro, D. L., Sheppard, B. H., & Cheraskin, L. (1992). Business on a handshake. *Negotiation Journal, 8*(4), 365–377.

Sias, P. M., Krone, K. J., & Jablin, F. M. (2002). An ecological systems perspective on workplace relationships. In M. Knapp & J. Daly (Eds.), *Handbook of interpersonal communication* (pp. 615–642). Thousand Oaks, CA: Sage.

Steinberg, L. D. (1981). Transformations in family relations at puberty. *Developmental Psychology, 17*, 833–840.

Strauss, A. (1978). *Negotiations: Varieties, contexts, processes, and social order.* San Francisco: Jossey-Bass.

Tenbrunsel, A. E., Wade-Benzoni, K. A., Moag, J., & Bazerman, M. H. (1999). The negotiation matching process: Relationships and partner selection. *Organizational Behavior and Human Decision Processes, 80*, 252–283.

Thompson, L. L., & DeHarpport, T. (1998). Relationships, goal incompatibility, and communal orientation in negotiations. *Basic and Applied Social Psychology, 20*(1), 33–44.

Thompson, L. L., Valley, K. L., & Kramer, R. M. (1995). The bittersweet feeling of success: An examination of social perception in negotiation. *Journal of Experimental Social Psychology, 31*, 467–492.

Tyler, T. R. (1989). The psychology of procedural justice: A test of the group-value model. *Journal of Personality and Social Psychology, 57*(5), 830–838.

Tyler, T. R. (1999). Why people cooperate with organizations: An identity-based perspective. In B. M. S. R. Sutton (Ed.), *Research in organizational behavior* (Vol. 21, pp. 201–246). Greenwich, CT: JAI.

Uzzi, B. (1997). Social structure and competition in interfirm networks: The paradox of embeddedness. *Administrative Science Quarterly, 42*(1), 35–67.

Uzzi, B. (1999). Embeddedness in the making of financial capital: How social relations and networks benefit firms seeking financing. *American Sociological Review, 64*, 481–505.

Walther, J. B. (1995). Relational aspects of computer-mediated communication: Experimental observations over time. *Organization Science, 6*(2), 186–203.

Wegner, D. M., Erber, R., & Raymond, P. (1991). Transactive memory in close relationships. *Journal of Personality and Social Psychology, 61*(6), 923–929.

8

Negotiation, Information Technology, and the Problem of the Faceless Other

JANICE NADLER and DONNA SHESTOWSKY

INTRODUCTION

*T*raditional approaches to research on negotiation do not typically consider the possibility that the type of communication media used by negotiators could be a factor affecting the negotiation itself. Early negotiation researchers had little reason to take note of the communication medium used by negotiators, because face-to-face negotiation was so typical that it was essentially assumed. But in the last two decades, the use of information technologies for general communication has grown exponentially. In fact, among Americans who are employed and have Internet access, 98% use e-mail at work (Fallows, 2002). Current estimates of instant messaging (IM) use indicate that some 53 million American adults use IM (representing 42% of those who have Internet access), and about 11 million American adults use it specifically to communicate at work (Shiu & Lenhart, 2004). Many people who use IM in the workplace report that it improves teamwork and saves time (Shiu & Lenhart, 2004). Outside of work, Internet users report that e-mail exchanges have improved their connections to family members and friends (Fallows, 2004). Thus, the use of information technology is increasingly pervasive both in and outside of the workplace.

The rapid increase in the use of information technology for communication generally makes it difficult to find reliable estimates of the frequency with which information technology is used for negotiation specifically. Two factors, however, give rise to an inference about the use of information technology for negotiations. First, we know that as a general matter, the use of information technology media such as e-mail has become mainstream in business communications, consumer transactions, and in interpersonal communication between friends and associates. Second, as pointed out by Fisher and Ury (1981), among others, negotiation is something that all of us do almost daily. Given these two fundamental realities, it is inevitable that we will have occasion to use technology in situations that involve negotiation.

In this chapter we focus on challenges imposed on negotiators by the use of communication technology. We refer to negotiations that take place using communication technology generally as "e-negotiations." Currently, a wide array of media is available to negotiators who communicate electronically. Some of these communication media have been available for many years, such as the telephone, fax machine, and videoconference. Other e-negotiations take place within the context of applications that are relatively new. For example, online dispute resolution systems such as onlineresolution.com provide individuals with a structured virtual forum for conducting negotiations. Similarly, Squaretrade, another well-known system, uses existing Web applications to provide a forum to mediate disputes arising from e-commerce (Nadler, 2001). E-negotiators can also opt to use traditional e-mail, or newer computer-mediated systems like IM. We occasionally address other forms of IT where they have been empirically examined, but we concentrate on e-mail for two primary reasons: first, e-mail has received the most attention in the existing empirical literature examining negotiation and information technology; and second, e-mail is now used so extensively to communicate.

Our focus on e-negotiations is situated within broader literatures that examine communication processes in virtual settings (DeSanctis & Monge, 1999; DeSanctis, Staudenmayer, & Wong, 1999; Hollingshead, McGrath, & O'Connor, 1993). The extent to which virtual organizations and teams are a viable alternative to those whose members work face to face is an issue that has received significant attention in the last decade (Griffith, Sawyer, & Neale, 2003). We examine one type of communication—negotiation—and explore the ways in which the use of information technology can shape the tone, the process, and even the outcome of negotiations. We argue that the extent to which the use of information technology helps or hinders negotiation processes and outcomes depends on how the technology in question interacts with other contextual variables, including the relationship between the parties, if any; the parties' sense of shared identity; the parties' perceptions of one another; how identifiable parties are to one another; and the nature and strength of the emotions evoked by the substance of the negotiation. We argue that these contextual variables are tied together by a common theme: the degree to which the negotiation counterpart is perceived, on the one hand, as a faceless, unknown stranger, or on the other hand, as a known, familiar person. Throughout this chapter we explore the various circumstances under which the use of communication technology leaves negotiators most vulnerable to erosion of the trust that is necessary for successful negotiation.

After briefly outlining our method of identifying the existing literature, we begin by discussing how the use of information technology can introduce perceptions of anonymity and lack of identifiability. We then discuss how these perceptions often have consequences for how negotiators perceive and behave toward their counterpart. As we turn to the specific context of negotiation, we discuss ways in which the diminished social cues that characterize e-negotiations can influence negotiator behavior. We assert that negotiator relationship is an important factor that interacts with the use of communication technology, but in the absence of a prior relationship, the potential hazards of using e-mail to negotiate with a stranger can be overcome to a large extent by establishing common ground beforehand. We conclude with a discussion of the overall normative implications of the research we reviewed, and a prospective look at how social psychological research can further advance our understanding of technology-mediated negotiation.

LITERATURE REVIEW

To organize our psychological review of the literature, we first conducted a thorough search of the English language published literature listed in the database PsychINFO. We limited our search to journal articles, books, and chapters that included "negotiation," "conflict," or "bargaining," as a keyword along with at least one of the following abstract terms: "technology," "online," "email," or "electronic communication." This search produced 60 citations dating from 1985 to 2004. We subsequently narrowed our search by reviewing the abstracts and omitting sources that, although technically inclusive with respect to the search terms, simply were not relevant to the theme of the chapter. We then broadened the search by adding relevant items listed in the reference lists of the set produced by the search. Although a thorough review of research outside the field of psychology is beyond the scope of this chapter, we expanded the theoretical component of our survey by examining how researchers in communications studies and organizational behavior have studied similar phenomena.

A snapshot of the overall field reveals that research results on e-negotiations have been, at times, seemingly contradictory. First, consider how economic outcomes might be influenced by the communication medium. Many negotiation exercises that are employed in experimental investigations are scored quantitatively, allowing for analysis and comparisons of how the parties fared economically (Thompson, 1990). For example, one can examine each individual negotiator's economic outcome separately to examine the absolute performance of each negotiator. Alternatively, one can sum two individual negotiators' outcome scores to obtain a "joint score," allowing examination of the extent to which an integrative outcome was reached (Thompson, 1990). Or, one can subtract one negotiator's score from her counterpart's score to examine the extent to which the economic outcome favored one party over the other. More broadly, one can examine the more general question of whether any agreement was reached. In situations in which the bargaining zone includes agreements that would make both parties better off than their respective alternatives to agreement, failure to agree (impasse) represents an economic failure for both parties.

Evidence on the question of whether negotiators' use of information technology influences the likelihood of achieving integrative agreements is mixed. Sometimes negotiators who interact via information technology are reported to have less success at achieving integrative outcomes than negotiators who interact face to face (Arunachalam & Dilla, 1995; Barefoot & Strickland, 1982), or by using paper and pencil (Griffith & Northcraft, 1994). Yet in other studies, information technology exerts no reliable observed effect on the ability to reach integrative agreements (Croson, 1999; Morris, Nadler, Kurtzberg, & Thompson, 2002; Naquin & Paulson, 2003; Purdy, Nye, & Balakrishnan, 2000).

A related question is whether using technology-mediated negotiation can advantage one party over the other, as measured by how equally the profit is split between the parties in the outcome that is eventually achieved. Sometimes it appears that negotiations conducted using information technology result in more equal outcomes than those conducted face to face (Croson, 1999), while other studies find no difference (Naquin & Paulson, 2003). Still others find that face-to-face negotiation results in more equal outcomes than does negotiation by e-mail (McGinn & Keros, 2002). In a study comparing e-mail with IM, negotiators who were given a technical advantage (they had better technical information on the items being negotiated) were able to "fast talk" their way into a better deal than their opponent when they used IM but not when they used e-mail; in this context e-mail negotiation resulted in more equal outcomes than negotiation via IM (Loewenstein, Morris, Chakravarti, Thompson, & Kopelman, in press).

Of course, there are other aspects of negotiation that are at least as important as *economic* outcomes (Curhan, Neale, Ross, & Rosencranz-Engelmann, 2004; Thompson, 1990). How does the use of information technology in negotiation affect social factors such as the parties' relationships, their experienced emotion during and after the negotiation, and their satisfaction with the process? Again, the evidence is inconclusive. On the one hand, parties who negotiate face to face have been reported to feel more confident in their performance and satisfied with the outcome than parties who negotiate via computer (Naquin & Paulson, 2003; Purdy et al., 2000; Thompson & Coovert, 2003). There is also evidence that compared to instances in which people negotiate face to face, negotiating via e-mail makes parties less likely to desire future interaction with their counterpart after the negotiation is finished (Naquin & Paulsen, 2003). On the other hand, other studies have compared the emotional content of messages in e-mail and face-to-face negotiations and found no differences (Morris et al., 2002). Finally, while some studies show that parties behave more cooperatively when negotiating face to face (Valley, Moag, & Bazerman, 1998, on face-to-face vs. writing; Purdy et al., 2000, on face-to-face vs. telephone or computer chat), others find that the cooperative advantage of face to face negotiation becomes less important when the parties are socially embedded in a relationship (McGinn & Keros, 2002); yet others find that negotiators behave *less* cooperatively when they have visual access to one another than when they do not (Carnevale & Isen, 1986; Carnevale, Pruitt, & Seilheimer, 1981). To begin understanding the differences in these findings, it helps to bear in mind the unique attributes of technology-mediated communication.

HOW IS COMMUNICATING VIA INFORMATION TECHNOLOGY DIFFERENT?

Communication using information technologies such as e-mail and IM differs structurally from face-to-face communication in important ways. Many of the features that are distinctive about electronic communication can create a context in which communicators experience the other person as more distant and unknown, and less salient and identifiable.[1] These distinguishing features of electronic media, we argue, have important implications for communication generally and negotiation in particular, especially when e-mail is the medium for negotiating with a counterpart with whom we have no prior relationship, no basis for in-group identification, and no reason to anticipate future interaction. These types of online interactions have already become common in the context of dispute resolution, as evidenced by the 30,000 eBay disputes mediated online in the year 2000 alone (Katsh & Rifkin, 2001). This phenomenon is bound to grow as government agencies, consumer groups, and industry associations are demanding that online businesses provide online dispute resolution mechanisms for their complaints (Yuan, Head, & Du, 2003). Deal-making e-negotiations are also likely to become more common as consumers negotiate some of their largest purchases, such as cars and mortgages, online (automiledirect.com, n.d.).

Although we briefly touch on the issue of relationships in the context of discussing the "faceless" other that figures in e-negotiations with strangers, a review of the negotiation literature on relationships more generally is the subject of the chapter by McGinn in chapter 7. In this section, we begin by explaining in more detail the distinguishing features of e-mail and similar information technologies, and the effects they can have on how we attend to our negotiation partner. We then describe more specifically how these features can intensify the perceived anonymity of our negotiation partner. Then, in the next section, we review evidence showing that, in general, perceived anonymity leads to lower perceived similarity, sympathy, and generosity toward the anonymous other—findings that have important implications for e-negotiations.

A fundamental characteristic of all of computer-mediated and online communication is that "they are, by definition, mediated by a machine and, therefore, relatively indirect means of interaction" (Spears & Lea, 1994, p. 691). The attributes of technology-mediated communication have been categorized and described in myriad ways by different researchers and theorists (e.g., Barry & Fulmer, 2004; Clark & Brennan, 1991; Daft & Lengel, 1984; Spears & Lea, 1994). One such attribute of technology is that it limits the dissemination of social information that comes from visual cues, cues that are common to face-to-face communication. As Friedman and Currall (2003) explain, when people communicate using e-mail or IM, for example, they are typically not present with one another in the same location at the same time, and cannot see one another, which limits visual and social cues. Visual cues convey information about the other person's facial expressions, gestures, and posture. In addition, visual cues allow each person to see what the other person is looking at and doing. When I see that your attention is directed toward me, I am likely to feel more involved in the interaction, and vice versa. Being in the same place at the same time also gives rise to a sense of shared surroundings. Communicating via e-mail or IM, by contrast, often involves being in a room alone, for many minutes or even hours at a time. E-mail and IM are text based, so that communicators are unable to hear one another's voice, which eliminates cues derived from intonation and the timing of speech.

E-mail messages also lack cotemporality; that is, when people communicate face to face, each person receives the other person's utterances at the time that they are spoken. By contrast, messages sent by e-mail are not typically read by the receiver at the same time they are sent, but often minutes, hours, or even days later. Lack of cotemporality can be useful for negotiators who want to think about their counterpart's last remark or confer with a colleague about the exchange, and gather more information or contemplate more deeply before formulating a response. Indeed, communicators are more likely to select e-mail when they desire greater control over the informational content of the interaction (Kayany, Wotring, & Forrest, 1996). For these reasons, the selection of e-mail as the mode of communication can be advantageous when the other party has more information or expertise than oneself. For example, in one study, negotiators playing the role of car seller were given an information advantage over the buyer, and when the negotiations were conducted using IM, sellers were able to take advantage of the buyer with "fast talk" (Loewenstein et al., in press). However, when negotiations were conducted via e-mail, "fast talk" was not effective, because buyers had greater latitude in timing their responses and reducing the seller's conversational dominance, resulting in buyers' and sellers' outcomes being more equal.

On the other hand, it is important to consider what is lost when cotemporality is absent. Smooth turn taking that normally characterizes face-to-face conversation depends on cotemporality, and without it the listener is unable to simultaneously and visually acknowledge attention, understanding, and agreement. Some types of electronic communication media, such as IM, are more cotemporal than e-mail, but the technology currently available still fails to provide parties to a communication with many of the cues that allow for the kind of smooth turn taking that characterizes face-to-face interaction.

The consequence is that the social bond that is formed in face-to-face conversation is attenuated, and instead people communicating via e-mail perceive the other person as less known and individualized than they would perceive the same partner face to face (Weisband & Atwater, 1999). This is a particular risk when people do not have much experience with e-mail as a medium. Inexperienced users are especially likely to miss opportunities to choose communication strategies that reduce equivocality in the message recipient (Carlson & Zmud, 1999). Perceptions of anonymity and lack of identifiability, as we will see in the next section, often have consequences for how we perceive and behave toward the other person.

ANONYMITY AND THE IDENTIFIABLE OTHER

The degree to which we perceive another person to be similar to ourselves in traits and attitudes, and to be worthy of our generosity or assistance, depends on the extent to which we perceive a personal connection with that person, no matter how trivial. The personal connection need not be friendship, acquaintanceship, or any kind of prior relationship. Instead, when we are asked to make predictions about the abilities or preferences of others, our predictions are strongly influenced by the extent to which we perceive these others as abstract and unknown on the one hand, or specific and real on the other hand (Alicke, Klotz, Breitenbecher, Yurak, & Vredenburg, 1995; Hsee & Weber, 1997). Thus, although we tend to rate ourselves more favorably than others on ambiguous traits like dependability, intelligence, and considerateness (Dunning, Meyerowitz, & Holzberg, 1989), these ratings are likely to depend on the abstractness of the others in question. If the other is the "average person" then my comparison tends to be more favorable toward myself than if the other is an individual stranger sitting next to me (Alicke et al., 1995). In other words, the less abstract the other person about whom I make a judgment, the more likely I am to judge that person as more similar to me. In addition to the abstractness of the other person, the degree of personal contact encourages feelings of similarity: specifically, I evaluate myself more favorably in reference to a stranger on a videotape than I do in reference to that same stranger who happens to be present in the room with me (Alicke et al., 1995).

The "identifiable other" effect extends to other judgments besides estimates of personality traits. For example, people estimate that an "average person" making a decision will choose a riskier option than themselves, but that the stranger sitting next to them will choose a similar option to the one they just chose for themselves (Hsee & Weber, 1997). Even more interesting for our purposes, the extent to which the other person is identifiable influences more than merely our judgments—it also affects our behavior toward other people. For example, responses to e-mail requests to participate in a survey have been shown to increase if the sender's photograph is included in the e-mail, thereby making the person more identifiable (Gueguen, Legoherel, & Jacob, 2003). In addition, the extent to which we are willing to give money to another person has also been shown to depend on how identifiable that person is (Bohnet & Frey, 1999; Small & Loewenstein, 2003). For example, in a dictator game experiment, half the participants received a card labeled "keep" (entitling them to keep $10 initially allocated to them) and half received a card labeled "lose" (obligating them to return their initial $10 allocation to the experimenter) (Small & Loewenstein, 2003). The "keep" recipients were then asked to decide how much, if any, of their $10 they would allocate to an anonymous participant in the "lose" condition. At some point, the "keep" participant drew a number that represented which particular "lose" participant would be assigned as their partner for the allocation. Strikingly, the "keep" participants whose partners were assigned *before* making the allocation decision allocated more money, on average, than the "keep" participants whose partners were assigned *after* making their allocation decision, even though all partners remained anonymous during and after the experiment.

Small and Loewenstein (2003) replicated this result in a field experiment in which citizens received five $1 bills in exchange for completing a survey, and were given the option to donate some or all of this money to the charity Habitat for Humanity. All participants were given brief descriptions of five different possible families who might receive the donation. Participants who were told that the recipient family *has already been chosen* allocated, on average, a greater portion of their $5 to the charity than participants who were told that the recipient family *will be chosen*, even though in both cases the recipient family was never actually disclosed. Taken together, these two studies show that people are more willing to help a target who is more identifiable than one who is more abstract, even when the act of identification conveys no information whatsoever about the characteristics of the target.

These findings regarding the identifiability of others have important implications for the use of information technology in negotiation. They suggest that, as a theoretical matter, we could expect that conceptualizing our negotiation counterpart as a specific, identifiable individual person reduces the perceived difference between the counterpart and ourselves (Alicke et al., 1995; Hsee & Weber, 1997), and under some circumstances could incline us to be more generous (Small & Loewenstein, 2003; Milgram, 1974) toward that person.

There is, in fact, some evidence that identifiability influences the outcomes of e-negotiations. Griffith and Northcraft (1994) conducted a job negotiation simulation in which the negotiators took turns submitting sealed bids, either by paper and pencil or through computer-mediated communication. Although all participants negotiated in the same room as their partners, some participants were informed as to the identity of their partner, and met and shook hands with that person; other partners remained anonymous to one another. Anonymous negotiators reached less integrative agreements than identified ones, suggesting that identifiability of the negotiation counterpart encourages cooperative behavior.

As detailed in the previous section, information technologies such as e-mail have characteristics that predispose negotiators to experience the counterpart as more unknown than the same counterpart would be viewed face to face. McGinn and Croson (2004) argue that properties of the communication medium (such as synchronicity and number of communication channels) are likely to affect social awareness—the extent to which a negotiator is conscious of and attentive to the other party. Social awareness itself reflects anonymity, similarity, liking, and expectation of future interaction, among other things. Kiesler, Zubrow, Moses, and Geller (1985) found that people using information technology (synchronous chat) to converse with another person rated that person less positively than did people communicating face to face. The former group also made more uninhibited comments, such as impolite remarks ("You are a jerk"), swearing, as well as statements of positive regard ("I like you"), and superlatives ("I like him best"). These kinds of uninhibited behaviors in this context may not be due to reduced social cues but, rather, to the norms that are relatively salient during the communication itself (Spears & Lea, 1994).

Research stemming from the SIDE (social identity model of deindividuation effects) model suggests that the effects of computer-mediated channels vary depending on whether the social context evokes individual identity or group identity (Spears & Lea, 1994). This model posits that the self is comprised of a range of self-categories including personal identities and social identities. These various identities, which are made more or less salient depending on the social context, prompt us to act in terms of the norms and standards associated with the salient identities. In one of many studies supporting the SIDE model, participants discussed a range of topics via a simple text-based synchronous computer-mediated system (Spears, Lea, & Lee, 1990). Participants were either separated from each other such that group members were relatively anonymous and isolated (i.e., they communicated using computers located in different rooms and did not meet each other), or they were able to have visual contact with one another (i.e., they communicated using computers located in the same room, facing each other). Of those who were anonymous and isolated, participants showed significantly greater opinion shift in the direction of group norms when their shared group identity was made salient than when individual identity was salient. Extending these results, we hypothesize that if negotiation counterparts are anonymous, then priming individual identities might produce less cooperation, and a greater desire on the part of each negotiator to pursue a highly favorable distributive outcome at the expense of the other, and the opposite tendency if a shared cooperative group identity is evoked. To the extent that negotiators can prime group identities associated with cooperation as they build rapport prior to exchanging offers, we would expect less competition and more integrative agreements.

When we communicate via technology, we attend less to the other person and more on the message they are disseminating (Matheson & Zanna, 1989). This focus on the message has potential benefits. For example, in a study comparing negoti-ations that took place either over the phone or in person (Morley & Stephenson, 1977), one negotiator in each dyad was given a strong case (i.e., a large number of high-quality arguments) to present whereas the other was assigned to present a weak case. The strong case was more successful in the phone condition (where negotiation partners were not visible) than in the face-to-face condition. By contrast, weak arguments were more successful when negotiations took place face to face as opposed to by phone. A clear implication of these findings is that the social constraint of the communication medium can affect the persuasion process that occurs during negotiations. In essence, with the availability of more social cues from a readily visualizable and identifiable counterpart participants were less affected by the quality of that counterpart's position during the negotiation. Thus, communicating via technology can lead negotiators to focus more on the content or quality of arguments made by their negotiation partner rather than being (mis)led into agreement by more peripheral factors like those made salient in face-to-face interactions (Dubrovsky, Kiesler, & Sethna, 1991; Hiltz, Johnson, & Turoff, 1986; Kiesler et al., 1985; Matheson, & Zanna, 1989).

This greater focus on the message content can have particularly negative consequences when the content of the message that one receives is negative or confrontational. Because we are more likely to react negatively when we encounter negative behaviors that we perceive as intentional and deliberate, and the reviewability feature of e-mail highlights the intentional communication behind the e-mails we receive, an e-mail that we perceive as negative can spark significant conflict (Friedman & Currall, 2003). Our ability to wait in response to a negative remark made over e-mail rather than responding immediately (which would be more likely if the remark were made during face-to-face conversation), provides us with the opportunity to ruminate over the negative communication. Such rumination can elevate anger (Rusting & Nolen-Hoeksema, 1998), which may in turn increase aggression and promote conflict. Insofar as emotional arousal enhances aggression when participants feel anonymous toward one another (Rogers & Ketchen, 1979), this path toward conflict has particular relevance to e-negotiations between strangers. As suggested by a recent study of online dispute resolution between strangers, particularly between buyers and sellers on eBay (Friedman et al., 2004), anger can inhibit conflict resolution.

In the sections that follow, we will see that when negotiators have a prior relationship, the anonymity inherent in e-mail makes little difference—negotiators rely on their prior relationship to keep the image of the counterpart salient, so that identifiability is not substantially diminished by the impoverished characteristics of electronic communication. People who communicate regularly with one another via e-mail can make up for some of the structural disadvantages associated with e-mail communication by finding ways to make the medium less impoverished (Carlson & Zmud, 1999). In fact, although computer-mediated group negotiations often produce worse outcomes compared to group negotiations that occur face-to-face, this media-based difference typically disappears when the same groups interact over time and negotiate again within a 9-week period (Hollingshead et al., 1993), suggesting that building working relationships can reduce some of the negative effects of computer-mediated communication. Indeed, we will see that the use of communication technology makes the biggest difference in negotiations when negotiators are strangers, or when they have not had the opportunity to connect socially beforehand, or when they have no basis to identify as members of the same in-group. The anonymous character of e-mail takes its greatest toll when no independent basis for social identification exists—in this context negotiators are left imagining a vague and abstract opponent whom they have never seen or met, making it more likely that negotiators will succumb to perceiving the counterpart as unlike themselves and unworthy of investing effort. In particular, we will focus on the contextual conditions in which the diminished social cues associated with the use of information technology are most likely to alter the process and outcomes of negotiations.

NEGOTIATORS' EXPECTATIONS ABOUT USING E-MAIL

Negotiators' expectations about the communication medium can be self-fulfilling. Anticipating a counterpart whose face we cannot see and voice we cannot hear can set up expectations about the counterpart's cooperativeness and the ultimate success of the negotiation. In particular, people who are preparing to negotiate face to face expect to trust the other party more than people who are preparing to negotiate using e-mail (Naquin & Paulsen, 2003). In this research, business students who were enrolled in different negotiation classes at the same university were randomly assigned by the experimenter to negotiate either face to face or using e-mail. Some students knew each other, some did not (these differences in relationship were randomly distributed across the different media). Yet, regardless of the existing relationship, negotiators who were about to negotiate via e-mail trusted the other party less than negotiators who were about to negotiate face to face. In both groups, trust increased slightly during the course of the negotiation, so that trust levels were slightly higher after the negotiation than they were before. Yet, media differences in trust persisted after the negotiation—even after an agreement was reached, negotiators who communicated via e-mail trusted the other party less than negotiators who communicated face to face.[2] In addition, negotiators who used e-mail expressed less interest in having future dealings with the other party compared with negotiators who communicated face to face. In this sense, the use of information technology can thwart the development of future relationships between the parties. Finally, e-mail negotiators were less satisfied with the outcome and less confident in their own performance compared to face-to-face negotiators.

This study demonstrates that for negotiators, the very idea of negotiating using e-mail sets up expectations of diminished trust, regardless of the existing relationship between the parties, and before the negotiation even begins (Naquin & Paulsen, 2003). More broadly, we hypothesize that the use of e-mail as a communication medium can influence the way in which negotiators make sense of the upcoming social interaction, which in turn influences perceptions of trust, satisfaction, and confidence, as well as the extent to which negotiators are willing to build a relationship with the counterpart afterward. The ways in which information technology interacts with negotiator relationship is addressed in the next section.

NEGOTIATOR RELATIONSHIP AND INFORMATION TECHNOLOGY

The relationship between negotiators is an important contextual variable that affects the extent to which negotiators successfully negotiate using information technology. As a general matter, it is easier for negotiators to reach integrative agreements if they already know and trust each other. For example, compared to mere acquaintances who negotiate, friends are more likely to achieve integrative agreements (Bazerman & Neale, 1992), and friends who use technology (either telephone or e-mail) to negotiate tend to behave more cooperatively, are more likely to strike a deal, and split the surplus more equally than strangers (McGinn & Keros, 2002).[3] Negotiations between dating couples are marked by greater information sharing and fewer pressure tactics compared to negotiations between mixed-sex strangers on the same negotiation task (Fry, Firestone, & Williams, 1983), and as a general matter, the stronger the relationship between negotiators, the more likely they are to share information (Greenhalgh & Chapman, 1998).

The greater likelihood of cooperation stemming from the existence of a prior relationship has been confirmed in the context of legal settlement negotiations. In a study of real legal disputes, Johnston and Waldfogel (2002) examined whether the existence of a prior relationship between opposing counsel would affect the likelihood of settlement in civil lawsuits. After examining thousands of cases, they found that cases were resolved more quickly and were less likely to go to trial when opposing counsel had faced each other in the past, than when the attorneys did not know each other.

Relationship Building and Information Technology

When negotiators do not begin with the advantage of a preexisting relationship, it may be possible to develop a relationship in the course of the negotiation. In fact, interpersonal relationships do develop even through computer-mediated communication channels, because people can adapt to the restrictions of the media (Walther & Burgoon, 1992). But building relationships can be much more challenging when negotiators use information technology because it generally takes longer to get to know one's negotiation partner.[4] In e-mail communication, physical appearance, accent, and other information frequently used to assign people to social categories are typically limited or absent, and one must use other sources, such as message content, to make these judgments (Krauss & Fussell, 1991). In fact, when people negotiate using technology they tend to focus on what is said rather than the individual characteristics of those who are communicating (Siegel, Dubrovsky, Kiesler, & McGuire, 1986). Ultimately, participants interacting via information technology often like their discussion partners less than those interacting face to face (Kiesler et al., 1985; Paese, Schrieber, & Taylor, 2003; Weisband & Atwater, 1999). This might be a particular risk when a negotiator forms a negative initial impression of his or her partner—under certain circumstances, those communicating via technology might amplify the perceptions they form about their partner, largely because they are apt to over-rely on the minimal amount of social information they have about this partner in making attributions (Lea & Spears, 1992).

Another difficulty stems from the fact that text-based messages are relatively deficient when it comes to conveying certain types of information (Kiesler, 1986; Matheson & Zanna, 1989; Trevino, Daft, & Lengel, 1990). Although there are ways to convey emotions via information technology, such as through explicit articulation of such states and the use of emoticons, more subtle information stemming from body language is generally absent. Because of the absence of nonverbal cues, e-mail communicators may find it difficult to send and receive affective or relational information, particularly in the context of newly developing relationships (Walther, 1995; Walther & Burgoon, 1992). Sometimes, of course, it may be possible to ascertain our negotiation partner's affective qualities even when face-to-face interaction does not take place—for example, their experienced emotions may "leak" from verbal expressions during the negotiation, or their moods may be learned from secondary sources of information, such as conversations with a third party prior to the negotiation (van Kleef, De Dreu, & Manstead, 2004; for a full review of the conceptual and empirical literature on affect in negotiation, see Barry, Fulmer, & Goates, chapter 6).

Although getting to know our negotiation partners' general temperament or feelings toward the specific negotiation issues at hand may be more difficult when we do not meet them face to face, a savvy negotiator may be able to make up for this "lost" information through other means. Indeed, there appear to be individual differences in the extent to which e-mail communicators convey affective information. For example, Thomson and Murachver (2001) conducted a discriminant analysis on e-mail content and found that compared to males, females made more references to emotion, provided more personal information, used more hedges (i.e., qualified language), and more intensive adverbs. This suggests that social cues are in fact present in electronic discourse, though they may be harder to detect than they would be in face-to-face communication.[5]

Nevertheless, in e-mail negotiations, the absence of smiles, nodding, handshakes, and the scarcity of questions about the other person or disclosures about the self might impede negotiators' attempts to establish a working relationship. One recent study compared text-only communication, text with audio, and text with both audio and video in a multi-issue negotiation involving the sale of a house (Yuan et al., 2003). It found that text-only communication was associated with less mutual understanding and acceptance, as well as less mutual trust compared to communication that included either audio or audio and video in addition to text.

The absence of nonverbal cues makes getting to know one's partner more difficult, and can thereby promote misunderstanding and conflict (Friedman & Currall, 2003). Relatedly, lack of nonverbal cues can also impede attempts to build the trust that is often considered necessary for creating an efficient and satisfactory agreement (Carnevale & Probst, 1997; Kramer & Tyler, 1996; Purdy et al., 2000). Indeed, trust is often cited as one of the critical hurdles to overcome in online negotiations (Katsh & Rifkin, 2001; Keen, Ballance, Chan, & Schrump, 2000). This notion is supported by findings that people with an informational advantage rarely exploited their partners when negotiating face to face but did so considerably when negotiating via written exchange (Valley et al., 1998). As we discuss in the next section, difficulties in establishing trust online between strangers has troubling implications for negotiation, where information exchange is crucial and lack of trust can form a barrier to information exchange.

Relationships and Information Exchange in Negotiation

Regardless of choice of communication medium, those who enter a negotiation as strangers must overcome a natural reluctance to share information openly. In general, people are more generous and empathic toward friends than toward strangers (Tesser, Pilkington, & McIntosh, 1989). The stronger the relationship between negotiators, the more likely they are to share information (Greenhalgh & Chapman, 1998; McGinn & Keros, 2002; see also McGinn, chapter 7). Lack of empathy and diminished trust in a negotiation between strangers might make the parties more reluctant to share information with one another. Failure to exchange sufficient information can be a barrier to successful negotiation, because sharing information about relative preferences and priorities is a necessary step in achieving efficient joint outcomes (Lax & Sebenius, 1987). Negotiators with an existing relationship may have already developed a sufficient basis for trust such that each believes that revealing some information about one's own preferences and priorities will be reciprocated by the other party, allowing for discovery of mutually beneficial negotiation solutions.

On the other hand, in the absence of an existing relationship, parties may have no reason to believe that revealing information will lead to mutually beneficial information exchange. Instead, revealing information to a stranger on the other side of the negotiation table might lead directly to that stranger using that information to that stranger's own benefit and one's own detriment. This in turn can lead the stranger-opponent to insist on a settlement that divides the surplus unequally or fails to leverage differences in preferences and priorities, and fails to increase the available pie of resources. An unequal division of the pie is a special concern for negotiators without a prior relationship, because an existing relationship increases negotiators' concern about the outcome of the other party (Loewenstein, Thompson, & Bazerman, 1989; Pruitt & Rubin, 1986). When we negotiate with a friend, we prefer that our counterpart's outcome be equal to our own; but when we negotiate with a stranger, we prefer to take more of the surplus for ourselves (Loewenstein et al., 1989). Negotiation with a stranger, therefore, poses a challenge for achieving outcomes that are efficient and fair to both sides.

Regardless of the existence of a prior relationship, the norm of reciprocity is fundamental in human behavior, even among strangers (Sober & Wilson, 1998). To what extent is reciprocity more likely in face-to-face negotiations compared to other media? The answer depends on the relationship and level of trust between the two parties. Valley, Thompson, Gibbons, and Bazerman (2002) assigned participants to roles of buyer or seller of a fictitious commodity. The experimenter randomly assigned each party's valuation of the commodity, and this valuation was known only to that party. Buyer/seller dyads then engaged in a double auction in which they each simultaneously submitted a sealed bid for the commodity, so that a trade would occur only if the buyer's bid exceeded the seller's asking price. All participants were strangers to one another, and in their opportunity to communicate prior to bidding, they rarely engaged in mutual revelation of their randomly assigned valuations (this occurred in only 4% of cases). Interestingly, McGinn and Keros (2002) used the identical bilateral bargaining game but with people belonging to the same social network (participants in a semester-long course), and found that mutual revelation of values occurred a great deal more often (26% of the cases). Although indirect media such as e-mail can promote competitive behavior between negotiators compared to face-to-face negotiations, reciprocity sparked by a cooperative gesture can make e-negotiations significantly less competitive. For example, when one party made a disclosure of private information regarding his BATNA (best alternative to a negotiated agreement)—and by implication, his reservation price—at the start of a purely distributive e-negotiation, competition was suppressed, leading the other party to both make less demanding offers as well as settle for less profit (Paese et al., 2003). Disclosing one's reservation price—ordinarily considered a very risky move—worked to the discloser's advantage in this context.

In fact, such disclosures promoted similar generosity even when negotiators were anonymous to one another (Paese et al., 2003).

In a different study involving e-mail negotiations among strangers, reciprocal exchange of crucial information about relative preferences and priorities was higher among negotiators who had schmoozed and developed a basis for trust (Nadler, 2004). That is, compared to negotiators who did not schmooze, negotiators who chatted with their counterpart prior to negotiating were more likely to receive multiple-issue priority information from their counterpart immediately following their own provision of such information. Negotiators who schmoozed expected more strongly to cooperate, did cooperate by sharing more relevant multiple-issue information, and received more cooperation in return from their counterpart. This pattern of multiple-issue information sharing is necessary for negotiators to avoid impasse by recognizing numerous, mutually beneficial solutions in the negotiation. In this mixed-motive negotiation, failing to exchange information resulted in negotiators failing to integrate their interests, leaving little or no joint surplus to share.

Gender differences in communication are also illustrative here. Guadagno and Cialdini (2002) hypothesized that because women attend more than men to interpersonal aspects of social exchange, there may be gender differences in persuasion that interact with communication medium because of the limited opportunity to build relationships using e-mail. They used a task in which participants communicated with a same-gender confederate regarding the desirability of comprehensive exams. In this task, women were more persuaded by the confederate when communicating face to face than when communicating via e-mail, whereas men showed no difference in openness to persuasion across media. In a follow-up study, they showed that women communicating via e-mail with *no* opportunity to build a relationship beforehand were least persuaded by the confederate; on the other hand, men communicating face to face who had established a *competitive* relationship with the confederate beforehand showed the least agreement with the confederate. The researchers argued that because women were more focused than men on relationship formation and cooperation, these goals were more salient and attainable when communicating face to face than via e-mail and when they had already established a relationship with their counterpart. Together, these studies suggest that the importance of establishing a relationship between parties conducting e-mail negotiations may be greater for women than for men.

As we have seen, there are reasons to anticipate that negotiations between strangers are more challenging when the parties cannot see or hear one another, and their messages are not cotemporal. It is in this context of e-mail negotiation with an abstract, anonymous, faceless other, with whom we have no basis for forming a shared identity, the medium of communication looms large in its effects on negotiator expectations, and on the negotiation itself. Information exchange requires cooperation, and there is evidence that the likelihood of cooperative behavior increases when people meet face to face.

Visual Access, Cooperation, and Negotiator Relationship

Experimental investigations in which bargainers playing a game communicate in intentionally impoverished environments (e.g., side by side, intercom, telephone, e-mail) have led to intriguing findings with respect to cooperative behavior. For example, when players of a repeated prisoner's dilemma game are permitted to have a face-to-face meeting prior to deciding whether to defect or cooperate, the cooperation rate is higher than when players are not permitted to communicate (Sally, 2000). Interestingly, being asked to *imagine* a face-to-face meeting with the other player and to write down what might be said during the imaginary meeting, leads to cooperation rates just as high as when a real meeting actually takes place. In other words, transforming the counterpart from a faceless, unknown stranger into a specific person (even if only in one's own imagination) leads to more cooperative behavior.

In another study examining the role of visual access in generating cooperation, all players had an initial meeting prior to playing a one-shot prisoner's dilemma game (Drolet & Morris, 2000). Players met either face to face or via speaker-phone. Cooperation rates were higher among players who met face to face compared with those who met using speakerphone. Rapport between players was rated by outside observers and by the players themselves; face-to-face meetings led to greater rapport, which in turn led to greater cooperation, as compared with speakerphone meetings. Again, the opportunity to perceive the opponent as more identifiable and salient led to more cooperative behavior toward that opponent.

The increased cooperation resulting from face-to-face contact (either real or imagined) in the prisoner's dilemma bargaining context also extends to the nego-tiation context. In fact, visual access, in and of itself, can dramatically increase cooperative behavior and, as a result, improve negotiated outcomes. For example, negotiators who played the roles of union and management representatives in a simulated strike negotiation were permitted to communicate only through exchange of written offers (Drolet & Morris, 2000). The sooner the strike was settled, the more beneficial the outcome for both parties. Some negotiators were permitted to sit face to face while silently exchanging written offers; others were asked to sit side by side instead. Compared to negotiators sitting side by side, negotiators who faced each other settled the strike more quickly and as a result, achieved better outcomes, simply by virtue of seeing the other person as written offers were silently exchanged.

McGinn and Croson (2004) argue that in settings where social perceptions and intimacy have not been established, such as negotiations between strangers, the lack of visual access, synchronicity, and efficacy inherent in e-mail can result in less cooperation, coordination, truth telling, and rapport building.[6] But where social perceptions and intimacy are already established, as in negotiations between friends, the medium might not make much or any difference. McGinn and Keros (2002) demonstrated this empirically. In a single-issue, distributive negotiation involving the sale of a lamp, friends who used information technology (telephone or e-mail) to negotiate behaved more cooperatively, were more likely to strike a

deal and split the surplus more equally than strangers. But when the nego
was conducted face to face, there was no difference between friends and strangers
in cooperation, likelihood of a deal, or equality of surplus. This finding suggests
that even in a purely distributive, single-issue negotiation, the use of information
technology can alter the likelihood of success depending on the extent to which
the other party is perceived as a stranger. In the absence of face-to-face contact,
the more a negotiator feels connected to the counterpart, the more likely they are
to trust the other person enough to behave cooperatively in such a way that leads
to a greater probability of agreement and more equal sharing of surplus. This
suggests that it takes relatively little work to be aware of, and receptive to, a similar
and liked other, even over the telephone or e-mail, but that it takes considerable
cognitive and emotional energy to imagine and attend to an e-mail counterpart
who is unknown and invisible.

Establishing Common Ground in the Absence of a Prior Relationship

The existence of a prior relationship with one's negotiation counterpart can confer
numerous advantages on negotiation outcomes and processes. One possible way
to remedy the drawbacks associated with negotiating with strangers using e-mail
is simply for negotiators to avoid using e-mail when negotiating with a stranger.
Of course, face-to-face negotiation will not always be an option. Constraints
imposed by distance, time, and other resources often preclude face-to-face negotiation. Given that e-negotiations are often unavoidable, we must consider the
possibility of establishing ties with the counterpart with whom we are about to
negotiate. Although we cannot always choose our negotiation counterpart, we
sometimes have the opportunity to modify, in advance of the negotiation, the
extent to which the counterpart is a perfect stranger.

Findings from three different studies on "schmoozing" prior to negotiating via
e-mail support the notion that getting to know one's counterpart, even a little,
prior to engaging in e-negotiation can contribute to greater cooperation and
likelihood of agreement. In all three studies, negotiators communicated exclusively
via e-mail; there was no face-to-face control group. And in all three studies,
negotiators were instructed to take steps to connect with the other person prior
to negotiating.

In the first study, prenegotiation contact with the counterpart was established
by exchanging minimal but personal information via e-mail (Moore, Kurtzberg,
Thompson, & Morris, 1999). Half of the participants negotiated via e-mail with a
counterpart from the same business school (in-group), and the other half negotiated via e-mail with a counterpart from a different business school (out-group).
In addition, half of the participants exchanged photographs and short biographies
and conducted a getting to know you e-mail conversation before negotiating
(schmoozing); the other half did not (no schmoozing). When negotiators were
from different schools, schmoozing made a big difference as to whether an agreement was reached (6% impasse rate with schmoozing; 29% impasse rate with no

schmoozing). But when negotiators were from the same school, schmoozing made no difference (about 7% to 8% rate in both groups). The most striking result here is that where there is no basis for common ground between negotiators (strangers who attend rival business schools who did not schmooze before negotiating), communication medium can break a deal, even though such a consequence is very unlikely between negotiators with some basis for common ground—even when common ground consists only of a brief chat, a photo, and a bio, or, alternatively, membership in the same in-group. Thus, in the presence of a basis for common ground—whether it is a prior relationship, in-group membership, or a brief personal e-mail chat before negotiating—information technology did not seem to hinder negotiations. But in the absence of some basis for common ground, the use of information technology as a negotiation medium was markedly problematic.

Exchange of personal information via e-mail is one way of establishing common ground sufficiently, at least in some contexts, to overcome the disadvantages conferred by the e-mail medium. Another approach to schmoozing is for negotiators to have a verbal conversation prior to using e-mail to negotiate. Two experimental investigations have examined negotiations conducted exclusively through e-mail, where each negotiator's counterpart was a student at a different school (Morris et al., 2002 [business students]; Nadler, 2004 [law students]). To induce schmoozing, half of the negotiators were instructed to have a 5- to 10-minute getting to know you telephone conversation with the counterpart prior to negotiating; the other half did not. In both studies, schmoozers had better social outcomes than nonschmoozers: They had more positive feelings toward their counterpart, as well as a better rating of their working relationship. Social lubrication improved outcomes in e-mail negotiation through the mechanism of increased felt rapport between negotiators. This result becomes quite impressive when we recall that the manipulation was simply a 5-minute phone call before a negotiation process that took, in many cases, a full week to complete.

Negotiators in these two studies who did not chat also found the process of e-mail communication more difficult. They ended up feeling significantly more angry, annoyed, and cold toward their opponent, as well as less friendly and pleasant, compared to negotiators who had the opportunity to chat with their opponent. The increased cooperation and trust that the telephone chat engendered led to smoother interactions and a friendlier attitude toward the opponent after the negotiation concluded. This attitude was also associated with respect: Negotiators who schmoozed formed an impression of their counterpart as significantly more accomplished, skilled, effective, and perceptive than the impression formed by negotiators who did not schmooze. Attitudes toward the counterpart at the conclusion of a negotiation are noteworthy, because how one feels at the *end* of an interaction is the critical factor in determining the person's overall subsequent evaluations of that interaction (Thompson, Medvec, Seiden, & Kopelman, 2001). If the counterpart leaves the negotiation feeling good about the process and outcome, that person is more likely to engage cooperatively in future negotiations and to fulfill the terms of the current agreement.

Schmoozing over the telephone prior to an e-mail negotiation not only improves the social process and outcome of negotiations, but can also dramatically improve the likelihood of a favorable outcome for both parties. In one study, negotiators who schmoozed prior to an e-mail negotiation were over *four times* as likely to reach an agreement for the purchase of a car, compared to negotiators who did not schmooze (Nadler, 2004). Only 9% of negotiators who schmoozed via a 5-minute telephone chat failed to reach an agreement, whereas nearly 40% of nonschmoozers failed to reach agreement. The high percentage of "no schmooze" pairs that were unable to reach agreement is especially noteworthy in light of the fact that a positive bargaining zone existed, making it economically desirable for each party to reach a negotiated agreement. Interestingly, negotiators who did not schmooze with their counterpart prior to negotiating reported feeling more competitive and less cooperative toward their counterpart than negotiators who did schmooze. Consistent with their cooperative mental model of the negotiation process, negotiators who schmoozed prior to negotiating exchanged significantly more information relating to their relative priorities on multiple issues compared to negotiators who did not schmooze. Thus, strangers who established common ground via a brief telephone chat prior to using e-mail to negotiate felt more cooperative in the negotiation and trusted the other negotiator enough to share the kind of information necessary to reach an efficient solution. In the absence of a prior relationship, the potential hazards of negotiating with a stranger using e-mail can be overcome to a large extent by establishing common ground beforehand.

Especially revealing in this study was an examination of precisely why some negotiators reached impasse. For all "schmooze" pairs that failed to reach agreement, the last offer on the table had a value below the reservation price of one of the parties. In other words, none (0%) of the "schmooze" pairs walked away from an offer that was more profitable than their outside option. Given the value of the last offer, it is understandable that one of the parties would refuse to agree to it. But the story for the "no schmooze" pairs was quite different: The value of the last offer on the table exceeded both parties' reservation price 64% percent of the time. Thus, most of the "no schmooze" negotiators who reached an impasse walked away from a deal that would have made each of them better off relative to impasse.

Finally, it is worthy of note how negotiators' use of information technology interact with the level of trust between the parties. One of the many ways to define trust is the expectation that the other person will cooperate with you when you are in a vulnerable position. Both Morris et al. (2002) and Nadler (2004) found that e-mail negotiators who had an initial telephone chat with their opponents left the negotiation with significantly more trust in their counterparts than did negotiators who did not chat initially. Note that it is in the particular context of the absence of any basis for common ground (here, strangers who had no opportunity to chat before negotiating and who had no basis for ingroup identification), that the use of information technology is most detrimental to the likelihood of negotiated agreement and building a basis for future exchange.

Yet, we have also seen that negotiators can take steps to increase the identifiability of their negotiation counterpart in an effort to offset the negative effects of anonymity. For example, the simple act of making personal telephone contact with the opponent prior to negotiating via e-mail enabled negotiators to substitute perceptions of an invisible, abstract opponent with a specific human being who shares one's own characteristics. As a result, negotiators who engaged in small talk prior to negotiating via e-mail were more successful at exchanging the right kind of information necessary to reach agreement, and at recognizing a beneficial agreement when the opportunity for such an agreement presented itself (Morris et al., 2002; Nadler, 2004). Alternatively, simple acknowledgment of shared social identity can also assist in reducing anonymity (Moore et al., 1999). Another possibility is to include a photograph in an e-mail (Gueguen, Legoherel, & Jacob, 2003), a technique that has been associated with gaining compliance with unsolicited requests sent by strangers.

Although mutual disclosure is generally at a minimum in low-efficacy, text-only negotiations (McGinn & Croson, 2004), there is also some evidence that, if left to their own devices, negotiators using e-mail will naturally attempt to establish common ground by engaging in an initial exchange of personal information that promotes cooperation and trust. Tidwell and Walther (2002) examined how computer-mediated communication partners spontaneously exchange personal information in initial interactions, focusing on the effects of communication channels on self-disclosure, question-asking, and how the communicating parties reduce uncertainty (i.e., lack of knowledge) about the stranger with whom they were interacting. Participants met either face to face or via information technology (using a semi-synchronous e-mail system) with a stranger for the purpose of solving a decision-making problem, or to simply get to know one another. Regardless of the task at hand, those communicating via technology used a significantly higher proportion of questions and produced a higher proportion of self-disclosures. By contrast, those interacting face to face displayed a greater proportion of *other* types of expressions, such as greetings, back-channeling statements, imperatives, statements about third parties, statements of fact that were not personal in nature, and other filler items that were neither questions nor statements of self-disclosure. Acquaintanceship can therefore develop spontaneously through mutual disclosure via information technology. Because the task in this study was getting to know the other person or jointly solving a problem, the conscious adoption of a problem-solving or getting to know you task orientation by negotiators prior to beginning the negotiation might be useful for establishing common ground and diminishing the problems discussed earlier associated with strangers negotiating via information technology.

CONCLUSION

The manner in which the use of information technology affects negotiation processes and outcomes depends on how the technology in question interacts with the parties' perceptions of one another. When the parties have no prior relationship, no prior contact, and no sense of shared identity, the conditions are ripe for

communication medium exerting the strongest influence on negotiator perceptions and behavior. In particular, when the structure of the negotiation is a
complex, potentially integrative negotiation that requires reciprocal information
sharing, the inability to see or hear the other person in conjunction with lack of
cotemporality can exacerbate initial distrust, leading to reluctance to engage in the
kind of reciprocal exchange of information required to reach a high-quality agreement, or any agreement at all, for that matter. Unlike a face-to-face negotiation,
where the rapport that results from visual access facilitates cooperation and mutually beneficial negotiation outcomes, e-mail negotiation is hampered by the
absence of information deriving from facial expressions, eye contact, gestures,
smooth turn taking, and cotemporality. As we have explored, the consequences of
these deficiencies that characterize e-mail and other communication technologies
are often minimal for negotiators who have already established common ground
with one another; at the same time, these characteristics can often make or break
a deal between unknown counterparts. Yet, thankfully, there are corrective measures that can be taken by negotiators to avoid the problems that arise when
negotiating with an unknown, anonymous counterpart. These measures entail, in
some sense, "unmasking" the faceless other. E-mail negotiators can rely on similarities between themselves and their counterpart as a basis for generating a sense
of shared social identity to facilitate a smooth negotiation process. In the absence
of either visual access or a prior relationship, negotiators can establish rapport and
common ground by schmoozing, by means of a prenegotiation, a getting to know
you chat, or mutual self-disclosure.

As research on technology-mediated negotiation continues, we expect to learn
more about how and why it differs from face-to-face negotiation. We also expect
to see more negotiation research on forms of technology other than text-based
e-mail. Industry analysts predict that IM will soon surpass e-mail as the primary
online communication tool (Heim, 2003). Surely research on the use of IM in
negotiations will also expand, thereby shedding greater light on the generalizability
of the faceless-other phenomenon to other technologies.

The future of the faceless other in technology-mediated negotiation is unclear.
Over time, as electronic communication media become richer in terms of impart-
ing understanding across communication partners, as negotiation via technology
becomes more common, and as people develop their own means for making the
media richer, the differences in how we negotiate online as opposed to face to
face might diminish. We might psychologically adapt to technology in such a way
that makes strangers with whom we negotiate seem less distant and anonymous.
It is also possible that, as technology continues to change, the structural gap
between face-to-face communication and technology-mediated communication
might become more narrow, thereby easing the adaptation process. For example,
as Westmyer, DiCioccio, and Rubin (1998) point out, "with the growth of technology, face-to-face communication is now available via computer-mediated systems, allowing two-dimensional, face-to-face interaction in real time" (pp. 45–46).
Is negotiation using this type of communication media akin to negotiating face to
face? Or will we continue to perceive our e-negotiation partner as distant and
unfamiliar? Will our expectations and perceptions with respect to any differences

between face-to-face and technology-mediated negotiation change as the use of technology becomes more familiar? These questions still remain unanswered. As Shell (1995) articulated a decade ago,

> As the telephone, computer, and television merge into a single, interactive, sound-and-picture technology, people are inevitably going to do deals and resolve disputes in cyberspace. The interesting question is what sort of help they are going to get from negotiation and ADR experts and whether the means can be found to use computers to promote wiser and more efficient outcomes. (p. 118)

As we have come ever closer to making this kind of hybrid technology mainstream, this question looms even larger.

Given the current state of technology options, people often prefer to negotiate face to face (Finholt, Sproull, & Kiesler, 1990). When a voice option is added to a text-based system to create a hybrid system, many people abandon the text function and opt to negotiate by voice (Yuan et al., 2003), suggesting that newer technologies that incorporate direct verbal communication might eventually trump the use of text-based e-mail as a preferred platform for remote negotiations. But our relative preference for face-to-face or direct verbal communication during negotiation may very well change. Media choice and adaptation tends to be shaped by individual preferences for using particular media in particular ways, as well as by one's skill in doing so (Westmyer et al., 1998). As we become more familiar with new technologies and adapt to their use for negotiation, our preferences and skills may develop such that we prefer to use technology for at least some stages of the majority of our negotiations. As Yuan and colleagues (2003) point out, "negotiations may involve many stages, such as greeting, background information exchange, agenda setting, issue discussion, and final agreement formulation, and different media may be used by negotiators to perform different tasks" (p. 107). Thus, we may develop a preference to rapport-build using face-to-face communication but to generate ideas and brainstorm possible settlements using technology (Mennecke, Valacich, & Wheeler, 2000). Future research might explore more deeply how preferences and utility for using technology at various stages of negotiation change over time, and as a function of experience with the related technology.

With the expected growth of online dispute resolution services, we also expect to see more research on real as opposed to simulated negotiations (e.g., Friedman et al., 2004). Online dispute resolution organizations are uniquely poised to contribute to our understanding of real-life negotiations via technology, which would be a valued complement to existing experimental research. We also expect to see more research on online disputes generally. As Brett and Gelfand (chapter 9) point out, some negotiation is geared primarily toward defining a future relationship between the two involved parties (i.e., "deal making"), whereas other negotiations, while also aimed at defining a future relationship, are concerned primarily with resolving past conflict between the parties (i.e., "dispute resolution"). To date, most of the research on negotiation via information technology investigated deal making; future research should follow Friedman et al. and Katsh and Rifkin (2001) in more closely examining the online resolution of disputes.

ACKNOWLEDGMENTS

We would like to thank Bruce Barry and Leigh L. Thompson for helpful suggestions. Preparation of this chapter was supported in part by the American Bar Foundation. Correspondence concerning this chapter should be addressed to: Janice Nadler, Northwestern University School of Law, 357 E. Chicago Ave., Chicago, IL 60611; jnadler@northwestern.edu.

NOTES

1. There are, however, situations where this is not the case. For example, when communicators have positive-valenced goals such as relationship-building, computer-mediated interactions can be highly personal, resulting in the development of close relationships (Walther, 1995). The development of virtual communities, online friendships, and Internet dating are examples of this phenomenon. By contrast, negotiations necessarily entail *competing* interests or goals, and the conflict inherent in negotiation can, as we argue in this chapter, be exacerbated in e-negotiations (Friedman & Currall, 2003).

2. Note that negotiators in this study were asked about trust only once—either before or after the negotiation, but not both. This avoided any possible contamination of postnegotiation trust ratings because of priming effects of prenegotiation trust ratings.

3. One study comparing dating couples and strangers found that dating couples underperformed compared to mixed-sex stranger dyads in terms of achieving high joint outcomes (Fry, Firestone & Williams, 1983). The researchers concluded that relationship maintenance goals may have contributed to this difference.

4. Social information processing theory from the communications field suggests that, given sufficient time and message exchanges for impression formation and relational development, relational communication in later stages of computer-mediated communication will parallel that which takes place face to face (Walther, 1995).

5. The SIDE model addresses a similar point. According to Spears and Lea (1994), despite the conventional wisdom that computer-mediated communication (CMC) restricts social cues generally and therefore reduces the effects of status and power, research in line with the SIDE model suggests that the social cues that do exist in indirect communication—which, they argue, are typically cues to role, status, and category membership—can become more important rather than less so. Thus, for this reason, "the 'faceless' nature of the communication in CMC may often reinforce the bureaucratic or hierarchical dimensions of interaction" (p. 452).

6. But some types of lies, namely monitor-dependent lies in which the deceiver stands to benefit from being able to monitor the target's reaction, are actually more common when negotiation partners have visual access to one another than when they do not (Schweitzer, Brodt, & Croson, 2002).

REFERENCES

Alicke, M. D., Klotz, M. L., Breitenbecher, D. L., Yurak, T. J., & Vredenburg, D. S. (1995). Personal contact, individuation, and the better-than-average effect. *Journal of Personality and Social Psychology, 68,* 804–805.

Arunachalam, V., & Dilla, W. (1995). Judgment accuracy and outcomes in negotiation: A causal modeling analysis of decision-aiding effects. *Organizational Behavior and Human Decision Processes, 61,* 289–304.

automiledirect.com. (n.d.) Why negotiate your purchase online. Retrieved October 20, 2004, from http://www.automiledirect.com/why_info

Barefoot, J. C., & Strickland, L. H. (1982). Conflict and dominances in television-mediated interactions. *Human Relations, 35*(7), 559–565.

Barry, B., & Fulmer, I. S. (2004). The medium and the message: The adaptive use of communication media in dyadic influence. *Academy of Management Review, 29,* 272–292.

Bazerman, M. H., & Neale, M. (1992). *Negotiating rationally.* New York: Free Press.

Bohnet, I., & Frey, B. S. (1999). The sound of silence in prisoner's dilemma and dictator games. *Journal of Economic Behavior and Organization, 38,* 43–57.

Carlson, J. R., & Zmud, R. W. (1999). Channel expansion theory and the experiential nature of richness perceptions. *Academy of Management Journal, 42,* 153–170.

Carnevale, P. J. D., & Isen, A. M. (1986). The influence of positive affect and visual access on the discovery of integrative solutions in bilateral negotiation. *Organizational Behavior and Human Decision Processes, 37,* 1–13.

Carnevale, P. J., & Probst, T. M. (1997). Conflict on the Internet. In S. Kiesler (Ed.), *Culture of the Internet* (pp. 233–255). Mahwah, NJ: Lawrence Erlbaum Associates.

Carnevale, P. J. D., Pruitt, D. G., & Seilheimer, S. D. (1981). Looking and competing: Visual access in integrative bargaining. *Journal of Personality and Social Psychology, 40,* 111–120.

Clark, H., & Brennan, S. (1991). Grounding in communication. In L. Resnick, J. Levine, & S. Teasley (Eds.), *Perspectives on socially shared cognition* (pp. 127–149). Washington, DC: American Psychological Association.

Croson, R. T. A. (1999). Look at me when you say that: An electronic negotiation simulation. *Simulation and Gaming, 30*(1), 23–37.

Curhan, J. R., Neale, M. A., Ross, L., & Rosencranz-Engelmann, J. (2004). *The O. Henry effect: The impact of relational norms on negotiation outcomes.* Manuscript submitted for publication.

Daft, R. L., & Lengel, R. H. (1984). Information richness: A new approach to managerial behavior and organizational design. In L. L. Cummings & B. M. Shaw (Eds.), *Research in organizational behavior* (Vol. 6, pp. 199–233). Homewood, IL: JAI Press.

DeSanctis, G., & Monge, P. (1999). Communication processes for virtual organizations. *Organization Science, 10,* 693–703.

DeSanctis, G., Staudenmayer, N., & Wong, S.-S. (1999). Interdependence in virtual organizations. In C. Cooper & D. Rousseau (Eds.), *Trends in organizational behavior* (pp. 81–104). New York: John Wiley.

Drolet, A. L., & Morris, M. (2000). Rapport in conflict resolution: Accounting for how face-to-face contact fosters mutual cooperation in mixed-motive conflicts. *Journal of Experimental Social Psychology, 36,* 26–50.

Dubrovsky, V. J., Kiesler, S., & Sethna, B. N. (1991). The equalization phenomenon: Effects in computer-mediated and face-to-face decision-making groups. *Human-Computer Interaction, 6,* 119–146.

Dunning, D., Meyerowitz, J. A., & Holzberg, A. D. (1989). Ambiguity and self-evaluation: The role of idiosyncratic trait definitions in self-serving assessments of ability. *Journal of Personality and Social Psychology, 57,* 1082–1090.

Fallows, D. (2002, December 8). Email at work. *Pew Internet & American Life Project.* Retrieved September 27, 2004, from http://www.pewinternet.org/pdfs/PIP_Work_Email_Report.pdf

Fallows, D. (2004, August 11). The Internet & daily life. *Pew Internet & American Life Project.* Retrieved September 27, 2004, from http://www.pewinternet.org/pdfs/PIP_Internet_and_Daily_Life.pdf

Finholt, T., Sproull, L., & Kiesler, S. (1990). Communication and performance in ad hoc task groups. In J. Galagher, R. E. Kraut, & C. Edigo (Eds.), *Intellectual teamwork: Social and technological foundations of cooperative work* (pp. 291–325). Hillsdale, NJ: Erlbaum.

Fisher, R., & Ury, W. (1981). *Getting to yes: Negotiating agreement without giving in.* Boston: Houghton Mifflin.

Friedman, R., Anderson, C., Brett, J., Olekalns, M., Goates, N., & Lisco, C. C. (2004). The positive and negative effects of anger on dispute resolution: Evidence from electronically mediated disputes. *Journal of Applied Psychology, 89,* 369–376.

Friedman, R. A., & Currall, S. C. (2003). Conflict escalation: Dispute exacerbating elements of e-mail communication. *Human Relations, 56,* 1325–1347.

Fry, W. R., Firestone, I. J., & Williams, D. L. (1983). Negotiation process and outcome of stranger dyads and dating couples: Do lovers lose? *Basic and Applied Social Psychology, 4*(1), 1–16.

Greenhalgh, L., & Chapman, D. I. (1998). Negotiator relationships: Construct measurement and demonstration of their impact on the process and outcomes of negotiation. *Group Decision and Negotiation, 7*(6), 465–489.

Griffith, T. L., & Northcraft, G. B. (1994). Distinguishing between the forest and the trees: Media, features, and methodology in electronic communication research. *Organization Science, 5,* 272–285.

Griffith, T. L., Sawyer, J. E., & Neale, M. A. (2003). Virtualness and knowledge in teams: Managing the love triangle in organizations, individuals, and information technology. *MIS Quarterly, 27,* 265–287.

Guadagno, R. E., & Cialdini, R. B. (2002). On-line persuasion: An examination of differences in computer-mediated interpersonal influence. *Group Dyanmics: Theory, Research and Practice, 6,* 38–51.

Gueguen, N., Legoherel, P., & Jacob, C. (2003). Solicitation of participation in an investigation by e-mail: Effect of the social presence of the physical attraction of the petitioner on the response rate [French]. *Canadian Journal of Behavioural Science, 35*(2), 84–96.

Heim K. (2003, March 7). Microsoft to push instant messaging for business. *San Jose Mercury News.* Retrieved on Novemeber 3, 2004, from http://www.siliconvalley.com/mld/siliconvalley/business/special_packages/ms_antitrust/5335953.htm.

Hiltz, S. R., Johnson, K., & Turoff, M. (1986). Experiments in group decision making: Communication process and outcome in face-to-face versus computerized conferences. *Human Communication Research, 13,* 225–252.

Hollingshead, A. B., McGrath, J. E., & O'Connor, K. M. (1993). Group task performance and communication technology: A longitudinal study of computer-mediated versus face-to-face work groups. *Small Group Research, 24*, 307–333.

Hsee, C. K., & Weber, E. U. (1997). A fundamental prediction error: Self-others discrepancies in risk preference. *Journal of Experimental Psychology: General, 126*, 45–53.

Johnston, J. S., & Waldfogel, J. (2002). Does repeat play elicit cooperation? Evidence from federal civil litigation. *Journal of Legal Studies, 31*, 39–60.

Katsh, E., & Rifkin, J. (2001). *Outline dispute resolution: Resolving conflicts in cyberspace.* San Francisco: Jossey-Bass.

Kayany, J. M., Wotring, C. E., & Forrest, E. J. (1996). Relational control and interactive media choice in technology-mediated communication situations. *Human Communication Research, 22*, 399–421.

Keen, P., Ballance, C., Chan, S., & Schrump, S. (2000). *Electronic commerce relationships: Trust by design.* Upper Saddle River, NJ: Prentice Hall.

Kiesler, S. (1986). The hidden messages in computer networks. *Harvard Business Review, 64*, 46–60.

Kiesler, S., Zubrow, D., Moses, A. M., & Geller, V. (1985). Affect in computer-mediated communication: An experiment in synchronous terminal-to-terminal discussion. *Human Computer Interaction, 1*, 77–107.

Kleef, G. A. van, De Dreu, C. K. W., & Manstead, A. S. R. (2004). The interpersonal effects of anger and happiness in negotiations. *Journal of Personality and Social Psychology, 86*, 57–76.

Kramer, R., & Tyler, T. R. (Eds.). (1996). *Trust in organizations.* Thousand Oaks, CA: Sage.

Krauss, R. M., & Fussell, S. R. (1991). Constructing shared communicative environments. In L. B. Resnick, J. Levine, & S. D. Teasley (Eds.), *Perspectives on socially shared cognition* (pp. 127–149). Washington, DC: American Psychological Association.

Lax, D. A., & Sebenius, J. K. (1987). *The manager as negotiator: Bargaining for cooperation and competitive gain.* New York: Free Press.

Lea, M., & Spears, R. (1992). Paralanguage and social perception in computer-mediated communication. *Journal of Organizational Computing, 2*, 321–341.

Loewenstein, G., Thompson, L., & Bazerman, M. H. (1989). Social utility and decision making in interpersonal contexts. *Journal of Personality and Social Psychology, 57*, 426, 432–433.

Loewenstein, J., Morris, M. W., Chakravarti, A., Thompson, L., & Kopelman, S. (in press). At a loss for words: Dominating the conversation and the outcome in negotiation as a function of intricate arguments and communication media. *Organizational Behavior and Human Decision Processes.*

Matheson, K., & Zanna, M. P. (1989). Persuasion as a function of self-awareness in computer-mediated communication. *Social Behaviour, 4*, 99–111.

McGinn, K. L., & Croson, R. (Eds.). (2004). *What do communication media mean for negotiators? A question of social awareness.* Palo Alto, CA: Stanford University Press.

McGinn, K. L., & Keros, A. (2002). Improvisation and the logic of exchange in embedded negotiations. *Administrative Science Quarterly, 47*, 442–473.

Mennecke, B. E., Valacich, J. S., & Wheeler, B. C. (2000). The effects of media and task on user performance: A test of the task-media fit hypothesis. *Group Decision and Negotiation, 9*, 507–529.

Milgram, S. (1974). *Obedience to authority: An experimental view.* New York: Harper & Row.

Moore, D. A., Kurtzberg, T. R., Thompson, L., & Morris, M. W. (1999). Long and short routes to success in electronically-mediated negotiations: Group affiliations and good vibrations. *Organizational Behavior and Human Decision Processes, 77,* 22–43.

Morley, I. E., & Stephenson, G. M. (1977). *The social psychology of bargaining.* London: Allen & Unwin.

Morris, M., Nadler, J., Kurtzberg, T. R., & Thompson, L. (2002). Schmooze or lose: Social friction and lubrication in e-mail negotiations. *Group Dynamics Theory, Research, and Practice,* 6(1), 89–100.

Nadler, J. (2001). Electronically-mediated dispute resolution and e-commerce, *Negotiation Journal 17,* 333–347.

Nadler, J. (2004). Rapport in legal negotiation: How small talk can facilitate e-mail deal-making. *Harvard Negotiation Law Journal, 9,* 225–253.

Naquin, C. E., & Paulson, G. D. (2003). Online bargaining and interpersonal trust. *Journal of Applied Psychology,* 88(1), 113–120.

Paese, P. W., Schreiber, A. M., & Taylor, A. W. (2003). Caught telling the truth: Effects of honesty and communication media in distributive negotiations. *Group Decision and Negotiation, 12,* 537–566.

Pruitt, D. G., & Rubin, J. Z. (1986). *Social conflict: Escalation, stalemate, and settlement.* New York: Random House.

Purdy, J. M., Nye, P., & Balakrishnan, P. V. (2000). The impact of communication media on negotiation outcomes. *International Journal of Conflict Management, 11,* 162–187.

Rogers, R. W., & Ketchen, C. M. (1979). Effects of anonymity and arousal on aggression. *Journal of Psychology, 102,* 13–19.

Rusting, C. L., & Nolen-Hoeksema, S. (1998). Regulating responses to anger: Effects of rumination and distraction on angry mood. *Journal of Personality and Social Psychology,* 74(3), 790–803.

Sally, D. (2000). A general theory of sympathy, mind-reading, and social interaction, with an application to the Prisoners' Dilemma. *Social Science Information sur les Sciences Sociales,* 39(4), 567–634.

Schweitzer, M. E., Brodt, S. E., & Croson. R. T. A. (2002). Seeing and believing: Visual access and the strategic use of deception. *International Journal of Conflict Management, 13,* 258–275.

Shell, R. G. (1995). Computer-assisted negotiation and mediation: Where we are and where we are going. *Negotiation Journal, 11,* 117–122.

Shiu, E., & Lenhart, A. (2004, September 1). How Americans use instant messaging. *Pew Internet & American Life Project.* Retrieved September 27, 2004, from http://www.pewinternet.org/pdfs/PIP_Instantmessage_Report.pdf

Siegel, J., Dubrovsky, V., Kiesler, S., & McGuire, T. W. (1986). Group processes in computer mediated communication. *Organizational Behavior and Human Decision Processes, 37,* 157–187.

Small, D. A., & Loewenstein, G. (2003). Helping the victim or helping a victim: Altruism and identifiability. *Journal of Risk and Uncertainty,* 26(1), 5–16.

Sober, E., & Wilson, D. (1998). *Unto others: The evolution and psychology of unselfish behavior.* Cambridge, MA: Harvard University Press.

Spears, R., & Lea, M. (1994). Panacea or panopticon? The hidden power in computer-mediated communication. *Communication Research, 21,* 427–459.

Spears, R., Lea, M., & Lee, S. (1990). De-individualization and group polarization in computer-mediated communication. *British Journal of Social Psychology, 29,* 121–134.

Tesser, A., Pilkington, C. J., & McIntosh, W. D. (1989). Self-evaluation maintenance and the mediational role of emotion: The perception of friends and strangers. *Journal of Personality and Social Psychology, 57,* 442–456.

Thompson, L. (1990). Negotiation behavior and outcomes: Empirical evidence and theoretical issues. *Psychological Bulletin, 108,* 515–532.

Thompson, L., Medvec, V., Seiden, V., & Kopelman, S. (2001). Poker face, smiley face, and rant and rave: Myths and realities about emotion in negotiation. In M. Hogg & R. S. Tindale (Eds.), *Blackwell handbook in social psychology.* Cambridge, UK: Blackwell.

Thompson, L. F., & Coovert, M. D. (2003). Teamwork online: The effects of computer conferencing on perceived confusion, satisfaction, and postdiscussion accuracy. *Group Dynamics: Theory, Research, and Practice, 7,* 135–151.

Thomson, R., & Murachver, T. (2001). Predicting gender from electronic discourse. *British Journal of Social Psychology, 40,* 193–208.

Tidwell, L. C., & Walther, J. B. (2002). Computer-mediated communication effects on disclosure, impressions, and interpersonal evaluations: Getting to know one another a bit at a time. *Human Communication Research, 28*(3), 317–348.

Trevino, L. K., Daft, R. L., & Lengel, R. H. (1990). *Understanding manager's media choices: A symbolic interactionist perspective.* Newbury Park, CA: Sage.

Valley, K. L., Moag, J., & Bazerman, M. H. (1998). "A matter of trust": Effects of communication on the efficiency and distribution of outcomes. *Journal of Economic Behavior and Organization, 34,* 211–238.

Valley, K. L., Thompson, L., Gibbons, R., & Bazerman, M. H. (2002). How communication improves efficiency in bargaining games. *Journal of Economic Behavior and Organization, 34,* 211–238.

Walther, J. B. (1995). Relational aspects of computer-mediated communication: Experimental and longitudinal observations. *Organization Science, 6,* 186–203.

Walther, J. B., & Burgoon, J. K. (1992). Relational communication in computer-mediated interaction. *Human Communication Research, 19,* 50–88.

Weisband, S., & Atwater, L. (1999). Evaluating self and others in electronic and face-to-face groups. *Journal of Applied Psychology, 84,* 632–639.

Westmyer, S. A., DiCioccio, R. L., & Rubin, R. B. (1998). Appropriateness and effectiveness of communication channels in competent interpersonal communication. *Journal of Communication, 48,* 27–48.

Yuan, Y., Head, M., & Du, M. (2003). The effects of multimedia communication on web-based negotiation, *Group Decision and Negotiation, 12,* 89–109.

9

A Cultural Analysis of the Underlying Assumptions of Negotiation Theory

JEANNE M. BRETT and MICHELE J. GELFAND

*N*egotiation theory and research has proliferated over the last several decades, causing Kramer and Messick (1995) to remark that "few areas of conflict research have enjoyed as much vogue . . . or can claim as much substantive progress, as negotiation theory" (p. vii). While true, we also contend that the negotiation theory that has evolved over the last 25 years of research in the United States and Northern Europe is laden with values and assumptions that are Western. Though it may be a historical accident that negotiation theory originated and proliferated in the West, a non-Western origin would surely generate a social science that would look very different, because social science theory reflects the dominant patterns of the culture in which it originates (Pruitt, 2004).

In this chapter, we take a *meta-theoretical* approach to the field of negotiation. Our purpose is to identify what the underlying assumptions of negotiation theory might look like from the point of view of non-Western culture, by which we mean primarily, but by no means exclusively, Asian cultures. Our purpose is not to provide a detailed review of all the negotiation and culture literature. Such a review is available in our edited volume *Handbook of Negotiation and Culture* (Gelfand & Brett, 2004). The *Handbook* has chapters on cognition, motivation, emotion, communication, conflict management, context, and so forth. Each chapter by a negotiation scholar is paired with a chapter by a scholar who studies culture and negotiation. In reading the *Handbook*, it is clear that the two sets of scholars are often working from contrasting assumptions about what is normative for social interaction.

We begin by defining culture and explaining the role of fundamental cultural assumptions in organizing social interaction. We then identify five assumptions that dominate Western culture theorizing about negotiations. We examine each assumption in terms of the fundamental problem of social interaction to which the assumption is a response, refer to the research that relies on the assumption, explain how the assumption reflects Western cultural traditions, describe an alternative assumption that reflects the solution that people from a non-Western culture have developed to cope with the same problem of social interaction in negotiation, document that alternative with research and theorizing, and develop a theoretical account that specifies the conditions that challenge the hegemony of the fundamental Western cultural assumption. Table 9.1 summarizes our analysis.

We conclude by returning to Pruitt's preface to the *Handbook of Negotiation and Culture* (2004), where he suggests that studying the way negotiation is conducted in other cultures provides insight that allows us to better understand the recessive nuances of our own culture.

CULTURE

Culture is the distinct character of a social group (Lytle, Brett, Barsness, Tinsley, & Janssens, 1995). It is manifest in the groups' values, beliefs, and norms, in the

TABLE 9.1   A Cultural Analysis of Negotiation Theory

Key Questions	Key Assumptions	Underlying Values and Norms	Scientific Artifacts	Alternative Assumptions
Judgment and concession-making: How to be persuasive?	Rationality in negotiation	Analytical thought Logic and intolerance of contradiction	Negotiating rationally and negotiation biases Art and science of negotiation	Emotionality Holistic thinking Tolerance of contradiction
Motivation: What energizes behavior?	Economic capital	Mastery Individualism Social networks that have weak ties and short in duration	Achieving Pareto Optimality Creating and claiming value	Social capital Strong ties and durable networks
Attributions: Why did this event occur?	Dispositional attributions	Individualism	Focus on traits of negotiators; resultant competition	Situational attributions; cooperation
Communication: How do I get information from the other party?	Direct information sharing	High versus low context	Importance of direct information sharing over trial and error	Indirect information sharing is superior for joint gain
Confrontation: How do we manage conflict?	Direct voice and "talk"	Individualism Egalitarianism	Avoidance is counterproductive and negative	Avoidance and indirectness is functional to conflict resolution

typical behavior patterns of cultural members, in their choice and use of rituals and symbols, and in artifacts. Social institutions carry culture in their ideology and reinforce that ideology by rewarding and sanctioning consistent social interaction within the culture (Brett, 2001). Culture grows out of the patterned ways that people in a group respond to the fundamental problems of social interaction (Trompenaars, 1996). Negotiation—a form of decision making when people are interdependent—is one of those fundamental problems. The beliefs that people have about negotiation, the values or goals that they try to validate in negotiation, the normative behaviors they exhibit in negotiation, and the structures of the institutions that they develop to contain and direct negotiations—all reflect fundamental assumptions of the culture about social interaction.

Examples of fundamental cultural assumptions abound (Lytle et al., 1995; Schwartz, 1994; Triandis, 1995). Some cultures assume that the needs of the individual should be subordinate to the needs of the collective, and the legal and social institutions of the culture reflect this priority. Some cultures assume that the way to maintain order in a society is to have an egalitarian social structure in which people participate in decision making, for example, by voting; other cultures assume a social hierarchy is the way to maintain order, and social institutions—ranging from government to economic entities to family—reflect these differences.

As these examples reveal, cultural assumptions are the building blocks of social interaction. They provide a basis for interpreting social situations and organizing and structuring social interaction. Because these assumptions are at the very deepest level of culture and do not vary much within a culture (Schein, 1985), it is not only difficult to "see" them, but even more difficult to test their limits. In this chapter, we provide a cultural analysis of the field of negotiation by unearthing assumptions fundamental to a Western culture analysis of negotiation. We do so by thoroughly analyzing the "artifacts" embedded in the scholarship of Western research on negotiations. Cross-cultural research provides the variation that allows us to "see" Western culture assumptions in stark relief, test their limits, and identify the conditions that define those limits.

The five assumptions about negotiations we discuss in this chapter are: persuasion via rationality versus emotionality; motivation; attributions for negotiators' behaviors; communication; and confrontation. We chose these assumptions because all address fundamental problems of social interaction to which a culture has to develop a standard response. All of the assumptions are reflected in the research questions that have received the most attention in Western culture negotiation research. However, non-Western culture research has already begun to identify the limitations of the Western cultural assumptions. In choosing these five assumptions we do not mean to imply that they are the only relevant assumptions fundamental to the Western conceptualization of negotiation, or that they are the only assumptions relevant to Western culture that are not supported in non-Western culture. Furthermore, we recognize that these assumptions are not totally discriminant, but tend to overlap in systematic and predictable ways that, we will show, have to do with their cultural origins. As Western culture negotiation research takes on a more social and a less cognitive perspective, and as non-Western culture negotiation research proliferates, we anticipate additional assumptions will surface that reflect differences in Western and non-Western cultural approaches to negotiation. Furthermore, we anticipate substantial development and explication of the cultural conditions that challenge the hegemony of the fundamental Western culture assumptions.

PERSUASION: RATIONALITY VERSUS EMOTION

One of the fundamental problems in negotiation is *How do I get the other party to make the concessions necessary to reach my desired endpoint?* Note this is an etic or universal problem, true of all negotiations and of negotiators all around the world. It is just that the solution to this problem is quite different depending on culture. One approach is to make rational appeals; another is to make emotional appeals.

The Western Culture Rationality Assumption

How does the use of rationality solve the problem of getting others to make the concessions? Rational argument relies on facts and reason (Glenn, Witmeyer, & Stevenson, 1977). The rational negotiator provides the other party with the true facts of the situation (as seen by the rational negotiator) and presumably the other party believes these facts, recognizes the error of her prior claim, and concedes. The rational negotiator may also provide the other negotiator with "reasons" why he should make concessions. Reasons may rely on power. For example, a threat communicates that the rational negotiator will harm the other negotiator if the other does not concede. If the threat is not credible because the recipient does not believe the rational negotiator will carry out the threat, or because the recipient believes that carrying out the threat will be more harmful to the rational negotiator than to him, the threat will not be effective. Reasons may also identify what the rational negotiator will do to benefit the other in return for a concession. This is the classic form of a tradeoff in which the rational negotiator makes a concession on a relatively low-valued issue in response for a concession on a high-valued issue. Recent research indicates that Western negotiators engage in sequences of rational persuasion and offers (or vice versa) more frequently than negotiators from non-Western cultures (Adair & Brett, 2005).

There are two aspects of the rational approach to persuasion in negotiation that are noteworthy beyond its relative frequency. The first is the assumption that the other party, relying on a cost-benefit analysis, is also rational. The rational negotiator assumes that the other has evaluated his or her alternatives to a negotiated agreement and has prioritized the issues. The second is the immediacy of the transaction. The persuasive appeal is supposed to generate an immediate concessionary response.

Rationality is deeply embedded in Western cultural perspectives on psychology. It implies a commitment to reason that follows certain rather explicit laws that should be instrumental in achieving the desired end states. In argument these laws are Aristotelian, by which we mean that they follow a logical process, while in negotiation they appear to be the avoidance of biases that restrict parties from jointly achieving Pareto Optimality (maximizing joint gain) or individually claiming value. There is substantial research that indicates that negotiators systematically depart from rationality (Neale & Bazerman, 1991; Thompson, 2005), primarily because they use faulty heuristics or cognitive shortcuts to process information relevant to negotiation. The entire Western culture enterprise of teaching negotiation skills is focused on replacing faulty heuristics with ones that are more rational. This perspective is institutionalized in the titles of the classics of negoti-ation: Raiffa's *The Art and Science of Negotiation* (1982), Bazerman and Neale's *Negotiating Rationally* (1992), and Thompson's *The Mind and Heart of the Nego-tiator* (2005). The common theme is that negotiators should be more rational, and the assumption is that rationality pays off.

The Western Cultural Basis of the Rationality Assumption

The rationality assumption seems to be embedded in several aspects of Western culture. In individualistic cultures, an *analytic* system of thought—character-ized by the practice of detaching an object from its context, using formal logic, and avoiding contradiction—is valued (Nisbett, Peng, Choi, & Norenzayan, 2001). Within this tradition, people attend to objects in social environments, abstract them from their context, and develop rules to categorize them while maintaining a sense of logical consistency. In Western cultures "psychological processes are likely to be established in such a way that seemingly inconsistent behaviors are readily re-construed to restore perceived consistency" (Kitayama & Markus, 1999, p. 261). Evidence of this can be seen in a study by Peng and Nisbett (1999). They presented Chinese and American participants with a series of contradictory propositions and found that Americans tended to favor one side over the other, while the Chinese were equally accepting of both sides and tried instead to explain the simultaneous existence of the contradictory propositions.

A focus on rationality is also fundamentally self and not other centered, which is consistent with the individualistic cultural values that dominant many Western cultures. Rationality is all about what I should and should not do in planning and executing negotiation, for example, identify my BATNA (best alternative to a negotiated agreement), set a walkaway, identify a target, and so forth. Negotiating rationally only seems to take into consideration the perspective of the other party, for example, "put yourself in the other party's shoes" when advising about avoiding the bias of failing to identify the differential priorities between negotiators' pref-erences, and so leaving value on the table. Finally, Western cultures tend to use low-context communication, and according to Hall (1976), rational argument is a mainstay of low-context communication. In low-context communication, meaning is on the surface of verbal and nonverbal behavior and can be understood regard-less of the situation in which it is communicated (Hall, 1976; Gibson, 1998).

Argument or persuasion in low-context cultures emphasizes facts, rationality, linear thinking, and the familiar "if-then" language of threats.

Emotion From a Western Cultural Perspective

In contrast to the dominance of a rational approach to negotiation, the study of emotion has been largely ignored in Western scholarship on negotiation that embraced cognition and rationality as its preferred topics of study. Emotions were viewed as disrupting ongoing social interaction. Emotion-related thought processes were viewed as lacking in direction and the principled orderliness of reason. Emotional expression was viewed as a reflection of the more primitive uncontrollable side of human nature that threatens social order (Morris & Keltner, 2000). Only recently has emotion grown more popular as a research topic; however, there has been very little research on emotion in negotiation (Barry & Fulmer, 2004), and a particular lack of attention to how emotions operate in real social interactions as opposed to those contrived in the laboratory (Morris & Keltner, 2000), or can be used to guide persuasion.

The Non-Western Culture Emotionality Assumption

In contrast to Western scholarship, rationality is not the dominant response to the question of persuasion: *How do I get the other party to make the concessions necessary to reach my desired endpoint?* In non-Western cultures, the dominant response is instead emotional appeals that remind parties of their status and responsibilities in the social order. For example, cross-cultural negotiation research reports that Taiwanese negotiators use normative statements referring to social roles and relationships to persuade more than U.S. negotiators who use an analytical system relying on logic and reasoning more than Taiwanese negotiators (Drake, 1995). In Japanese social interchange, the script of *naniwabushi* relies on an emotional appeal that takes place in three stages: opening with *kikkake*, where the negotiator conveys his/her feelings about the relationship; followed by *seme*, which is a discussion of the events that have made the social relationship difficult; and concluding with *urei* or an expression of great sorrow or self-pity, which is intended to persuade the other to be benevolent (March, 1990). According to March, the more emotionally moving the appeal, the more likely it is to be persuasive, because to refuse to make a concession in the face of such a plea, the recipient would have to ignore his role as a higher status party in the culture. As we discuss below, the assumption of using emotions, not rational appeals, to persuade others, is grounded in non-Western values and norms.

The Non-Western Cultural Basis of the Emotionality Assumption

In non-Western cultures, cognition is characterized by a holistic system of thought, as opposed to a rational state of mind, individuals view themselves as embedded and interdependent with a larger social context, and the focus of cognitive attention is on relationships and the context (Peng & Nisbett, 1999). A hallmark of this system of thought is the recognition that there are many social contexts and roles that collectively define any given person, and there is a large tolerance for contradiction (Kitayama & Markus, 1999). Emotional appeals, like apology and sympathy, generate attention to the social problem and highlight the role that the party appealed to is supposed to play in the context. Emotional appeals help people sort out which of their many social roles is important in the context. Once the role is identified, norms cue appropriate behavior.

The Japanese script of naniwabushi discussed above illustrates high-context communication. The fact that non-Western cultures tend also to be high-context communication cultures provides further insight into emotions and negotiations (Gibson, 1998; Hall, 1976; Ting-Toomey, 1988). High-context communication is indirect and implicit. Meaning is conveyed not just by verbal or nonverbal behavior, but by the context in which those behaviors were exhibited. High-context communication requires considerable familiarity with the cultural interpretation of the context of social interaction. Persuasion in high context cultures tends to be based on appeals to emotions and affect (Glenn et al., 1977; Johnstone, 1989). Such appeals do not tell the receiver explicitly what he or she should do, as emotional appeals are likely to do in Western cultures (Schroth, Bain-Chekal, & Caldwell, 2004), but send implicit messages that cue role- and context-specific behavior. In another example, March (1990) describes a persuasive performance strategy that is consistent with high-context communication and hierarchical culture. First, subordinates in the status hierarchy seek acceptance of their dependency from superiors in the hierarchy (they are asking superiors to take responsibility for them), *amae*; their behavior produces social obligations, *gimu*, to them on the part of the social superiors that will ultimately be repaid on in one form or another.

Other subtle, high-context emotional signals include behaviors referred to as relational aggressive, including withholding of information (Gelfand, Major, Raver, Nishii, & O'Brein, in press). Contempt—to scorn or disgrace, to offend against dignity—is another subtle form of emotional expression. Contempt may solve the concession problem because it conveys information about status—yours is low—and evoke a concession to win back approval and status (Morris & Keltner, 2000). Although this persuasion strategy may work in a hierarchical culture, data from a study of online auction dispute resolution in the United States indicate that in Western culture, expressions of contempt significantly slow down the process of dispute resolution (Brett et al., 2005).

In sum, the role of emotions in persuasion has long been discussed in the non-Western scholarship on conflict and negotiation. Emotions are functional in non-Western cultures because they signal important meaning about status and obligations. The use of logic and "rational appeals" is generally eschewed and seen as "cold hearted" (March, 1990). The reliance on emotional appeals for persuasion has its basis in the non-Western culture's dominant values and norms that affect everyday behavior.

The Conditions That Challenge the Hegemony of the Western Culture Rationality Assumption

The evidence of biases possibly should have been sufficient to abandon the assumption of rationality in negotiation. Many of these biases are clearly relational and emotional: escalation of commitment, reactive devaluation, fixed pie—as they originate in the perception of the self in the social environment (see Morris & Gelfand, 2004). Emotions, of course, are not unimportant in Western cultures. It is just that historically, they have not been a major subject in negotiation research. As discussed above, this is in part due to the value for rationality in Western cultures, a phenomenon dating back to ancient Greece. Yet, it is also likely due to the fact that research on negotiation is often conducted in the laboratory—a context in which the range of authentic emotional expression is limited (see Barry, Fulmer, & van Kleef, 2004). Recent studies in the laboratory manipulating emotion (van Kleef, De Dreu, & Manstead, 2004) and in the field of naturally occurring disputes and emotion (Friedman et al., 2004) have begun to open the emotional black box in negotiation research. Scholars should also look beyond Western borders for clues on how negotiation is emotion laden, as it is the non-Western cultural perspective with its emphasis on subtle emotional argument that provides excellent insight into the important role of emotions in negotiation and social interchange in Western culture.

MOTIVATION

Motivation, the focused and persistent energy that drives cognition and behavior, (Mook, 2000) answers the social interaction question, *How should we evaluate the outcome of the negotiation?* This evaluation question like the prior question of *How do I get the other party to make concessions?* is etic or universal to negotiations around the world. People in social interaction engage in motivated behavior selected to fulfill their goals. This, too, appears to be etic behavior. It is just that the goals that people seek to realize in negotiations are not all the same. A major cultural distinction is between goals to accumulate economic capital versus goals to accumulate relational capital (Gelfand et al., in press)

The Western Culture Assumption of Economic Capital as a Criterion for Negotiation Outcomes

Economic capital refers to the individual and joint value that negotiators try to create and claim (Lax & Sebenius, 1986). Economic capital is the result of claiming for yourself as much value created in negotiations as possible. Individual gains and joint gains have been the criteria of choice for Western culture research on negotiations (e.g., Raiffa, Bazerman, Neale, or Thompson). These criteria interestingly are also enlisted by researchers taking a more social and motivational approach (e.g., Pruitt, Carnevale, De Dreu).

In brief, the research that uses the economic capital criterion shows that negotiators fail to maximize joint gains because of biases (Bazerman & Neale, 1992), and because of failures to seek the information they need to make trade-offs or use that information properly, if by chance they get it (Pruitt, 1981). Setting high goals appears to facilitate both individual and joint gains, since high goals appear to be translated into aggressive opening offers, and aggressive openings have two distinct effects. First, they can anchor negotiations in the value claiming direction of the party making the opening offer (Huber & Neale, 1986; 1987; Neale & Bazerman, 1985; Rosette, Brett, Barsness, & Lytle, 2004). Second, they can motivate the search for a solution that will come close to meeting those high goals (Rosette et al., 2004; White & Neale, 1994).

The Western Cultural Basis for the Economic Capital Assumption

Maximizing economic capital is wholly consistent with the individualist values of most Western cultures. The accumulation of economic capital confirms individualists' conceptions of themselves as achievers (Schwartz, 1994), who through their own enterprise and personal attributes are able to extract value from the socially interdependent situation that is negotiation. Accumulating economic capital in negotiation is self-verifying in that its accomplishment provides feedback against the individualists' self-interested goals.

The Non-Western Relational Capital Criterion for Evaluating Negotiations

Relational capital is similar to the notion of social capital from sociology, which refers to the investments and returns associated with being a part of a loosely or tightly linked social network (Granovetter, 1985). Yet relational capital in negotiation refers to the assets that accumulate within a specific dyadic negotiation relationship, rather than the overall pattern of relationships among many individuals, which is typically the subject of social capital theory. Relational capital as a criterion for evaluating negotiations refers to the accumulation of assets of mutual liking, mutual knowledge, mutual trust, and mutual commitment to the relationship (Gelfand et al., in press). Accumulating relational capital may be inconsistent with achieving economic capital, at least in the short run. To build trust and mutual commitment to the relationship, parties may have to forgo the hard bargaining associated with the accumulation of economic capital in Western cultures.

The Non-Western Cultural Basis for the Relational Capital Assumption

Evidence that relational capital is a prominent criterion for motivating and evaluating performance in negotiation in non-Western cultures comes from a variety of sources. For example, Yamagishi and Yamagishi (1994) show that individuals from Japan are much more likely to prefer, if not insist on negotiating with individuals with whom they have relationship connections, even if it means forgoing potential economic benefits (see also Graham & Sano, 1989). Likewise, in China, negotiation relationships are more likely to occur through *guanxi* networks, since such networks provide assurances of mutual cooperation, even if an alternative partner outside of the network could provide higher economic value (Gelfand & Cai, 2004). This is not to imply that negotiators are unconcerned with economic issues in non-Western cultures. Instead, in non-Western cultures relationships are the dominant motive, and economic capital is the subordinate motive. Furthermore, relationships are viewed as a force for later economic benefits. Recently, when running a research focus group with Taiwanese students who had just done a dispute resolution negotiation, we were bombarded with questions about the relationship between two disputants—How long had the disputants known each other? How had they met? Students asked, "Why should we try to maximize points for ourselves the negotiation?" They wanted to know why we had them negotiate face to face when it would have been much more normative to send a mutual friend to do the negotiation. In short, relational concerns loom large in non-Western cultures, and until the relational concerns are addressed, concerns for economic capital are not the primary focus of attention. Put differently, relational issues provide the base for building economic capital in non-Western cultures.

The Conditions That Challenge the Hegemony of the Western Cultural Assumption of Economic Capital

The importance of relational capital in non-Western cultures is intricately linked to the structure of social networks in these cultures that tend to have stronger ties, greater density (e.g., individuals all know each other), and multiplex roles (e.g., parties know each other based on friendship, kinship, etc.) than the social networks characteristic of individualistic cultures. All of these network features make it more difficult to enter and exit relationships in collective as compared to individualistic cultures (Barley, 1991; Gelfand & Cai, 2004; Morris, Podolny, & Ariel, 2000). However, there are distinct benefits of accumulating relational capital, especially in the negotiation situation. For example, negotiators who have a lot of trust, liking, mutual knowledge, and mutual commitment will be more willing to comply with and implement negotiated agreements. They will also be more likely to have an interest in engaging in future negotiations, even ones that are not economically advantageous to themselves (Gelfand et al., in press). Moreover, as relationships develop over the course of a negotiation, each negotiator's social network expands to include the other negotiator and ultimately those in the other negotiator's social network who might provide future social succor.

Maximizing relational capital also is consistent with values for social harmony and hierarchy that characterize non-Western cultures (Hofstede, 1980; Schwartz, 1994). Having relational capital confirms that the individual is embedded and interdependent with others, that the individual is an important actor within a larger social system. Once relational capital is established, individuals work to maintain social harmony and to preserve their own and others' face, because disharmony or affronts to face threaten the social system on which the individual's self-construal is dependent.

The accumulation of relational capital is also consistent with the view in non-Western culture that time is continuous (Hall, 1976). It is not that there are no expectations of payback in non-Western culture. Reciprocity appears to be a universal norm (Adair, 2004; Cialdini, 1983; Gouldner, 1960). It is just that payback is not viewed in the form of the immediate accumulation of economic capital. Payback comes when the relational capital needs to be called in (Brett, 2001), when, for example, a downturn in the economy means a contract needs to be reopened, or when an opportunity that requires risk sharing becomes available.

The Conditions That Challenge the Hegemony of the Western Cultural Assumption of Economic Capital as the Criterion for Evaluating Negotiations

Social relationships are not unimportant in Western culture. Indeed, the emphasis on networking and social capital in sociology points out just how important relationships are in Western culture (Granovetter, 1985). It is just that in negotiation research, relationships, especially long-term relationships that transcend the boundaries of the current negotiation, have not been a focus of attention. There is a very simple reason for this. Most Western culture research on negotiation is based on simulations with a discrete beginning and end, being negotiated by students or managers who may or may not be acquainted, and who know that they are participating in a simulation. The design of the research encourages a game type perspective and provides no long-term outcomes. Deals are negotiated, but there is no implementation, hence, no way of evaluating whether the deal was somehow "good" in the long run.

Also, social relationships probably are more important in non-Western cultures than Western cultures. The reason is that in non-Western cultures people are motivated to accumulate relational capital first; they do so because the values in those cultures both stimulate and reward the accumulation of relational capital. In Western cultures people are motivated to accumulate economic capital first, and they do so because the values in Western cultures stimulate and reward the accumulation of economic capital.

ATTRIBUTIONS

Attributions are causal interpretations of events (Kelley & Michela, 1980). They answer the social interaction question, *Why did this event occur?*, which is extremely important when interpreting novel or equivocal events and motivating subsequent behavior. Attributions are particularly important in dispute resolution negotiations because in these negotiations, unlike deal-making negotiations, there has been some kind of unsatisfactory prior interaction between the parties. An event has occurred. Furthermore, one of the parties (possibly both) is sufficiently unhappy about the event that she (the claimant) makes a claim for restitution against the other (respondent). Note that by making a claim directly to another person, the implication is that the other person is responsible for the event and therefore should be responsible for its restitution. A dispute occurs when the respondent rejects the claim, thereby refusing to take responsibility for it (Felsteiner, Able, & Sarat, 1980/81). There are two major cultural distinctions inherent in the dispute situation. One is direct versus indirect confrontation, which is the subject of a later section. The other is the causal attributions that people from different cultures are likely to make. Two dimensions of causal attributions, situational and dispositional, distinguish Western and non-Western cultures.

Attributions are important because they affect perceptions, preferences, and subsequent behaviors. Consider the situation of Rubbermaid's contract to supply their kitchen and bath products to WalMart (Kaufman, 2000). About a year into the contract Rubbermaid asked WalMart to reopen negotiations. Rubbermaid was having margin problems with the contract they had negotiated with WalMart. Why? The situational attribution is that the cost of their raw materials increased dramatically with the rise in oil prices over which they had no control. The dispositional attribution is that Rubbermaid did not negotiate a very good contract; they should have thought of this contingency and planned for it. The dispositional attribution casts aspersion on Rubbermaid's management—a generalization of perceptions. Such perceptions at their most cynical might be that Rubbermaid intentionally avoided negotiating a contingency in the contract based on raw material costs because they hoped to take advantage of lower raw material costs and planned to reopen negotiations if raw materials became more expensive, which would have implications for WalMart's willingness to renegotiate the contract and their negotiating behavior. In contrast, the situational attribution implies no bad faith bargaining but events outside of parties' control make reopening negotiations perfectly reasonable. What attribution does WalMart make? If it is situational, it seems likely WalMart would be willing to return to the negotiating table. If it is dispositional, they may not.

The Western Culture Dispositional Attributions

Western culture observers making causal attributions about events, including others' behaviors, typically make the fundamental attribution error—they underestimate the impact of situational factors and overestimate the impact of dispositional factors (Ross, 1977). In short, they make dispositional attributions. There is a great deal of research evidence confirming the fundamental attribution error in psychology, see Kelley (1967, 1973); Weiner (1985); Weiner and associates (1971); and for a recent review Martinko and Thomson (1998). In the negotiation literature, Morris, Larrick, and Su (1999) showed that U.S. negotiators made dispositional attributions for their counterparts' behaviors and tended to ignore potential situational attributions. Furthermore, these researchers showed that there were negative consequences associated with making dispositional attributions in interpersonal contexts, including more competitive perceptions of the situation and behaviors, such as choosing to resolve conflicts through adversarial procedures.

The Western Cultural Basis
for the Dispositional Attribution

Dispositionalism is an implicit theory about social behavior that is more widespread in individualist than collective cultures (Miller, 1984; Morris & Peng, 1994). Implicit theories are acquired from culturally bound experiences, including but not limited to public institutions like laws, art, artifacts, and literature. In Western culture, social conceptions are person centered; people presume that social behavior is shaped by personal preferences and dispositions (Hsu, 1953). People's behaviors are viewed in terms of motives (Heider & Simmel, 1944), one of which is the value for achievement (Schwartz, 1994). If individuals act in situations to bring about events, then the reason that events occur is due to individual action.

The Non-Western Culture Situational Attributions

Situational attributions are explanations of cause that emphasize concrete situations, the temporal occasion, and the social context (Geertz, 1975). In the example of WalMart and Rubbermaid, the situational attribution has all of these characteristics: There is a concrete situation (Rubbermaid is in financial trouble); there is a temporal occasion (oil prices have skyrocketed); and there is a social context (this event was outside of Rubbermaid's control). Anthropologists have reported for many years that attributional patterns reflect different cultural contexts (Morris & Peng, 1994). For example, Geertz concluded that the Balinese attributed behavior to social roles not dispositions, because Balinese social norms directed attention to roles not dispositions. Selby (1975), studying American Indian culture, reported that even rare and deviant behaviors like murder were explained in terms of context and situation, not dispositions. Further, Selby reported that since contextual and situational events were unlikely to come together in exactly the same way again, there was little concern that the person would again commit murder.

Note, the implications for treatment for a person or company involved in a conflict are therefore very different depending on whether the attribution is dispositional or situational. If the attribution is situational, then the person or company is treated with respect and even sympathy. The party making such an attribution is likely to cooperate in resolving the situation, because he/she views it as the result of a unique set of circumstances. If the attribution is dispositional, then the person or company is treated with disrespect, perhaps even viewed as bargaining in bad faith. As the previous section on emotional persuasion suggests, such a negative emotional attribution is likely to stimulate uncooperative or even downright competitive behaviors.

Research by Bond (1983), Shweder and Bourne (1982), Miller (1984), and most recently Morris and Peng (1994), has documented that Asians make more situational attributions while Americans make more dispositional ones. Morris and Peng concluded that Chinese process events with a situation-centered theory that produces a mental representation that preserves contextual information.

The Non-Western Cultural Basis
for Situational Attributions

In non-Western cultures, social conceptions are group centered, reflecting inter-dependence (Markus & Kitayama, 1991). People believe that human behavior is constrained by roles and role constraints, by group norms to preserve relationships with others, and by scripts that prescribe proper situational behavior. This perspective is highly consistent with making situational attributions. It is also consistent with the hierarchical values of these cultures (Schwartz, 1994).

Note that the situation prevails in East Asian causal accounts despite the fact that these cultures are extremely relationship oriented. At first this may seem somewhat counterintuitive if the focus is on the relationship; when something goes wrong with the relationship, why should the attribution of cause not be dispositional? The answer is probably that a situational attribution is less harmful to the relationship than a dispositional one, and in a culture that values harmony and relationships, preservation of them is paramount. A situational attribution also provides more flexibility for restitution that saves face and preserves respect despite the conflict, which is a less than ideal circumstance. For example, new arrangements can be negotiated to avoid the concrete situation, change the context, or hedge against temporal uncertainty. Or, the parties can assume that such a confluence of events just will not happen again.

The Conditions That Challenge the Hegemony of the
Western Culture Assumption of Dispositional Attributions

Had attribution theory been developed in East Asia to explain people's responses to unfamiliar or novel events or situations, the hegemony would have been situational causal accounts, not dispositional ones. The fundamental attribution error would have been to ascribe cause to concrete situations, temporal events, and or context. Given the same information about an event, people from different cultures give very different attributions (Miller, 1984; Morris & Peng, 1994; Stevenson & Stigler, 1992), and construct causal explanations that are consistent with their culturally instantiated belief system. Of course the truth of the situation is irrelevant. Are the East Asians correct? Are the Americans correct? It does not matter because these culturally linked attribution patterns occur, affecting perceptions, reasoning, and other cognitive processes, as well as negotiation and other behavior.

COMMUNICATION

One of the major social challenges in negotiation is: *How do I get the information I need about the other party's interests and priorities without giving up too much information about my own interests, thereby making myself vulnerable to exploitation?* Knowledge of the other party's preferences and priorities is essential if value is to be created in the negotiation (Thompson, 2005). There are two rather different approaches for how to do so, one based on questioning and the other on using proposals.

The Western Culture Questioning Approach to Information Sharing

The Western research on information exchange in negotiations leading to Pareto Optimal outcomes identified two strategies (series of motive-directed behaviors). The questioning strategy follows the script of asking the other party questions about his preferences and priorities, assuming he is telling the truth, reciprocating with information about your own preferences and priorities, and thereby slowly building a complete understanding of the tradeoffs in the negotiation and formulating multi-issue proposals to capture those tradeoffs (Weingart & Olekalns, 2004). The research demonstrating the value of sharing information about priorities for joint gain originated with Pruitt (Pruitt & Lewis, 1975) and has been confirmed in studies by Putnam and Wilson (1989); Thompson (1991); Weingart, Thompson, Bazerman, and Carroll (1990); Weingart, Hyder, and Prietula (1996); Olekalns and Smith (2000, 2003); Olekalns, Smith, and Walsh (1996). Other research indicates that information sharing is not enough, that it has to be accompanied by insight into the other party's payoffs if negotiators are to create joint gain (Olekalns & Smith, 2003; Thompson & Hastie, 1990; Tutzauer & Roloff, 1988).

The other strategy identified by Pruitt and Lewis (1975) is hardly a strategy at all. They call it heuristic trial-and-error processing, which means that negotiators test out lots of alternative proposals for settlement with no particular strategy guiding choice of a proposal other than if the prior one was not acceptable, try another. There has not been further discussion of trial and error processing in the literature.

The Western Cultural Basis for the Questioning Approach

As previously discussed in the section on persuasion, Western culture uses what is called a low-context communication (Gibson, 1998; Gudykunst, Matsumoto, Ting-Toomey, & Nishida, 1996; Hall, 1976). Low-context communication is direct; meaning is explicit and on the surface of verbal or nonverbal behavior. Interpretation of low-context communication requires familiarity with verbal and nonverbal behavior, but it does not require familiarity with the context or situation in which the behavior occurs.

There have been several cross-cultural studies contrasting low-context U.S. negotiators with negotiators from several different high-context cultures. In one study, U.S. negotiators used more *no's* than high-context Chinese negotiators (Adler, Braham, & Graham, 1992). In another study, U.S. negotiators engaged in more direct information sharing, explicitly sharing information when questions were asked, making statements about their own priorities, commenting on commonalities or differences between parties' priorities, and directly responding to the other party's suggestions or offers than Japanese negotiators (Adair, Okumura, & Brett, 2001). In a third study of negotiation over time (Adair & Brett, 2005), U.S. and other low-context negotiators from cultures such as Germany, Sweden, and Israel (all negotiating intraculturally) shared information directly throughout the negotiation at a higher rate than low-context negotiators from Hong Kong, Japan, Russia, and Thailand. Sharing information directly in negotiation is consistent with the low context, "say what you mean" communication style that is pervasive in Western cultures.

The Non-Western Culture Proposal Approach

The research on intracultural negotiations in non-Western cultures has identified an approach to information exchange based on proposals. Four studies have now documented this pattern (Adair, 2004; Adair & Brett, 2005; Adair et al., 2001; Rosette et al., 2004). The strategy is to make proposals, both single-issue and multi-issue proposals, and draw inferences about the other parties' priorities from the patterning of proposals and counterproposals. Using proposals in a high-context setting is not a trial-and-error process as observed by Pruitt and Lewis (1975) in a low-context setting. It is a highly sophisticated inferential search routine that is effective in identifying joint gain (Adair & Brett, 2005).

Inferences about the other party's preferences and priorities should be relatively simple to make (and therefore accessible to Western culture negotiators) if the negotiators are using multi-issue proposals that include all the issues in the negotiation. The reason is that one multi-issue proposal can be compared directly to another. However, negotiators in non-Western cultures do not limit themselves to multi-issue proposals; they also make more single-issue proposals than Western negotiators (Adair & Brett, 2005; Adair et al., 2001). Drawing inferences from a pattern of single-issue proposals requires a heavy focus on context. For example, in a three-issue deal-making negotiation we may have to decide price, volume, and delivery date. If I make you a proposal on delivery date, and you do not explicitly reject it but move on to price giving me an offer on price, I need to start building a concept of the settlement based on my delivery date and your price. If your price is not acceptable to me, I make you an alternative offer on price, keeping in mind my prior offer on delivery date, but not explicitly restating it. As the number of issues and options per issue increase, inferring a pattern of priorities becomes more and more complex and probably less and less accessible to negotiators without experience in high-context communication cultures (Adair & Brett, 2004). Yet, negotiators from non-Western high-context cultures seem to be able to use this approach to generate joint value (Adair, 2004; Adair & Brett, 2005; Adair et al., 2001; Rosette et al., 2004).

Each of the four studies documenting the proposal approach to information extraction in negotiations is important in different ways. The Adair et al. (2001) study documents the more frequent use of the proposal approach among Japanese than U.S. intracultural negotiators. There were no differences in this study between Japanese and U.S. intracultural negotiators on joint gain, indicating that both the question and answer and the proposal strategies for information sharing were equally valid in uncovering the information needed to make tradeoffs. The Adair (2004) study extends this finding by documenting that negotiators from a variety of high-context cultures (Russia, Thailand, Hong Kong, and Japan) use the proposal strategy more frequently than negotiators from a variety of low-context cultures (U.S., Germany, Israel, Sweden). Adair reports that the impact of proposals on joint gain was higher for high- than low-context negotiators, suggesting that negotiators from the two different types of communication cultures were using proposals differently.

The Adair and Brett (2005) study contributes several further new insights. This study used the same multiculture sample as the Adair (2004) study, but it analyzed sequences of negotiator behavior—what one said and the other replied—and it did so over time, dividing the negotiations into quarters based on number of speaking turns. First, reciprocity of offers was greater in high- than in low-context negotiations. Second, this pattern began in the first quarter of the negotiation and continued through the third quarter. Only in the fourth quarter of the negotiation did the low-context negotiators start reciprocating offers at the same rate as the high-context negotiators. Third, there were also intercultural dyads in this study (U.S.–Japan and U.S.–Hong Kong, negotiating in English in the U.S.). These mixed-context negotiators used sequences of questions and answers indistinguishably from the low-context negotiators. However, they lagged both the high- and the low-context negotiators in the sequential use of proposals, and unlike the low-context negotiators, they did not catch up in the fourth quarter. They also claimed less value than either the high- or the low-context negotiators.

Finally, the Rosette et al. (2004) study contrasted high-context Hong Kong Chinese negotiators with low-context U.S. negotiators negotiating via e-mail. E-mail is a communication medium that is particularly amenable to the use of multi-issue proposals because it is text-based communication. In this comparative study, Hong Kong Chinese intracultural negotiators used more multi-issue proposals than their U.S. counterparts; they demonstrated a better understanding of the other party's priorities, and they negotiated higher joint gains than the U.S. intracultural negotiators.

The Non-Western Cultural Basis for Proposals

The theory of culture and communication postulates that communication should be more indirect in high- than low-context cultures (Hall, 1976; Okabe, 1983). Non-Western cultures use high-context communication more than Western cultures (Gibson, 1998; Gudykunst et al., 1996; Hall, 1976). High-context communication is indirect and implicit, meaning is embedded in the context surrounding the words or acts, and words and acts cannot be interpreted without a cultural understanding of the context in which they are communicated. In the negotiation studies reviewed in the prior section, the researchers operationalized high-context communication in terms of proposals. At first, this may seem odd. Afterall, an offer expresses something I want, and that would seem to be evidence of direct, low-context communication. However, it is the context in which an offer is made, the context of the prior offers, whether single- or multi-issues are proposed that provides the information from which high-context inferences about priorities can be made. This is why the researchers argue that offers are an indirect, high-context means of identifying preferences, priorities, tradeoffs, in short, in generating insight.

The Conditions That Challenge the Hegemony of the Western Cultural Questioning Approach to Information Exchange

Western culture negotiators can and do use proposals. Indeed, the Adair and Brett (2005) study showed that by the final quarter of the negotiation Western and non-Western culture negotiators were using proposals at the same rate. The difference appears not only in timing, but also in utility. High-context culture provides cultural experience in drawing inferences from complex and embedded patterns. Negotiators from these cultures use that experience to draw inferences about the other's preferences and priorities in negotiation.

Once again the Western culture hegemony limits what we can see within our own culture. By studying non-Western cultural negotiators' use of information-sharing strategy, researchers were able to uncover a substantially different, and effectively equivalent, strategy (using the Western culture criterion of economic capital). Furthermore, it is a strategy that Western negotiators might benefit from using themselves, intraculturally, when negotiating with someone who is reluctant to answer questions and share information, or interculturally, when negotiating with someone from a high-context culture.

CONFRONTATION OF CONFLICT

In this last section, we focus on one last universal social problem, namely, *How do we manage conflict?* This question refers to managing the conflicting interests of parties after an event has occurred that is sufficiently unsatisfactory to one or both parties that they would like at a minimum the event to end and a return to past practices, and quite frequently restitution for damages perceived as resulting from the event. The cultural responses to social conflict are consistent and reflect very distinct underlying assumptions. One approach is to confront the other party directly, *Let's talk!* Another approach is to avoid direct confrontation. (For a more extended discussion of the assumptions underlying direct confrontation in the conflict management research, see Shapiro and Kulik, 2004.)

The Western Culture Assumption—
Direct Confrontation: Let's Talk!

"Can we *talk*?," a colloquial expression made famous by comedienne Joan Rivers, expresses a desire to discuss negative feelings about an event and if possible repair the situation (Von Glinow, Shapiro, & Brett, 2004). It also implies direct confrontation between the parties. Western conflict management scholars suggest that talk is effective in repairing relationships (De Dreu, Weingart, & Kwon, 2000; Montoya-Weiss, Massey, & Song, 2001; Moore, 1986; Shapiro & Kulik 2004). These scholars also identify conflict management styles such as avoidance or withdrawal as less effective than those that emphasize confrontation (DeDreu et al., 2000; Montoya-Weiss et al., 2001; Shapiro & Kulik, 2004). Avoidance, after all, leaves the conflict unresolved (Shapiro & Kulik, 2004). Although note that the assumption is that resolution is the goal of those in conflict, when expression of grievances or retaliation may actually be the goal of at least one of the parties (Shapiro & Kulik, 2004). Von Glinow et al. (2004) conclude that cumulatively there is a protalk view of what conflicted parties ought to do.

The Western Culture Basis for Direct Confrontation

The candid nature of talk shares characteristics with low-context communication (Gudykunst & Ting-Toomey, 1988; Leung & Lind, 1986; Ting-Toomey, 1988; Wolfson & Norden, 1984). Talk is direct and explicit. The meaning is embedded in the words chosen for talk not in the context. The assumption that talk is good dates back to ancient Western intellectual traditions. Kim (2002), for example, discusses how poets and philosophers in ancient Greece (from Homer to Socrates to Plato) preached that talking was one of the most important skills to develop in order to succeed in debating and to develop excellent thinking. The assumption that talk is good is entirely consistent with modern-day cultural individualism, in which the focus is on separating the self from the social context (Markus, Kitayama, & Heiman, 1996) and expressing one's unique attributes. In the conflict literature, talk, or the direct confrontation of conflict, is seen to be productive because it leads to isolating disputes between parties from what is often a more general context of conflict between them (Felsteiner et al., 1980/81). Once a dispute is defined in this way, parties can use negotiation skills to discover underlying interests and resolve conflict (Tinsley, 2004). Talk, in short, represents a Western perspective on conflict management (Brett, 2001; Cameron, 2000).

The Non-Western Cultural Assumption—Indirect
Confrontation

In non-Western cultures, the assumption that *not* talking is good predominates. The value of silence in East Asian culture, for example, can be seen in ancient philosophical traditions, including Buddhist and Taoist practices where meditation, silence, and internal visualization are seen as beneficial for high levels of thinking (Kim, 2002). In Japan, several famous proverbs capture this essence: "Out of the mouth comes all evil," "Silence is golden," and "The tongue is sharper than the sword." In a recent psychological analysis, Kim showed that East Asians were indeed more likely to believe that silence was superior for thinking and that parents encouraged silence and nonverbal communication, whereas European Americans were more likely to believe that talking was superior for thinking and reported that parents encouraged the use of verbal over nonverbal communication. Thus, *talking beliefs* and *talking practices* vary dramatically across cultural groups.

Differences in beliefs about talk across cultures are manifested in preferred ways for dealing with conflict. Early cross-cultural research on conflict management using the Rahim scale of preferences for conflict management styles identified non-Westerners as conflict avoiders (Kirkbride, Tang, & Westwood, 1991; Tang & Kirkbride, 1986; Trubisky, Ting-Toomey, & Lin, 1991). However, these conclusions seem to be bound to the Western culture theory and methods that generated them. There are no choices on the Rahim scale for indirect confrontation behaviors that can be used with the supreme subtlety of high context communication.

People in non-Western cultures prefer expressing conflict in indirect ways, both verbally and especially behaviorally (Brett, 2001). From a verbal perspective, non-Westerners in conflict prefer using words whose meaning requires inference, for example, contempt rather than anger; words that are less blunt (Gudykunst & Ting-Toomey, 1988; Trubisky et al., 1991) and words that are more ambiguous and "avoid leaving an assertive impression" (Okabe, 1983, p. 26). The behaviors that non-Westerners use to manage conflict are also indirect.

There are many different types of indirect confrontation behaviors. One set involves using diffused voice, which means broadcasting concerns publicly to a diffused audience rather than directly to the other person (Shapiro & Kulik, 2004). That audience in a non-Western culture would most certainly include the superior of the person with whom you are in conflict. For example, Tse, Francis, and Walls (1994) found that executives from China were much more likely to consult a superior about a conflict as compared to executives from Canada. Leung (1987) also showed that compared to Americans, Chinese preferred indirect procedures involving third parties, such as mediation, to direct face-to-face adversarial procedures, because the indirect procedures were seen as more conducive to reducing animosity among the parties. In the Japanese context, Lebra (1984) has shown that people have evolved a number of other indirect mechanisms by which conflict is contained, including anticipatory management (i.e., preventing a conflict from occurring in the first place), situational code switching (being cordial only when the situation calls for it), and triadic management (involving a third party). Similarly, Ohbuchi and Takahashi (1994) found that disputants in Japan used indirect strategies of ingratiation, impression management, and appeasement in order to deal with conflict.

Another indirect example that nevertheless involves the two disputants directly is illustrated by the problem of the rattling bicycles in Brett (2001). A Westerner, visiting a plant that was producing bicycles that the Westerner had sold to a German buyer, determined that the bicycles rattled. Concerned that the buyer would not accept the shipment, he took the plant manager out for a ride, remarked that the German buyer of the bicycles was concerned about precision engineering, and went back to Hong Kong. The bicycles were free of rattles when they arrived in Germany.

Why take this risk that the rattling bicycles would be shipped and rejected? Because in non-Western culture *face* is highly valued, both your own and others' (see Earley, 1997; Ho, 1976; Leung, 1997). The concept of face translates loosely into respect. By not getting *into the face* of the plant manager and telling him in no uncertain terms that the rattles had to be taken care of, the Western manager conveyed his respect to the plant manager. Yes there was a problem, yes both parties knew about the problem. But by using indirect confrontation, the Western manager avoided conveying disrespect and blame. He avoided adding an emotional element to the conflict. Interestingly, adding an emotional element to a conflict always occurs when there is a formal dispute (Brett, 2001; Brett et al., 2004) but does not have to occur when parties are in conflict. Adding an emotional element may speed up settlement by calling attention to the importance of resolving the conflict, or by adding a second issue that can be used in a tradeoff, or it may slow it down if the emotional element generates an increasing conflict spiral (Brett et al., 2005).

If the person telling the bicycle story had been non-Western, he might have taken a different but still indirect approach. A major conflict management strategy followed in non-Western cultures is to have a third party act as a go-between, and the preference seems to be a third party with some clout. A good choice in the bicycle situation might be another contractor who is having goods manufactured at the same plant: *I understand there have been some quality control problems with Chen's order.*

Why take an indirect approach? One reason is that in non-Western cultures, conflict is rarely viewed as an isolated incident between two parties but a threat to the harmony of the social network in which these parties are embedded (Ting-Toomey, 1988; Tinsley, 2004). Thus, how to go about resolving the dispute concerns not just the principals but also the broader community.

Indirect confrontation does not mean an eschewal of power. Indeed, Tinsley (2004) comments that power strategies tend to be used in non-Western cultures where social stratification and hierarchical values are more common. With social status, she points out, comes the ability to pronounce a resolution to the conflict, since the higher status party has the resources to impose damages on the lower status party, and the lower status party has few alternatives to impost costs to the other side. (Not that anything would ever be said explicitly about damages.)

The Cultural Basis for Indirect Confrontation

The reason for the preference for indirect confrontation in non-Western cultures relates to the characteristics of non-Western cultures, including values for collective interests and social harmony, and even hierarchy, in addition to high-context communication. Collectivism and high-context culture provide a contextual focus for conflict and dispute. In order to maintain social harmony when parties are viewed as embedded in a social network, the collective interests of the network need to be engaged. In order to understand a conflict between two parties the context of their conflict and the implications of their conflict for others need to be understood. Third parties are frequently involved because they should have the broader perspective that takes context into account. Hierarchical culture is also consistent with involving powerful third parties in the resolution of conflict. Those with status in the hierarchy of course have the resources to harm those with less status without causing disrespect or offense. One might think that this would lead people to avoid the risks of involving third parties. However, in a hierarchical culture with its structured web of status based social obligations, powerful parties are constrained from imposing a settlement that disregards the well-being of lower status parties (Hu, 1944; Yang, 1993).

The Conditions That Challenge the Cultural Hegemony of Direct Confrontation

Direct confrontation is normative in individualistic, low-context communication cultures; indirect confrontation is normative in collective, hierarchical, and high-context cultures. The question left unaddressed is whether one strategy is more effective than another? One might assume that direct confrontation is more effective in Western cultures and indirect confrontation in non-Western cultures. But, Shapiro and Kulik (2004) and Von Glinow et al. (2004) raise serious questions about just how affective talk is as a conflict management strategy even in Western cultures. (See also Jackson, Peterson, Mannix, and Trochim, 2002, who report that the most effective MBA project teams are ones that do not confront interpersonal conflicts but rather impose structure on group process to prevent them from disrupting task accomplishment.) This may be an example of a cultural assumption—namely, directness—that is maladaptive in conflict and negotiation situations and needs to be recognized as such.

CONCLUSION

In this chapter, we provided a cultural analysis of some of the major assumptions underlying negotiation theory. Negotiation as a field of scholarly inquiry has largely developed and evolved within the context of Western culture. Science is not value free (Lacey, 1999). Western values and assumptions, we argued, are reflected in the ways in which the science has developed. We showed how a number of key assumptions including the role of rationality versus emotionality, the importance of economic versus relational capital, the attributions that are made, and the role of communication and confrontation, reflect important values and norms that are cultivated in Western culture. We provided evidence of these assumptions, in the scientific "artifacts" in which they are manifested, and alternative assumptions that are more congruent with other cultural contexts.

We conclude with two observations. First, our analysis illustrates the importance of going beyond Western borders in order to *expand the assumptions* that guide thinking and research on negotiation. A science that is developed only in the West will ultimately reflect a partial view of the phenomenon of interest. Second, our analysis illustrates the importance of going beyond Western borders in order to *understand more about our own cultural context* and the ways in which we view negotiations. Culture, although omnipresent, is often invisible. It is only when we study other cultures that we are able to see clearly how our own beliefs are constituted through cultural practices, values, and norms (Gelfand & Brett, 2004). As Pruitt (2004, p. xii) cogently noted, "Social scientists tend to notice first the characteristics that stand out in their society. Hence they are likely to miss more subtle features that may, nevertheless, be important. By studying other societies where these features are dominant, they can develop concepts and theories that will eventually be useful for understanding their own." Put differently, cross-cultural research helps us understand the *recessive* nuances of our own culture (Tinsley, 2004).

For example, although heuristic trial-and-error search had been identified as a strategy for the development of joint gain, this technique received very little attention in Western scholarship. Yet, a nonrandom variant of this search strategy is well developed in non-Western culture. Identifying the use of offers and understanding how relevant information is extracted from them, provides insight and strategic alternatives for Western negotiators (Adair & Brett, 2004). Similarly, although avoidance and indirectness have generally been viewed negatively in the Western conflict literature, with Western scholars arguing that *talk is good* (and even possible). Recent theorizing (Shapiro & Kulik, 2004; Von Glinow et al., 2004) argues that talk is not necessarily functional in modern-day disputes in which disputants are faceless and need to communicate indirectly. Further Western culture discussion of the *nontalk* alternative would benefit from looking at the rich literature that exists in Asian cultures on this phenomenon. To be sure, it is not possible to merely adapt beliefs and practices from other cultures into the West. Yet, by looking beyond our borders to other cultures where different beliefs and practices have long cultural traditions, we will be better able to understand our own culture.

ACKNOWLEDGMENTS

We would like to acknowledge the Melbourne Business School, which supported the first author during the drafting of this chapter. We would also like to thank Wendi Adair and Ray Friedman for their comments on an earlier draft of this chapter.

REFERENCES

Adair, W. (2004). Reciprocal information sharing and negotiation outcome in East-West negotiations. *International Journal of Conflict Management, 14,* 273–296.
Adair, W. L., & Brett, J. M. (2004). Culture and negotiation processes. In M. J. Gelfand & J. M. Brett (Eds.), *Handbook of negotiation and culture* (pp. 158–176). Palo Alto, CA: Stanford University Press.

Adair, W. L., & Brett, J. M. (2005). The negotiation dance: Time, culture, and behavioral sequences in negotiation. *Organizational Science., 16*(1), 33–51.

Adair, W., Okumura, T., & Brett, J. (2001). Negotiation behavior when cultures collide: The United States and Japan. *Journal of Applied Psychology, 86*(3), 371–385.

Adler, N. J., Braham, R., & Graham, J. L. (1992). Strategy implementations: A comparison of face-to-face negotiations in the People's Republic of China and the US. *Strategic Management Journal, 13*, 449–266.

Barley, S. R. (1991). Contextualizing conflict: Notes on the anthropology of disputes and negotiations. In M. H. Bazerman, R. J. Lewicki, & B. H. Sheppard (Eds.), *Research on negotiation in organizations* (Vol. 3, pp. 165–199). Greenwich, CT: JAI Press.

Barry, B., & Fulmer, I. S., Kleef, G. A. van (2004). I laughed, I cried, I settled: The role of emotion in negotiation. In M. J. Gelfand & J. M. Brett (Eds.), *Handbook of negotiation and culture* (pp. 71–94). Palo Alto, CA: Stanford University Press.

Bazerman, M. H., & Neale, M. A. (1992). *Negotiating rationally.* New York: Free Press.

Bond, M. H. (1983). A proposal for cross-cultural studies of attribution processes. In M. H. Hewstone (Ed.), *Attribution theory: Social and applied extensions* (pp. 144–157). Oxford, UK: Basil Blackwell.

Brett, J. (2001). *Negotiating globally: How to negotiate deals, resolve disputes, and make decisions across cultural boundaries.* San Francisco: Jossey-Bass.

Brett, J. M., Olekalns, M., Goates, N., Friedman, R., Anderson, C., & Lisco C. C. (2005). *Emotionally tinged communications and the speed of settling disputes.* Dispute Resolution Research Center Working Paper, Northwestern University.

Cameron, D. (2000). *Good to talk?: Living and working in a communication culture.* Thousand Oaks, CA: Sage.

Cialdini, R. B. (1983). *Influence: The psychology of persuasion.* New York: William Morrow.

De Dreu, C. K. W., Weingart, L. R., & Kwon, S. (2000). Influence of social motives on integrative negotiations: A meta-analytic review and test of two theories. *Journal of Personality and Social Psychology, 7*, 889–905.

Drake, L. E. (1995). Negotiation styles in intercultural communication. *International Journal of Conflict Management, 6*(1), 72–90.

Earley, P. C. (1997). *Face, harmony and social structure: An analysis of organizational behavior across cultures.* Oxford, UK: Oxford University Press.

Felsteiner, W. L. F., Able, R. L., & Sarat, A. (1980/81). The emergence and transformation of disputes: Naming, blaming, and claiming. *Law and Society Review, 15*, 631–654.

Friedman, R., Anderson, C. Brett, J., Olekalns, M., Goates, N., & Lisco, C. C. (2004). The positive and negative effects of anger on dispute resolution: Evidence from electronically-mediated disputes. *Journal of Applied Psychology, 89*, 369–376.

Geertz, C. (1975). On the nature of anthropological understanding. *American Scientist, 63*, 47–53.

Gelfand, M. J., & Brett, J. M. (2004). Introduction. In M. J. Gelfand & J. M. Brett (Eds.), *Handbook of negotiation and culture* (pp. 3–6). Palo Alto, CA: Stanford University Press.

Gelfand, M. J., & Cai, D. A. (2004). The cultural structuring of the social context of negotiation. In M. J. Gelfand & J. M. Brett (Eds.), *Handbook of negotiation: Theoretical advances and cultural perspectives* (pp. 238–257). Palo Alto, CA: Stanford University Press.

Gelfand M. J., Major, V. S., Raver, J., Nishii, L., & O'Brien, K. M. (in press). Negotiating relationally: The dynamics of the relational self in negotiations. *Academy of Management Review.*

Gibson, C. B. (1998). Do you hear what I hear: A model for reconciling intercultural communication difficulties arising from cognitive styles and cultural values. In P. C. Earley & M. Erez (Eds.), *New perspectives on international industrial/organizational psychology* (pp. 335–362). San Francisco: New Lexington Press.

Glenn, E. S., Witmeyer, D., & Stevenson, K. A. (1977). Cultural styles of persuasion. *International Journal of Intercultural Relations, 1*(3), 52–66.

Glinow, M. A. Von, Shapiro, D. L., & Brett, J. M. (2004). Can we *talk*, and should we? Managing emotional conflict in multicultural teams. *Academy of Management Review, 29*(4), 578–592.

Gouldner, A. W. (1960). The norm of reciprocity: A preliminary statement. *American Sociological Review, 25*(2), 161–178.

Graham, J. L., & Sano, Y. (1989). *Smart bargaining*. New York: Harper Business.

Granovetter, M. (1985). Economic and social structure: The problem of embeddedness. *American Journal of Sociology, 91*, 481–510.

Gudykunst, W. B., & Ting-Toomey, S. (1988). *Culture and interpersonal communication*. Beverly Hills, CA: Sage.

Gudykunst, W. B., Matsumoto. Y., Ting-Toomey, S., & Nishida, T. (1996). The influence of cultural individualism-collectivism, self-construals, and individual values on communication styles across cultures. *Human Communication Research, 22*, 510–543.

Hall, E. T. (1976). *Beyond culture*. New York: Anchor Press.

Heider, F., & Simmel, M. (1944). An experimental study of apparent behavior. *American Journal of Psychology, 57*, 243–259.

Ho, D. Y. F. (1976). On the concept of face. *American Journal of Sociology, 81*, 867–884.

Hofstede, G. (1980). *Culture's consequences: International differences in work-related values*. Beverly Hills, CA: Sage.

Hsu, F. L. K. (1953). *Americans and Chinese: Two ways of life*. New York: Schuman.

Hu, H. C. (1944). The Chinese concepts of "face." *American Anthropologist, 46*, 61–64.

Huber, V. L., & Neale, M. A. (1986). Effects of cognitive heuristics and goals on negotiator performance and subsequent goal setting. *Organizational Behavior and Human Decision Processes, 38*, 342–365.

Jackson, K., Peterson, R., Mannix, E., & Trochim, W. (2002, August). *Conflict resolution strategies in leaderless groups: An exploratory study of their impact*. Paper presented at the Academy of Management, Denver, CO.

Johnstone, B. (1989). Linguistic strategies and cultural styles for persuasive discourse. In S. Ting-Toomey & F. Korzenny (Eds.), *Language, communication and culture* (pp. 139–156). Newbury Park, CA: Sage.

Kaufman, L. (2000). As biggest business WalMart propels changes elsewhere. *New York Times* (October 22, 2000).

Kelley, H. H. (1967). Attribution theory in social psychology. In D. Levine (Ed.), *Nebraska symposium on motivation* (pp. 192–238). Lincoln: University of Nebraska Press.

Kelley, H. H. (1973). The process of causal attribution. *American Psychologist, 28*, 107–128.

Kelly, H. H., & Michela, J. L. (1980). Attribution theory and research. *Annual Review of Psychology, 31*, 457–501.

Kim, H. S. (2002). We talk, therefore we think? A cultural analysis of the effect of talking on thinking. *Journal of Personality and Social Psychology, 83*, 828–842.

Kirkbride, P. S., Tang, S. F., & Westwood, R. I. (1991). Chinese conflict preferences and negotiation behavior: Cultural and psychological influences. *Organizational Studies, 12*, 365–386.

Kitayama, S., & Markus, H. R. (1999). The yin and yang of the Japanese self: The cultural psychology of personality coherence. In D. Cervone & Y. Shoda (Eds.), *The coherence of personality: Social-cognitive bases of consistency, variability, and organization* (pp. 242–302). New York: Guilford Press.

Kleef, G. A. van, De Dreu, C. K. W., & Manstead, A. S. R. (2004). The interpersonal effects of emotions in negotiations: A motivated information processing approach. *Journal of Personality and Social Psychology, 87,* 510–528.

Kramer, R., & Messick, D. (1995). *The social context of negotiation.* Newbury Park, CA: Sage.

Lacey, H. (1999). *Is science value free? Values and scientific understanding.* New York: Routledge.

Lax, D. A., & Sebenius, J. K. (1986). *The manager as negotiator: Bargaining for cooperation and competitive gain.* New York: Free Press.

Lebra, T. S. (1984). Nonconfrontational strategies for the management of interpersonal conflicts. In E. S. Krauss, T. P. Rohlen, & P. G. Steinhoff (Eds.), *Conflict in Japan* (pp. 41–60). Honolulu: University of Hawaii Press.

Leung, K. (1987). Some determinants of reactions to procedural models for conflict resolution: A cross-national study. *Journal of Personality and Social Psychology, 53,* 898–908.

Leung, K. (1997). Negotiation and reward allocation across cultures. In P. C. Earley & J. Erez (Eds.), *New perspectives on international industrial/organizational psychology* (pp. 640–675). San Francisco: New Lexington Press.

Leung, K., & Lind, E. A. (1986). Procedure and culture: Effects of culture, gender, and investigator status on procedural preferences. *Journal of Personality and Social Psychology, 19,* 35–49.

Lytle, A. L., Brett, J. M., Barsness, Z. I., Tinsley, C. H., & Janssens, M. (1995). A paradigm for confirmatory cross-cultural research in organizational behavior. In L. L. Cummings & B. M. Staw (Eds.), *Research in organizational behavior* (Vol. 17, pp. 167–214). Greenwich, CT: JAI Press.

March, R. M. (1990). *The Japanese negotiator: Subtlety and strategy beyond Western logic.* New York: Kodansha International.

Markus, H. R., & Kitayama, S. (1991). Culture and the self: Implications for cognition, emotion, and motivation. *Psychological Review, 98,* 224–253.

Markus, H. R., Kitayama, S., & Heiman, R. J. (1996). Culture and "basic" psychological principles. In E. T. Higgins & A. W. Kruglanski (Eds.), *Social psychology: Handbook of basic principles* (pp. 857–913). New York: Guilford Press.

Martinko, M. J., & Thomson, N. F. (1998). A synthesis and extension of the Weiner and Kelly attribution models. *Basic and Applied Psychology, 20,* 271–284.

Miller, J. G. (1984). Culture and the development of everyday social explanation. *Journal of Personality and Social Psychology, 46,* 961–978.

Montoya-Weiss, M. M., Massey, A. P., & Song, M. (2001). Getting it together: Temporal coordination and conflict management in global virtual teams. *Academy of Management Journal, 44*(6), 1251–1262.

Mook, J. (2000). *Motivation.* New York: Prentice Hall.

Moore, C. W. (1986). *The mediation process: Practical strategies for resolving conflict.* San Francisco: Jossey-Bass.

Morris, M. W., & Gelfand, M. J. (2004). Cultural differences and cognitive dynamics: Expanding the cognitive perspective on negotiation. In M. J. Gelfand & J. M. Brett (Eds.), *Handbook of negotiation and culture* (pp. 45–70). Palo Alto, CA: Stanford University Press.

Morris. M. W., & Keltner, D. (2000). How emotions work: The social functions of emotional expression in negotiations. *Research in Organizational Behaviour*, 22, 1–50.

Morris, M. W., Larrick, R. P., & Su, S. K. (1999). Misperceiving negotiation counterparts: When situationally determined bargaining behaviors are attributed to personality traits. *Journal of Personality and Social Psychology*, 77, 52–67.

Morris, M. W., & Peng, K. (1994). Culture and cause: American and Chinese attributions for social and physical events. *Journal of Personality and Social Psychology*, 67(6), 949–971.

Morris, M. W., Podolny, J., & Ariel, S. (2000). Missing relations: Incorporating relational constructs into models of culture. In P. C. Earley & H. Singh (Eds.), *Innovations in international and cross-cultural management* (pp. 52–90). Thousand Oaks, CA: Sage.

Neale, M., & Bazerman, M. (1985). The effect of externally set goals on reaching integrative agreements in competitive markets. *Journal of Occupational Behavior*, 6, 19–32.

Neale, M., & Bazerman, M. (1991). *Cognition and rationality in negotiation*. New York: Free Press.

Nisbett, R. E., Peng, K., Choi, I., & Norenzayan, A. (2001). Culture and systems of thought: Holistic versus analytic cognition. *Psychological Review*, 108(2), 291–310.

Ohbuchi, K., & Takahashi, Y. (1994). Cultural styles of conflict management in Japanese and Americans: Passivity, covertness, and effectiveness of strategies. *Journal of Applied Social Psychology*, 24, 1345–1366.

Okabe, R. (1983). Cultural assumptions of East and West: Japan and United States. In W. B. Gudykunst (Ed.), *Intercultural communication theory: Current perspectives* (Vol. 7, pp. 21–44). Beverly Hills, CA: Sage.

Olekalns, M., & Smith, P. L. (2000). Negotiating optimal outcomes: The role of strategic sequences in competitive negotiations. *Human Communication Research*, 26, 527–557.

Olekalns, M., & Smith, P. L. (2003). Testing the relationships among negotiators motivational orientations, strategy choices and outcomes. *Journal of Experimental Social Psychology*, 39, 101–117.

Olekalns, M., Smith, P., & Walsh, T. (1996). The process of negotiating: Strategy and timing as predictors of outcomes. *Organizational Behavior and Human Decision Processes*, 68(1), 68–77.

Peng, K., & Nisbett, R. E. (1999). Culture, dialectics, and reasoning about contradiction. *American Psychologist*, 54, 741–754.

Pruitt, D. (2004). Foreword. In M. J. Gelfand & J. M. Brett (Eds.), *Handbook of negotiation and culture* (pp. xi–xiii). Palo Alto, CA: Stanford University Press.

Pruitt, D. G. (1981). *Negotiation behavior*. New York: Academic Press.

Pruitt, D. G., & Lewis, S. A. (1975). Development of integrative solutions in bilateral negotiation. *Journal of Personality and Social Psychology*, 31, 621–630.

Putnam L. L., & Wilson, S. R. (1989). Argumentation and bargaining strategies as discriminators of integrative outcomes. In M. A. Rahim (Ed.), *Managing conflict: An interdisciplinary approach* (pp. 549–599). Newbury Park, CA: Sage.

Raiffa, H. (1982). *The art and science of negotiation*. Cambridge, MA: Harvard University Press.

Rosette, A. S., Brett, J. M., Barsness, Z., Lytle A. L. (2004). *When cultures clash electronically: The impact of e-mail and culture on negotiation behavior*. DRRC Working Paper #302, Northwestern University.

Ross, L. D. (1977). The intuitive psychologist and his shortcomings: Distortions in the attribution process. In L. Berkowitz (Ed.), *Advances in experimental social psychology* (Vol. 10, pp. 173–220). New York: Random House.

Schein, E. H. (1985). *Organizational culture and leadership*. San Francisco: Jossey-Bass.

Schroth, H. A., Bain-Chekal, J., & Caldwell, D. F. (2004). *Sticks and stones may break some bones and words CAN hurt me: Words and phrases that trigger emotions in negotiations and their effects*. University of California Haas School of Business Working Paper.

Schwartz, S. (1994). Beyond individualism/collectivism: New cultural dimensions of values. In U. Kim, H. C. Triandis, & G. Yoon (Eds.), *Individualism and collectivism* (pp. 85–123). London: Sage.

Selby, H. A. (1975). Semantics and causality in the study of deviance. In M. Sanches & B. Blount (Eds.), *Sociocultural dimensions of language use* (pp. 11–24). New York: Academic Press.

Shapiro, D. L., & Kulik, C. T. (2004). Resolving disputes between faceless disputants: New challenges for conflict management theory. In M. J. Gelfand & J. M. Brett (Eds.), *Handbook of negotiation and culture* (pp. 177–192). Palo Alto, CA: Stanford University Press.

Shweder, R. A., & Bourne, E. J. (1982). Does the concept of the person vary cross-culturally? In A. J. Marsella & G. M. White (Eds.), *Cultural conceptions of mental health and therapy* (pp. 97–137). New York: Kluwer Academic Publishers.

Stevenson, H. W., & Stigler, J. W. (1992). *The learning gap: Why our schools are failing and what we can learn from Japanese and Chinese education.* New York: Summit Books.

Tang, S. F., & Kirkbride, P. S. (1986). Developing conflict management skills in Hong Kong: An analysis of some cross-cultural implications. *Management Education and Development, 17,* 287–301.

Thompson, L. (1991). Information exchange in negotiation. *Journal of Experimental Social Psychology, 27,* 161–179.

Thompson, L. (2005). *The mind and heart of the negotiator* (3rd ed.). Upper Saddle River, NJ: Pearson Prentice Hall.

Thompson, L., & Hastie, R. (1990). Social perception in negotiation. *Organizational Behavior and Human Decision Processes, 47,* 98–123.

Ting-Toomey, S. (1988). Intercultural conflict styles: A face-negotiation theory. In Y. Y. Kim & W. B. Gudykunst (Eds.), *Theories in intercultural communication* (pp. 213–235). Thousand Oaks, CA: Sage.

Tinsley, C. (2004). Culture and conflict: Enlarging our dispute resolution framework. In M. J. Gelfand & J. M. Brett (Eds.), *Handbook of negotiation and culture* (pp. 193–210). Palo Alto, CA: Stanford University Press.

Triandis, H. C. (1995). *Individualism and collectivism*. New York: Simon & Schuster.

Trompenaars, F. (1996). Resolving international conflict: Culture and business strategy. *Business Strategy Review, 7,* 51.

Trubisky, P., Ting-Toomey, S., & Lin, S. (1991). The influence of individualism-collectivism and self-monitoring on conflict styles. *International Journal of Intercultural Relations, 15,* 65–84.

Tse, D. K. J., Francis, J., & Walls, J. (1994). Cultural differences in concluding intracultural and intercultural negotiations: A Sino-Canadian comparison. *Journal of International Business Studies, 24,* 537–555.

Tutzauer, F., & Roloff, M. E. (1988). Communication processes leading to integrative agreements: Three paths to joint benefit. *Communication Research, 15,* 360–380.

Weiner, B. (1985). "Spontaneous" causal thinking. *Psychological Bulletin, 97,* 74–84.

Weiner, B., Frieze, I., Kukla, A., Reed, L., Rest, S., & Rosenbaum, R. M. (1971). *Perceiving the causes of success and failure*. Morristown, NJ: General Learning Press.

Weingart, L. R., & Olekalns, M. (2004). Communication processes in negotiations: Frequencies, sequences, and phases. In M. J. Gelfand & J. M. Brett (Eds.), *Handbook of negotiation and culture* (pp. 143–157). Palo Alto, CA: Stanford University Press.

Weingart, L. R., Hyder, E. B., & Prietula, M. J. (1996). Knowledge matters: The effect of tactical descriptions on negotiation behavior and outcome. *Journal of Personality and Social Psychology, 70*(6), 1205–1217.

Weingart, L. R., Thompson, L. L., Bazerman, M. H., & Carroll, J. S. (1990). Tactical behavior and negotiation outcomes. *International Journal of Conflict Management, 1*, 7–31.

White, S. B., & Neale, M. A. (1994). The role of negotiator aspirations and settlement expectancies in bargaining outcomes. *Organizational Behavior and Human Decision Processes, 57*, 303–317.

Wolfson, K., & Norden, M. (1984). Measuring responses to filmed interpersonal conflict: A roles approach. In W. Gudykunst & Y. Kim (Eds.), *Methods for intercultural communication research* (pp. 155–166). Beverly Hills, CA: Sage.

Yamagishi, T., & Yamagishi, M. (1994). Trust and commitment in the United States and Japan. *Motivation and Emotion, 18*, 129–166.

Yang, K. S. (1993). Chinese social orientation: An integrative analysis. In L. Y. Cheng, R. M. C. Cheung, & C. N. Chen (Eds.), *Psychotherapy for the Chinese: Selected papers from the First International Cconference* (pp. 117–158). Hong Kong: Chinese University Press.

10

Gender in Negotiations: A Motivated Social Cognitive Analysis

LAURA KRAY and LINDA BABCOCK

Social psychologists have long recognized that what is salient in a given situation has a profound influence on behavior (Fiske & Taylor, 1991). Gender is one of the most salient characteristics of an individual, causing observers to notice and process it immediately in a social situation (Deaux & LaFrance, 1998). Despite the widespread application of social psychological perspectives to the negotiation domain, the investigation of gender's capability of explaining negotiating behavior has been relatively sparse. Two factors speak to the failure of gender to capture the attention of negotiation researchers. First, this type of investigation is generally regarded to be atheoretical. Documenting a gender difference does not speak to what caused the difference to emerge, and explorations of gender in negotiations have typically fallen short of adequately explaining the process through which gender matters. Another reason why researchers have been reluctant to study gender is the perception that it accounts for little variation in behavior in a complex, mixed-motive context such as negotiations. To the extent that gender has been recognized as a predictor of competitive behaviors and the division of resources (Stuhlmacher & Walters, 1999; Walters, Stuhlmacher, & Meyer, 1998), its documented impact has been relatively weak.

With these criticisms in mind, we try to dispel the misperception that gender is irrelevant for understanding bargaining behavior. At least two reasons speak to why the perception that gender has relatively little explanatory power in negotiations is inaccurate. First, even gender differences in negotiation behavior and outcomes that are small in magnitude add up to very large amounts over time because these differences accumulate. Martell, Lane, and Emrich (1996), using a simulation approach, show that even if gender explains only 1% of the variation in performance evaluations, this difference has a large negative impact on the proportion of women who end up at senior levels in an organization. Likewise, gender differences in the initiation of a negotiation at the beginning of a career can add up to more than a half-million dollars in lost income over a lifetime (Babcock & Laschever, 2003). Therefore, even gender differences that seem small in magnitude may have a large meaningful impact on gender differences in outcomes.

Second, recent scholarship has argued that the effect of gender on negotiation outcomes has been obfuscated because most research has tended to take an individual difference perspective rather than a situational perspective (Bowles, Babcock, & McGinn, 2004; Kray, Galinsky, & Thompson, 2002; Kray, Thompson, & Galinsky, 2001; Stuhlmacher & Walters, 1999; Walters et al., 1998). Because gender may affect negotiation behavior in some situations and not others, when researchers compare results across studies and do not account for the different situational factors across these same studies, it may appear that gender has an inconsistent impact. For example, Kray et al. (2001) only observed gender differences in one study when the negotiation task was thought to be highly diagnostic of core negotiating abilities; otherwise, men and women performed comparably. Similarly, Bowles et al. (2004) found large gender differences in negotiation outcomes when concrete goals were not provided to the negotiation participants; however, these differences disappeared when participants were given clear negotiation targets. Therefore, careful attention to aspects of the negotiation situation will help to clarify the impact of gender on negotiations.

The purpose of this chapter is to provide a broader theoretical framework in which to analyze the situational complexity of gender in negotiations. We focus on differences that emerge between men and women in their underlying motivations and cognitions, which ultimately guide behavior at the bargaining table. Through the lens of motivation and cognition, we aim to demonstrate that the situational context shapes negotiators' expectations, judgments, goals, and aspirations—all of which subsequently influences performance. By exploring the full range of contextual factors that differentiate men and women, we seek to develop a framework for understanding when gender emerges as a predictor of behavior and outcomes at the bargaining table. We believe that this approach will foster an appreciation of the substantial explanatory power of gender and help to guide future empirical research in this area.

AN EXAMINATION OF GENDER THROUGH THE MOTIVATED SOCIAL COGNITIVE LENS

Building on many of the insights from the social-cognitive perspective of negotiation (see Neale & Fragale, chapter 3; Neale & Fragale, 2004), we explore the social cognitive and motivational differences between women and men at the bargaining table. We also draw heavily on a wide range of social psychological theories to offer insight into why these differences emerge when they do. In so doing, we detail the many situational factors that determine whether gender differences are pronounced or muted at the bargaining table. Finally, we conclude by identifying several pressing questions that we believe should be prioritized in future research on gender and negotiations.

Gender and Motivation

Two classes of negotiator motivations are relevant for understanding gender differences between men and women: task-specific goals and interaction goals. While it is uncertain which type of goal is more important in general, it is clear that the relative weight on each type of goal will depend on the situation. For example, when buying a used car, the task-specific goal is likely to figure more prominently than interaction goals, whereas the latter will potentially be more important when two friends are deciding what movie to see. We believe as well that the relative weight of the goals will depend on gender, with women placing greater relative weight on interaction goals than do men. Below we review the evidence that speaks to this hypothesis.

Task-Specific Motivations An important negotiator motivation is the outcome goal that negotiators set for the negotiation. High-outcome goals lead to more persistence and, ultimately, better outcomes (Bazerman, Magliozzi, & Neale, 1985; Huber & Neale, 1987; Locke & Latham, 1990; Neale & Bazerman, 1985). One reason that this goal is so important is that it has a strong relationship with the negotiator's opening offer, which tends to anchor the negotiation and influence the ultimate agreement that is reached (Galinsky & Mussweiler, 2001).

Several negotiation studies have measured what tangible outcomes male and female negotiators hope to attain. Stevens, Bavetta, and Gist (1993) measured negotiators' goals before a mock salary negotiation. Among their sample of MBA students, they found that men's goals were nearly 5% higher than the goals of women, despite the fact that they scored identically in terms of their tactical knowledge entering into the negotiation. Not surprisingly, the salaries that men ultimately achieved were proportionally superior to those of their female counterparts. Kray et al. (2002) recently observed that in a baseline condition of mixed-gender dyads, men's target sale prices were higher than their female counterparts' targets. They also showed that goal differences mediated the relationship between their experimental manipulation of stereotype activation and performance. Finally, Bowles et al. (2004) provide further evidence that, in mixed-gender dyads, men set higher performance targets than females. The size of their gender differences was relatively large—male buyers set goals that were 9.8% more aggressive than female buyers'. In combination, these studies support the proposition that men and women differ in the task-specific goals they set before reaching the bargaining table. It suggests that women may be weighting other goals, such as interaction goals, more heavily compared to men.

How men and women negotiate varies on the basis of their outcome goals, with greater gender variation in negotiation strategies in competitive environments. Deal (2000) observed that the intentional use of information to support a particular point of view was greater for male negotiators than female negotiators in a competitive negotiation context (i.e., one in which a "winner" would be declared), but men and women exhibited similar patterns of information use in a more collaborative negotiation context. Consistent with this finding is the emergence of a performance gap between men and women in solving computerized mazes when they competed with each other for rewards in a tournament, but comparable performance on the same task when rewards were paid according to piece rate (Gneezy, Niederle, & Rustichini, 2004). These findings suggest that gender differences emerge when rewards are structured in such a way that negotiators are motivated to compete against one another. This is consistent with evidence from Stuhlmacher and Walters (1999), which showed that, across a wide range of studies, gender differences in negotiated outcomes were greater in distributive negotiations than in integrative ones.

Another relevant task-specific motivation concerns negotiators' interest in engaging in negotiations. The degree of interest that individuals express for a task influences their motivation to expend effort and persevere in the face of difficulties (Butler, 1987; Dweck & Elliot, 1983). Women report being less interested in negotiation tasks than men, and this gender difference appears to be greatest when negotiators are charged with a high aspiration that is difficult to attain (Kimmel, Pruitt, Magenau, Konar-Goldband, & Carnevale, 1980). Men appear to believe that participating in negotiations is a much more positive experience than do women. Gelfand and McCusker (2004) presented a list of scenarios and asked participants to select those scenarios that they associated with negotiations. Although the study focused on culture differences in choosing metaphors, they also found that men were more likely to equate negotiations with a wrestling match or winning a ballgame than women, who tended to equate negotiating with going to the dentist.[1] In another study, participants rated how much a set of adjectives described how they thought about the prospect of conducting a negotiation. Whereas men selected words like "exciting" and "fun," women tended to select adjectives like "scary" (Babcock, Gelfand, Small, & Stayn, 2004). Also consistent with the idea that gender affects negotiators' motivations to engage in the bargaining process is the observation that male negotiators reap better outcomes and spend more time negotiating than female negotiators (Neu, Graham, & Gilly, 1988). Likewise, King and Hinson (1994) demonstrated that negotiating dyads with a male seller exchanged more offers than dyads with a female seller, contributing to the male seller's superior performance.

Interaction-Specific Motivations   Going as far back as Rubin and Brown's (1975) treatise on negotiation behavior, men and women have been assumed to differ in their interpersonal orientation (IO). Interpersonal orientation is an individual difference measure that concerns the degree to which individuals are interested in and responsive to the interpersonal aspects of their relationships (Swap & Rubin, 1983). Individuals who are characterized by a high IO tend to adjust their behavior on the basis of their negotiating partner's behavior. That is, they behave cooperatively with a cooperative partner and behave competitively with a competitive partner. In contrast, low-IO individuals tend to be unresponsive to their partner's behavior. With regard to gender, women are argued to be more sensitive and reactive to the interpersonal aspects of the negotiation than men. Consistent with this argument, men and women have been shown to differ in how they prioritize various negotiation-relevant values. Specifically, men report being more concerned with a comfortable life and being logical, whereas women report being more concerned with fostering positive relationships through honesty, being loving, and maintaining self-respect (Feather, 1984).

Specific to negotiations, Barron (2003) interviewed male and female negotiators in an effort to understand their motivations. Whereas the vast majority of men reported a motivation to further their own interests as a primary goal in the negotiation, the majority of women endorsed the view that the purpose of the negotiation was to further their acceptance by others. Accordingly, Halpern and Parks (1996) observed female–female dyads engaging in far more self-disclosures about personal information during the course of their negotiation than male–male dyads did.

Interpersonal orientation is an important gauge of motivation in negotiations because it directly influences individuals' preferences for dividing resources. The influence of gender and IO on resource allocation between two same-sex partners working on a joint cooperative task was examined by Major and Adams (1983). Before commencing the task, women were found to score higher on IO than men. Upon completion of the cooperative task, one dyad member was asked to decide the division of performance points. Women's subsequent reward allocations between themselves and their partner were more equal than men's allocations, which were more favorable to themselves. Kimmel et al. (1980) also provided evidence that male dyads engaged in distributive bargaining tactics to a greater extent than female dyads, which may be evidence of men's lower concern about the relationship relative to concern about their own outcome.

Apart from the differential concern that men and women appear to have for the outcomes of their negotiating counterpart is their concern with the state of the relationship itself. Whereas most negotiation studies measure performance in terms of economic outcomes, negotiation performance can also be measured relationally. The importance of the relationship in a one-shot laboratory context is likely diminished, yet in many negotiations outside of the laboratory it is likely that the development of a relationship is a primary goal. Consistent with this idea, Fry, Firestone, and Williams (1983) observed that dating couples, who were presumably highly concerned with keeping their relationship intact, had lower joint economic outcomes than negotiating dyads comprised of strangers. Preliminary research by Curhan, Neale, Ross, and Rosencranz-Engelmann (2004) suggests a tradeoff between economic gains and relational satisfaction at the bargaining table. With this realization in mind, we consider whether men and women differ in the outcome goal that they emphasize.

Cross and Madson (1997) argue that women's self-schemas are inherently interdependent, meaning that they define themselves in terms of their interpersonal relationships, to a larger extent than men's self-schemas. Likewise, Kolb and Coolidge (1991) argue that women rarely see negotiations as not having a relationship dimension. If this argument is true, then it suggests that the desire to use the negotiation as an opportunity to foster the negotiators' relationship should figure more prominently for women than men. Accordingly, King and Hinson (1994) showed that, in a postnegotiation assessment, women were more likely than men to endorse the view that they treated their opponent fairly, they were motivated to maintain a good relationship with their opponent during the negotiation, and that they were concerned with their opponent's feelings during the negotiation. Likewise, the inferences that negotiators made about their negotiating partner's concerns for the relationship varied across gender, with women holding more charitable views of their partner's actions than men. Lastly, Gelfand, Smith-Major, Raver, and Nishii (2004) introduce a concept they call *relational self-construal*, which is the degree to which one views one's self as connected to others. They argue that women's scores on this construct are significantly greater than the scores for men.

Another way in which self-schemas can affect negotiating behavior is by influencing how negotiators utilize power. Chen, Lee-Chai, and Bargh (2001) showed that individuals characterized by a communal relationship orientation used power to meet social responsibility goals in an interpersonal context to a greater degree than individuals characterized by an exchange relationship orientation, who used power to further self-interest goals. If women are more communally oriented than men are (Cross & Madsen, 1997), then it might create a difference in how they use power.

Another negotiator motivation that may differ across gender is the degree of concern with managing the impressions formed by negotiating partners and third parties. According to this perspective, normative expectations dictate that women behave in a more communally oriented manner than men, thereby creating a correspondingly larger self-presentational concern for women who behave in a self-interested manner.[2] Rudman's (1998) research suggests that this concern might not be unfounded, as women who were self-promoting in an interview context suffered a backlash in terms of their perceived likeability. Likewise, Carli, LaFleur, & Loeber (1995) found that women who used a very task-oriented style (e.g., rapid speech, direct eye contact) with a male audience to whom they were delivering a persuasive message were perceived to be less likeable and competent than men who delivered the same message using the same style. Finally, Burgoon, Dillard, and Doran (1983) found that men and women who presented an argument in a manner that violated gender stereotype expectations were less persuasive than men and women who presented the same argument in a stereotype-consistent manner.

Evidence that women understand they are more burdened than men by self-presentational concerns would come from the observation that their behavior in competitive situations differs in public and private contexts to a greater extent than does the behavior of men. Kidder, Bellettirie, and Cohn (1977) found that women allocated rewards between themselves and an inferiorly performing partner more equally in public and when they expected future interactions than they did in private and when no future interaction was expected. In contrast, men actually rewarded more points to themselves in public than in private. Similarly, Major, McFarlin, and Gagnon (1984) found that the amount of time that women worked for a fixed amount of pay, although always longer than what men worked, was considerably less when they believe the work was unmonitored than when they believed it was monitored. In contrast, the amount of time that men worked did not vary across different monitoring conditions. Finally, Wade (2001) found that the amount of salary requested by women for a hypothetical job depended on whether they were making the request for themselves or another individual.

Arguably constrained by the self-presentational desire to appear not greedy, women requested less for themselves than men did, and they requested far less for themselves than they did for another woman. Presumably, women's impression management concerns about selfishness were diminished when advocating on the behalf of someone else.

Impression management concerns of men and women might also differ to the extent that they typically possess different levels of power in negotiations. Low-power individuals have been shown to be more motivated to manage impressions than high-power individuals (Copeland, 1994; Jones, 1986). A large body of research suggests that women are typically thought to be less influential and enjoy lower status than do men (Eagly, 1983), suggesting that structural factors apart from the negotiation context itself might contribute to the greater impression management burdens carried by women.

If men and women differ in their motivations, then negotiation studies that gauge performance solely on the basis of economic gains implicitly devalue women's skills. Women's relatively greater cooperative motivation has generally been equated with weakness (Watson, 1994), leading women to devalue their abilities (Kolb, 2000). However, cooperation is often important in the construction of integrative agreements. Women's cooperative motivation appears to be associated with less contentious bargaining strategies than those employed by men (Kimmel et al., 1980). Theoretically, a strong relationship between negotiators should increase the likelihood of crafting integrative agreements in the future (Pruitt & Rubin, 1986). However, consistent with the dual-concern prediction, Calhoun and Smith (1999) found that integrative outcomes were greater in same-sex female dyads when women had a high concern both for the other party and oneself compared to when their concern for themselves was low and their concern for the other party was high. This finding suggests that women's habitual tendency to be cooperative is an asset when it is coupled with a high regard for their own interests.

A final motivational factor that speaks to the interpersonal aspect of the negotiation is the extent to which women are motivated to react against the disadvantage that they sometimes experience in the negotiation arena. Explicitly connecting gender to negotiating ability prior to a mixed-gender negotiation leads women to react against the stereotype by setting higher goals than they otherwise would, thereby reaping better outcomes than their male counterparts (Kray et al., 2001). Although a chivalrous norm has been shown to emerge when negotiating on behalf of a woman (Pruitt, Carnevale, Forcey, & van Slyck, 1986), Kray et al. were able to rule out this explanation for the documented reversal of the typical gender gap by providing valuable performance incentives to both male and female negotiators. What appears to account for women's superior performance is an increased motivation to overcome the implications of the limiting stereotype.

Gender and Cognition

Beliefs About Bargaining Zone Negotiators' beliefs about the range of possible and appropriate outcomes shape the offers that they make and what concessions they deem acceptable. In an investigation specifically aimed at comparing women's and men's estimates of the bargaining zone, Kaman and Hartel (1994) presented a hypothetical job description to participants and asked them to assess the target and resistance points of the job recruiter and the candidate (i.e., themselves). Relative to men, women candidates set lower target and resistance points, and their estimates of the job recruiters' resistance points were lower. Given these differences in estimates of the bargaining zone, it is perhaps not surprising that Pruitt et al. (1986) reported that male negotiators expected to take a more competitive approach in a mixed-motive negotiation than women did.

Beliefs About Ability and Worth   As detailed above, men and women differ in their estimates of the bargaining zone. One factor that likely influences negotiators' beliefs about the bargaining zone is their own perceived worth. Barron (2003) documented a striking divergence in how men and women determine their worth in salary negotiations. Whereas the vast majority of men indicated their worth was self-determined, the overwhelming majority of women felt that their worth was determined by what the company would pay them. Similarly, Major and Konar (1984) documented that men expected to earn over 15% more money than women the first year on the job and over 45% more during their peak salary-earning year. Women consistently pay themselves less than men do (Callahan-Levy & Messe, 1979), which has been attributed to a weaker connection between work and monetary rewards for women than men.

To the extent that negotiators use social comparison information to gauge their worth and the bargaining zone, differences in the quantity and quality of information available may account for the emergence of a gender gap. Consistent with this reasoning, Major and Konar (1984) found that what women expected other people in a similar job to be earning was lower than what men expected. In an experimental piece exploring the use of comparison information in affecting personal entitlement beliefs, Major et al. (1984) found that women paid themselves less than men for a fixed amount of work when social comparison information was absent. When comparison information was present, men and women paid themselves comparably. In a follow-up investigation, McFarlin, Frone, Major, and Konar (1989) found that reference group comparison information was a better predictor of expected pay than other plausible factors, such as different career paths and motivation levels.

A related cognitive factor that impacts how negotiators view themselves is their confidence in the negotiation arena. If men and women differ on this dimension, then it could influence how forcefully they assert their interests at the bargaining table (Mowday, 1978, 1979). In fact, women typically report less confidence in masculine or competitive tasks (Beyer, 1990; Lenney, 1977; Ragins & Sundstrom, 1989) and in the influence domain (Instone, Major, & Bunker, 1983) than men do. If women and men have different beliefs about their worth, then they would be expected to experience different levels of threat by a task purported to uncover their worth. Accordingly, Kray et al. (2001) showed that, in a diagnostic negotiation that negotiators believed would reveal their true negotiating ability, male negotiators expected to get a larger portion of the "bargaining pie" than their female counterparts. When the negotiation was described as a nondiagnostic exercise, however, no differences in expectations emerged between men and women.

Presumably, confidence is influenced by the degree of control negotiators expect to have over the process. Stevens et al. (1993) observed that differences in the degree to which women and men believed that they could influence and control their negotiation experience mediated the relationship between various training programs and subsequent negotiated salaries. In an early demonstration of self-evaluation differences in the negotiation arena, Benton (1973) observed that men rated themselves as more competent in settling conflicts of interest involving money than their female negotiating partners. Accordingly, men indicated a greater expectation of winning than their female counterparts. One reason why this confidence gap is particularly troubling is that it often leads to an underestimation of performance for women (Beyer, 1990). For example, although men and women performed comparably on a bargaining task, women reported less confidence in their ability prior to the negotiation and less satisfaction with their outcome after the negotiation than men did (Watson & Hoffman, 1996).

Differences in perceived negotiating ability of men and women may be caused by beliefs about what personal characteristics people ascribe to effective negotiators in general. Many of the traits that characterize effective negotiators are perceived to be masculine in nature, and many of the traits of ineffective negotiators are perceived to be feminine (Williams & Best, 1982). Kray et al. (2001) documented a mapping between the traits that negotiators associated with effective bargaining and gender. MBA student respondents were asked to indicate whether they believed one gender had an advantage in negotiations and, if so, which one. In line with the dominant cultural stereotype, the modal response supported the view that men have a negotiation advantage. When asked to justify their response, the vast majority of reasons offered characterized men in terms of their strength and assertiveness and women in terms of their emotion and concern for others.

Quite apart from the traits that people ascribe to effective negotiators is whether they believe negotiating ability is fixed versus malleable. Negotiators' implicit beliefs as to whether negotiating ability is a trait one is born with (or not) or a skill that can be developed through practice and instruction affects how they bargain. Building on Dweck and Leggett's (1988) approach to motivation and personality, Kray and Haselhuhn (2004) have demonstrated that negotiators who believe negotiating ability is malleable fare better at the bargaining table compared to negotiators who believe that negotiating skill is fixed. Importantly for understanding how these beliefs speak to gender is their finding that only women who held the belief that negotiating ability was malleable reacted against the blatant activation of a negative gender stereotype and outperformed their male counterpart; women who believed negotiating ability was fixed succumbed to the negative stereotype.

To the extent that stereotypes shape beliefs about negotiating style and ability, knowing the gender of one's bargaining opponent should influence what behavior is expected of him or her. Matheson (1991) found that knowing the gender of one's negotiating partner impacted how cooperative and exploitative they were expected to be, with female negotiators expected to be more cooperative and less exploitative than male negotiators. In a related study, women as a category were expected to be more cooperative in a prisoner's dilemma game than were men, although in this case the gender of individual players did not affect the extent to which their partners expected them to be cooperative (Orbell, Dawes, & Schwartz-Shea, 1994). In addition to affecting what is expected of a negotiating partner, gender stereotypes also appear to affect the gender attributions that are made for an interaction partner's behavior. King, Miles, and Kniska (1991) asked participants in a prisoner's dilemma game to infer the gender of their partner whose behavior was manipulated to be competitive, cooperative, or tit-for-tat. Participants were more likely to infer their partner was male in the competitive condition than the other two conditions.

The expectations that a negotiator has about his or her counterpart are important to consider because perceiver expectations can elicit target behaviors that are consistent with the perceiver's expectations (Snyder, Tanke, & Berscheid, 1977). For example, Skrypnek and Snyder (1982) examined the behavioral confirmation process in a mixed-gender negotiation over the division of tasks that had gender connotations. By manipulating the male negotiator's beliefs about his female partner's gender (unbeknownst to her), the researchers were able to examine the impact of these beliefs on the female partner's behavior. Consistent with the idea that a perceiver's expectations of a target influence a target's actions, when the male perceiver mistakenly believed that his negotiating partner was male, she subsequently chose more stereotypically masculine tasks than when the male perceiver correctly believed that his negotiating partner was female. Presumably, subtle cues elicited by the male perceiver guided the behavior of the female target in a manner consistent with his beliefs about her gender. The molding of negotiator behavior on the basis of what is expected of them by others extends to situations involving surveillance by constituents. Pruitt et al. (1986) observed that surveillance by a male constituent made negotiators more contentious and resulted in relatively unequal outcomes compared to when negotiators believed they were being monitored by a female constituent. They argued that this effect was the result of negotiators' beliefs regarding what their constituent expected of them. Because high-power perceivers have been shown to affect behavioral confirmation processes to a greater extent than low-power perceivers (Copeland, 1994), it is likely that gender-based power asymmetries will disproportionately affect women (Ragins & Sundstrom, 1989).

Mental Model of the Negotiation Situation

One aspect in which the negotiation context might differ between men and women concerns how they mentally represent the negotiation domain. We argue that how the negotiation situation is framed influences concerns about how gender stereotypes speak to a negotiator's performance. As described in the previous section on beliefs about negotiating parties, gender stereotypes shape expectations and attributions for negotiators' behaviors. If women are expected to fare relatively poorly due to their gender, then being in a competitive negotiation may trigger stereotype threat, or the concern that their behavior at the bargaining table will confirm this negative stereotype about their gender (Steele, 1997). This concern poses an additional burden that women carry with them to the bargaining table, rendering the very meaning of the negotiation different than what their male counterparts understand the negotiation to be about. One particular set of beliefs that can trigger stereotype threat at the bargaining table is the understanding that the task is diagnostic of one's core negotiating abilities (Kray et al., 2001). This diagnostic framing leads negotiators to assess what skills are needed to succeed, which activates gender stereotypical traits and unwittingly leads to behaviors that confirm the stereotype (Kray et al., 2001). When the negotiation is framed as a learning exercise, these stereotypical thoughts are not conjured up, and men and women perform comparably. Beliefs about the relevance of gender stereotypes can contribute to a gender gap in negotiations.

Yet another factor influencing how negotiators frame the situation concerns whether they recognize an issue as negotiable and then choose to initiate a negotiation. Perhaps because men perceive less risk in engaging in various activities than women do (Lerner, Gonzalez, Small, & Fischhoff, 2003; Slovic, 2000), gender may differentially affect women and men's propensity to negotiate. In a Web-based field survey of a diverse population, Babcock et al. (2004) discovered that women indicated a greater period of time since their last negotiation and when they expected to negotiate next than men did. Likewise, Small, Babcock, Gelfand, and Gettman (2004) observed that men were nearly nine times more likely to ask for additional compensation over and above a baseline rate after completing a task than women were, despite the fact that men and women evaluated their performance on the task comparably. Also consistent with the view that men perceive more opportunities for legitimate negotiations than women is the observation that male job candidates perceived a wider range between a job recruiter's target point and resistance point than female candidates did (Kaman & Hartel, 1994). One notable exception to this finding is the observation that male and female MBA students were equally likely to report having negotiated for a higher salary than what was initially offered by their new employer (Gerhart & Rynes, 1991). Gerhart and Rynes suggested that the relatively similar opportunity sets among their sample of MBA graduates at an Ivy League school may have diminished the impact of gender on the propensity to negotiate. In addition, this study took place in a strong situation in which there were clear norms suggesting that negotiation is possible and appropriate.

The strategies that women and men believe to be appropriate in negotiations appear to differ. Instone et al. (1983) observed a tendency for men to engage in a wider range of influence strategies and to make more influence attempts than women did. Likewise, Kaman and Hartel (1994) showed that men assigned a higher probability than women to engaging in an active negotiation strategy, involving behaviors such as asking for a specific salary that is higher than what they expect an employer might be willing to accept. In contrast, women indicated a higher likelihood than men of engaging in behaviors that indirectly suggest a higher strategy was appropriate, such as emphasizing their skills and motivation to work.

One reason that women are less inclined to engage in active negotiation behaviors than men is that they may be less effective at them. For example, women who used a quid pro quo influence tactic negotiated lower salaries than men who used the same tactic (Dreher, Dougherty, & Whitely, 1989). Likewise, women who negotiated a job offer received a lower return on the negotiation in terms of the difference between the initial salary offer and the final accepted offer than their male counterparts (Gerhart & Rynes, 1991). In an ultimatum game, women were expected to concede more and were offered less than their male counterparts (Solnick & Schweitzer, 1999), providing a disincentive for women to participate in negotiations. Finally, women were more likely than men to fail to match the extremity of their negotiating partner's requests (i.e., responding to an opponent's low demand with a high demand), thereby disrupting the flow of the negotiation process (Pruitt & Syna, 1985). This mismatching effect may indicate both a greater willingness of women to exploit a weak opponent and/or a divergent understanding between male and female negotiators of how the negotiation process should unfold.

A final set of beliefs that can distinguish male and female negotiators concerns the time horizon, or whether a negotiation is interpreted as a one-shot deal versus one with long-term consequences. In the previous section on negotiator motivations we identified the degree to which negotiators' self-schemas are relationship-oriented as one way of distinguishing men and women. This distinction is important for determining the expected time horizon of a negotiation. Greenhalgh and Gilkey (1993) manipulated whether negotiators were relationship- versus transaction-oriented and showed that the former type of negotiators were more likely to view the relationships with other parties as continuous rather than episodic relative to the latter type of negotiators. When high performing members of a dyad perceive the relationship to extend to the future, they are more likely to distribute rewards equally than when they believe no future interaction will occur, in which case they allocate rewards equitably (Shapiro, 1975). Differing perceptions of the time horizon between men and women might affect their preferences for equality.

Situational Factors Affecting Negotiators' Motivation and Cognition

A key situational factor that we expect to influence whether gender differences emerge in negotiations is the salience of gender. Kanter (1977) argues that gender is particularly salient when the gender composition of a group is skewed. If women negotiate less frequently than men, when a negotiator faces a woman on the other side of the bargaining table, her gender will be more salient than a comparable male negotiator's gender would be. When a woman is a numerical minority, her token status increases her visibility, polarizes gender differences, and leads others to see her in stereotypical terms. As the previous section described, expecting an individual to behave in stereotypical terms can unwittingly lead to behaviors that are consistent with these expectations.

Another factor that can increase the salience of gender is the gender composition of the negotiating dyad, with gender being more prominent in mixed-gender negotiations than same-gender negotiations. In their investigation of stereotype threat in negotiations, Kray et al. (2001) included both same-gender and mixed-gender negotiating dyads. Only when gender was salient due to a mixed-gender composition did stereotype threat and reactance processes occur. Presumably, the fact that a particular stereotype applied equally to both negotiators in same-gender dyads rendered the stereotype irrelevant to the interaction. Although mixed-gender dyads have been shown to be as efficient as same-gender dyads in face-to-face negotiations, mixed-gender dyads appear to drag out the negotiations when the negotiators are physically separated (Vallacher, Callahan-Levy, & Messe, 1979). One reason why physical separation may impair the negotiation process is that gender becomes the only salient social cue available to negotiators to guide their expectations of their negotiating partner. These findings suggest that gender differences can be reduced by negotiating with individuals of the same gender or in mixed-gender contexts that provide individuating information to facilitate the process.

The role constraints and demands impacting negotiators are also likely to contribute to an emergence of a gender gap. When negotiators are advocating on the behalf of others, they behave differently than when they are negotiating on their own behalf. Wade (2001) argued that women negotiate more forcefully when advocating on behalf of another person than when negotiating for themselves because they are more comfortable and satisfied when they work to produce change in the former case, and advocating forcefully for another person is consistent with the normative expectations of female communal behavior. Furthermore, women advocating on behalf of themselves would feel constrained by normative expectations to not behave too aggressively. Consistent with this hypothesis, Bowles et al. (2004) observed that female and male negotiators' prenegotiation expectations were more aligned when they expected to negotiate on behalf of someone else than when they expected to negotiate on their own behalf, in which case men's targets and intended offers were more aggressive than were women's. Because negotiating in an advocacy role necessarily introduces a constituent into the situation, it is also important to consider whether the gender of one's constituents matters. As described earlier, Pruitt et al. (1986) observed more contentious bargaining behavior when one's constituent was male than when the constituent was female.

The strength of the negotiation situation is also likely to determine whether gender differences emerge. Mischel (1977) argued that situations can be characterized along a continuum ranging from strong to weak. His person x situation interactionist perspective advances the view that individual differences are likely to emerge in weak situations, which tend to involve relatively ambiguous behavioral cues. Recent work by Bowles et al. (2004) extends this framework to the domain of gender and negotiations. They identify weak situations, or those in which sufficient ambiguity exists as to appropriate goals for the negotiation, as ones in which different beliefs and motivations between women and men are likely to impact behavior at the bargaining table. In several empirical tests of this hypothesis, they observed more favorable negotiation terms for male negotiators than female negotiators when negotiation goals were ill-defined relative to when they were clearly specified.

Whether negotiators conceive a negotiation as professional versus personal in nature is another situational factor that appears to distinguish men's and women's bargaining behaviors. In an examination of women's and men's distributive justice preferences, Major, Bylsma, and Cozzarelli (1989) determined that women's preferences were more benevolent (less entitled) than men in work domains, but gender did not impact resource allocation preferences in personal settings. This finding suggests that whether negotiators conceive their interaction as "all business" versus occurring within the context of a personal relationship impacts the similarity of men's and women's preferences for dividing resources. Consistent with this reasoning, Babcock et al. (2004) observed that women were less likely to initiate negotiations in a hypothetical work scenario than men were, but gender did not impact the propensity to negotiate in scenarios outside of work.

Another situational factor that influences how men and women negotiate is the power dynamic of the negotiation. Because the ability to walk away from the bargaining table affords a negotiator a great deal of power (Pinkley, Neale, & Bennett, 1994), the degree to which negotiators possess similarly attractive alternatives to a negotiated agreement is a key source of leverage. Kray, Reb, Galinsky, and Thompson (2004) observed that the ability of women to react against a negative stereotype is limited to situations in which they possess this type of bargaining power. There is reason to believe that how men and women respond to powerlessness may differ. Specifically, in an investigation of critical incidents in the workplace, Mainiero (1986) documented a greater tendency among women than men to respond to powerlessness by using an acquiescence strategy, or acting in a helpless manner that implies an acceptance of the power imbalance. In the context of negotiations, this strategy could perpetuate and potentially magnify existing power asymmetries.

Leveling the Playing Field

In this section, we consider interventions that can help to eliminate the barriers that women face in negotiating the outcomes they desire and the constraints that women face on their behavior documented in the preceding sections. Although the ideas described in this section most directly speak to improving women's economic outcomes, they are also relevant to male negotiators who prefer not to negotiate on the basis of gender or anyone interested in mentoring a female negotiator. Men that manage female employees may also be interested in finding ways to improve their employees' negotiating performance (Babcock, Laschever, Gelfand, & Small, 2003). Because this section also describes interventions that lead female negotiators to outperform their male counterparts, even a purely self-interested male negotiator would be wise to consider the various factors that lead to a reversal of the gender gap. In keeping with the framework outlines above, we distinguish between motivational, cognitive, and situational factors.

Motivational Interventions   Impression management motivations appear to
differ across gender in the context of competitive situations. One reason why these
concerns may differ between men and women is the fact that women experience
a backlash when they behave in a self-promoting manner (Rudman, 1998). In this
research, women who self-promoted while being considered for a job benefited
in terms of their interaction partner's competence ratings of them, but suffered
in terms of their social attractiveness and hireability ratings. When women pair
communal behavior with agentic behavior necessary for self-promotion, it is more
likely to be successful than simply engaging in agentic behavior alone (Rudman
& Glick, 2001). One notable exception to this pattern emerged in the ratings of
males who were outcome-dependent, who did not negatively evaluate their female
counterpart when she engaged in self-promotion. Presumably, the fact that men
were dependent on self-promoting women led them to seek to develop an accurate
perception of their female counterparts (Hilton & Darley, 1991). This research
suggests that, by emphasizing the mutual dependency of the two negotiators to
achieve outcomes that exceed their alternatives, women can be relieved of the
external pressure to "soften" their style by using communal behavior and can be
freer in their choice of actions.

Negotiators' motivations can also be altered to affect performance vis-à-vis the
salience of gender stereotypes. Generally speaking, people are motivated to protect
their freedom and modify their behavior accordingly when they perceive a restriction being imposed (Brehm, 1966). In the context of negotiations, this reactance
process can lead to a somewhat ironic outcome. Specifically, asserting that women
are less skilled in the negotiation domain than men can lead women to outperform
their male counterparts (Kray et al., 2001). Presumably, blatantly connecting
gender to performance increases the desire of women to prove the stereotype to
be inaccurate. By increasing negotiators' consideration of the validity of gender
stereotypes in the negotiation arena, explicitly connecting gender to performance
can lead women to disidentify with the limiting stereotype and thereby assertively
put forward their interests at the bargaining table.

Cognitive Interventions   In addition to the powerful influence that tangible
alternatives have on the negotiation process, power mindsets can also be instantiated to affect behavior (Galinsky, Gruenfeld, & Magee, 2003). By recalling
instances in which an individual possessed (versus lacked) power, subsequent
actions that are consistent with being powerful (versus powerless) are elicited.
Consistent with this reasoning, female and male negotiators achieved comparable
outcomes and higher joint gain when they individually recognized superordinate
identities and goals prior to negotiating (Kray et al., 2001). Presumably, focusing
on their commonalities reduced perceptions of power asymmetries, thereby min-
imizing performance differentials.

Another way that the female negotiators' power mindset can be strengthened
is through a process of stereotype regeneration (Kray et al., 2002), which involves
modifying the traits that are connected to negotiation effectiveness to include
stereotypically feminine traits (e.g., listening skills, empathy). In so doing, the
performance gap reverses, with women outperforming their male counterparts at

the bargaining table. In a similar vein, Stevens et al. (1993) observed that increasing perceptions of control among women through a self-management training session, which involved identifying obstacles and setting goals to overcome them, improved their performance relative to a baseline condition. These findings suggest that, in addition to the comparability of the alternatives male and female negotiators have available to them, the content of negotiators' thoughts affects how they mutually agree to divide resources.

The cognitive landscape can also be changed to level the playing field through the clarification of the negotiation parameters. Bowles et al. (2004) observed that gender parity in performance was observed when goals were clearly defined for the negotiators, but emerged when goals were poorly defined. This finding suggests that organizations that are committed to gender equality can level the playing field by improving access to information that is relevant for setting the negotiation parameters. Greater information flow can be instituted by formal mechanisms such as mentoring programs that redirect the channeling of information toward men and women equally (Noe, 1988). Armed with the same information ammunition, men and women are expected to use this information comparably to obtain favorable negotiating terms.

Situational Interventions   A key equalizing factor in negotiations concerns power. Given the identical set of power dynamics, female and male negotiators perform comparably. In line with this view is Gerhart and Rynes's (1991) observation that male and female MBAs' propensity to negotiate a salary offer was largely determined by structural factors, such as the attractiveness of the initial offer they received and the availability of alternatives. Given very clear negotiation parameters (characteristic of a strong situation), men and women were equally likely to negotiate. Consistent with this proposition, Watson and Hoffman (1996) examined the relationship between organizational power and negotiating behavior across gender. Although women expressed less satisfaction and confidence than men, gender did not affect bargaining behavior and outcomes. More recently, Kray et al. (2004) observed that the negotiator with a more attractive alternative prevailed in mixed-gender negotiations, regardless of gender. Whereas the ability of women to react against a negative stereotype was hindered when they were disadvantaged by an unattractive alternative to a negotiated agreement, women's outcomes exceeded men's outcomes when women had the power advantage. Finally, Chen and Welland (2002) observed that different combinations of power and self-construals (in interdependent versus independent terms) led men and women to pursue comparable goals in response to a vignette over the division of labor for an onerous task. This perspective suggests that power is an effective equalizer in that men and women tend to use it comparably.

Another situational intervention is to modify the roles that women assume in important negotiations. Because differences between the genders are reduced when advocating on the behalf of others (Bowles et al., 2004), framing a negotiation in terms of its broader impact on other women or members of an organization in general might reduce the extent to which women feel constrained to conform to gender role expectations.

CONCLUSIONS

In this chapter, we have put forth a framework for understanding the relationship between gender and negotiations. At its core, we argue that gender's ability to explain behavior at the bargaining table is enhanced when we consider how and when men and women differ in their motivations and cognitions. Rather than viewing gender as an innate determinant of who prevails in negotiations, we have identified the host of situational factors that lead to different expectations, beliefs, goals, and concerns for women and men, and concomitant differences in bargaining outcomes.

Although the focus of the current chapter has been motivation and cognition, we acknowledge that negotiators' behaviors are likely also influenced by their emotions. Given that one component of the feminine stereotype is an expectation that women are more emotional than men, we might expect the expression and suppression of emotion to have a differential impact on male and female negotiators. Recent research has found that an induction of anger before a negotiation (relative to a neutral condition) reduces negotiators' ability to recall information about their own preferences and about the preferences of the other side (Gonzalez, Lerner, Moore, & Babcock, 2004). Although this study did not explore the impact of gender, if men are more used to suppressing emotion than are women, the presence of emotion may have a more detrimental impact on women than men. Another interesting direction concerning emotion is: Under what bargaining circumstances do women benefit from the (stereotypically) greater ease with which they display and read emotions? An emotionally hot-headed woman might gain concessions from her male counterpart based on his desire to bring the emotional tone of the exchange down a few notches.

Another pressing question is to what extent do gender differences in motivation and cognition remain constant as negotiators gain expertise? Because most of the research reviewed in this chapter was conducted with students who presumably lacked much formal negotiating experience, the question of whether these findings apply to more experienced negotiators is somewhat open. One possibility is that the extent to which gender-based cognitions and motivations can account for the behavior of experienced negotiators is overridden by the knowledge acquired and goal setting skills honed over time, suggesting a natural leveling of the playing field among those people who do not self-select out of the domain entirely. Conversely, it is possible that the small differences observed with novice negotiators accumulate over time, simultaneously reinforcing and widening the gap in expectations and motivations that characterizes men and women (see Wood, Corcoran, & Courant, 1993).

Our goal in viewing gender through a motivated social-cognitive lens is to provide a deeper theoretical understanding of how gender influences negotiator behavior. We hope that this framework provides empirical researchers with a guide for hypothesizing and testing the factors that mediate gender differences in negotiation behavior and invigorates the study of gender in negotiation. It is only with this deeper understanding that a level playing field can be attained.

NOTES

1. Personal communication from Michele Gelfand.
2. Note that this is not to say that women always have greater self-presentational concerns. Negotiation is a relatively competitive situation—one that may be at odds with normative expectations for female behavior.

REFERENCES

Babcock, L., Gelfand, M. J., Small, D. A., & Stayn, H. (2004). *Propensity to initiate negotiations: Toward a broader understanding of negotiation behavior.* Unpublished manuscript, Carnegie Mellon University.

Babcock, L., & Laschever, S. (2003). *Women don't ask.* Princeton, NJ: Princeton University Press.

Babcock, L., Laschever, S., Gelfand, M., & Small, D. (2003). Nice girls don't ask. *Harvard Business Review, 81*(10), 14–16.

Barron, L. A. (2003). Gender differences in negotiators' beliefs. *Human Relations, 56,* 635–662.

Bazerman, M. H., Magliozzi, T., & Neale, M. A. (1985). Integrative bargaining in a competitive market. *Organizational Behavior and Human Decision Processes, 35,* 294–313.

Benton, A. A. (1973). Reactions to demands to win from an opposite sex opponent. *Journal of Personality, 41,* 430–442.

Beyer, S. (1990). Gender differences in the accuracy of self-evaluations of performance. *Journal of Personality and Social Psychology, 59,* 960–970.

Bowles, H. R., Babcock, L., & McGinn, K. (2004). *Gender as a situational phenomenon in negotiation.* Unpublished manuscript, Carnegie Mellon University.

Brehm, J. W. (1966). *A theory of psychological reactance.* New York: Academic Press.

Burgoon, M., Dillard, J. P., & Doran, N. E. (1983). Friendly or unfriendly persuasion: The effects of violations of expectations by males and females. *Human Communication Research, 10,* 283–294.

Butler, R. (1987). Task-involving and ego-involving properties of evaluations: Effects of different feedback conditions on motivational perceptions, interest, and performance. *Journal of Educational Psychology, 79,* 474–482.

Calhoun, P. S., & Smith, W. P. (1999). Integrative bargaining: Does gender make a difference? *International Journal of Conflict Management, 10,* 203–224.

Callahan-Levy, C. M., & Messe, L. A. (1979). Sex differences in the allocation of pay. *Journal of Personality and Social Psychology, 37,* 433–446.

Carli, L. L., LaFleur, S. J., & Loeber, C. C. (1995). Nonverbal behavior, gender, and influence. *Journal of Personality and Social Psychology, 68,* 1030–1041.

Chen, S., Lee-Chai, A. Y., & Bargh, J. A. (2001). Relationship orientation as a moderator of the effects of social power. *Journal of Personality and Social Psychology, 80,* 173–187.

Chen, S., & Welland, J. (2002). Examining the effects of power as a function of self-construals and gender. *Self and Identity, 1,* 251–269.

Copeland, J. T. (1994). Prophecies of power: Motivational implications of social power for behavioral confirmation. *Journal of Personality and Social Psychology, 67,* 264–277.

Cross, S. E., & Madson, L. (1997). Models of the self: Self-construals and gender. *Psychological Bulletin, 122,* 5–37.

Curhan, J. R., Neale, M. A., Ross, L., & Rosencranz-Engelmann, J. (2004). *The O'Henry effect: The impact of relational norms on negotiation outcomes.* Unpublished manuscript, Massachusetts Institute of Technology.

Deal, J. J. (2000). Gender differences in the intentional use of information in competitive negotiations. *Small Group Research, 31*, 702–723.

Deaux, K., & LaFrance, M. (1998). Gender. In D. T. Gilbert & S. T. Fiske (Eds.), *Handbook of social psychology* (4th ed., pp. 788–827). New York: McGraw-Hill.

Dreher, G. F., Dougherty, T. W., & Whitely, W. (1989). Influence tactics and salary attainment: A gender-specific analysis. *Sex Roles, 20*, 535–550.

Dweck, C., & Elliot, E. S. (1983). Achievement motivation. In E. M. Hetherminton (Ed.), *Handbook of child psychology: Social and personality development* (Vol. 4, pp. 643–691). New York: John Wiley.

Dweck, C. S., & Legget, E. L. (1988). A social-cognitive approach to motivation and personality. *Psychological Review, 95*, 256–273.

Eagly, A. H. (1983). Gender and social influence: A social psychological analysis. *American Psychologist, 38*, 971–981.

Fiske, S., & Taylor, S. E. (1991). *Social cognition.* New York: Random House.

Feather, N. T. (1984). Masculinity, femininity, psychological androgyny, and the structure of values. *Journal of Personality and Social Psychology, 47*, 604–620.

Fry, W. R., Firestone, I. J., & Williams, D. J. (1983). Negotiation process and outcome of stranger dyads and dating couples: Do lovers lose? *Basic and Applied Social Psychology, 4*, 1–16.

Galinsky, A. D., Gruenfeld, D. H., & Magee, J. C. (2003). From power to action. *Journal of Personality and Social Psychology, 85*, 453–466.

Galinsky, A. D., & Mussweiler, T. (2001). First offers as anchors: The role of perspective-taking and negotiator focus. *Journal of Personality and Social Psychology, 81*, 657–669.

Gelfand, M. J., Smith-Major, V., Raver, J., & Nishii, L. (2004). *Gender, self, and negotiation: Implications of relational self-construals for negotiations.* Unpublished manuscript, University of Maryland.

Gelfand, M. J., & McCusker, C. (2004). *Metaphor and the cultural construction of negotiation: A paradigm for research and practice.* Unpublished manuscript, University of Maryland.

Gerhart, B., & Rynes, S. (1991). Determinants and consequences of salary negotiations by male and female MBA graduates. *Journal of Applied Psychology, 76*, 256–262.

Gneezy, U., Niederle, M., & Rustichini, A. (2004). *Performance in competitive environments.* Unpublished manuscript, Harvard University.

Gonzalez, R., Lerner, J., Moore, D., & Babcock, L. (2004). *Mad, mean, and mistaken: The effects of anger on strategic social perception and behavior.* Unpublished manuscript, Carnegie Mellon University.

Greenhalgh, L., & Gilkey, R. W. (1993). The effect of relationship orientation on negotiators' cognitions and tactics. *Group Decision and Negotiation, 2*, 167–186.

Halpern, J. J., & Park, J. M. (1996). Vive la difference: Differences between males and females in process and outcomes in a low-conflict negotiation. *International Journal of Conflict Management, 7*, 45–70.

Hilton, J. L., & Darley, J. M. (1991). The effects of interaction goals on person perception. *Advances in Experimental Social Psychology, 24*, 235–267.

Huber, V. L., & Neale, M. A. (1987). Effects of self- and competitor goals on performance in an interdependent bargaining task. *Journal of Applied Psychology, 72*, 197–203.

Instone, D., Major, B., & Bunker, B. B. (1983). Gender, self confidence, and social influence strategies: An organizational simulation. *Journal of Personality and Social Psychology, 44*, 322–333.

Jones, E. (1986). Interpreting interpersonal behavior: The effects of expectancies. *Science,* *234,* 41–46.

Kaman, V. S., & Hartel, C. E. (1994). Gender differences in anticipated pay negotiation strategies and outcomes. *Journal of Business and Psychology, 9,* 183–197.

Kanter, R. M. (1977). *Men and women of the corporation.* New York: Basic Books.

Kidder, L. G., Bellettirie, G., & Cohn, E. S. (1977). Secret ambitions and public performances: The effects of anonymity on reward allocations made by men and women. *Journal of Experimental Social Psychology, 13,* 70–80.

Kimmel, M., Pruitt, D. G., Magenau, J. M., Konar-Goldband, E., & Carnevale, P. J. D. (1980). Effects of trust, aspiration, and gender on negotiation tactics. *Journal of Personality and Social Psychology, 38,* 9–22.

King, W. C., & Hinson, T. D. (1994). The influence of sex and equity sensitivity on relationship preferences, assessment of opponent, and outcomes in a negotiation experiment. *Journal of Management, 20,* 605–624.

King, W. C., Miles, E. W., & Kniska, J. (1991). Boys will be boys (and girls will be girls): The attribution of gender roles stereotypes in a gaming situation. *Sex Roles, 15,* 607–623.

Kolb, D. (2000). *Renewing our interest in gender negotiations: What's new or what would really be new?* Paper presented at the Academy of Management meetings, Toronto, Ontario, Canada, August 2000.

Kolb, D. M., & Coolidge, G. C. (1991). Her place at the table: A consideration of gender issues in negotiation. In J. W. Breslin & J. Z. Rubin (Eds.), *Negotiation theory and practice* (pp. 261–277). Cambridge, MA: PON Books.

Kray, L. J., Galinsky, A. D., & Thompson, L. (2002). Reversing the gender gap in negotiations: An exploration of stereotype regeneration. *Organizational Behavior and Human Decision Processes, 87,* 386–409.

Kray, L. J., & Haselhuhn, M. (2004). *Implicit negotiation theories, gender stereotypes, and the division of resources at the bargaining table.* Unpublished manuscript, University of California, Berkeley.

Kray, L. J., Reb, J., Galinsky, A., & Thompson, L. (2004). Stereotype reactance at the bargaining table: The effect of stereotype activation and power on claiming and creating value. *Personality and Social Psychology Bulletin, 30,* 399–411.

Kray, L. J., Thompson, L., & Galinsky, A. D. (2001). Battle of the sexes: Stereotype confirmation and reactance in negotiations. *Journal of Personality and Social Psychology, 80,* 942–958.

Lenney, E. (1977). Women's self-confidence in achievement settings. *Psychological Bulletin, 84,* 1–13.

Lerner, J. S., Gonzalez, R. M., Small, D. A., & Fischhoff, B. (2003). Emotion and perceived risks of terrorism: A national field experiment. *Psychological Science, 14,* 144–150.

Locke, E. A., & Latham, G. P. (1990). *A theory of goal setting and task performance.* Englewood Cliffs, NJ: Prentice Hall.

Mainiero, L. A. (1986). Coping with powerlessness: The relationship of gender and job dependency to empowerment-strategy usage. *Administrative Science Quarterly, 31,* 633–653.

Major, B., & Adams, J. B. (1983). Role of gender, interpersonal orientation, and self-presentation in distributive-justice behavior. *Journal of Personality and Social Psychology, 45,* 598–608.

Major, B., Bylsma, W. H., & Cozzarelli, C. (1989). Gender differences in distributive justice preferences: The impact of domain. *Sex Roles, 21,* 487–497.

Major, B., & Konar, E. (1984). An investigation of sex differences in pay expectations and their possible causes. *Academy of Management Journal, 27,* 777–792.

Major, B., McFarlin, D. B., & Gagnon, D. (1984). Overworked and underpaid: On the nature of gender differences in personal entitlement. *Journal of Personality and Social Psychology, 47*, 1399–1412.

Martell, R. F., Lane, D. M., & Emrich, C. (1996). Male-female differences: A computer simulation. *American Psychologist, 51*, 157–158.

Matheson, K. (1991). Social cues in computer-mediated negotiations: Gender makes a difference. *Computers in Human Behavior, 7*, 137–145.

McFarlin, D. B., Frone, M. R., Major, B., & Konar, E. (1989). Predicting career-entry pay expectations: The role of gender-based comparisons. *Journal of Business & Psychology, 3*, 331–340.

Mischel, W. (1977). On the future of personality measurement. *American Psychologist, 32*, 246–254.

Mowday, R. T. (1978). The exercise of influence in organizations. *Administrative Science Quarterly, 23*, 137–156.

Mowday, R. T. (1979). Leader characteristics, self-confidence, and methods of upward influence in organizational decision situations. *Academy of Management Journal, 22*, 709–725.

Neale, M. A., & Bazerman, M. H. (1985). The effect of externally set goals on integrative agreements in competitive markets. *Journal of Occupational Behavior, 6*, 19–32.

Neale, M. A., & Fragale, A. (2004). Social cognition, attribution, and perception in negotiation. In A. Kruglanski & J. Forgas (Eds.), *Frontiers in social psychology.* New York: Psychology Press.

Neu, J., Graham, J. L., & Gilly, M. C. (1988). The influence of gender on behaviors and outcomes in a retail buyer-seller negotiation simulation. *Journal of Retailing, 64*, 427–451.

Noe, R. A. (1988). Women and mentoring: A review and research agenda. *Academy of Management Review, 13*, 65–78.

Orbell, J., Dawes, R., & Schwartz-Shea, P. (1994). Trust, social categories, and individuals: The case of gender. *Motivation and Emotion, 18*, 109–128.

Pinkley, R. L., Neale, M. A., & Bennett, R. J. (1994). The impact of alternatives to settlement in dyadic negotiations. *Organizational Behavior and Human Decision Processes, 57*, 97–116.

Pruitt, D. G., Carnevale, P. J. D., Forcey, B., & van Slyck, M. (1986). Gender effects in negotiation: Constituent surveillance and contentious behavior. *Journal of Experimental Social Psychology, 22*, 264–275.

Pruitt, D., & Rubin, J. (1986). *Social conflict: Escalation, stalemate, and settlement.* New York: Random House.

Pruitt, D. G., & Syna, H. (1985). Mismatching the opponent's offers in negotiations. *Journal of Experimental Social Psychology, 21*, 103–113.

Ragins, B. R., & Sundstrom, E. (1989). Gender and power in organizations: A longitudinal perspective. *Psychological Bulletin, 105*, 51–88.

Rubin, J. Z., & Brown, B. R. (1975). *The social psychology of bargaining and negotiation.* New York: Academic Press.

Rudman, L. A. (1998). Self-promotion as a risk factor for women: The costs and benefits of counterstereotypical impression management. *Journal of Personality and Social Psychology, 74*, 629–646.

Rudman, L., & Glick, P. (2001). Prescriptive gender stereotypes and backlash toward agentic women. *Journal of Social Issues, 57*, 743–762.

Shapiro, E. G. (1975). Effect of expectations of future interaction on reward allocations in dyads: Equity or equality? *Journal of Personality and Social Psychology, 31*, 873–880.

Skrypnek, B. J., & Snyder, M. (1982). On the self-perpetuating nature of stereotypes about women and men. *Journal of Experimental Social Psychology, 18*, 277–291.

Slovic, P. (2000). *The perception of risk.* London; Sterling, VA: Earthscan Publications.

Small, D., Babcock, L., Gelfand, M., & Gettman, H. (2004). *Who gets to the bargaining table? Understanding gender variation in the initiation of negotiations.* Unpublished manuscript, Carnegie Mellon University.

Snyder, M., Tanke, E. D., & Berscheid, E. (1977). Social perception and interpersonal behavior: On the self-fulfilling nature of social stereotypes. *Journal of Personality and Social Psychology, 35*, 656–666.

Solnick, S., & Schweitzer, M. E. (1999). The influence of physical attractiveness and gender on ultimatum game decisions. *Organizational Behavior and Human Decision Processes, 79*, 199–215.

Steele, C. M. (1997). A threat in the air: How stereotypes shape intellectual identity and performance. *American Psychologist, 52*, 613–629.

Stevens, C. K., Bavetta, A. G., & Gist, M. E. (1993). Gender differences in the acquisition of salary negotiation skills: The role of goals, self-efficacy, and perceived control. *Journal of Applied Psychology, 78*, 723–735.

Stuhlmacher, A. F., & Walters, A. E. (1999). Gender differences in negotiation outcome: A meta-analysis. *Personnel Psychology, 52*, 653–677.

Swap, W. C., & Rubin, J. Z. (1983). Measurement of interpersonal orientation. *Journal of Personality and Social Psychology, 44*, 208–219.

Vallacher, R. R., Callahan-Levy, C. M., & Messe, L. A. (1979). Sex effects on bilateral bargaining as a function of interpersonal context. *Personality and Social Psychology Bulletin, 5*, 104–109.

Wade, M. E. (2001). Women and salary negotiation: The costs of self-advocacy. *Psychology of Women Quarterly, 25*, 65–76

Walters, A. E., Stuhlmacher, A. F., & Meyer, L. L. (1998). Gender and negotiator competitiveness: A meta-analysis. *Organizational Behavior and Human Decision Processes, 76*, 1–29.

Watson, C. (1994). Gender versus power as a predictor of negotiation behavior and outcomes. *Negotiation Journal, 10*, 117–127.

Watson, C., & Hoffman, L. R. (1996). Managers as negotiators: A test of power versus gender as predictors of feelings, behavior, and outcomes. *Leadership Quarterly, 7*, 63–85.

Williams, J. E., & Best, D. L. (1982). *Measuring sex stereotypes: A thirty nation study.* Beverly Hills, CA: Sage.

Wood, R. G., Corcoran, M. E., & Courant, P. N. (1993). Pay differences among the highly paid: The male-female earnings gap in lawyers' salaries. *Journal of Labor Economics, 11*, 417–441.

Index

A

Ability, gender differences in beliefs about, 210–212

Accuracy motivation, 47

Acquiring a company game, 16–17, 19

Actor effects, 139

Adaptive supply and demand, and success of negotiation research, 2

Advocacy role, gender differences in, 215

Affect

    and cognitive goals, 105

    conceptual/theoretical approaches, 101–103

    contexts in negotiation, 109–112

    in crisis negotiation, 109–110

    defined, 100–101

    as dependent variable, 106–107

    empirical studies of, 103–108

    and long-term memory, 114

    as mediator in negotiation, 107–108

    paucity of research on, 101

    predicting in negotiation, 106–107

    as predictor of negotiation outcome and process, 103–106

    priming of information processing by, 102

Affect heuristic, 13

Affect infusion model (AIM), 101

Affective experience, 103

Affective forecasting, 114

Affective primacy, 13

Agreement, emotional context of, 101

Allocentrism, 67

Ambiguity, in feedback, 84

Analogical encoding, 87, 91

Anchoring, 3

    effects on negotiation outcomes, 59

    and gender differences, 205

Anger

    correlation with cooperation, 65, 104

    defection punished by, 102

    inhibiting conflict resolution on e-media, 154

    reduced joint gains with, 104

    and tendency to reject profitable offers, 9

Anonymity

    consequences for electronic negotiation, 150–154

    perceptions in e-negotiation, 146, 150, 153

    reducing prior to e-negotiation, 164

Antecedent-focused emotion regulation, 116

Anticipatory management, 192

Appeasement strategies, 192

Applied research, 3

Arbitration, 110–112. *See also* Third-party conflict resolution

Arm's-length transactions, 132

    vs. socially embedded transactions, 129

Art and Science of Negotiation, 7

Asian cultural assumptions. *See* Assumptions; Non-Western cultural biases

Aspiration, 57, 68

    in dual concern theory, 59–62

    gender differences in, 206

    and motive in negotiation, 57–59

Aspiration level theory, and goal setting, 58

Aspiration price, 29

    and intrapersonal comparisons, 41

Aspirations, 4

    vs. reservations, 29–32

Assumptions

    cultural differences in underlying, 173–174, 194–195

    direct *vs.* indirect confrontation, 190–194

    dispositional *vs.* situational attribution, 183–186

    economic *vs.* relational capital, 180–183

    rationality *vs.* emotionality, 176–180

Asynchronous communication

    detrimental effects on outcomes, 112

    encouragement of rumination by, 154

    in e-negotiation, 150

Attention, relationship to perception, 11–12

Attribution, 27–28, 47–48

    cross-cultural approaches to, 174

    dispositional *vs.* situational, 183–186

    and influence of relationships on negotiation process, 132–133

    influence of relationship on negotiation through, 132–133

    situational and personality, 85

Attribution error, 38, 45

Availability concept, 14–15

Avoidance, non-Western use of, 174

Avoidance stages, 110

M

Machiavellianism, links to cooperative behavior and emotion, 104
Mastery goals, 88
McGinn, Kathleen L., 129
Mediation, 110–112. *See also* Third-party conflict resolution
    Asian preferences for third-party, 182, 193
Mediator emotions, 111
Memory encoding, affective experiences and, 112, 113
Message valence, in crisis negotiation, 110
Mimicry, 117
    transmission of emotional information by, 102
Mixed feelings, need for research on, 118
Mixed-motive conflicts, 32, 55
    gender differences in, 203
    generous behavior among related individuals in, 134
Monitoring conditions
    gender differences in behavior with, 212
    and negotiator behavior, 208
Monty Hall game, 15–16
Mood. *See also* Affect; Emotion
    defined, 100
    effect on cognitive processes, 112–114
    effect on cooperative/competitive goal adoption, 33, 34
    and heuristic processing, 113
    role in negotiation, 4, 65
Motivated information processing model, 56
Motivated social cognition, 5
Motivational interventions, 217
Motivational orientation. *See also* Motives; Social motives
    cross-cultural approaches to, 174
    cultural differences in, 180–183
    economic *vs.* relational capital, 180–183
    effects on joint outcome, 64
    gender differences in, 205–209
    interaction-specific motivations, 206–209
    and learning processes, 88
    situational factors affecting gender differences in, 214–216
    task-specific, 205–206
Motivational shifts, 85
Motives, 4
    and aspirations in negotiation, 57–59
    culture as basis for, 67–68
    epistemic, 65–66
    four classes of, 57
    identity related, 66–67
    as negotiators' raison d'être, 55–56, 68–70

    social, 59
    taxonomy of, 56–57
Multi-issue proposals, 189
Multi-party ultimatums, 17–21

N

Nadler, Janice, 145
Naniwabushi, 178–179
Narrow assumptions, 12–13, 19
Neale, Margaret A., 27
Negative-ability feedback, 34
Negative emotion
    and affective consequences of impasse, 107
    cooperative behavior triggered by, 104–105
    encouraged by asynchronous e-communication, 154
    introversion and low emotional stability effects on, 114
    productive social functions of, 108
    in retaliatory conflict model, 102
Negative framing, 8, 17
Negative mood, and competition, 34
Negative outcomes, desire to avoid, 30
Negotiated order perspective, 130
Negotiating ability
    and diagnostic framing, 213
    fixed *vs.* malleable, 211
Negotiation
    bounded awareness and focusing failures in, 7, 15–21
    and context of relationships, 129–130
    as decision making among interdependent parties, 175
    decision perspective to, 7–10
    effects of electronic technology on, 145–147
    ethical shortcomings in, 3
    failure to exchange information as barrier in, 157–158
    four-stage model of, 102–103
    gender differences in, 203–204, 218–219
    influence on relationships, 135–136
    learning, 77–78, 91–92
    mental model gender differences in, 212–214
    as mixed-motive conflict, 32
    motivated information processing model of, 56
    paucity of research on affect in, 101
    social context of emotion in, 99–100
    success as topic of scholarly inquiry, 1
    superstars of, 3

Negotiation instruction
    academic achievement increased by, 77
    implications of negotiation experience for, 90–91
    teaching methods in, 91
Negotiation partners. *See* Interaction partner choice
Negotiation research, 1, 4–5
    adaptive supply and demand, 2
    best practices, 3
    community of scholars, 3
    cross-citation rate in, 3
    dependent measures for, 2
    on gender differences, 204
    underperformance, 2
Negotiation strategies
    cooperative *vs.* competitive, 83
    gender differences in, 213–214
Negotiation theory
    cultural analysis of underlying assumptions, 173–174, 194–195
    culture defined in, 174–176
    dispositional *vs.* situational attributions, 183–186
    economic *vs.* relational capital as goal motivation, 180–183
    rationality *vs.* emotion in persuasion, 176–180
Negotiator cognition, social motivation and, 62–63
Negotiator effectiveness, prescriptive approach to improving, 8
Negotiator judgment, 4
Negotiator preferences, uncertainty about, 39–40
Negotiator satisfaction
    and affective states, 106
    in context of prior relationships, 136
    in e-negotiation, 148
    and internal comparisons, 42
    outcome as determinant of, 40–41
    social comparison as determinant of, 40–41
Negotiators, novice *vs.* experienced, 77–78, 91–92
Non-Western cultural biases
    emotionality as tool of persuasion, 178–180
    indirect communication and proposal approach, 188–190
    indirect confrontation in conflict resolution, 191–194
    relational capital as outcome criterion, 181–183
    situational attributions to save face, 185–186
Noncooperative motivation, 56
    and idiocentrism, 67
Nonverbal cues, 34, 156, 157
    emphasis in Asian cultures, 192–194
    missing in e-mail negotiation, 112

Northwestern University, vii
Novice negotiators, 77–78, 91–92
    characterizing, 88–90
    fixed-pie assumptions of, 88–89
    focus on single issues, 89
    motivational shifts in, 85
    social comparison and, 107

O

Objective payoff, primacy in negotiations among related parties, 135
Observational learning, 90, 91
Observed behaviors, and cooperative/competitive stance, 34–35
Online mediation. *See also* E-mail negotiation; Electronic communication
    dispute resolution by, 149
    role of emotion in, 112
    Squaretrade Web applications for, 146
Opening moves, in four-stage model of negotiation, 102
Opening up, 82
Opponents' preferences
    increased logrolling association with accurate inferences about, 78, 79
    uncertainty about, 36–38
Opponents' reputation, effect on negotiated outcomes, 80
Organizational behavior, 1
Other-concern, levels and outcomes, 60
Out-group members, 108
    and interpersonal comparisons, 42
Outcomes
    beneficial effects of uncertainty on, 44
    as determinant of negotiator satisfaction, 40–41
    in disputes, 138
    economic capital as criterion for, 180–181
    economic/objective payoff, 135
    effect of information technology on, 4, 146
    effects of cultural frameworks on, 5
    effects of face-to-face interaction on, 4–5
    effects of social cognition, attribution, perception on, 27–28, 47–48
    and experience in impasse situations, 79
    and focus on goals or limits, 59
    impeded by strong emotions, 111
    influence of prior relationships on, 135
    of negotiators making first offers, 30–31
    psychological influences on, 27
    relatedness, 136
    relational capital as non-Western criterion for, 181–183